Populist Challenges to Constitutional Interpretation in Europe and Beyond

This book explores the relationship between populism or populist regimes and constitutional interpretation used in those regimes.

The volume discusses the question of whether contemporary populist governments and movements have developed or encouraged new and specific constitutional theories, doctrines and methods of interpretation, or whether their constitutional and other high courts continue to use the old, traditional interpretative tools in constitutional adjudication. The book is divided into four parts. Part I contains three chapters elaborating the theoretical basis for the discussion. Part II examines the topic from a comparative perspective, representing those European countries where populism is most prevalent, including Austria, Croatia, the Czech Republic, Greece, Hungary, Italy, Poland, Romania, Spain, and the United Kingdom. Part III extends the focus to the United States, reflecting how American jurisprudence and academia have produced the most important contributions to the theory of constitutional interpretation, and how recent political developments in that country might challenge the traditional understanding of judicial review. This section also includes a general overview on Latin America, where there are also some populist governments and strong populist movements. Finally, the editors' closing study analyses the outcomes of the comparative research, summarizing the conclusions of the book.

Written by renowned national constitutional scholars, the book will be essential reading for students, academics and researchers working in constitutional law and politics.

Fruzsina Gárdos-Orosz is Director and Senior Research Fellow of the Institute for Legal Studies, Centre for Social Sciences, Hungary, and also Associate Professor in Constitutional Law at the ELTE Law School in Budapest, Hungary.

Zoltán Szente is Professor of Law at the Department of Constitutional Law, National University of Public Service, and he holds a Research Professor at the Institute for Legal Studies, Centre for Social Sciences of the Hungarian Academy of Sciences, Budapest. He is a co-chair of the IACL Research Group on Constitutional Interpretation, and a vice-president of the Independent Group of Experts of the Council of Europe.

Comparative Constitutional Change

Comparative Constitutional Change has developed into a distinct field of constitutional law. It encompasses the study of constitutions through the way they change and covers a wide scope of topics and methodologies. Books in this series include work on developments in the functions of the constitution, the organization of powers and the protection of rights, as well as research that focuses on formal amendment rules and the relation between constituent and constituted power. The series includes comparative approaches along with books that focus on single jurisdictions, and brings together research monographs and edited collections which allow the expression of different schools of thought. While the focus is primarily on law, where relevant the series may also include political science, historical, philosophical and empirical approaches that explore constitutional change.

Series editors:
Xenophon Contiades is Professor of Public Law, Panteion University, Athens, Greece and Managing Director, Centre for European Constitutional Law, Athens, Greece.

Thomas Fleiner is Emeritus Professor of Law at the University of Fribourg, Switzerland. He teaches and researches in the areas of Federalism, Rule of Law, Multicultural State; Comparative Administrative and Constitutional Law; Political Theory and Philosophy; Swiss Constitutional and Administrative Law; and Legislative Drafting. He has published widely in these and related areas.

Alkmene Fotiadou is Research Associate at the Centre for European Constitutional Law, Athens.

Richard Albert is Professor of Law at the University of Texas at Austin.

Also in the series:
Icelandic Constitutional Reform
People, Processes, Politics
Edited by Ágúst Þór Árnason and Catherine Dupré

Dynamic Federalism
A New Theory for Cohesion and Regional Autonomy
Patricia Popelier

Peace, Discontent and Constitutional Law
Challenges to Constitutional Order and Democracy
Edited by Martin Belov

New Challenges to Constitutional Adjudication in Europe
A Comparative Perspective
Edited by Zoltán Szente & Fruzsina Gárdos-Orosz

Constitutional Change and Popular Sovereignty
Populism, Politics and the Law in Ireland
Edited by Maria Cahill, Colm Ó Cinnéide, Seán Ó Conaill, and Conor O'Mahony

For more information about this series, please visit:
www.routledge.com/Comparative-Constitutional-Change/book-series/COMPCONST

Populist Challenges to Constitutional Interpretation in Europe and Beyond

Edited by Fruzsina Gárdos-Orosz and Zoltán Szente

Routledge
Taylor & Francis Group
LONDON AND NEW YORK

First published 2021
by Routledge
2 Park Square, Milton Park, Abingdon, Oxon OX14 4RN

and by Routledge
52 Vanderbilt Avenue, New York, NY 10017

Routledge is an imprint of the Taylor & Francis Group, an informa business

British Library Cataloguing-in-Publication Data
A catalogue record for this book is available from the British Library

Library of Congress Cataloging-in-Publication Data
Names: Gárdos-Orosz, Fruzsina, editor. | Szente, Zoltán, editor.
Title: Populist challenges to constitutional interpretation in Europe and beyond / edited by Fruzsina Gárdos-Orosz & Zoltán Szente.
Description: Milton Park, Abingdon, Oxon ; New York, NY : Routledge, 2021.
| Series: Comparative constitutional change | Includes bibliographical references and index.
Identifiers: LCCN 2020052991 (print) | LCCN 2020052992 (ebook) | ISBN 9780367710095 (hardback) | ISBN 9781003148944 (ebook)
Subjects: LCSH: Constitutional law. | Populism.
Classification: LCC K3165 .P673 2021 (print) | LCC K3165 (ebook) | DDC 342.4/0011--dc23
LC record available at https://lccn.loc.gov/2020052991
LC ebook record available at https://lccn.loc.gov/2020052992

ISBN: 978-0-367-71009-5 (hbk)
ISBN: 978-0-367-71013-2 (pbk)
ISBN: 978-1-003-14894-4 (ebk)

Typeset in Galliard
by SPi Global, India

Contents

List of Authors

Balaguer Callejón, Francisco, is Professor of Constitutional Law at the University of Granada

Brzozowski, Wojciech, is Associate Professor at the University of Warsaw

Demuro, Gianmario, is Professor of Constitutional Law at the University of Cagliari

Gamper, Anna, is Professor of Public Law at the University of Innsbruck

Gardasevic, Djordje, is Associate Professor at the Zagreb Law School

Gárdos-Orosz, Fruzsina, is Director of the Institute for Legal Studies, Centre of Social Sciences, and Associate Professor at the Eötvös Loránd University (Budapest)

Graber, Mark A., is Regents Professor at the University of Maryland Carey School of Law

Kühn, Zdeněk, is Associate Professor of Jurisprudence, Charles University Law School (Prague), and a Justice of the Supreme Administrative Court of the Czech Republic

Lachmayer, Konrad, is Professor for Public Law at the Sigmund Freud University in Vienna

Loughlin, Martin, is Professor of Public Law at the London School of Economics and Political Science

McEldowney, John, is Professor of Law at the University of Warwick Law School

Mercescu, Alexandra, is a research assistant, West University of Timisoara

Montaldo, Riccardo, is a doctoral candidate at the University of Kassel and the University of Cagliari

Riberi, Pablo, is Constitutional Law Professor at the School of Law of the National University of Córdoba and at the School of Political Science of the Catholic University of Córdoba (Argentina)

Szente, Zoltán, is Research Professor, Centre of Social Sciences, Institute for Legal Studies, and Professor of Law, National University of Public Service (Budapest)

Tushnet, Mark, is William Nelson Cromwell Professor of Law, Harvard Law School

Vlachogiannis, Apostolos, is a teaching assistant at the Hellenic Open University (Athens)

Introduction and Acknowledgements

In our age, the rise of populism seems to be a worldwide trend in politics. Even if there is no consensus whether it is a particular political ideology, a style of governance, or mere rhetoric, most scholars are likely to agree that it brings about a challenge to the traditional values and institutions of constitutional democracies. Although populism is an essentially political phenomenon, it undoubtedly has significant constitutional implications as well. The birth and spread of the term 'populist constitutionalism' shows that one of the distinctive features of modern populism is that it has specific constitutional ambitions insofar as it seeks to achieve its political goals through constitutional means. This perception has inspired a growing literature and has provoked scholarly debates about whether populism has evolved a specific constitutional theory or not. Since populist constitutionalism, like populism itself, is an essentially contested concept, much of this discourse is about the conceptualization of this phenomenon.

Our book attempts to go beyond conceptual debates, and it is not intended to describe the constitutional changes brought about by populist politics. The topic of our book is much more specialized; namely, it examines the impact of populist politics on the methods of constitutional interpretation. We presumed that if populists really see the constitution and the constitutional changes as tools necessary to reach their power goals, then the same is true of constitutional interpretation. Some experience clearly shows that when authoritarian populism, the dominant form of contemporary populism, comes to power, it makes the constitutional court an instrument of the executive power and, presumably, wants to change the meaning of the constitution by constitutional interpretation. If populists control constitutional interpretation, they can use that influence to legitimize unconstitutional laws by the courts, qualifying them as constitutional, and they can refuse the review or repeal of earlier laws that thwarted populist aspirations. At the end of the day, these political aspirations neutralize constitutional or other equivalent courts as institutional counterweights to legislative and the executive power. Consequently, in populist times, constitutional review may not lose its role, but its function changes significantly, as the 'executive control of the constitutional court indirectly gives the government an important say in how the constitution should be interpreted'.[1] In this process, the influence over the methods of constitutional interpretation can be an effective weapon in political struggles. All these ambitions can plausibly be justified by the populist creed, which usually considers constitutional and other high-level judges to be part of the elite that only hinders the realization of the popular will, and this is particularly unacceptable, as they are not officials directly elected by the people.

If this is so, it seems reasonable to assume that populist goals are better served by certain methods of interpretation than others. When, for example, populism has a significant influence over legislation, populists likely support the plain meaning rule (textualism), or the interpretation based on the original intent, because, in principle, these methods may provide most deference to the lawmakers, while the moral reading of the constitution or an objective purposive interpretation give greater leeway for judicial discretion. However, historical experience testifies that it is advisable to be cautious in this regard. While, for example, the grammatical-logical interpretive method had the greatest influence in the jurisprudence of the Weimar Republic, the Nazi regime, maybe the most extreme form of autocratic populism, distrusted legal textualism (because of the Nazis' lack of respect for the surviving laws of the Weimar Republic), and preferred a specific interpretive method reflecting and realizing the spirit of National Socialism and based on dubious and uncertain ("contradiction-transcending") legal concepts.[2] Therefore, depending on different contexts and legal cultures, populists are likely to prefer different methods of interpretation. If no specific modalities of constitutional interpretation can be closely associated with populist constitutionalism, perhaps the outcomes of interpretation can be effectively changed by reinterpreting substantive constitutional concepts.

However, these assumptions apply only to populist aspirations, which can prevail only if they can be passed through the courts that perform the function of constitutional review of laws. Courts can respond to these claims in different ways.[3] For example, they can engage in an activist stance, resisting the attempts that endanger the established constitutional order; or, alternatively, they can defer to the changing constitutional policy of the political branches; or, possibly, they can try to keep their distance from political struggles as if nothing had happened.

But whatever constitutional claims the populists have, and whatever strategy the courts choose in response to them, it is certain that the well-admitted methods of constitutional interpretation are affected. Therefore, the core

1 Pablo Castillo-Ortiz, 'The Illiberal Abuse of Constitutional Courts in Europe' (2019) 15 European Constitutional Law Review 70.

2 Oliver Lepsius, 'The Problem of Perceptions of National Socialist Law or: Was there a Constitutional Theory of National Socialism?' in Christian Joerges and Navraj Singh Ghaleigh (eds.), *Darker Legacies of Law in Europe. The Shadow of National Socialism and Fascism over Europe and its Legal Traditions* (Hart Publishing 2003) 38–39.

3 Yaniv Roznai, 'Who will Save the Redheads? Towards an Anti-Bully Theory of Judicial Review and Protection of Democracy' (2020) 29 William & Mary Bill of Rights Journal 27.

question of this volume is whether populist politics influences the way the constitution is interpreted in the countries examined, and if so, how populism affects the constitutional interpretation in those European countries where this movement has recently gained tangible political influence.

As is well known, populism has no clear or consensual concept, just as the methods of constitutional interpretation are defined and classified in diverse ways. Our book does not have any ambition to give an authoritative definition either, but the first two chapters provide a comprehensive overview of the literature on populism and populist constitutionalism, as well as on the most basic knowledge of the methods of constitutional interpretation. These chapters are followed by a wide-ranging comparative study exploring the relationship between the political system and the preferred methods of constitutional interpretation, and a theoretical examination of the possibility of autochthonous interpretive tools that are characteristic of the various nations or legal cultures. Then, the subject-matter is explored in ten European country studies with an outlook to the United States and the Latin American countries; the former is justified by the rich traditions of constitutional interpretation, the latter by the spread of populism. The authors of the volume examine the possible effects of populism on constitutional interpretation in different ways; while some of them provide a general picture on the changes of constitutional jurisprudence, others present case studies that characterize judicial responses to populist actions. Nevertheless, they all identify the challenges that can be classified as 'populist' aspirations attempting to influence the methods of constitutional interpretation. The final chapter briefly summarizes the main findings of the book, and it also seeks to explain why populism affects the constitutional interpretation so differently in the various countries.

The reason for choosing this topic was not only that it focuses on a research field that has not been studied so far, but that it also had other antecedents. In 2018, we edited a book which examined how global challenges, such as the world economic crisis, terrorism or mass migration, affected the jurisprudence of some European constitutional courts and the case law of the European courts.[4] In the same year, we initiated the establishment of the Research Group on Constitutional Interpretation within the framework of the International Association of Constitutional Law. This Group was formed by 26 renowned scholars of the topic as founding members from 17 countries. After holding an international conference on *Constitutional Interpretation in European Populist Regimes* in Budapest in 2019, this volume is the first result of the cooperation of the members of the Group.

Another relevant research has been going on for two years, in which we are involved and which has received support also from the European Union's Horizon 2020 research and innovation programme under grant agreement No 822590 on 'Democratic Efficacy and the Varieties of Populism in

4 Zoltán Szente and Fruzsina Gárdos-Orosz (eds.), *New Challenges to Constitutional Adjudication in Europe: A Comparative Perspective* (Routledge 2018).

Europe' (DEMOS) and from the 129245 'Populism in Public Policy and Legislation' project supported by the National Research, Development and Innovation Office.

Our book is intended as a contribution to the scholarly discourse on populist constitutionalism and constitutional interpretation in the hope that it provides useful knowledge for further research and for other researchers.

Fruzsina Gárdos-Orosz
Zoltán Szente

Budapest, November 2020

Part I

Theoretical implications

1 Populism and populist constitutionalism

Zoltán Szente

1.1 Introduction

In order to get closer to answering the questions set out in the Introduction, i.e. to understand the relationship between populism and constitutional interpretation, it is necessary to provide the framework of the academic discourse and the major attempts to conceptualize the two key concepts of this book. Populist constitutionalism is a kind of intermediate category between these two concepts and refers to the constitutional approach, aspirations, or activities of populism. Having regard to the great variety of relevant definitions, this study has no ambition to develop authentic conceptualizations – our goal is simply to bring the reader closer to the academic discourse on populism, populist constitutionalism, and constitutional interpretation, and to provide help for a better understanding of the studies collected in this volume. In doing so, we use the classical conceptualization technique which determines the subject of the research by identifying its most important conceptual criteria.

Among the sources of these criteria, we can find both normative theories and descriptive works; in fact, this chapter aims to provide a comprehensive literature review of these categories.

1.2 The impalpable concept of populism

The conceptualization of populism is difficult not only because it is a very abstract concept, but also because it signifies a phenomenon that does not fit, or fits only with difficulty, into other existing conceptual frameworks. This means that the various manifestations of populism cannot be placed in the traditional dichotomies of the political right and left, democracy and autocracy, and cannot be attributed to specific time periods or geographical regions. There is not even a consensus as to whether this concept actually refers to a particular political organization, ideology, political aspiration, or style. Therefore, as a specific political phenomenon, it is often compared to a chameleon that adapts to the colour of its environment.[1]

1 Paul Taggart, *Populism* (Open University Press, 2000) 4.

Some claim that almost every scholar has an individual definition of populism that suits his or her own interests.[2] Indeed, the conceptualization of populism has a specific, ever-expanding literature, but no consensual concept has emerged as a result. This may also be due to the fact that populism does not have an exemplar, a universally accepted ideal-type that exists in reality, and, by the same token, different conceptualizations are attempted in the discourse on the topic. It is common to highlight only one defining criterion, but many seek to identify populist policies or movements on the basis of several criteria,[3] and there are even examples which define primary and secondary aspects (on the basis of which different types of populism can also be distinguished).[4] Some definitions of populism are normative, classifying certain political phenomena as populist according to whether they meet a pre-established general conceptualization, while others approach the notion of populism on an empirical basis by generalizing the main characteristics of certain political systems or movements. As a consequence, '[a] persistent feature of the literature on populism is its reluctance – or difficulty – in giving the concept any precise meaning', and any '[n]otional clarity – let alone definition – is conspicuously absent'.[5]

Therefore, some suggest that populism should be given a 'minimalist' definition that includes as many of the cases discussed as possible in its own conceptual scope,[6] although an overly broad definition would call into question the use of this category for scientific analysis.

Due to this conceptual diversity and indeterminacy, it is not surprising that there are also authors who think that the concept of populism as such is less suitable for exploration by the social sciences.[7]

However, the use of the term is extremely widespread in political science and even in constitutional scholarship, and, in addition, despite different attempts at conceptualization, this phenomenon has several features on which there is a broad consensus among scholars. Therefore, it is still worth taking a closer look at the best-known definitions of populism and the criteria most often attributed to populists.

2 Jürgen Mackert, 'Introduction. Is There Such a Thing as Populism?' in Gregor Fitzi, Jürgen Mackert, and Bryan S. Turner (eds.), *Populism and the Crisis of Democracy. Volume 1: Concepts and Theory* (Routledge 2018) 2.

3 Yves Mény and Yves Surel, 'The Constitutive Ambiguity of Populism' in Yves Mény and Yves Surel (eds.), *Democracies and the Populist Challenge* (Palgrave MacMillan 2002) 1–21.

4 For the latter, see for example Paul Taggart, 'Populism and "Unpolitics"' in Gregor Fitzi, Jürgen Mackert, and Bryan S. Turner (eds.), *Populism and the Crisis of Democracy. Volume 1: Concepts and Theory* (Routledge 2018) 80.

5 Ernesto Laclau, *On Populist Reason* (Verso 2005) 3.

6 Cristóbal Rovira Kaltwasser, 'How to Define Populism? Reflections on a Contested Concept and its (Mis)use in the Social Sciences' in Gregor Fitzi, Jürgen Mackert, and Bryan S. Turner (eds.), *Populism and the Crisis of Democracy. Volume 1: Concepts and Theory* (Routledge 2018) 64.

7 Cathérine Colliot-Thélène, 'Populism as a Conceptual Problem' in Gregor Fitzi, Jürgen Mackert, and Bryan S. Turner (eds.), *Populism and the Crisis of Democracy. Volume 1: Concepts and Theory* (Routledge 2018) 19.

1.3 Conceptualizing populism

1.3.1 Historical background

Populism is not a recently discovered concept; its roots go back to the 19th century, and it was first used, perhaps, for the Populist Party in the United States and for the Narodnik movement in Russia at the end of that century. In reality, however, its use became widespread in post-World War II Europe, when it began to be applied to various political organizations, such as the French Poujade movement, the right-wing Development Party of the Danish Mogens Glistrup, and the left-wing movements that emerged in the 1970s and 1980s, such as the green parties in Western Europe.[8] These movements had different ideologies and political aspirations, but their common features were radicalism and opposition to the ruling political establishment.

Subsequently, populism emerged in various waves and was most often linked in the 1990s and 2000s to radical right-wing parties such as the Freedom Party (FPÖ) led by Jörg Haider in Austria, the French National Front by Jean-Marie Le Pen, Forza Italia in Italy which was founded and led by Silvio Berlusconi, or the Pim Fortuyn List (LPF) in the Netherlands. At the same time, some radical leftist movements have also been characterized as populists, such as the German The Left (*Die Linke*) or, at the same time, the Dutch and Scottish socialist parties. Although mostly outsider parties have been labelled in this way, some claim that 'since the early 1990s populism has become a regular feature of politics in western democracies'.[9]

However, populism also emerged outside Europe in the 20th century, and one of its best-known examples was the movement of Juan Perón in Argentina, which actually created traditions that persist to this day; and several other Latin American regimes have been considered populists since the 1960s. In the USA such a trait has often been assigned to the so-called alternative (i.e. not supported by the two major parties) presidential candidates, such as Ross Perot, Ralph Nader, and Pat Buchanan, but some also consider McCarthyism, which has been developing since the 1940s, to be populist.[10] Furthermore, populism was not limited to outsider or alternative movements, parties, or politicians, since many observers described such leading politicians as Tony Blair as populists, on the basis of his third-way program,[11] and this is how US President Jimmy Carter described himself.[12]

The latest surge of populism emerged in the 2010s and has now become so prevalent that it definitely deserves special attention. It is believed that the global economic crisis that erupted in 2008, the refugee crisis that peaked in 2015, and the terrorist attacks of 2010s all fuelled increasingly authoritarian

8 Cas Mudde, 'The Populist Zeitgeist' (2004) 39 Government and Opposition 548.

9 Ibid. 551. See also Jack Haward, *Elitism, Populism, and European Politics* (Oxford University Press 1996) 10.

10 Jan-Werner Müller, *What Is Populism?* (University of Pennsylvania Press 2016) 91.

11 Mudde (n 8) 551.

12 Müller (n 10) 91.

populist regimes in several post-communist countries in Central and Eastern Europe, strengthened the anti-immigrant and EU-sceptical populist movements in Western Europe, and played a role in events such as the withdrawal of the United Kingdom from the European Union. In 2014, 24 of the then 28 member states of the EU had populist parties in their parliaments.[13]

In the United States, the appearance, and subsequent development, of the Tea Party since the early 2000s, a process that reportedly culminated in the election of Donald Trump in 2016, is seen as part of a populist wave. But populism is present in several countries in Latin America (especially in Venezuela, Bolivia, Ecuador, and Brazil) and Asia (in the Philippines).

According to some, the novelty of today's populism is precisely its intensity and prevalence in constitutional democracies.[14]

1.3.2 The dimensions of populism

But what connects these vastly different politicians, movements, and political systems?

According to perhaps the most quoted definition, populism is

> a thin-centered ideology that considers society to be ultimately separated into two homogeneous and antagonistic camps, 'the pure people' versus the 'corrupt elite', and which argues that politics should be an expression of the volonté générale (general will) of the people.[15]

In this sense, populism only provides a framework that can be filled with substantive ideologies such as socialism or conservatism.[16] This means that although it can be considered an ideology, it is not a system of ideas that provides a comprehensive explanation for social coexistence or that defines the ideal of the best political system. Its central idea is to represent the 'real' interests of the people,[17] as opposed to the political elite that holds

13 Sofie Blombäck, 'Populism as a Challenge to Liberal Democracy in Europe' in Antonia Bakardjieva, Engelbrekt Niklas Bremberg, Anna Michalski, and Lars Oxelheim (eds.), *The European Union in a Changing World Order. Interdisciplinary European Studies* (Palgrave Macmillan 2020) 227–229.

14 Nadia Urbinati, 'Political Theory of Populism' (2018) 22 Annual Review of Political Science 112.

15 Cas Mudde and Rovira Kaltwasser, *Populism: A Very Short Introduction* (2nd ed. OUP 2017) 5.

16 Axel Mueller, 'The Meaning of 'Populism'' (2019) 45 Philosophy and Social Criticism, 1029; Bojan Bugarič, 'The Two Faces of Populism: Between Authoritarian and Democratic Populism' (2019) 20 German Law Journal 392; Théo Fournier, 'From Rhetoric to Action, a Constitutional Analysis of Populism' (2019) 20 German Law Journal 363; Mudde (n 8) 544.

17 Julian Scholtes, 'The Complacency of Legality: Constitutionalist Vulnerabilities to Populist Constituent Power' (2019) 20 German Law Journal 352.

(or usurps) power.[18] In other words, its defining characteristics are popular sovereignty and anti-elitism, which overrides the traditional left-right dichotomy of political ideologies[19] and is therefore difficult to classify among their traditional forms.

As has been stated by Jan-Werner Müller, who wrote a short monograph on the concept, populism is a specific moral conception of politics that contrasts a morally clean and united people with an elite that is supposed to be corrupt.[20] This kind of interpretation already leads to a conception of populism that identifies the concept with specific political aspirations. In this framework of conceptualization, the main objective of populism is to protect the ordinary citizens from elites and foreign groups (such as immigrants), and to replace corrupt elites.[21] It is a political trend that 'is inherently hostile to the idea and institutions of liberal democracy or constitutional democracy'.[22]

One of the crucial questions in the conceptualization of populism is its relationship to democracy, which is the most widely discussed topic in the relevant political science academic discourse. In this respect, the range of positions to found in the literature is particularly wide. At one end of the range of opinions are perceptions that view populism as a challenge to liberal democracy (or its elite) which is not in itself anti-democratic, even if its concept differs from that of Western-type constitutional democracy.[23] According to this view, populism can also be seen as an attempt at a correction of democracy that gives voice to groups that are not represented by elites.[24] Proponents of this position often cite examples that did not lead to an authoritarian system[25] but, on the contrary, attempted to make democracy more inclusive.[26] And although authoritarian populism has indeed taken on the hegemonic form today, many authors believe that democratic populism is also possible. This line has historically included in the United States the presidency of Andrew Jackson and the New Deal policy of Franklin Delano Roosevelt, and today in Europe the populism represented by the Spanish Podemos or the Greek Syriza Party.[27] Overall, therefore, after coming to

18 Margaret Canovan, 'Trust the People! Populism and the Two Faces of Democracy' (1999) 47 Political Studies 3; Mudde (n 8) 543.

19 Bojan Bugarič and Alenka Kuhelj, 'Varieties of Populism in Europe: Is the Rule of Law in Danger?' (2018) 10 Hague Journal on the Rule of Law 22.

20 Müller (n 10) 39.

21 Roger Eatwell and Matthew Goodwin, *National Populism: The Revolt Against Liberal Democracy* (Penguin 2018) 55–56.

22 Mudde (n 8) 561.

23 Eatwell and Goodwin (n 21) xi–xii.

24 Cristóbal Rovira Kaltwasser, 'The Ambivalence of Populism: Threat and Corrective for Democracy' (2012) 19 Democratization 185.

25 Paul Blokker, 'Varieties of Populist Constitutionalism: The Transnational Dimension' (2019) 20 German Law Journal 350.

26 Bojan Bugarič, 'Could Populism Be Good for Constitutional Democracy?' (2019) 15 Annual Review of Law and Social Science 43.

27 Ibid. 43, 46.

power, despite transforming democratic principles, populism does not break with democracy itself.[28]

However, according to the opposite view, a historical comparison shows that if populists come to power, they will build a system that is democratic but not liberal in that it merely imitates liberal principles and institutions but ultimately undermines liberal democracy.[29] In fact, this is a more frequent view, which sees populism as an authoritarian challenge to liberal democracy, which does not reject the principle of representation in modern democracies but is not considered democratic precisely because it promotes a conception of representation that claims exclusiveness inasmuch as populists consider themselves as the only legitimate representatives of the people. By this means, they are a real threat to democracy,[30] and, in the long run, they dismantle constitutional democracy[31] and do not introduce an open dictatorship simply because this would come at too high a political price.[32] Kim Lane Scheppele openly views politicians, otherwise characterized as populists, as autocrats who capture state institutions and use constitutional and democratic tools to destroy constitutional democracy. The new autocrats not only exploit popular distrust of public institutions but also attack the principles of liberal and democratic constitutionalism because they want to consolidate their own power and, while maintaining the appearance of democracy and the rule of law, use their democratic authorization to remove the limits on executive power.[33]

However, many authors think that the relationship between populism and democracy cannot be characterized in general terms, because any assessment of this issue largely depends on the normative presuppositions regarding democracy: thus, for example, adherents of liberal democracy generally see populism as a pathological phenomenon, while proponents of radical democracy hold that it strengthens representation; therefore, the evaluation of the relationship is less an empirical but rather a theoretical question, the answer to which depends on speculation as to how democracy should work.[34]

Some scholars simply use the concept of populism to denote political systems, parties, or movements that promote populist principles or follow such an ideology. Populism is accordingly a 'wide contemplative frame', marking very different left- and right-wing political regimes, which have in common

28 Urbinati (n 14) 118.

29 Takis S. Pappas, 'Populists in Power' (2019) 30 Journal of Democracy 70, 72, 82.

30 Müller (n 10) 103.

31 Jan-Werner Müller, 'Populism and Constitutionalism' in Cristóbal Rovira Kaltwasser, Paul Taggart, Paulina Espejo Ochoa, Pierre Ostiguy (eds.), *The Oxford Handbook of Populism* (Oxford University Press 2017) 603.

32 Müller (n 10) 50.

33 Kim Lane Scheppele, 'Autocratic Legalism' (2018) 85 The University of Chicago Law Review 547.

34 Kaltwasser (n 24) 185.

that they refer to the unified people as the ultimate source of political morality and public power.[35]

Others see populism only as a specific political style or rhetoric that refers to the power of the people or is based on anti-minority policies and attitudes.[36]

1.3.3 Types of populism

The vagueness of the concept of populism is counterbalanced by several authors by distinguishing between its types, often classifying extremely different groups or ideological creeds into this category. As already mentioned, the loose ideological frameworks of populism make it inclusive for traditional political streams, so it is not surprising that many differentiate between left-wing and right-wing populism and populists according to what values are associated with their ideology or ambitions, or from which social group they expect electoral support.[37] For example, Viktor Orbán and his party, Fidesz in Hungary, the informal leader in Poland, Jarosław Kaczyński and the ruling Law and Justice Party (*Prawo i Sprawiedliwość*, PiS), or the German opposition party Alternative for Germany (*Alternative für Deutschland*, AfD), are considered right-wing populists. In contrast, the Greek ruling party, Syriza and the Spanish opposition Podemos, or Bernie Sanders, a Democratic presidential candidate in 2016 and 2020, are generally characterized as leftists. It should also be noted that there are occasionally significant political-ideological cleavages between like-minded populist parties and movements, which makes the picture even less clear. In Europe, for example, some left-wing and right-wing parties support both the euro and European integration, while many other populist parties are Eurosceptic.[38]

Similarly, it is common to distinguish between 'negative' and 'positive',[39] 'good' and 'bad', 'authoritarian' and 'emancipatory'[40] populism, groups which are in fact based on the relationship of a particular populist policy regarding democracy, and accordingly the distinction is made between authoritarian and democratic populism. Thus, the populist regimes in Hungary and Poland are often seen as authoritarian based on their nationalism and the semi-authoritarian nature of their legal and political reforms,[41] as opposed to Western European populism, which has not destroyed liberal

35 Neil Walker, 'Populism and Constitutional Tension' (2019) 17 International Journal of Constitutional Law 517, 519; Fournier (n 16) 363.

36 See on this, Aziz Z. Huq, 'The People Against the Constitution' (2018) 116 Michigan Law Review 1124; and Mueller (n 16) 1130; Fournier (n 16) 365; Blombäck (n 13) 219.

37 Mark Tushnet, 'Comparing Right Wing and Left Wing Populism', in Mark A. Graber, Sanford Levinson and Mark Tushnet (eds.), *Constitutional Democracy in Crisis?* (Oxford University Press 2018).

38 Bugarič (n 16) 396.

39 See on this, Henrik Bang and David Marsh, 'Populism: A Major Threat to Democracy?' (2018) 39 Policy Studies 3.

40 Bugarič (n 26) 42.

41 For example, Bugarič (n 16) 393, Bugarič and Kuhelj (n 19) 22.

constitutionalism and the rule of law.[42] In particular, there are those who emphasize the democratic features of populism, arguing that populism provides responses to the real problems of liberal democracies, such as the gap between the representative institutions and the represented people,[43] or the 'lack of possibilities for meaningful civic engagement' in public decision-making.[44]

One of the best-known scholars of populism, Margaret Canovan, says there can be different varieties of populism depending on against what type of establishment they mobilize, because her approach is to define someone as populist because of how he or she relates to the power structure.[45] Other views suggest that while the original notion of populism, based on the juxtaposition of mass and elite, is often associated with authoritarianism and xenophobia, the latter phenomena should not necessarily be classified as populism because this kind of conceptualization is not useful for the analysis.[46]

1.4 The mysterious notion of populist constitutionalism

The debates on populism have also reached the constitutional discourse, recognizing that one of the distinguishing features of modern populism is its 'constitutional project', that is, the ambitions of populists to pursue constitutional changes to achieve their goals when they come to power.[47] It should be noted, however, that some opinions, as far as authoritarian populism is concerned, do not attach particular importance to formal rules because they believe that these regimes use primarily informal means; and they are rather characterized by the way they manipulate, circumvent, or evade constitutional and legal rules that would limit their power. Such systems, which are sometimes referred to as competitive authoritarian regimes, often operate within the framework of seemingly democratic constitutions but neutralize control of power by informal means.[48]

Nevertheless, after having come to power in several countries, those generally considered 'authoritarian populists' adopted new constitutions to serve their purposes (such as in Peru in 1995, Venezuela in 1999, Ecuador in 2008, Bolivia in 2009, and Hungary in 2011), or they achieved significant constitutional reforms (such as in Turkey in 2017, or in Poland after 2015). As a result, it is now common to believe that it would be erroneous to underestimate the importance of formal constitutional rules in the so-called

42 Bugarič and Kuhelj (n 19) 23.

43 Andrew Arato, 'How We Got Here? Transition Failures, Their Causes and the Populist Interest in the Constitution' (2019) 45 Philosophy and Social Criticism 1108.

44 Paul Blokker, 'Populism as a Constitutional Project' (2019) 17 International Journal of Constitutional Law 552.

45 Canovan (n 18) 4.

46 David Fontana, 'Unbundling Populism' (2018) 65 UCLA Law Review 1496.

47 Blokker (n 44).

48 Steven Levitsky and Lucan A. Way, *Competitive Authoritarianism: Hybrid Regimes After the Cold War* (Cambridge University Press 2010) 78–81.

'hybrid regimes' that also include populist governments. This is shown by the success and spread of the term 'populist constitutionalism', which, however, has several rival concepts depending on how observers classify the main aspirations of these movements and their relationship to constitutional democracy.

1.4.1 'Authoritarian', 'illiberal', or 'populist' constitutionalism?

Although some scholars suppose that after the recent threats of constitutional democracy, which have now become a global phenomenon, no new model of constitutional systems has emerged,[49] the constitutional effects of populism are considered by most academics to be so significant that it is treated as a separate category.[50]

The contemporary decline or backsliding of liberal democracies are defined in various ways, but many of the widely used labels such as 'constitutional breakdown',[51] 'stealth authoritarianism',[52] or 'democratic recession'[53] indicate the process rather than the substance.

The political systems that emerge as a result of these tendencies are often referred to in political science works as 'hybrid regimes',[54] or competitive[55] or electoral[56] authoritarianism. For many authors, some of the competing terms are interchangeable concepts or are related to each other as main and sub-groups.

Other scholars prefer to classify this legal transformation as, for example, 'autocratic legalism'[57] or 'counter-constitutionalism'.[58] Among the often-used terms, 'abusive constitutionalism' is frequently cited, according to which modern authoritarian regimes seek constitutional changes through which they can consolidate or preserve their power. However, a constitution or constitutional amendment for such a purpose can be considered abusive, as it is basically aimed at weakening or breaking down the limits of governmental power or making it more difficult for the opposition to come to power.[59]

49 Mark A. Graber, Sanford Levinson, and Mark Tushnet, 'Introduction' in Mark A. Graber, Sanford Levinson, and Mark Tushnet (eds.), *Constitutional Democracy in Crisis?* (Oxford University Press 2018) 3.

50 These oppositional categories, however, are not strictly correct, if we consider the question of whether or not populism has produced its own constitutional theory.

51 Wojciech Sadurski, *Poland's Constitutional Breakdown* (Oxford University Press 2019).

52 Ozan O. Varol, 'Stealth Authoritarianism' (2015) 100 Iowa Law Review 1673–1742.

53 Larry Diamond, 'Facing Up to the Democratic Recession' (2015) 26 *Journal of Democracy* 142.

54 Matthijs Bogaards, 'How to Classify Hybrid Regimes? Defective Democracy and Electoral Authoritarianism' (2009) 16 Democratization 399–423.

55 Levitsky and Way (n 48).

56 Andreas Schedler, *The Politics of Uncertainty Sustaining and Subverting Electoral Authoritarianism* (Oxford University Press 2013).

57 Scheppele (n 33) 545–583.

58 Paul Blokker, 'Populist Counter-Constitutionalism, Conservatism, and Legal Fundamentalism' (2019) 15 European Constitutional Law Review 519–543.

59 David Landau, 'Abusive Constitutionalism' (2013) 47 UC Davis Law Review 213.

According to other approaches, populism is a political phenomenon whose constitutional ambitions are better expressed by the terms 'illiberal' or 'non-liberal constitutionalism',[60] which is a stage in the process of a transition from liberal democracy to an authoritarian system, a special form of constitutional development that relativizes the rule of law, democracy, and human rights in politically sensitive matters and institutionalizes populist nationalism.[61] The term can be traced back to a frequently cited article by Fareed Zakaria,[62] but many politicians use the term for their own definition,[63] maintaining however that their illiberal regimes – such as in Poland and Hungary – can be classified as constitutional democracies.[64]

The effects of populism on the constitutional system are most often referred to as 'populist constitutionalism',[65] a term which is often preferred because it refers specifically to changes brought about by populist politics, while the epithets 'authoritarian' or 'illiberal' have broader meanings that can also be applied to non-populist regimes.

1.4.2 Populist constitutionalism: an oxymoron, or a special kind of constitutional system?

The political theory debate about the relationship between populism and democracy appears in the constitutional discourse mostly in the form of the dichotomy of populism and constitutionalism, which indicates the only existing consensus, i.e. that there is a tension between the two pillars of modern democracies, popular will and constitutionalism.[66]

While some scholars argue that constitutionalism also makes sense without a liberal character,[67] many claim that illiberal constitutionalism is an oxymoron because constitutionalism as such can only be liberal, whereas Central and Eastern European and Latin American populist regimes are seen as authoritarian regimes.[68]

60 Graham Walker, 'The Idea of Non-Liberal Constitutionalism' in Ian Shapiro and Will Kymlicka (eds.), *Ethnicity and Group Rights* (New York University Press 1997) 169.

61 Tímea Drinóczi and Agnieszka Bień-Kacała, 'Illiberal Constitutionalism: The Case of Hungary and Poland' (2019) 20 German Law Journal 1141, 1165; Aron Buzogány, 'Illiberal Democracy in Hungary: Authoritarian Diffusion or Domestic Causation?' (2017) 24 Democratization 1307–1325.

62 Fareed Zakaria, 'The Rise of Illiberal Democracy' (1997) 76 Foreign Affairs 22–43.

63 Drinóczi and Bień-Kacała (n 61) 1148.

64 Ibid. 1149.

65 For instance, in Paul Blokker, 'Populist Constitutionalism' Verfassungsblog, 2017/5/04. https://verfassungsblog.de/populist-constitutionalism/; David Landau, 'Populist Constitutions' (2018) 85 The University of Chicago Law Review 521–543.

66 Mény and Surel (n 3) 7–11.

67 Mark Tushnet, 'The Possibility of Illiberal Constitutionalism?' (2017) 69 Florida Law Review 1367–1384; Tom Ginsburg and Aziz Z. Huq, *How to Save a Constitutional Democracy* (The University of Chicago Press 2018).

68 See for example Gábor Attila Tóth, 'Constitutional Markers of Authoritarianism' (2019) 11 Hague Journal on the Rule of Law 37–61; Gábor Halmai, 'Populism, Authoritarianism and Constitutionalism' (2019) 20 German Law Journal 296–313.

Others suppose, however, that '[p]opulist constitutionalism is, ... limited to a procedural vision of democracy',[69] that is, populism does not necessarily undermine constitutional democracy, and the claim that populism is unconstitutional because of its inherent characteristics is erroneous.[70] In the United States, for example, just as populism has a positive, democratic tradition, populist constitutionalism has also a progressive trend that would give the people a greater role in determining the content of the constitution,[71] together with questioning or proposing at least a more moderate form of judicial review.[72] Although the new wave of populism in Europe has a primarily negative reputation, it is a Janus-faced concept that has different types, and that can be authoritarian or democratic; the point is that a populist constitutionalism that combines the principles of liberal constitutionalism and democracy is possible.[73] Populist constitutionalism is not a contradiction in terms if we mean by constitutionalism only that governmental practice complies with the constitutional requirements (whatever these are), and 'it is a theory of constitutions and constitutional practices that emphasizes their populist character and recommends that they develop along a populist trajectory'.[74]

According to its characteristics, populist constitutionalism can also be understood as a coherent political theory.[75] In this view, populist regimes are fighting not for an improved liberal constitutionalism, but for an alternative one based on direct legitimacy through the people.[76] Just as liberal constitutionalism is in fact an aspirational idea, so illiberal constitutionalism can also be a normative concept, albeit in the opposite direction.[77] Populism has a sui generis constitutionalism, a counterpart of liberal constitutionalism, and 'constitutional populism' is characteristic of government-run, institutionalized populism that pursues populist constitutional reforms, such as in Venezuela, Bolivia, or Hungary.[78] Unlike anti-constitutional regimes, such systems have constitutions that limit power, but they are not centred on individual rights, and are not ideologically neutral, but are based on the

69 Fournier (n 16) 381.

70 Bugarič (n 16) 390, 395.

71 See on this, Lucia Corso, 'What Does Populism Have to Do with Constitutional Law? Discussing Populist Constitutionalism and Its Assumptions' (2014) III Rivista di filosofia del diritto, 443–470.

72 As, for example, in Mark Tushnet, *Taking the Constitution Away from the Courts* (Princeton University Press 1999).

73 Ibid. 391. That is, there is not only exclusionary but also inclusive populism. Cédrich M. Koch, 'Varieties of Populism and the Challenges to Global Constitutionalism: Dangers, Promises and Implications' (2020) Global Constitutionalism 9.

74 Oran Doyle, 'Populist Constitutionalism and Constituent Power' (2019) 20 German Law Journal 164.

75 Ibid. 165.

76 Landau (n 59) 541.

77 Tushnet (n 67) 1368, 1371.

78 Manuel Anselmi, *Populism. An Introduction* (Routledge 2018) 87.

substantive values of ethnic, religious, or communitarian morality.[79] The constitutional policy of populists creates a radically different constitutional polity compared to the liberal legal-constitutional system; that is, it is a kind of response to constitutional orthodoxy,[80] even if in some countries, such as Poland or Hungary, there is a kind of counter-constitutionalism.[81]

However, the opposing view is that populist or illiberal constitutionalism is an oxymoron as far as authoritarian populism is concerned because liberalism is not only a restriction of the majority principle but also a precondition for democracy that guarantees the rule of law, a system of checks and balances and fundamental rights. If the main feature of constitutionalism is the legally limited power of government, then this requirement is not met, neither by authoritarian nor illiberal constitutionalism.[82] In other words, as populists reject the limits of political power, they also deny the very idea of constitutionalism,[83] because constitutionalism *per se* means that laws must conform to liberal principles.[84] As the inherent ambition of populism is to enforce the homogeneous will of a united people, it removes the limitations of the *vox populi* such as the separation of power, the autonomy of politically neutral bodies, or the rights of minorities.[85] Thus, it does not make sense to talk about populist constitutionalism in a meaningful way, because populists undermine not only its technical and organizational characteristics, but its basic values.[86] Some authors point out that this is not a static situation, but populist governance slowly, peacefully and, in a formal sense, legitimately abolishes constitutionalism, and illiberal democracy becomes an oxymoron only in the long run.[87]

In a sense, between these two opposing positions is the theory of 'abusive constitutionalism', which means 'the use of the mechanisms of constitutional change – constitutional amendment and constitutional replacement – to undermine democracy'. This approach sees the novelty of the contemporary global decline of liberal constitutionalism in the fact that autocrats today no longer come to power through coups and do not preserve it by open violence, but form governments through democratic elections and retain

79 Li-Ann Thio, 'Constitutionalism in Illiberal Polities' in Michael Rosenfeld and András Sajó (eds.), *The Oxford Handbook of Comparative Constitutional Law* (Oxford University Press 2013) 136.

80 Walker (n 35) 529.

81 Blokker (n 58) 520.

82 Halmai (n 68) 311–312.

83 Scholtes (n 17) 353.

84 Scheppele (n 33) 563.

85 Müller (n 31) 598.

86 Martin Krygier, 'The Challenge of Institutionalisation: Post-Communist "Transition", Populism, and the Rule of Law' (2019) 15 European Constitutional Law Review 570.

87 Wojciech Sadurski, 'Constitutional Crisis in Poland' in Mark A. Graber, Sanford Levinson, and Mark Tushnet (eds.), *Constitutional Democracy in Crisis?* (Oxford University Press 2018) 272; Gábor Attila Tóth, 'Breaking the Equilibrium: From Distrust of Representative Government to an Authoritarian Executive' (2019) 28 Washington International Law Journal 321.

their power by constitutional means. Such constitutional systems seem distantly democratic and contain many elements that can also be found in liberal constitutions; in reality, however, on closer inspection, they undermine democracy, as in Colombia, Venezuela, and Hungary. 'They are increasingly turning towards constitutional amendment and replacement as tools to help them construct a more authoritarian order', and use 'mechanisms of constitutional change in order to make a state significantly less democratic than it was before'.[88]

The background of these conceptualization debates is that while some accept the formal(ist) notion of constitutionalism, according to which it means the mere existence and enforcement of a constitution regardless of its content, others view constitutionalism in a 'material' sense; that is, according to them, it is possible to talk about constitutionalism in a meaningful way, only if certain (liberal) constitutional principles prevail in practice.

It is also worth noting that some authors distinguish between different forms of populist constitutionalism within its conceptual scope, making a distinction between, for example, 'inclusive' and 'exclusionary',[89] 'cosmopolitan' and 'communitarian'[90] constitutionalism (which are, in fact, repercussions of the liberal–illiberal dichotomy in other contexts), national and transnational constitutional populism,[91] and so on.

1.4.3 Defining populist constitutionalism: positive and negative criteria

Despite these conceptual debates, there is a broad consensus that populism has now posed a significant challenge to the institutions and principles of constitutional democracies, and that the category of populist constitutionalism has become so widespread that its use or exploration, even in a critical sense, can hardly be ignored if we want to understand this challenge.

Populist constitutionalism is often defined not only as the antithesis of liberal constitutionalism, but also on the basis of one or more of its characteristics. Many authors highlight a single aspect as a defining feature. Of course, these criteria are very often the same as the different conceptualizations of populism, or their constitutional transformations. Thus, for example, according to one conceptual attempt, populist constitutionalism is a constitutional practice based on the conflict between two homogeneous and antagonistic groups (a homogeneous people on the one side, and special interest groups such as the power establishment, technocrats, international organizations, immigrants, certain minority groups on the other) which redefines the balance between individual and collective interests.[92] Others suppose it to be a

88 Landau (n 59) 191, 195.
89 Blokker (n 25) 343.
90 Koch (n 73) 3.
91 Blokker (n 25) 344.
92 Walker (n 35) 516, 533.

constitutional strategy aimed at consolidating power,[93] while some identify this concept with the specific perception of the nature of constituent power and popular sovereignty.[94]

Some conceptual criteria that can be identified from the literature are negative ones, in the sense that populism and populist constitutionalism are often defined as criticisms or denials of certain key features of traditional constitutional democracies. At the same time, there are also positive criteria that relate to the main values, principles, and institutional solutions of this type of constitutionalism.

Most of these criteria, as we shall see, are characteristic of authoritarian populism and its constitutional conception; this is hardly surprising, since in practice this is the prevailing trend today. It is also important to note that the following characteristics are not specific to all populist governments or movements but are present in various countries to different degrees and in different combinations, and in the end, the various traits cannot be sharply separated from each other, i.e. there may be significant overlaps between them.

1.4.3.1 Negative criteria of populist constitutionalism

1.4.3.1.1 CRITICISM OF THE SEPARATION OF LAW AND POLITICS

Populists are usually critical of the liberal conception of constitutionalism and the rule of law, criticizing its depoliticization because it removes people from institutions. According to Paul Blokker, there is no difference between right-wing and left-wing populism in that both oppose the separation of law and politics, which means that populism rejects the restriction of political power by legal norms.[95]

Some scholars apply the theory of political constitutionalism to populist constitutional policy, claiming that the constitutional ambitions of populism represent a shift from legal to political constitutionalism; that is, they aim to establish a new constitutional order that supports the will of the people and the common good against particular interests.[96] However, this interpretation has also provoked controversy in the literature, as some authors argue that populist or illiberal constitutional aspirations, insofar as they seek to dismantle checks and balances, do not meet the democratic requirements of political

93 Simone Chambers, 'Democracy and Constitutional Reform: Deliberative versus Populist Constitutionalism' (2019) 45 Philosophy and Social Criticism 118.

94 Luigi Corrias, 'Populism in a Constitutional Key: Constituent Power, Popular Sovereignty and Constitutional Identity' (2016) 12 European Constitutional Law Review 9; Doyle (n 74) 164.

95 Blokker (n 44) 535–537, 539.

96 Lech Morawski, 'A Critical Response' Verfassungsblog, June 3, 2017.; Blokker (n 58) 531–532, Blokker (n 44) 539.

constitutionalism, as the latter does not mean unlimited public power, but this theory stresses that the restriction of power is of a political nature.[97]

Some argue that populists' 'legal resentment' is motivated by the fact that the politically neutral conception of law in a liberal democracy undermines the representation of the national interest because, for example, it allows constitutional courts and other supreme courts to obstruct the popular will.[98]

1.4.3.1.2 ANTI-ELITISM

It is a common feature of the various approaches of populism that one, if not the most essential, characteristic of this political phenomenon is the juxtaposition of the virtuous people and the corrupt elite, and their opposition to the elite's interests. In addition, populists refer to a united people (nation, community), or 'ordinary' people as opposed to a privileged cosmopolitan elite, i.e. to average people whose interests are suppressed by an arrogant elite, corrupt politicians, or minorities.[99] 'Populists are anti-establishment politicians – figures who, claiming to represent the voice of "the people", wage war on what they depict as a corrupt and conspiratorial elite'.[100] Notably, it is a radical anti-elitism that recognizes the will of the people as the only source of constitutional legitimacy.[101] Populism differs from other anti-regime groupings in that it questions not only those in power but also the values of the elite.[102] Not only does it sharply criticize the power elite, but in its political program, it also promises that by coming to power, people will take back control or take their country back from elites who usurp power.[103]

Nevertheless, there is some variety as to what groups are designated as part of the elite. Most often, politicians and parties in power (if they are not the populists themselves) are classified in this circle, but officials of the most anti-majoritarian institutions, such as the judges of the constitutional courts or ordinary courts, are frequently seen as elitist groups against whom the real will of the people must be enforced. But international organizations or EU institutions are also often seen as obstacles to popular will.

97 Pablo Castillo-Ortiz, 'The Illiberal Abuse of Constitutional Courts in Europe' (2019) 15 European Constitutional Law Review 63, 65; Halmai (n 68) 302, 304; Drinóczi and Bień-Kacała (n 61) 1161–1162.

98 Blokker (n 44) 549, 551.

99 Canovan (n 18) 5.

100 Steven Levitsky and Daniel Ziblatt, *How Democracies Die* (Crown Publishing 2018) 22.

101 Valerio Fabbrizi, 'Constitutional Democracy in the Age of Populisms: A Commentary to Mark Tushnet's Populist Constitutional Law' (2019) Res Publica, https://doi.org/10.1007/s11158-019-09430-7; Bojan Bugarič, 'Central Europe's Descent into Autocracy: A Constitutional Analysis of Authoritarian Populism' (2019) 17 International Journal of Constitutional Law 598; B. Guy Peters and Jon Pierre, 'A Typology of Populism: Understanding the Different Forms of Populism and Their Implications' (2020) Democratization, DOI: 10.1080/13510347.2020.1751615; Mudde (n 8) 543, 546; Müller (n 10) 2; Müller (n 31) 593.

102 Canovan (n 18) 3.

103 Mueller (n 16) 1026.

It is to be noted, however, that anti-elitism is often merely rhetoric, used mostly by populist opposition movements and politicians, and not infrequently selective – at least as is shown by the fact that some politicians generally classified as populists themselves belonged to the political (like the Hungarian Viktor Orbán or the Polish Jarosław Kaczyński) or the economic elite (like Silvio Berlusconi in Italy or Donald Trump in the United States) when they came to power. On the other hand, experience shows that populist governments are not inherently or generally anti-elitists, as they themselves often pursue elitist policies once they come to power, i.e., their political program is indeed more about only replacing the ruling or former elite.

The 'people', which is postulated as a uniform one, is often opposed by populist politicians not only to the ruling elite, but also to certain minority groups, such as LGBTQ communities or immigrants, whose distinctive features differ from the morality or identity of the majority. Populist governments can discriminate against enemy groups by legal means, also stigmatizing NGOs and alternative churches, or restricting their operations.

1.4.3.1.3 ANTI-INSTITUTIONALISM

Populism is usually characterized not only by its radical anti-elitism but also by its distrust of traditional institutions. This is often explained by the fact that populists see these institutions as obstacles to the will of the people, and when they come to power they weaken or dismantle them if they obstruct populist governance.[104] The illiberal version of populism rejects the constitutional limits of state power and the protection of minority rights.[105] Because non-majoritarian public bodies are generally seen as unnecessary intermediaries between the government and the people, anti-institutionalism can be characteristic even of populist movements that are considered democratic.

As we have pointed out, this kind of mistrust tends to manifest itself primarily against non-elected or anti-majoritarian institutions, in particular the constitutional courts, supreme and ordinary courts, and other politically neutral bodies such as election commissions or ombudsmen. Political attacks and structural changes can also target different types of supervisory bodies (such as media authorities, or economic competition authorities). This can take place in a number of ways, from political pressure to packing the institutions with loyal people, but here formal legal changes have special significance.

Constitutional changes offer an effective framework for these efforts, and populist governments in several countries have attempted to pass a new constitution or substantially amend the existing basic law. In Venezuela, for example, President Hugo Chávez convened a Constituent Assembly in 1999 to draft a new constitution, which was confirmed in a referendum in the

104 Bugarič and Kuhelj (n 19) 27, 69, Scheppele (n 33) 549.
105 Castillo-Ortiz (n 97) 49.

same year, and in 2009 another referendum abolished the constitutional limitation on presidential re-election. The same took place in Ecuador after the election of President Rafael Correa in 2007. In Hungary, the MPs of the ruling party coalition, which won a constitution-making majority in the 2010 general elections, voted for a new constitution in 2011, which has since been adapted nine times in favour of the current political interests of the governing parties. Russia and Turkey accomplished several constitutional reforms in the 2000s that strengthened presidential power, while in Poland, without formal constitutional amendments, significant structural changes were made, including through parliamentary legislation which put the Constitutional Court and the Judiciary under political control.

The lack of confidence in the existing institutional system naturally stems from a populist political view that identifies public bodies with a corrupt elite,[106] but perhaps more weight is given to power interests, that is, to neutralizing independent countervailing bodies and dismantling the system of checks and balances.

As a matter of fact, what we have seen with anti-elitism also applies in this respect: populists are not generally anti-institutional, for when they come to power, they try to put public authorities at the service of their own ends.[107] As Levitsky and Ziblatt claim, for autocrats, independent institutions are both a threat and an opportunity, so they are transformed so as to serve as an effective means of selectively enforcing laws, punishing opponents, and protecting their own people.[108] Institutional changes are therefore devoted to strengthening the executive and occupying and weakening countervailing powers.[109]

Overall, populist constitutions do not abolish the institutions of liberal democracy but merely imitate their operation, as they do not work in accordance with their original function but serve the interests of the authoritarian government.[110]

1.4.3.1.4 ANTI-PLURALISM

There is also a broad consensus among scholars that populists are against pluralism, considering themselves the only genuine representatives of the real interests of the people.[111] Most populist parties are critical of the functioning of representative democracy and often question the legitimacy and role of traditional parties.[112] This is because, according to the populist political view,

106 Landau (n 59) 526.

107 Müller (n 31) 598; Müller (n 10) 39; Landau (n 59) 537–539.

108 Levitsky and Ziblatt (n 100) 78.

109 Chris Thornhill, 'Constitutionalism and Populism: National Political Integration and Global Legal Integration' (2020) 12 International Theory 2.

110 Tóth (n 68) 52–53.

111 Mudde (n 8) 543; Müller (n 31) 593; Müller (n 10) 3; Bugarič and Kuhelj (n 19) 26.

112 Blombäck (n 13) 221; Urbinati (n 14) 113.

the people are united and indivisible, with a clear and recognizable will, and pluralism is a threat in their eyes to the real public interest.[113]

Anti-pluralism can be mere rhetoric, or in the constitutional sense it can mostly mean the restriction of freedom of expression and other political rights, the biased transformation of the electoral system, the obstruction of the operation of opposition parties, and so on.

1.4.3.1.5 ILLIBERALISM

As has been said, the emergence of populist movements is often seen as a challenge to liberal democracy, and their aspirations or views on the constitution are frequently referred to by many as illiberal constitutionalism. This is emphasized by many authors because this category is sufficiently broad to include politicians and parties that are not anti-democratic[114] within a populist conception. Certainly, this definition is not acceptable for those who identify democracy with its liberal form, supposing that populist constitutionalism rejects, or at least limits, the system of checks and balances, judicial review of laws, and in general any players with a veto which restricts the real will of the people,[115] because these guarantees are considered by many to be essential requirements and accessories of modern democracies.

However, the populist form of constitutionalism can be considered anti-liberal not only because of the rejection of power-sharing, but also because of the limitation of the protection of minorities and individual rights, which follows from the foundations of communitarian populism, according to which the public interest and the general will of the people should take precedence over individual and particular interests.

Both the dismantling of institutional barriers and the erosion of the rule of law, as well as the restriction of the protection of minorities and individual rights require constitutional-legal changes, as exemplified by populist constitutions and recent constitutional developments in countries with populist governments. Although there have been few or no examples of such institutional changes in several Central and Eastern European post-Soviet states, Poland's and Hungary's performance have deteriorated significantly in various independent surveys, rule of law and corruption indices, and reports of international human rights organizations since they have been ruled by populists, while Russia, Turkey, and Venezuela have generally been classified as consolidated autocracies.

1.4.3.2 Positive criteria of populist constitutionalism

Nevertheless, there are not only negative indicators among the criteria of populist constitutionalism, denying or criticizing certain constitutional

113 Blokker (n 44) 543.
114 Fabbrizi (n 101).
115 Ibid.

principles and institutions, but also positive criteria that offer a kind of answer or solution to the perceived or real democratic deficit of liberal constitutionalism. Some say, for example, that in Poland and Hungary, conservative populists want to build an alternative, 'counter-constitutional' order to replace liberal constitutionalism.[116]

Among these positive characteristics, those on which there is a broad consensus can be considered 'primary' criteria, while others are 'secondary' features that are attributed to populist constitutionalism by some academics but do not have a general recognition in scholarship. Many of these criteria are also closely related to and overlap each other, but it is worth separating them for analysis and clarity.

1.4.3.2.1 POPULAR SOVEREIGNTY AND DIRECT DEMOCRACY

Populist constitutionalism arises with the claim to directly represent the 'average people', that is, to enforce popular sovereignty.[117] As the public interest is uniform and can precisely be defined,[118] the function of representation is to implement it consistently and without hindrance.[119] This is based on a conception of popular sovereignty that sees the majority formed in elections as the sole source of democratic legitimacy.[120]

Consequently, the people are the constituent power, not in the institutionalized, indirect form as in liberal democracies, but as an imaginary entity whose will is not limited by the existing constitutional order. In other words, a populist interpretation of constituent power puts the rule of the people above the rule of law,[121] whatever that means.

Several authors point out that populists do not mean people in the empirical sense, that is, the community of citizens, but that there is no longer any consensus on what the constructivist conception of the people exactly signifies. Some say populism identifies the people with the majority of the electorate,[122] but they can think of the sovereign in the abstract sense, the 'ordinary people' or the nation[123] (ethnic community), while the concept of people often appears as a sort of mystical, homogeneous, and moral entity,[124] a 'collective subject' stuck together by tradition, common suffering, and destiny.[125]

116 Blokker (n 44) 542.
117 Ibid. 536–537.
118 Müller (n 10) 26; Corrias (n 94) 11.
119 Scholtes (n 17) 354.
120 Mueller (n 16) 1033.
121 Corrias (n 94) 9.
122 Mueller (n 16) 1036).
123 Mudde and Kaltwasser (n 15) 9.
124 Mudde (n 8) 546; Müller (n 10) 28.
125 Blokker (n 44) 542.

Yet, references to 'people' may lead to different value choices, depending on whether they are referred to in terms of *plebs*, *demos*, or *ethnos*.[126]

Some authors argue, however, that this reference to the people in terms of an abstract and unified entity is merely rhetoric, and populism is in fact a plebiscite conception of democracy in which the expression of the will of the electorate is limited to participation in elections.[127] Populists more often than not consider the people to be a passive mass, and once the representation of the genuine will of the people has taken place, there is no need for further popular participation.[128] In contrast, many authors argue that populism is characterized by a preference for direct democracy over institutionalized representation.[129]

In practice, the picture is very controversial. For example, while the Brexit referendum, generally held to be a populist enterprise, brought about significant political and constitutional changes in the United Kingdom, which is traditionally averse to direct democracy, unrestricted populist governance in Hungary confined the institution of referendum to serve governmental interests.[130]

1.4.3.2.2 AUTHENTIC POPULAR REPRESENTATION

According to a significant part of the literature on populism, this political ideology, style, or rhetoric is characterized by the claim to be an authentic and exclusive representation of the people imagined in the aforementioned sense.[131] Populist parties differentiate themselves from other parties by claiming that they represent the real interests of the people instead of the elite,[132] and they build their legitimacy on this base.[133] It is clear that the claim to authentically represent the people is a logical consequence of the aforementioned anti-pluralism, and that populists have as little trouble with

126 Rogers Brubaker, 'Why Populism?' in Gregor Fitzi, Jürgen Mackert, and Bryan S. Turner (eds.), *Populism and the Crisis of Democracy. Volume 1: Concepts and Theory* (Routledge 2018) 28.

127 Thornhill (n 109) 3.

128 Müller (n 31) 594.

129 Bugarič (n 16) 392; Bojan Bugarič, 'Central Europe's Descent into Autocracy: A Constitutional Analysis of Authoritarian Populism' (2019) 17 International Journal of Constitutional Law 598, Fabbrizi (n 101), Chambers (n 93) 117, Corrias (n 94) 12, 19.

130 Since 2010, hundreds of referendum initiatives have been rejected by the Fidesz-controlled National Electoral Commission, and only one national referendum, initiated by the government in an obviously unconstitutional manner, has taken place. See for this Zoltán Szente, 'The Controversial Anti-Migrant Referendum in Hungary Is Invalid' https://constitutional-change.com/the-controversial-anti-migrant-referendum-in-hungary-is-invalid/.

131 Müller (n 31) 593; Gábor Halmai, 'A Coup Against Constitutional Democracy. The Case of Hungary' in Mark A. Graber, Sanford Levinson, and Mark Tushnet (eds.), *Constitutional Democracy in Crisis?* (Oxford University Press 2018) 253.

132 Corrias (n 94) 11.

133 Canovan (n 18) 4.

representation if they are the representatives, just as political-administrative elitism is not the devil's work if they themselves make up the elite.[134] The almost natural consequence of this is the de-legitimization of the opposition, the limitation of its resources, and the disregarding of its proposals and initiatives, and the elimination of political discourse with the opposition parties.

Although the claim to be the authentic representatives of the people is often only part of the communication of populist politicians and movements, ample evidence indicates that in practice, populist governments, when they have the opportunity, seek to consolidate their power using constitutional or legal means. There are several ways to do this. Whereas government control of the media, widespread patronage, smear campaigns against the opposition, and their delegitimization are basically elements of the political toolbox,[135] such efforts can be effectively facilitated by various legal techniques. For example, biased intervention in the electoral system to provide illegitimate advantage for the governing parties over the opposition can most effectively be achieved through constitutional and legal reforms.

In the populist mindset, the authentic representation of the people also legitimizes the desire to see the one-time election victory – that is, the populist parliamentary majority – as a permanent but at least long-lasting mandate, so that later general elections become mere electoral approval of government policy.[136]

1.4.3.2.3 EXTREME MAJORITARIANISM

Populist constitutionalism can be characterized by the absolutization of the majority principle as long as the 'right' parties have won the election.[137] This majoritarian conception of democracy regards electoral empowerment as an expression of the will of the people and, on that basis, rejects the constitutional restriction of power.[138] This vision looks at politics as a zero-based struggle for dominance between political adversaries, claiming that only parties or politicians that have won a majority in elections can legitimately participate in political decision-making.[139] This idea may justify weakening non-elected controlling institutions, rejecting any veto of majority decisions based on legal or constitutional considerations, and ultimately contrasting the majority principle with the rule of law.[140] Here again, the repudiation of

134 Müller (n 10) 30.
135 Landau (n 59) 199; Mueller (n 16) 1037, 1041.
136 Müller (n 10) 63; Mueller (n 16) 1041.
137 Blokker (n 44) 543.
138 Landau (n 59) 533; Mudde (n 8) 561; Mueller (n 16) 1035; Scheppele (n 33) 562; Urbinati (n 14) 113.
139 Mueller (n 16) 1036.
140 Fournier (n 16) 366.

pluralism can be observed, as it considers the actual governing majority as a permanent one rather than a result or outcome of the continuous political struggle between rival parties, and it is reluctant to recognize minority interests' need for protection against the will of the majority.[141]

In reality, this does not mean a total denial of the protection of minorities or individual rights, but it does mean that these rights, depending on the weight of the presumed or real community interests, can be restricted to a much greater extent than in the practice of consolidated constitutional democracies.

1.4.3.2.4 THE STRONG LEADER (PERSONIFICATION OF POWER) AND THE STRENGTHENING OF EXECUTIVE POWER

Another widely recognized feature of populist constitutionalism is the concentration of power in the hands of a charismatic, strong leader.[142] Populists such as the American Donald Trump, the Russian Vladimir Putin, Recep Tayyip Erdoğan in Turkey, the Venezuelan President Nicolás Maduro, the Hungarian Prime Minister Viktor Orbán, and even the Polish Jarosław Kaczyński, who is without any leading position in government, and the French and Dutch opposition party leaders Marine Le Pen and Geert Wilders are all allegedly claiming that they are the genuine leaders of their people against corrupt elites.[143]

One of the characteristics of populist political leaders is that they differentiate themselves from the traditional elite by not following conventional forms of political behaviour in their politics or communication style,[144] by blending visions, and by flexibly alternating their statements and opinions. They also need to do so because, in fact, they often belonged to the former elite themselves, sometimes for decades,[145] such as the aforementioned politicians Orbán or Wilders; or Trump or Berlusconi, who belonged to the economic elite before starting their political careers.

Constitutional law can also be an effective tool for centralizing power, either by strengthening the executive (see, for example, the institutionalization of Latin American 'super-presidential' systems or the Turkish presidential system) or by neutralizing counterbalancing institutions or removing re-election barriers (as occurred in several South American countries or in Russia with the 2020 constitutional amendment).

141 Fontana (n 46) 365.

142 Bugarič and Kuhelj (n 19) 27; Drinóczi and Bień-Kacała (n 61) 1159; Landau (59) 539; Müller (n 10) 33; Pappas (n 29) 71–72. However, some do not consider this, together with some other criteria, to be a criterion for populism. See Kaltwasser (n 6) 68.

143 Bugarič (n 129) 598.

144 Blombäck (n 13) 220.

145 Fontana (n 46) 1502; Müller (n 10) 34; Mudde (n 8) 560; Peters and Pierre (n 91) 5.

1.4.3.2.5 THE INSTRUMENTALIZATION OF LAW

As has been said earlier, one of the peculiarities of contemporary populism is the recognition that the constitution can provide an effective toolbox for preserving power and breaking down checks and balances, so populist regimes are characterized by active constitution-making, as far as this is possible for them.

Nevertheless, the perception of law as an instrument of power itself is not one of the openly acknowledged values of populist political ideology, although in practice, this approach makes it easier to realize these values. Consequently, we can identify it as a common feature of populist constitutionalism. This way of thinking regards law on the one hand as a means of realizing political will, and on the other hand as a necessary condition for the preservation of power.[146] Besides this, in authoritarian populist systems, the formal legitimization of political decisions and the maintenance of the appearance of democracy and rule of law are important functions of the legal system.[147]

Constitutional changes provide particularly effective opportunities for all this, provided that the populists are able to enforce their perception of the role and normative nature of the constitution. This is because constitutional changes override all previous rules and can have a lasting effect. At the same time, in a case in which the aim of the constitution-making is to radically change the political system and to consolidate governmental power, the function of the basic law will change significantly: it will be no longer a guarantee of the status quo, but an engine of transformation. This necessarily conflicts with the normative and permanent nature of the constitution, not only where populists have the opportunity to amend the constitutional text as they wish (such as in Hungary, Russia, or Turkey), but also where – in the absence of a constitution-making majority – they achieve the same effect through the reinterpretation of the constitution (as in Poland).

Some scholars point out that the legalization of political decisions, regardless of their content, merely formally upholds constitutionalism; that is, it actually only imitates legality.[148] For this purpose, populists actually adopt 'pseudo-' or 'façade constitutions'[149] which, instead of restricting power, help to secure and perpetuate the power of populists, and with which autocrats disguise the true character of the system. And while many researchers on populism note that populist regimes carefully maintain formal legalism, in reality they very often circumvent or simply ignore their own constitution.[150]

146 Blokker (n 44) 545; Landau (n 59) 532; Müller (n 10) 63; Müller (n 31) 598.
147 Tóth (n 68) 52.
148 Levitsky and Ziblatt (n 100) 77; Scheppele (n 33) 573.
149 See Giovanni Sartori, 'Constitutionalism: A Preliminary Discussion' (1962) 56 American Political Science Review 853, 861; David S. Law and Mila Versteeg, 'Sham Constitutions' (2013) 101 California Law Review 863–952; and Tóth (n 68) 51.
150 Walker (n 35) 520.

1.4.3.2.6 OTHER (SECONDARY) CRITERIA

These 'secondary' criteria are often specific to certain regions or countries, or only to populist politics associated with specific ideologies, or deserve to be mentioned precisely because of their constitutional significance.

One of these characteristics is the preference for the concept of *constitutional identity*. Some argue that populists aim to define and defend the identity of the community,[151] or to set in stone their own image of the people[152] through constitutional changes. Moreover, constitutionalization can be a means of giving the nation a nationalist and religious concept and thus supporting authoritarian intentions.[153] The background motivation can be to symbolically strengthen the political unity of the people (or the supporters) and, through this, to legitimize populist governance,[154] despite the fact that, according to experience, the values included in the constitutions do not usually contain the real popular values.[155]

The legitimacy of populist rule is also supported by the *abusive legal borrowing* of certain legal institutions or procedures; more precisely, the way of argumentation which justifies some controversial constitutional-legal solutions by the fact that they also occur in consolidated democracies. These regimes frequently refer to the institutional patterns of developed Western democracies[156] and object to the 'double standard' that is used by those who criticize the populist institutional and legal reforms. Indeed, there are examples of almost all of the institutional settings brought about by populist regimes in consolidated democracies, but they meet the requirements of the rule of law individually and not as a whole.[157] The use of foreign patterns taken out of their context leads to a 'Frankenstein state' that 'is composed of various perfectly reasonable pieces, and [whose] monstrous quality comes from the horrible way that those pieces interact when stitched together'.[158]

Some scholars also specify *crisis management* as a source of legitimacy for populism because an external threat gives populists the opportunity to legally break free from the limits of power.[159] In Turkey, for example, the failed coup in 2016 provided an opportunity for the government to impose repressive measures, followed by the introduction of a presidential system in 2017 with a referendum strengthening President Recep Tayyip Erdoğan's power, while

151 Blokker (58).
152 Müller (n 31) 603; Corrias (n 94) 23.
153 Halmai (n 68) 310; Cesare Pinelli, 'The Rise of Populism and the Malaise of Democracy' in Sacha Garben, Inge Govaere, Paul Nemitz (eds.), *Critical Reflections on Constitutional Democracy in the European Union* (Hart 2019) 42.
154 Thornhill (n 109) 2; Walker (n 35) 522.
155 Mila Versteeg, 'Unpopular Constitutionalism' (2014) 89 Indiana Law Journal 1137.
156 Rosalind Dixon and David Landau, '1989–2019: From Democratic to Abusive Constitutional Borrowing' (2019) 17 International Journal of Constitutional Law 493.
157 Mark Tushnet, 'Varieties of Populism' (2019) 20 German Law Journal 386.
158 Kim Lane Scheppele, 'The Rule of Law and the Frankenstate: Why Governance Checklists Do Not Work' (2016) 26 Governance 560.
159 Levitsky and Ziblatt (n 100) 93.

in Hungary the outbreak of the coronavirus pandemic in 2020 led to the declaration of an emergency situation providing an unlimited authorization for the Orbán government, the most important elements of which were later enacted, i.e. perpetuated, by the two-thirds parliamentary majority of Fidesz after the end of the special legal order. Some authors presume that populists sometimes invent or exacerbate a crisis situation themselves because citizens are more tolerant or even supportive of authoritarian measures in times of crisis that threaten their security.[160] Populism usually does not emerge in stable, orderly conditions, which is also the reason why populist governance is said to be difficult to maintain in the long run, or after normalcy returns.[161]

Among the operational characteristics of populist, illiberal states, the *restriction of certain fundamental rights*, as well as the *intolerance of or discrimination against certain minorities*, can be highlighted. This usually affects political rights, especially freedom of expression, academic freedom, and the right of assembly and association. Presumably, the more authoritarian a populist system becomes, the more likely it is that personal freedom will be restricted.[162] Negative campaigning, and direct and indirect discrimination against Roma, immigrants, LGBTQ communities or certain religious 'sects' that do not belong to the people or endanger their culture and identity, are also frequent phenomena. These actions may not only be taken through political or administrative measures, but they may also gain a legal-constitutional basis through legal preference, for example, for the traditional family model, the discriminatory regulation of the status of churches and NGOs, or the tightening of certain fundamental rights restrictions.

These manifestations of 'nativism' are often associated with *anti-globalism*, insofar as populism is hostile to all 'foreign' political values because it sees them as a threat to national sovereignty or to the true will of the people. In populist rhetoric, this threat is most often represented in Europe by the EU institutions and the European courts, but the alleged evidence of the threat can be, for example, EU immigration policy or criticisms from international organizations (interpreted as attacks on 'Hungarians', 'Poles', or 'Turks'). It is important to add, however, that some views also see progressive political tendencies (such as the Greek Syriza Party) which are not characterized by anti-liberalism and nativism, as populist.[163]

Clientelism, *state capture*, and the '*Gleichschaltung*' of certain social systems (putting them under direct political control), which are also characteristic of populist governments, require the use of legal instruments as well.

160 Levitsky and Ziblatt (n 100) 94, 208; Müller (n 10) 43; Blombäck (n 13) 223.

161 Paul Taggart, 'Populism and the Pathology of Representative Politics' in Yves Mény and Yves Surel (eds.), *Democracies and the Populist Challenge* (Palgrave MacMillan 2002) 69.

162 See e.g. Sadurski (n 51); Sadurski (n 87) 268–270; Tóth (n 68) 54; Bugarič (n 129) 607–608.

163 Robert Howse, 'In Defense of Disruptive Democracy – A Critique of Anti-Populism' (2019) 17 International Journal of Constitutional Law 643. Howse defines populism as any action against the elitist policies of advanced liberal democracies. Ibid. 641.

According to some authors, the systematic patronage, clientelism,[164] and the 'colonization' of the state – that is, the 'occupation' of the most important institutions (filling them with politically loyal people) – are features of populism.[165] In a sense it is not surprising, because if populists consider themselves to be the only true representatives of the people, it is justified to take possession of public institutions and to take action against those who obstruct the pursuit of the genuine public interest.[166] It is to be noted, furthermore, that the power ambitions of populists are not limited to political institutions, but are also aimed at influencing certain social sub-systems, as a consequence of their identity-based ideology. This can be manifested by stigmatizing the politically suspicious non-governmental organizations, restricting their operation, interfering in the scientific and artistic sphere and in the system of public education, for which legislation provides opportunities, as is also the case in the often statist, protectionist economic policy.

Whatever combination of the aforementioned primary and secondary criteria of populist constitutionalism is achieved in a country, it is sure that they raise a significant challenge to traditional representative government and liberal constitutionalism. And if they have, or may have, such an important effect on the functioning constitutional systems, then it can be rightly assumed that this influence extends to the methods of constitutional interpretation and, of course, to its outcome. However, in order to assess this effect, it is necessary to clarify the nature and definition of the constitutional interpretation which is as controversial as the concepts of populism and populist constitutionalism themselves. It is discussed in the next chapter.

164 Müller (n 31) 597; Pappas (n 29) 72, 74.
165 Pappas (n 29) 73; Landau (n 59) 200.
166 Müller (n 31) 596.

2 The art of constitutional interpretation

Fruzsina Gárdos-Orosz and Zoltán Szente

2.1 Defining constitutional interpretation

The concept of legal interpretation has several meanings. It is usually understood as determining the meaning of a legal norm; that is, this definition treats the process as a rational activity by which a meaning is derived from a linguistic formula.[1] This general definition can also be applied to the interpretation of the constitution: on the basis of this, constitutional interpretation is the process of giving concrete meaning to the particular provisions of the constitution.[2]

Beyond this definition, there are already differing views on the conceptualization of legal interpretation. Some argue that this category should be used in a narrower sense, claiming that interpretation is needed only if the meaning of the text is not clear[3] and there is a difference between the comprehension and interpretation on the one hand, and the application of a legal text on the other,[4] while others argue that interpretation is essential to reveal the meaning of a legal norm in all cases.[5] The narrower concept of interpretation follows the principle of *in claris non fit interpretatio* (the clear rule does not require interpretation), while the rival approach claims that this statement – namely that a rule is not clear – is itself a result of interpretation. For a text to be able to behave as a rule, it must have a rational meaning, that is, an identifiable content that can be justified to some level of certainty for all participants in the constitutional discourse.

According to another view, the fundamental question of legal interpretation is how the legal norm as a general rule is applied to a specific case, i.e. the

1 Jerzy Wróblewski, 'Legal Language and Legal Interpretation' (1985) 4 Law and Philosophy 243; Andrei Marmor, *Interpretation and Legal Theory* (Clarendon Press 1992) 13; Aharon Barak, *Purposive Interpretation of Law* (Princeton University Press 2005) 3, 18.
2 Donald P. Kommers, John E. Finn and Gary J. Jacobsohn, *American Constitutional Law. Essays, Cases and Comparative Notes. Vol. 1: Governmental Powers and Democracy* (Rowman & Littlefield Publishers 2009) 34.
3 Wróblewski (n 1) 243.
4 Marmor (n 1) 12–13, 31, 122.
5 Barak (n 1) xv. Barak argues that it is not possible to determine in advance whether a text has a clear or unclear meaning: this can be determined only by interpretation. Ibid. 273.

interpretation of each norm comes to the fore during its execution,[6] while other scholars conceptually separate this process of legal thinking – as subsumption – from interpretation. Nevertheless, in the value-based conception of constitutional interpretation, the function of interpretation is basically to ensure that state actions remain within the framework of the provisions and principles of the constitution.[7]

As to the circumscription of interpretation, there is a broad consensus that the linguistic limitations of a text are also limitations of interpretation, and the latter is an activity that attributes a meaning to the norm which is consistent with the grammatical meaning of the text. However, this does not provide sufficient guidance to distinguish between interpretation and other forms of legal thinking, as language is not a completely precise form of expression and, moreover, its meaning can be explicit or implicit. It is therefore clear, empirically, that the same text may be understood differently even by speakers of the same language, whereas the expectation is that the law, as a set of general and enforceable rules of conduct, will form a system of norms that is comprehensible and predictable in advance. This is the reason why legal interpretation is such a fashionable and frequent subject in legal discourse, and why so many attempts have been made and will continue to be made to describe and explain it (to justify the best method of interpretation).

In fact, constitutions often use ambiguous, uncertain and contradictory terms, or remain silent on issues that need to be resolved in constitutional disputes. In such cases, an interpretation is needed because the constitutional text does not provide full guidance on how to answer the question involved in the particular constitutional controversy.[8] There may be several reasons why the constitution is not clear. First, this is the case for all legal norms, as they are *per se* normative in nature, i.e. general rules that contain binding provisions for a large number of individual cases. Second, the subjects of the constitutions are also very complex social relations. Their text is often the result of political compromises, and it is also possible that the original ideas of the constitution makers were not clear either, or even that they deliberately used terms with abstract, vague meanings.[9]

The uncertainty or multiple meanings of the text make certain legal disputes 'hard cases' that can be resolved only by interpretation. Although the problem of hard cases leads us back to debates about the necessity of interpretation,[10] it is certain that resolving such cases requires legal interpretation,

6 Hans Kelsen, 'On the Theory of Interpretation' (1990) 10 Legal Studies 127.

7 Sotirios A. Barber and James E. Fleming, *Constitutional Interpretation: The Basic Questions* (Oxford University Press 2007) 13.

8 Kommers, Finn and Jacobsohn (n 2) 34.

9 Walter F. Murphy, James E. Fleming, and William F. Harris II, *American Constitutional Interpretation* (The Foundation Press 1986) 5.

10 Whereas Ronald Dworkin, for example, says that resolving both 'easy' and 'hard cases' presupposes interpretation, others claim that easy cases are those in which the rule (and the way it is implemented), even without interpretation, is known. See Ronald Dworkin, *Law's Empire* (Belknap Press 1986) 266, 353–354, and Timothy A. O. Endicott, 'Putting Interpretation in Its Place' (1994) 13 Law and Philosophy 466.

as these cases are usually difficult precisely because it is not clear what rule applies to them, or because the rule applicable to them is fuzzy and vague. Besides that, especially in the case of old constitutions, the original constitutional principles no longer meet the requirements of the modern age, and due to the inflexibility of the constitution, interpretation remains the only reasonable way to adjust its content to social change.[11] Moreover, certain otherwise important provisions (empowerments, restrictions) are missing from the constitutional text, or at least there is no directly and clearly applicable rule. One of the most famous such shortcomings in constitutional history is that the judicial review of federal legislation is not explicitly recognized by the US Constitution, although it is a fundamental institution of US constitutional law. Missing provisions often cause problems in fundamental rights matters, not only if the text does not include an explicit entrenchment of a universally accepted freedom, but also when the constitution does not provide guidance on how to restrict fundamental rights or to reconcile them when they come into conflict with each other. Creating institutions, guarantees and procedures, or constructing unenumerated rights absent from the constitutional text by way of judicial decisions is always controversial, because it is difficult to justify that courts merely realize the will of constitution makers, rather than replace it with their own convictions. In any case, it does not seem to be a compelling argument that what is not included in the constitutional text could surely not be the intention of the constituent power, as social, economic, technical, etc., developments from time to time create new needs and situations that the constituent power could not even imagine. When drafting constitutions decades ago, for example, constitution makers clearly could not have known of the future existence of antibiotics, space research, organ transplantation, human cloning, microchips or the Internet – that is, so many things that can cause urgent constitutional problems that must be resolved even if the constitution cannot be properly amended for any reason.

2.2 Classifying interpretive theories

2.2.1 Monist and pluralistic theories

Clearly, whatever concept of constitutional interpretation is accepted, the definition of which interpretive method should be followed does not include a judgement on which one is the most authentic or the best. The authority of the constitutional text alone does not imply the primacy of any particular modality of interpretation.[12] This is because the concept of interpretation is quite abstract and flexible, so any choice of how a judge should interpret

11 Jeffrey Goldsworthy, 'Introduction' in Jeffrey Goldsworthy (ed.), *Interpreting Constitutions. A Comparative Study* (Oxford University Press 2007) 1.

12 Frederick Schauer, 'An Essay on Constitutional Language' (1982) 29 UCLA Law Review 812, 817, 828.

a legal text can be based on several different factors, from the purpose of interpretation to legal culture.[13] The possible interpretive methods are, in fact, '*axiomes fondés sur l'expérience*' (axioms based on experience), and they themselves are not legal norms. The choice between them in a particular case is, however, important, because it does not follow from the fact that the text has a multifarious or multilayered meaning which has to be interpreted in several different ways.

Although some constitutions contain provisions as to how their own texts should be interpreted,[14] most of them do not provide any guidance in this regard. But even where such provisions can be found in the constitution itself, their validity is not general, and especially not exclusive, as in modern constitutional democracies, constitutional and legal interpretation falls within the scope of the authority of courts.

The theories of constitutional interpretation are normative approaches about how the constitution should be interpreted in general. In order to be able to choose from among different interpretive theories, or simply from among the various methods of interpretation, it is necessary to determine what their function is and what requirements a consistent theory should meet. For this aim, several different aspects are defined, such as that interpretive theories should properly describe the practice of constitutional interpretation, provide strong normative justification for their preferred methods, produce satisfactory results resolving constitutional disputes, and limit the scope for judicial discretion; in brief, they should provide, as far as possible, objective methods. The problem is, however, that different interpretive philosophies adjust the expectations of 'proper' interpretive methods to their own conceptions. Thus, for example, the originalists like to postulate a fundamental requirement for theories of interpretation that they ensure the realization of the original intentions of the constitution-makers, which is clearly an unacceptable criterion for the adherents of a dynamic approach to the constitution. Among the possible options, perhaps the most common is the sceptical perception that there is no 'true' or 'genuine' method of interpretation – the only option available is to determine the most plausible method for a given case.

The interpretive rules must ensure the reasonableness of the whole process of discovering the meaning of the text and justify the preferred method(s). Obviously, they have the important function of safeguarding constitutionalism and the rule of law, because if everyone were to be free to interpret the constitution in the way they wanted, the supremacy of the constitution and legal certainty in general could not be maintained.

Some interpretive theories claim that their preferred method is suitable for interpreting any or every type of legal text. Those that are based on the primacy of a particular method we call monistic theories. Of course, there may also be significant differences between them in terms of their ambitions and

13 Endicott (n 10) 451.

14 See Gamper, Chapter 3 in this volume.

scope, and depending on whether their preferred method takes precedence in all cases,[15] or only in the so-called hard cases,[16] that is in deciding problems that cannot be solved by grammatical or traditional means of interpretation in general.[17] The possibilities of language are limited, so the use of an interpretive theory is needed to determine how the meaning of a legal text should be revealed, if it is not clear.

The other group of interpretive theories can be called pluralistic approaches, which deny the prominent role of a particular method, except for the textualism or grammatical-logical interpretation, which in most perceptions is an indispensable part of the process of interpretation. Instead, they suppose that deciding which method leads to the best result depends on the particular text or constitutional provision (or, possibly, on the specificity of the concrete dispute). While this view seems to be pessimistic as regards objectivity – a celebrated value of law (and legal interpretation) – it seems to be much closer to the day-by-day practice of constitutional interpretation.

At the same time, some take a sceptical position against such theories, disputing their justifiability or usefulness. This is not surprising from those who argue that interpretation should enforce pragmatic considerations rather than follow the prescriptions of a normative theory. The usefulness of interpretive theories is also questioned by some because judges in a significant number of cases achieve the same result regardless of the preferred method of interpretation, and even similar interpretive results would be produced in many other cases that do not go to court precisely because of the broad consensus.[18] However, neither is the need for theorization reinforced by the fact that most well-known normative conceptions do not lead to a definite result in a number of cases, or in their pure form often reach unacceptable conclusions.[19] Finally, such theories are often invented by law professors, who present them to other scholars without their having any significant impact on legal practitioners.[20]

As I have already pointed out, there is a broad consensus between monistic and pluralist interpretive theories that the correct interpretation should be based on, or at least traceable to, the constitutional text.[21] Beyond that, however, practice shows that courts rarely commit themselves to a particular

15 See, for example, Aharon Barak's theory of purposive interpretation. Barak (n 1) 2005.

16 For example, Dworkin's moral interpretive theory. Ronald Dworkin, *Taking Rights Seriously* (Duckworth 1991) 81–130; Ronald Dworkin, *Freedom's Law: The Moral Reading of the American Constitution* (Oxford University Press 1999).

17 In contrast, those cases are considered 'easy cases' in which there is agreement in the constitutional scholarship on the content of the relevant constitutional provisions and the method of interpretation to be applied. Robert Justin Lipkin, 'Indeterminacy, Justification and Truth in Constitutional Theory' (1992) 60 Fordham Law Review 609.

18 Adam M. Samaha, 'Low Stakes and Constitutional Interpretation' (2010) 13 Journal of Constitutional Law 312–313.

19 Ibid. 313–315.

20 Richard A. Posner, 'Against Constitutional Theory' (1998) 73 New York University Law Review 4.

21 Kommers, Finn, and Jacobsohn (n 2) 36.

method of interpretation; instead, they usually represent an eclectic, pragmatic approach. Yet this is not only a practical consideration, but also a theoretically defensible position, because it can be strongly argued that in a hermeneutical sense it is the best output of interpretation to which most interpretive methods lead. This is why some constitutional thinkers suppose that it is a hermeneutical requirement for the interpreter to consider all canons of interpretation. However, for those who think that some methods are better than others, this is hardly a convincing view, especially if the case before the court can be easily resolved in the preferred way.

2.2.2 Other classifications of interpretive theories

Experience shows that the debates over the principles of constitutional interpretation have nowhere led to any generally accepted or exclusive method.[22] In contrast, there are a number of more or less well-accepted ways of interpretation in constitutional law.

In general, a number of tools of legal interpretation are identified,[23] and there is a broad consensus that judicial practice is characterized by the pluralism of applied methods, and by the combined and variable use of interpretive modalities.[24]

In Europe, the most classic categorization of the methods of legal interpretation is linked to the German jurist Carl Friedrich von Savigny, who distinguished between grammatical, logical, historical (referring to the original intent of the lawmaker) and systematic ways of interpretation.[25] Laws were

22 Dieter Grimm, 'Constitutional Adjudication and Interpretation' (2011) NUJS Law Review 23.

23 Fritz Ossenbühl, 'Grundsätze und Grundrechtsinterpretation' in Detlef Mertem and Hans-Jürgen Papier (eds.), *Handbuch der Grundrechte in Deutschland und Europa. Band I. Entwicklung und Grundlagen* (C.F. Müller 2004) 600; Klaus Stern, 'Die Auslegung des Verfassungsrechts' in Klaus Stern (ed.), *Das Staatsrecht der Bundesrepublik Deutschland. Band I. Grundbegriffe und Grundlagen des Staatsrechts, Strukturprinzipien der Verfassung* (C. H. Bech'sche Verlagsbuchhandlung 1984) § 4, III. 1.

24 The U.S. Supreme Court, for example, in *Griswold v. Connecticut*, 381 U.S. 497 (1965), used at least six different methods of interpretation. Kommers, Finn, and Jacobsohn (n 2) 47.

25 Friedrich Carl von Savigny, *Vorlesungen über juristische Methodologie, 1802–1842* (Vittorio Klostermann 2004) 91–95, 215–246; Friedrich Carl von Savigny, *Das System des heutigen Römischen Rechts. Erster Band* (Veit und Camp 1840) 213–214. Although Savigny applied these methods of interpretation to private law, his classification is generally considered valid also in constitutional law, supplemented, possibly, by a method of comparative law, encouraged by the practical benefits of comparing EU law, the case law of the European Court of Human Rights and national constitutions. See 11 BVerfGE 126, 129 (1960); Michael Sachs 'Einführung' in Michael Sachs (ed.) *Grundgesetz. Kommentar* (Verlag C. H. Beck 2011) 15–16; Winfried Brugger, 'Legal Interpretation, Schools of Jurisprudence, and Anthropology: Some Remarks from a German Point of View' (1994) 42 The American Journal of Comparative Law 397; Christian Starck, 'Die Verfassungsauslegung' in Josef Isensee and Paul Kirchhof (eds.), *Handbuch des Staatsrechts dr Bundesrepublik Deutschland. Band VII. Normativität und Schutz der Verfassung – Internationale Beziehungen* (C. F. Müller 1992) 200.

obviously interpreted from the very beginnings (in Hungary, for example, István Werbőczy's *Tripartitum*, a collection of medieval customary law published in 1517, already contained references to the methods of legal interpretation). Savigny's significance lies primarily in systematizing and theorizing the possible interpretive methods. According to conventional wisdom, judges must interpret the law using these methods and choose between them according to which leads to the best solution.

In the United States, the American lawyer Joseph Story had already dealt with the issue of correct constitutional interpretation before Savigny, when, in his voluminous commentary on the American Constitution, the first edition of which was published in 1833, he wrote: '[t]he first and fundamental rule in the interpretation of all instruments is, to construe them according to the sense of the terms, and the intention of the parties',[26] while a scientific systematization of interpretive methods appeared in American legal literature as early as 1837.[27]

Constitutional interpretation theories can be descriptive or normative. While the former instantiate, explain and systematize the practice of interpretation, the latter also claim that there are correct and incorrect interpretive methods and include the principles of choosing between them.[28]

These theories can also be labelled according to whether or not a hierarchy is defined between different interpretation methods. As we have seen, monistic theories favour the primacy of a particular method, but pluralistic interpretive philosophies do not reject this claim, either. So it is broadly accepted that the exercise of interpretation should start with the exploration of the grammatical-logical meaning of the text, and any other methods may be used only if an appropriate interpretive result cannot be established, or an absurd conclusion would be reached in this way. Theories other than textualism therefore do not dispute the grammatical interpretation itself or its legitimacy, but only its exclusive or primary nature.[29] The alternative methods generally do not replace but merely supplement the grammatical interpretation.[30] But even in the absence of a strict and permanent hierarchy of interpretive methods, some scholars argue that although multiple methods can be legitimately used in the course of constitutional interpretation, some of them are better than others, and the recognition of the multiplicity of interpretive principles does not exclude the fact that in

26 Joseph Story, *Commentaries on the Constitution of the United States, Vol. I* (Hilliard, Gray, and Company 1833) 383.

27 Francis Lieber, *Legal and Political Hermeneutics* (F. H. Thomas 1837). On Lieber's legal and political hermeneutics see also the special issue of *Cardozo Law Review*, Vol. 16, No. 6, April 1995.

28 Susan J. Brison and Walter Sinnott-Armstrong, *Contemporary Perspectives on Constitutional Interpretation* (Westview Press 1993); Richard Fallon Jr., 'How to Choose a Constitutional Theory' (1999) 87 California Law Review 537.

29 Sachs (n 25) 15; Frank B. Cross, 'The Significance of Statutory Interpretive Methodologies' (2006–2007) 82 Notre Dame Law Review 1973.

30 Cross (n 29) 1974.

individual cases some can be more effective than others, and, therefore, it may be preferred to move from the more concrete to the more abstract in the process of interpretation.[31] In Germany, for example, it is a widespread perception that, although traditional principles of interpretation are equally applicable, the plain meaning of the text must be respected in the course of interpretation.[32]

In the American legal literature, the distinction between interpretivism and non-interpretivism has been widespread since the mid-1970s.[33] In this classification, the methods based on the semantic meaning as well as the originalist approach were classified in the first group, while the second group includes those – mainly natural and moral – schools which legitimize or prefer the use of non-textual sources for interpretation. So-called 'interpretivism' is the approach that 'it is the Constitution alone which is authoritative, whereas noninterpretivism is the view that in at least certain classes of cases some set of supplementary, extra-constitutional norms are authoritative as well'.[34] Interpretivism is based on legal positivism according to which, in the absence of a consensus on the exact content and requirements of natural rights or moral principles, the social consensus necessary for the constitution to prevail can be grounded only on positive, consensual agreements between the people. By contrast, 'non-interpretive' theories state that the constitution includes, in addition to the written text, unwritten, more general moral or political principles which must also be taken into account in the course of interpretation.[35]

Some distinguish 'substantive' theories that see the representation of certain moral or political values as the main task of constitutional interpretation, while 'formalist' theories are those that determine what kinds of considerations judges should follow when they adjudicate.[36]

In principle, a further distinction can also be made between 'static' and dynamic (or evolutive) schools of interpretation on the basis that while the

31 Thus, for example, in statutory interpretation through the examination of the legal text, the original legislative process, the legal purpose, the history of the development of the law, and the current aspirations. William N. Eskridge Jr. and Philip P. Frickey, 'Statutory Interpretation as Practical Reasoning' (1990) 42 Stanford Law Review 353.

32 Brugger (n 25) 400. It is to be noted that Savigny, who is still considered a classic of interpretation theory throughout Europe, did not establish any hierarchy between the various principles. 'So there are not four kinds of interpretation from which one could choose according to taste or preference, but there are different activities that must be combined, when interpretation is to be done'. Savigny, *Das System des heutigen Römischen Rechts* (n 191) 215.

33 Michael Perry, *Morality, Politics and Law* (Oxford University Press 1988) 10–11.

34 Dennis J. Goldford, 'The Political Character of Constitutional Interpretation' (1990) 23 Polity 262.

35 Ibid. 264–265.

36 Fallon (n 28) 562–563. Notably, the substantive–formalist division is not the same as the interpretivism–non-interpretivism dichotomy. In this respect, for example, both moral and pragmatic interpretation are formalistic because they refer to the need to strive for the morally best decision, or for the most effective solution. Ibid. 563–564.

former claims that constitutional interpretations are framed by the original intentions (or objectives) of the constitution-makers, the latter emphasizes that interpretation develops through constant changes, because the constitution does not have eternal meaning, but should be accommodated to continuously changing circumstances and values.[37]

Notwithstanding, practical experience shows not only that there is no authentic method or exact ranking among competing interpretive theories or principles,[38] but also that none of them play a decisive role in building consensus among judges. According to some surveys, consensus can be reached at most around the results of pragmatic interpretation,[39] which is not very surprising based on the great variety of interpretive modalities. The variety and pluralism of these methods provide the greatest leeway for judges in constitutional interpretation. The possibility to choose between different methods, on the basis of the particularities of the given case, allows judges to 'borrow' the opportunity to find and justify the best solution. Empirical research usually proves that in practice, judicial interpretation is characterized by the varied, combined and mixed application of interpretive methods. There may be differences in the frequency, emphasis or scope of the use of each method, but this does not change the fact that a wide variety of methods are used in many different forms.[40] The only exception to this is textualist interpretation, because it is considered everywhere to be the starting point of the whole process, and only exceptionally is it permissible to deviate from the plain meaning rule.

2.3 Main interpretive theories

2.3.1 Interpretive modalities

As we have seen, there are several possible classifications of the methods of constitutional interpretation which often distinguish between different interpretive principles and theories.[41] The identification of each specific method

37 Terrance Sandalow, 'Constitutional Interpretation' (1981) 79 Michigan Law Review 1033–1034.

38 Christian Starck, 'Constitutional Review and the Theory of Interpretation' in Thomas Ellwein, Dieter Grimm, Joachim-Jens Hesse, and Gunnar Folke Schuppert (eds.), *Jahrbuch zur Staats- und Verwaltungswissenschaft. Band 7.* (Nomos 1994) 51; Starck (n 25) 203.

39 Cross (n 29).

40 See, for example, Vicki C. Jackson and Jamal Greene, 'Constitutional Interpretation in Comparative Perspective: Comparing Judges or Courts?' in Tim Ginsburg and Rosalind Dixon (eds.), *Comparative Constitutional Law* (Edward Elgar 2011) 604–605; Stephen M. Griffin, 'Pluralism in Constitutional Interpretation' (1994) 72 Texas Law Review 1757, 1760–1761.

41 On the major explanatory factors of the differences in constitutional interpretation in the various constitutional polities, see Jeffrey Goldsworthy, 'Constitutional Interpretation' in Michael Rosenfeld and András Sajó (eds.) *The Oxford Handbook of Comparative Constitutional Law* (Oxford University Press 2013) 706–717.

depends on the chosen normative theory and the conceptualization of the constitutional interpretation. Nevertheless, the most commonly identified interpretation theories (which themselves are generic concepts) are:

- textualism (grammatical-logical interpretation),
- originalism (intentionalism, interpretivism),
- contextual (systematic, structural) interpretation,
- purposive interpretation (teleology),
- moral and natural law interpretation,
- pragmatic interpretation, and
- common law interpretation.

In line with textualism, the meaning of a legal text is given by the ordinary or technical meaning of the words or phrases it uses. The interpretation is thus based on the conventional rules and the internal logic of the language. The primary and even almost exclusive source of grammatical-logical interpretation is, of course, the text itself, because the constitutional text itself is what the constituent power adopted as such.

Pursuant to originalism, the main purpose of constitutional interpretation is to execute the original intention of the constituent power. Consequently, that meaning must be attributed to the text which the constitution-makers intended to give to it when the constitution was adopted. The basic conception of this idea is that the constitution-makers have the exclusive power to adopt or amend the constitution. So the execution of the will of those who were empowered to lay down constitutional rules is an absolute requirement arising from the authority of the constituent power, which cannot be replaced by any other intention or consideration.

The essence of the structural or contextual interpretation is that the words, expressions and even provisions of the constitutional text should not be interpreted in isolation, but instead in accordance with other rules and principles of the constitution as a whole. This is based on the fact that the constitution is not a set of logically separate rules, but a coherent group of norms aimed at establishing the whole legal system.

Purposive (theological) interpretation in constitutional law attaches meaning to the text in accordance with the purpose of the constitutional provisions or the whole constitution (*telos, ratio legis, ratio iuris*). The theoretical basis of this sort of interpretation is the consideration that a piece of legislation always has a purpose; that is, it is designed to have a specific effect.

Although moral and natural law interpretations are not the same, their common feature is that they attach decisive importance to extra-constitutional values and principles, and thereby often endorse interpretive solutions that do not follow compellingly from the constitution. In fact, the adherents of these theories see the constitutional text as only a starting point and reach interpretive results derived from some philosophical conviction. Natural law theories claim that the authority of the constitution does not stem from the mandate of the constitution makers or the special authority granted to them;

in contrast, the needs for the limitation of power and for human rights are of natural origin, so their enforcement cannot be entrusted to the political majority of the day. The moral reading of the constitution puts fundamental moral values at the centre of legal reasoning. According to this conception, constitutions consist not only of individual rules, but also of moral principles, the interpretation of which must seek the best moral solution, that is, the solution that best enforces the basic values of the constitution.

It is not clear whether the conception of legal pragmatism can be considered an independent philosophy of interpretation. In a sense, it can be described as a 'theory without a theory', as one of its central ideas is that in the course of interpretation, the court should find the best solution for the given situation, not a meaning arising from a special interpretive principle. In this view, courts must always take into account the social consequences of their possible decisions.

The common law constitutional interpretation can be seen as a separate type of interpretive theory, not only because it is used in most Anglo-Saxon countries, but also because of its specific logic supposing that the meaning of the constitution must be determined on the basis of the principle of *stare decisis*; that is, following previous judicial decisions in similar cases. Although this respect for precedents is unique to Anglo-Saxon legal systems, many constitutional courts have developed (or at least sought to establish) a kind of constitutional case law over the years; thus, this method has gained some importance in civil law systems as well. In practice, this means that the previous decisions of the constitutional court, which build on each other to produce a unified doctrinal system, can play a prominent role in their constitutional polities.

2.3.2 Substantive interpretation

Another group of theories of constitutional interpretation can be classified as conceptions based on specific value choices, which are either aimed at defining the purpose of interpretation or enforcing certain constitutional values.

There are a large number of examples of 'substantive interpretation' conceived in this sense, such as John Hart Ely's theory claiming that the constitution primarily provides for procedural democracy, and judicial review should also support this goal. The constitution and the courts are otherwise value-neutral; the importance of the constitution is to provide an open forum for discussing all competing values until the majority decides. It is not the job of the courts to override specific value choices, but to ensure that all values have an equal chance in the decision-making process.[42] Another American thinker, Michael Perry, proposes the consensus theory, according to which judicial review should be aimed at preserving values in which there is a high degree of social consensus, as opposed to

42 John Hart Ely, *Democracy and Distrust: A Theory of Judicial Review* (Harvard University Press 1980).

matters that deeply and ultimately divide society. In the latter, the courts should be reluctant to decide, and rather leave the decision to the democratic legislatures.[43] The theory of 'popular constitutionalism' has been present in the literature since a famous 1957 article by Robert Dahl. He claimed that experience shows that the Supreme Court, which is inevitably a policy-making body itself, cannot for an extended period successfully prevent the will of a strong legislative majority from prevailing, or it can act only against a weak legislative majority.[44] A more recent version of this approach supposes that, in the long run, the interpretive practice of the US Supreme Court follows the evolution of public opinion.[45]

Substantive interpretation often focuses on certain constitutional values, such as the notion of human dignity or 'general freedom of action' in the practice of the German Federal Constitutional Court,[46] and the interpretive practices that define the protection of the basic structure of the constitution as a main function of judicial review can also be listed here.[47]

However, while the formal modalities of constitutional interpretation are primarily aimed at standardizing the process of interpretation, and constitutional changes in this way can be achieved mainly by alternating different methods, in this form of interpretation the same results can be reached only by reinterpreting the content of substantive constitutional values.[48]

2.3.3 Other interpretive aids: judicial doctrines, constructions, standards, tests and legal maxims

Beyond interpretive theories, there are a number of other special tools and technics of interpretation, such as constitutional doctrines (constructions) standards (tests) and interpretive sub-principles and guidelines (canons, maxims). They help the interpretation process in different ways, and the techniques and tools of their various groups have certain common features. However, the differentiation between these methods is only relative, so they can often not be precisely separated from each other. Consequently, their existence and specification have usually no statutory basis but primarily serve as an analytical framework.

Constitutional doctrines are judicial constructions that set out certain general rules or criteria for interpretation in order to decide certain types

43 Perry (n 33).

44 Robert Dahl, 'Decision-Making in a Democracy: The Supreme Court as a National Policy-Maker' (1957) 6 Journal of Public Law 286.

45 Larry D. Kramer, *The People Themselves: Popular Constitutionalism and Judicial Review* (Oxford University Press 2004).

46 Donald P. Kommers, 'Germany: Balancing Rights and Duties' in Jeffrey Goldsworthy (ed.) *Interpreting Constitutions: A Comparative Study* (Oxford University Press 2007) 323.

47 See e.g. this doctrine in Indian constitutional law: Sudhir Krishnaswamy, *Democracy and Constitutionalism in India: a Study of the Basic Structure Doctrine* (Oxford University Press 2009).

48 See e.g. Gárdos-Orosz, Chapter 9 in this volume.

of cases. There is usually some important constitutional value behind them that the court must uphold in its proceedings. The doctrines are mostly formulated by the constitutional and other high courts; that is, they are not included in the constitutional text. Nevertheless, they adopt special legal approaches and conceptions that are useful instruments for judges to determine the content of constitutional principles or build a coherent analytical framework.[49] The doctrine of the so-called 'living constitution',[50] the 'unity of the constitution',[51] the 'interpretation conforming the constitution'[52] or the 'autonomous concepts'[53] can be included, among others, in this group.

The standards and tests used in constitutional interpretation are also judicial constructions, aiming to make judicial review predictable and transparent and thus, in a sense, controllable. Basically, these are technical requirements for the interpretive process, which determine what aspects (and how) the court will scrutinize in its proceeding. This includes fundamental rights tests such as the necessity-proportionality test,[54] constitutional balancing,[55] or such specific methods as the strict scrutiny test in the United States[56] or the so-called Wednesbury reasonableness in the UK.[57]

The legal nature of some other interpretive rules, canons, maxims and guidelines is vague, and their legal status is uncertain; at least, they are much weaker than those of principles, doctrines, or tests of interpretation in constitutional law, even though in some cases they may play a decisive role in finding the right solution to the case. These interpretive aids merely assist the judge but do not in themselves have legal force; usually, they are based solely on the consensus of a legal community. Consequently, there is no authoritative list of interpretive canons, and their use varies in case law, as do their generality and scope: some maxims are specific, applicable only in some cases; others are more similar to general principles of law. Among them, there are primarily interpretive canons such as 'the rule against surplusage' or '*ejusdem generis*' ('of the same kind'), maxims of legal logics such as '*argumentum a maiore ad minus*' ('from the larger scale to the smaller one'), '*argumentum a contrario*' ('argument from the contrary'), or '*idem per idem*' ('the same through the same'), conflict resolution rules, as '*lex superior derogat legi inferiori*' ('the higher law repeals the lower one'), '*lex specialis derogat legi generali*' ('the special law repeals the general law') '*lex posterior*

49 Craig R. Ducat, *Constitutional Interpretation* (Wadsworth 2009) 80; Kommers, Finn, and Jacobsohn (n 2) 40.

50 Sandalow (n 37) 1053.

51 Kommers (n 46) 178; Stern (n 23) § 4, III. 8.

52 Sachs (n 25), 18–19; Starck (n 25) 210.

53 George Letsas, *A Theory of Interpretation of the European Convention on Human Rights* (Oxford University Press 2010) 41–43.

54 Alec Stone Sweet and Jud Mathews, 'Proportionality, Judicial Review, and Global Constitutionalism' in Giorgio Bongiovanni, Giovanni Sartor, and Chiara Valentini (eds.) *Reasonableness and Law* (Springer 2009) 173.

55 Louis Henkin, 'Infallibility under Law: Constitutional Balancing' (1978) 78 Columbia Law Review 1029.

56 Richard H. Fallon Jr., 'Strict Judicial Scrutiny' (2007) 54 UCLA Law Review 1273.

57 Stone Sweet and Mathews (n 54) 175.

derogat legi priori' ('the later law repeals the prior one') and value-laden interpretive aids such as '*nullum crimen sine lege*' ('no crime without law' and 'no punishment without law') '*contra bono mores*' ('against good morals').

2.4 Conclusion

In sum, it can be concluded that a number of theories and methods of constitutional interpretation have been developed both in scholarship and jurisprudence. By reason of the vagueness and indeterminacy of the constitutional text, however, choosing between them is unavoidable, as in many cases the plain meaning does not provide sufficient guidance to resolve the dispute.

Beyond the exigency of interpretation, the next question is who should be the ultimate interpreter of the constitution. Without engaging here in the never-ending dispute around the counter-majoritarian difficulty, but assuming that constitutional interpretation, at least in the countries examined in this volume (perhaps with the sole exception of the UK) is essentially a judicial function, the art of interpretation lies primarily in deciding which interpretive methods lead to the best outcome in various constitutional debates. The real difficulty is how to justify the application of the chosen interpretive methods or principles. As a matter of fact, there is no natural hierarchy between the various theories of constitutional interpretation and the modalities and substantive concepts attached to them (as we will see in reality, even if the constitution itself prefers certain methods); that is, one can choose between them only on the basis of a certain (political, moral, etc.) value judgement.

Whatever choice is made between competing interpretive methods, now it is sufficient for us to conclude that the courts undeniably encounter constitutional disputes generated by the contemporary wave of populism and therefore are forced to decide whether or not to change their previous interpretive practices, and if so, how they do this. This is what this book is about.

3 An 'Instrument of Government' or 'Instrument of Courts'?

The impact of political systems on constitutional interpretation and the case of populism

Anna Gamper

3.1 Introduction

Lately, the Janus face of populism has been addressed in the illuminating opening address of the cantonal governor of the Swiss canton Appenzell Inner Rhodes delivered at the Landsgemeinde on 28 April 2019, the annual gathering of cantonal voters:[1]

> Recently, the term 'populism' … has become used to an almost inflationary degree, particularly with a view to accuse the other side of a lack of real arguments. It is sometimes overlooked that politics is always guided by the sentiment of the people. This is, per se, neither condemnable nor dangerous, but democratic as long as the people has the actual say. Understood in this sense, populism is not the end of democracy, but, on the contrary, a request to defend democracy against demagogy and dramatization, with self-assertiveness and the willingness to reform and consensus. For even democracies can die.[2]

Liberal constitutions should not and do not want democracies to die. Rather, their task is to help democracies – and, thus, the rule of the *demos* (the Greek synonym for the Latin *populus*) – survive. But can they themselves survive in a populist environment?

1 Cantonal voters directly elect their representatives as well as vote on cantonal laws in these gatherings that have a medieval origin. Even though direct democracy is sometimes associated with populism, populists derive their power essentially from elections and their claim to represent the people. See, also, on the frequency of liberal outcomes of referenda, Robert Howse, 'Epilogue: In Defense of Disruptive Democracy – A Critique of Anti-populism' (2019) International Journal of Constitutional Law 641, 648.

2 Opening address by Landammann Daniel Fässler, http://www.ai.ch/politik/landsgemeinde/archiv-landsgemeinden/28-april-2019/ftw-simplelayout-filelistingblock/landsgemeindeansprache-landammann-daniel-fassler.pdf accessed 14 October 2019, 2–3.

Although legal resentment is considered to be a prominent dimension of populism,[3] constitutional law is regarded as an important matter by populists – even if from a different lens than that of liberal democracy.[4] This has induced scholars to speak of 'constitutional populism'[5] or 'populist constitutionalism'.[6] By and large, populists engage with constitutions either because they use them, where necessary, as their own protective shields or because they criticize them or because they interfere with them, e.g. by a constitutional amendment.

Their engagement with constitutions necessarily implies that constitutional interpretation, too, is an important matter for populist governments in Europe and elsewhere. Most often, it is the constitutional interpretation by constitutional or other courts that collides with populist attitudes. This may prompt a populist government to counteract either with or without the means of constitutional law. Conversely, courts may also critically respond to populist measures by counteracting even constitutional amendments.

In this chapter, I will first attempt to sketch a general framework of how the nature of a political system corresponds to constitutional interpretation, based on three hypotheses: (i) political systems – that are, for the purposes of this study, classed as liberal democracies, illiberal democracies and non-democracies[7] – require constitutional interpretation that implements and furthers their aims, (ii) both liberal and illiberal democracies seek for formal legitimacy of constitutional interpretation and (iii) illiberal democracies are – despite or perhaps exactly because of this notion of formal legitimacy – more disposed to amend the constitution for interpretive purposes if necessary. In order to test these hypotheses, I undertake to examine written constitutions worldwide

3 Paul Blokker, 'Populism as a Constitutional Project' (2019) 17 International Journal of Constitutional Law 535, 548–551; Paul Blokker, 'Populist Constitutionalism' (Blog of the International Journal of Constitutional Law, 4 May 2017) www.iconnectblog.com/2017/05/populist-constitutionalism accessed 14 October 2019; Paul Blokker, 'Populist Constitutionalism' in Carlos de la Torre (ed.), *Routledge Handbook of Global Populism* (Routledge 2018) 113, 115, 120–123.

4 Blokker, 'Constitutionalism' (n 3); Jan-Werner Müller, 'Populist Constitutions' (Blog of the International Journal of Constitutional Law, 23 April 2017) www.iconnectblog.com/2017/04/populist-constitutions-a-contradiction-in-terms accessed 14 October 2019; Neil Walker, 'Populism and Constitutional Tension' (2019) 17 International Journal of Constitutional Law 515, 519–522; Blokker, 'Constitutionalism' (n 3) 115; Blokker, 'Populism' (n 3) 535–553; Luigi Corrias, 'Populism in a Constitutional Key' (2016) 12 European Constitutional Law Review 6, 9–10.

5 Ana Micaela Alterio, 'Reactive vs Structural Approach' (2019) 8 Global Constitutionalism 270, 273.

6 Blokker, 'Constitutionalism' (n 3); Müller (n 4); Walker (n 4) 519; Blokker, 'Constitutionalism' (n 3); Paul Blokker, 'Varieties of populist constitutionalism' [2019] 20 German Law Journal 332.

7 While both liberal and illiberal democracies are based on constitutions that provide a democratic form of government, the constitutions of non-democracies lack a democratic design or only pretend a kind of 'semantic' democracy. The constitutional difference between liberal and illiberal democracies may often be less striking than in political terms but focuses on the hierarchical position and constitutional resilience of fundamental rights.

(again categorizing between those of liberal democracies, illiberal democracies and non-democracies) as to whether they contain explicit rules on the methods and standards of constitutional interpretation. Do these rules correspond to the political character of the respective system? Are they enacted originally with a view to establish a political system? Or are they enacted in order to counteract a previous constitutional interpretation by courts?

Secondly, the relation between political systems and constitutional interpretation will be examined in the specific case of populism. Do populist systems generate their own constitutional interpretation, either by the entrenchment of rules on constitutional interpretation or by other, organizational or procedural measures that may at least indirectly influence constitutional interpretation? Have populist systems invented new instruments to safeguard the constitutional interpretation they desire, or do they just play the usual constitutional repertoire? Lastly, the article will examine the possible approaches of constitutional and other apex courts regarding constitutional interpretation, namely as to whether they serve to escalate or de-escalate populism. The pending question is whether the constitutional lawmaker or constitutional courts have the final say on constitutional interpretation.

3.2 Do political systems generate their own rules of constitutional interpretation?

3.2.1 Hypotheses

Constitutional interpretation is an inexhaustible topic that has been explored under innumerable aspects. A large part of the recent literature on constitutional interpretation takes a court perspective, e.g. which kind of interpretation methods and style of reasoning courts use, whether they lead an interpretive dialogue with other courts or even governments and legislatures, whether they exercise strong- or weak-form review, etc.[8] The question of if and how the nature of a political system and constitutional interpretation correlate, however, goes much beyond the perspective of courts – or of governments, either.

My first hypothesis is that a political system requires constitutional interpretation that implements and furthers its own aims. Whether this is done in accordance with the constitution or not, depends, though. Non-democracies do not even formally seek to be guided by the constitution when it comes to constitutional interpretation. In some non-democracies a semi-liberal

8 See, e.g., most recently: Mark Tushnet, *Weak Courts, Strong Rights* (Princeton University Press 2008); Karen J Alter, 'National Perspectives on International Constitutional Review' in Erin F. Delaney and Rosalind Dixon (eds.), *Comparative Judicial Review* (Edward Elgar Publishing 2018) 244, 269; András Jakab, Arthur Dyevre, and Giulio Itzcovich (eds.), *Comparative Constitutional Reasoning* (Cambridge University Press 2017); Tania Groppi and Marie-Claire Ponthoreau, *The Use of Foreign Precedents by Constitutional Judges* (Hart Publishing 2013).

constitution may formally be in place but is nevertheless not respected in practice: whatever rule on interpretive methods, independent courts or other related issues may formally be provided, it will still not be obeyed. In both cases, therefore, the political system seeks to maintain its non-democratic character, either within the semantic framework of the constitution or outside.

In liberal and illiberal democracies, instead, the constitution as such will be heeded since in both types of democracies the commitment to popular sovereignty as the source of the constituent power vests the constitution with a status that cannot be overthrown easily. However, this does not exclude that constitutions are amended as long as this is done in accordance with the amendment rules provided by the constitution. My second hypothesis is, therefore, that democracies of both types are characterized by a commitment to make constitutional interpretation formally legitimate – either in terms of organization, procedures, methods or even constitutional amendment if needed for a change in constitutional interpretation.

My third hypothesis, however, is that fewer attempts to amend constitutions with the view to alter prevailing constitutional interpretation will be made in liberal democracies, whereas illiberal democracies show a greater preference for amendments that directly or indirectly bring about changes in constitutional interpretation. Liberal democracies and their constitutions might be more liberal also with regard to constitutional interpretation, at least with regard to methods which are largely entrusted to the discretion of courts. Illiberal democracies, however, might be more restrictive with regard to desired constitutional interpretation and may thus be more likely to seek constitutional amendments in order to change undesired constitutional interpretation. However, whether this possibility can be used at all will also depend on a variety of other factors examined later in this chapter.[9]

3.2.2 Written rules on constitutional interpretation – in the liberal world and beyond

In order to test these hypotheses empirically, written rules on constitutional interpretation which are explicitly entrenched in constitutions around the globe shall be examined as to if and how they reflect a political system. While constitutional interpretation often occurs without or perhaps even despite such rules in practice, the worldwide comparison of written interpretive rules nevertheless delivers a very interesting sample of how constitutional interpretation may be shaped constitutionally.[10]

The rules considered to be relevant in this context are rules that guide the interpretive organs with regard to method and yardstick of constitutional

9 See Section 3.3.

10 See the more exhaustive survey in Anna Gamper, *Regeln der Verfassungsinterpretation* (Springer 2012); Anna Gamper, 'Explicit' Interpretation in Comparative Constitutional Law' in Luigi Melica, Luca Mezzetti, and Valeria Piergigli (eds.), *Studi in onore di Giuseppe De Vergottini* (Wolters Kluwer 2015) 417.

interpretation. According to this understanding, they neither comprise constitutional rules targeted at the interpretation of subconstitutional[11] law nor rules on constitutional interpretation entrenched in subconstitutional law nor rules concerned with the organizational or procedural aspects of constitutional interpretation, such as, e.g., the establishment of organs that are explicitly authorized to interpret the constitution. Constitutions of countries with a British legal tradition, in particular, often contain a final chapter or schedule titled 'interpretation' which, however, does not normally include abstract rules of constitutional interpretation but concretized definitions of terms used by the constitution. Such definitions operate like 'crystallized' interpretation rules inasmuch as a certain content which is suggested as the meaning of a constitutional term is already determined by the constitution itself and not left to the discretion of courts or other interpretive bodies.[12] Similarly, many constitutions provide that a certain term or content must or must not be 'deemed' in such and such manner; in particular, this concerns cases where a *lex generalis* regulates a constitutional matter, with exceptions provided by a *lex specialis*. In truth, however, this is less an issue of constitutional interpretation than a regulatory technique. In many constitutions, the positive or negative definition of a constitutional term is accompanied by a clause such as 'unless the context otherwise requires' or 'unless the contrary intention appears' which requires a systematic or teleological interpretation method that takes precedence over the definition where applicable.

Even the limited range of rules considered to be relevant here, however, comprises a relatively large set of provisions that either positively stipulate or prohibit the use of a certain method or methods for interpreting constitutional law or the parameters which may or must be used as a yardstick for such interpretation.

Perhaps the most striking empirical observation is that the constitutions of consolidated liberal democracies within Europe, North America and Australia hardly contain such written rules. Rare examples are Sec 27 Canadian Constitution Act 1982 according to which the Canadian Charter of Rights and Freedoms shall be interpreted in a manner consistent with the preservation and enhancement of the multicultural heritage of Canadians – a provision which was inserted only in 1982 and is limited to the interpretation of rights; or Sec 10 para 2 Constitution of Spain 1978, which was the first liberal and democratic Spanish constitution after the Franco regime, which stipulates that provisions relating to the fundamental rights and liberties recognized by the Constitution shall be construed in conformity with the Universal Declaration of Human Rights and international treaties and agreements thereon ratified by Spain. A special case is constituted by the UK's unwritten constitution as, indeed, several Acts that are considered to be constitutional in nature include interpretive rules ranging from the Human

11 Some Islamic constitutions include rules on the interpretation of the Sharia, such as the preamble to the Constitution of Egypt, similarly Art 4 constitutional draft for Yemen or Art 8 Constitutional Draft for Libya.

12 Gamper, *Regeln* (n 10) 35–43.

Rights Act's provision on the requirement to consistent interpretation[13] to the various rules[14] of interpreting devolved competences.

On the whole, however, neither the original nor amended constitutions of mature Western democracies entrench rules on constitutional interpretation in the sense explained here. The fact that constitutional amendments in these states have generally not been made with a view to shape constitutional interpretation in a politically desired way suggests that liberal democracies of this type see no need to directly determine constitutional interpretation.

Admittedly, a majority of mature liberal democracies underlies, apart from other international treaties, the European Convention on Human Rights as well as the EU Charter of Fundamental Freedoms and, thus, both liberal and unifying interpretation by the European Court of Human Rights and the European Court of Justice. This does not sufficiently explain, however, why these constitutions lack interpretation rules also with regard to other constitutional issues than fundamental rights. It rather seems that democracies governed by the rule of law regard constitutional interpretation as an essential domain of independent courts – their constitutions are, in fact, not really silent on this issue but decide to let the courts decide on constitutional interpretation.[15]

Other constitutions, however, include interpretation rules in great number and diversity. Among these, we find mostly younger Western-style constitutions that, in contrast to the aforementioned category, were enacted in environments lacking a mature liberal tradition. In these cases, the obvious intention of entrenched interpretation rules was mostly to guarantee the existence, maintenance and promotion of liberal democracy. Newly established constitutional courts or other interpretive organs should be guided by these rules in order to interpret the constitution in accordance with liberal values, to avoid interpretive uncertainty or even open misuse.

In most of these cases, interpretation rules are targeted not at the interpretation of the constitution as a whole, but at that of fundamental rights as a specific constitutional segment.[16] A number of – particularly, Eastern European and African – constitutions include explicit rules on the interpretation of fundamental rights that are quite similar to the aforementioned Spanish example, namely, to interpret fundamental rights in line with certain or all international covenants on human rights[17] or in line with the respective

13 Sec 3 para 1 HRA 1998.

14 Sec 29 para 3 and 101 Scotland Act 1998, Sec 94 para 7 in conjunction with Sec 154 para 2 Government of Wales Act 2006, Sec 83 Northern Ireland Act 1998.

15 Martin Loughlin, 'The Silences of Constitutions' (2018) 16 International Journal of Constitutional Law 930.

16 See, for a survey Gamper, *Regeln* (n 10) 7–28.

17 See, e.g., Art 26 para 2 Constitution of Angola, Art 13 para IV Constitution of Bolivia, Art 17 para 3 Constitution of Cape Verde, Art 93 Constitution of Colombia, Art 13 para 2 Constitution of Ethiopia, Art 29 no 2 Constitution of Guinea-Bissau, Art 68 Constitution of Maldives, Art 4 para 1 Constitution of Moldova, Art 43 Constitution of Mozambique, Fourth Final and Transitory Provision Constitution of Peru, Art 16 para 2 Constitution of Portugal, Art 20 para 1 Constitution of Romania, Art 48 Constitution of Seychelles, Sec 10 subsection 2 Constitution of Spain, Art 23 Constitution of Timor-Leste.

international case law[18] which seeks to both maximize and internationalize fundamental rights as far as possible.

A similar type of such rules can be found in those rare cases where a constitution demands or at least allows for an interpretation that is guided by foreign law: the most prominent of these rules is Sec 39 para 1 subpara c Constitution of South Africa, but other examples can also be found in Art 46 para 1 subpara e Constitution of Zimbabwe ('relevant foreign law') as well as – even with regard to the general interpretation of the constitution – Sec 11 para 2 subpara c Constitution of Malawi ('comparable foreign case law') and Art 3 para 1 Constitution of the Marshall Islands ('decisions of the courts of other countries having [similar] constitutions').[19] Moreover, Art 1 subpara d Schedule 2.3 to the Constitution of Papua New Guinea demands that, *inter alia*, judges have to regard the 'legislation of, and ... relevant decisions of the courts of, any country that in the opinion of the court has a legal system similar to that of Papua New Guinea'.

Other rules on the interpretation of fundamental rights often demand a liberal interpretation by entrenching certain values such as an open and free society, freedom, human dignity, etc., as interpretive standards, by requesting a systematic and purposive interpretation in line with the liberal spirit of the bill of rights or by prohibiting a restrictive interpretation of human rights or an extensive interpretation of limitation or derogation clauses respectively.[20]

A number of constitutions include more general interpretive rules that concern the interpretation not only of fundamental rights but of the constitution as a whole. European constitutions hardly contain such rules, but one important, although not particularly liberal and certainly not 'cosmopolitan-friendly' or evolutive example is constituted by Art R para 3 Constitution of Hungary, according to which the provisions of the Constitution shall be interpreted in accordance with their purposes, the National Avowal contained therein and the achievements of the 'historic constitution'; also the preamble to the Hungarian Constitution, with its strong references to history and Christianity, has thus to be taken into consideration. Further to that, Art 28 of the same Constitution stipulates that courts, when interpreting the Constitution, shall presume that it serves moral and economic purposes which are in accordance with common sense and the public good – all standards oriented rather at collective interests than individual rights. However, most of the non-European constitutions that include general guidelines on constitutional interpretation positively combine an interpretation method with a liberal yardstick, i.e. they demand an interpretation that conforms to all or certain aims and values or even the whole spirit of a liberal constitution which implies both a teleological and systematic interpretation.[21] Art 259 para 1 Constitution of Kenya is an illustrative example, as it entrenches

18 See, e.g., Art 53 Constitution of Kosovo.

19 See, with more detail, Gamper, *Regeln* (n 10) 12–21.

20 See, e.g., Art 20 para 4 Constitution of Kenya, Sec 7 Constitution of Fiji, Sec 36 and 39 Constitution of South Africa.

21 See details in Fruzsina Gárdos-Orosz, Chapter 9 in this volume.

several standards (purposes, values and principles of the Constitution [subpara a]; the rule of law, human rights and fundamental freedoms in the Bill of Rights [subpara b]) which shall be promoted and advanced when the constitution is interpreted. Further, constitutional interpretation shall contribute to good governance (subpara d), which is another standard. Remarkably, constitutional interpretation shall permit the development of the law (subpara c) which is in line with Art 259 para 3 according to which every provision of the constitution shall be construed according to the doctrine of interpretation that the law is always speaking. While the first category of standards immanently suggests a systematic and teleological interpretation, the latter category refers to a dynamic 'living tree' instead of an originalist interpretation. However, the standards within the first category are partly overlapping, since some are 'principles' that have to be promoted, while 'purposes' may themselves be related to (all or some) 'values' and 'principles', without forming a substantive content themselves. A very similar though slightly shorter provision can be found in Art 267 para 1 and 3 Constitution of Zambia. Art 3 Constitution of Fiji requires an interpretation that promotes the spirit, purpose and objects of the constitution as a whole, and the values that underlie a democratic society based on human dignity, equality and freedom, which, again, combines methods with substantive standards. Sec 4 para 3 Constitution of Tuvalu requires that the Constitution shall be interpreted and applied in such a way as to achieve the aims of fair and democratic government, in the light of reason and experience and of Tuvaluan values as well as consistently with the principles set out in the preamble. Among these principles, Tuvaluan values, culture and tradition are emphasized as well as human dignity and the need for the constitution not to hamper a gradual change of these principles in a changing world. Again, this is an example of how substantive standards – in this case oriented at both autochthonous traditions and liberal democracy – are combined with a systematic and teleological interpretation method. By referring to its preamble the Constitution also clarifies that the preamble has binding force, at least for interpretive purposes.

In all of these cases, the respective rules were part of the original constitution and not inserted at a later stage. However, none of these constitutions were enacted prior to, and most of them even later than, the 1980s. Generally speaking, older constitutions contain interpretation rules to a much lesser extent than younger constitutions. Looking at the concrete states that entrenched such rules in their constitutions, this was obviously done with a view to overcoming former constitutional crises caused by revolutions, civil war, authoritarian regimes, economic troubles or other tensions. Far from governing mature liberal democracies, these constitutions and their interpretation rules rather seek to pave the way for establishing liberal democracies.

All of them seek legal clarity, and certainty inasmuch as the interpretive bodies are explicitly bound to obey certain standards and/or methods when they interpret the constitution. This resembles the aim of many legal definitions referred to earlier, namely to leave as little doubt as possible on the construction of constitutional terms and provisions in general – which is also token of a certain fear or mistrust that interpretive bodies might interpret the constitution in an undesired manner. In all of the referred cases, moreover, these rules seek to implement substantive goals that are liberal in nature. This is not only the case in the particularly rich field of fundamental rights interpretation, but also where general rules on constitutional interpretation apply. Interpretive bodies such as courts and (ordinary) legislatures should be motivated to consolidate these overall values when they enact judgments or ordinary legislation; but should also be deterred from undermining liberal democracy by attributing to the constitution any other meaning, or, in the case of courts, be protected from external pressure in this regard. Moreover, the referral to abstract principles, international or foreign law or 'an' open and democratic society seeks to guarantee a uniform liberal understanding of principles beyond the nation state – that is, shared by liberal democracies globally.[22]

It is quite another question, however, whether these aims can be truly realized in the desired manner. Firstly, even the most sophisticated interpretation rules cannot avoid the fact that they themselves need to be interpreted. Where these rules are self-applicable – provided that they generally apply to the respective constitution as a whole and, accordingly, also to themselves – this problem can at least theoretically be resolved by interpreting them in exactly the way which is prescribed by them. This resolves the problem only formally, though; the vaguer the wording is, the more complex or even contradictory the standards are, the more difficult will it be to discern their exact meaning. Secondly, moreover, constitutional practice may turn out very differently from what is formally prescribed by a constitutional text. Where the constitution is not really effective, also the interpretive rules entrenched therein will have little or no effect. Still, however, even though this possibility exists, it does not argue against the entrenchment of interpretation rules as such – in other words, it will not be their fault if they are not heeded.

Even though the majority of interpretation rules form part of the respective original version of the constitution, there are cases where constitutions were amended exactly with a view to change prevailing constitutional interpretation. Such an example is the Constitution of Bangladesh which, until 2011, had stipulated that, *inter alia*, the 'principles of absolute trust and faith in the Almighty Allah' should guide constitutional interpretation.[23] Since its 15th amendment, however, which introduced secularism among the fundamental principles of state policy, constitutional interpretation has had to be guided by secularism, among other principles.

A further category of constitutions contains 'neutral' interpretive rules that do not positively demand a liberal (or any) yardstick but restrict themselves

22 Cheryl Saunders, 'Judicial Engagement with Comparative Law' in Tom Ginsburg and Rosalind Dixon (eds.), *Comparative Constitutional Law* (Edward Elgar Publishing 2011) 571, 574.

23 Similarly, Art 8 Constitutional Draft for Libya stipulates that the Constitution shall be interpreted and bound in accordance with the Sharia.

to determining the interpretive method. Some Latin American constitutions, for example, require an originalist interpretation of the constitution in line with the will of the constitution's framers. The most impressive of these is Art 268 Constitution of El Salvador that reads as follows:

> Trustworthy documents for the interpretation of this Constitution will be, in addition to the proceedings of the plenary session of the Constituent Assembly, the audio and video recordings which contain the incidents and participation of the Constituent Deputies in its discussion and approval, as well as similar documents elaborated by the Editing Commission of the proposed Constitution. The Managing Board of the Legislative Assembly must dictate the pertinent dispositions to guarantee the authenticity and conversation of said documents.

A similar, though less concrete provision is Art 196 para II Constitution of Bolivia which stipulates that the Pluri-National Constitutional Court shall give preference to the intent of the constituent assembly as demonstrated in its documents, acts and resolutions, as well as the literal tenor of the text. Also Art 427 Constitution of Ecuador requires an originalist understanding of the constitution, even though only among other interpretive methods and subsidiarily:

> Constitutional provisions shall be interpreted by the literal meaning of its wording that is most closely in line with the Constitution as a whole. In the event of any doubt, it is the most favorable interpretation of the full and effective force of rights and that best respects the will of the constituent, in accordance with the general principles of constitutional interpretation, that shall prevail.

Art 24 Constitution of Papua New Guinea mentions 'the official records of debates and of votes and proceedings', enumerating them in some detail, as materials that can be used as aids to constitutional interpretation. Another example within this method-restricted category, namely of a required systematic and consistent interpretation, is Art 146 Constitution of Tunisia which stipulates that the Constitution's provisions shall be understood and interpreted in harmony, as in indissoluble whole.

In the latter category of cases, the respective interpretive rule lacks any reference to a substantive standard and limits itself to determine the interpretive method. Indirectly, however, the method has impact on the substance, because either the will of the framers or a consistent interpretation of the constitution implies a yardstick – which, in turn, may have a more or less liberal character. A consistent interpretation of the Tunisian Constitution, for example, which shows a strong preference for Islam, being also the state religion,[24] while at the same time guaranteeing religious freedom and stressing

24 This status is also protected by the eternity clause under Art 1 Constitution of Tunisia.

Islam's aims as 'characterized by openness and moderation',[25] cannot follow the same liberal yardstick as if a secular interpretation of the constitution is explicitly stipulated.[26] As a result, mere references to interpretive methodology suggest formal neutrality, but if the method determines an immanent yardstick, such as in the case of considering the 'context of the whole constitution' or the 'will of the constituent', the method indirectly demands interpretive orientation by a certain content.

Another type of prima facie neutrality with a 'hidden' content dimension can be found in Art 239 Constitution of Poland and Sec 5 of the Closing and Miscellaneous Provisions of the Constitution of Hungary. These rules do not positively request an interpretive method but just negate past constitutional interpretation. Without directly determining the interpretive method or yardstick, they indirectly invalidate the interpretive force of judgments made under the respective former constitution by the respective constitutional court. Whilst the individual decision taken by a judgment does not lose its legal effect, its remaining content – and this is, more or less, the applied authoritative interpretation of the constitution which, apart from the parties to the case, addresses a general legal audience – does. Art 239 Constitution of Poland refers, however, to the interpretation of statutes and not specifically to the interpretation of the constitution, and only to a limited period of time;[27] while para 1 deals with judgments of the Constitutional Court regarding the nonconformity to the Constitution of statutes adopted before its coming into force which are to be considered by the Parliament's first chamber, para 2 and 3 are concerned with the same court's resolutions regarding the universally binding interpretation of statutes which lose their universally binding force or shall, in case of pending proceedings, not be passed at all.

In the Hungarian case, however, Sec 5 of the Closing and Miscellaneous Provisions stipulates that decisions of the Constitutional Court taken prior to the entry into force of the Fundamental Law are repealed, but that this shall be without prejudice to the legal effects produced by those decisions. This provision, unlike the aforementioned positive interpretive rules, formed no part of the original Hungarian Constitution of 2011, but was inserted in 2013 by the Fourth Amendment and severely criticized by the Venice Commission.[28] Here, it is not the repeal of judgments with regard to the universally binding interpretation of statutes, but it is the repeal of the decisions as such, apart from the individual legal effects produced by those decisions. The prescribed repeal does not, however, prevent the Constitutional Court

25 Preamble to the Constitution of Tunisia.

26 Similarly, on this ambiguity Hanna Lerner, 'Interpreting Constitutions in Divided Societies' in Erin F. Delaney and Rosalind Dixon (eds.), *Comparative Judicial Review* (Edward Elgar Publishing 2018) 99, 112–113.

27 Venice Commission, 'Opinion on the Fourth Amendment to the Fundamental Law of Hungary' CDL-AD(2013)012, 22.

28 Ibid.

from applying a certain interpretation that was applied already in those former decisions.[29]

In terms of constitutional interpretation, Sec 5 is a formally neutral provision inasmuch as it does not positively prescribe an interpretive method or standard. Negatively, however, it invalidates any kind of legal bondage to former constitutional interpretation of whatever content. Taken together with organizational measures, such as, e.g., the retirement of old and appointment of new judges or the appointment of additional judges, such an invalidation may indeed create different constitutional interpretation – because a 'new' court, unlike perhaps an 'old' court, will not necessarily feel disposed to interpret the constitution in the same manner as before – and is at any rate not required to do so. This dilemma is obviously alluded to by the Venice Commission that spoke of 'a systematic limitation of the position of the Constitutional Court' by constitutional amendments 'in reaction to decisions of the Constitutional Court'.[30] Nevertheless, the provision as such does not force the Constitutional Court either to apply its former interpretation or to disapply it, and in fact the Constitutional Court has not even abandoned using its former case law when appropriate.[31] The provision only prohibits the Constitutional Court from regarding former case law and, thus, constitutional interpretation as binding. That constitutional courts are not constitutionally bound to stick to their former interpretation, however, is nothing *per se* that established civil-law liberal democracies would be unfamiliar with.[32] On the contrary, we often find constitutional courts that develop their case law in unexpected ways, deviating from their former interpretation, because of 'societal changes' or other 'factual developments'. As long as these changes are explained in a reasoned way and targeted at promoting liberal values, an evolutive or 'living tree' interpretation is much less criticized.[33] In truth, the pathology of the Hungarian provision lies in its nexus with the aforementioned substantive rules on constitutional interpretation which are indeed binding also to the Constitutional Court.

There is not much to add on non-democratic constitutions in this context, since they regularly do not include any written rules on constitutional interpretation. Nor do they provide any independent interpretive organs in charge of constitutional interpretation. The North Korean Constitution, e.g., entrusts the Presidium of the Supreme People's Assembly (not even the Supreme People's Assembly itself) with the task of constitutional interpretation[34] – instead of courts, apart from the fact that the Central Court is not

29 See also ibid. 21.

30 Ibid. 22.

31 András Jakab and Johanna Fröhlich, 'The Constitutional Court of Hungary' in András Jakab, Arthur Dyevre, and Giulio Itzcovich (eds.), *Comparative Constitutional Reasoning* (Cambridge University Press 2017) 433.

32 Venice Commission (n 27) 21.

33 Anna Gamper, 'Legal Certainty' in Werner Schroeder (ed.), *Strengthening the Rule of Law in Europe* (Hart Publishing 2016) 80, 88–95.

34 Art 116 para 4 Constitution of North Korea.

independent, but accountable to the Supreme People's Assembly.[35] These constitutions have a merely semantic value which is set aside whenever occasion arises; they do certainly not provide possibilities to overrule the political will of the governing power by the means of constitutional interpretation.

3.3 Populist constitutionalism and constitutional interpretation – instruments and limits

Not all populist systems are illiberal democracies,[36] and not all liberal democracies are free of populism. Populist emphasis on popular sovereignty and democracy even includes a commitment to voting and plebiscitarian rights.[37] Indeed, the engagement of populists with constitutional interpretation often has a fundamental rights background, either because they want to be more restrictive with regard to certain rights, related, for example, to the media, private life or asylum, or because they even want to extend some of them, e.g. with regard to rights relating to direct democracy.

Remarkably, the most direct instrument to influence constitutional interpretation, namely the entrenchment of an interpretive rule in the respective constitution, has so far been used only in the case of Hungary. In Turkey, the original interpretation rule embedded in Art 174, 'No provision of the Constitution shall be construed or interpreted as rendering unconstitutional the Reform Laws … which aim to raise Turkish society above the level of contemporary civilization and to safeguard the secular character of the Republic', as well as the liberal principles mentioned in the preamble as guidelines of interpretation, are still in force despite the constitutional amendment of 2017.

Another, more indirect instrument used by populist systems in the context of constitutional interpretation concerns the change of the organizational and procedural rules relating to (constitutional or other) courts, such as experienced, e.g., in the recent Polish, Hungarian and Turkish cases. They, *inter alia*, include: the early retirement of judges; to increase the number of judges; to appoint new judges (and chief justices) in accordance with the government's political wishes as well as to enact new political appointment procedures and terms of office; to curtail the staff and finances of courts; to bind certain judgments to qualified majorities in judges' commissions which will be difficult to be reached; to establish certain time limits for courts to decide cases; to establish new courts and channels of instances in which some courts are eclipsed and others not; to use even emergency powers for

35 Art 168 Constitution of North Korea.

36 Howse (n 1) 645. See also, on the relationship between illiberalism and populism, Pablo Castillo-Ortiz, 'The Illiberal Abuse of Constitutional Courts in Europe' (2019) 15 European Constitutional Law Review 48, 49.

37 Andrew Arato, 'Populism and the Courts' (Blog of the International Journal of Constitutional Law, 25 April 2017) www.iconnectblog.com/2017/04/populism-and-the-courts accessed 14 October 2019.

implementing these measures.[38] While these measures cannot directly influence constitutional interpretation, the desired result, namely that judges interpret the constitution due to the government's wishes, may be exactly the same.

The use of these instruments, however, will be difficult for a government if they require a constitutional amendment.[39] All written constitutions include rules on constitutional amendments which regularly stipulate a qualified quorum and majority, but in many cases also additional elements, such as a referendum, parliamentary elections, approval by constituent states (in federal systems), repeated approval by parliament (parliamentary chambers), etc.[40] Populist governments may or may not meet these requirements, either because they do not have a constitutional majority in Parliament or one of its chambers or in the constituent states, or because a referendum will not turn out in accordance with their wishes. The aforementioned constitutional reform in Hungary, however, encountered no legal obstacles because the government commanded a constitutional majority in the Parliament.[41] The Turkish constitutional reform of 2017, too, could be enacted after a successful, if controversial referendum.[42] Provided that constitutions are at all amendable, the constitutional lawmaker, at any rate, proves to be the strongest – and always political (populist or not) – power. Inasmuch as the bodies of which the constitutional lawmaker is composed (primarily an elected parliament, but perhaps also an elected head of state that signs the bill or other elected bodies

38 On these possibilities, as actually exercised in populist systems, such as Hungary, Poland or Turkey, Müller (n 4); Konrad Lachmayer, 'Counter-Developments to Global Constitutionalism' in Martin Belov (ed.), *Global Constitutionalism and Its Challenges to Westphalian Constitutional Law* (Hart Publishing 2018) 81, 98; Emilio Peluso Neder Meyer and Thomas da Rosa de Bustamante, 'The Chief Justice of the Brazilian Supreme Court' (Blog of the International Journal of Constitutional Law, 24 August 2019) www.iconnectblog.com/2019/08/the-chief-justice-of-the-brazilian-supreme-court-institutional-and-constitutional-self-destruction accessed 15 October 2019; Bertil Emrah Oder, 'Populism and the Turkish Constitutional Court' (Verfassungsblog, 2 May 2017) verfassungsblog.de/populism-and-the-turkish-constitutional-court-the-game-broker-the-populist-and-the-popular accessed 15 October, 2019; Bojan Bugarič, 'Central Europe's Descent into Autocracy' (2019) 17 International Journal of Constitutional Law 597, 602–608; Castillo-Ortiz (n 36) 49. On general contents of populist constitutional amendments see Alterio (n 5) 278–279.

39 Alterio (n 5) 277–278. Constitutional instrumentalism – as supposedly expressed by the frequency of amendments (Blokker, 'Populism' [n 3] 545–548) – is, moreover, no exclusive characteristic of populist systems, but mainly depends on the amendability rules. The Austrian Federal Constitutional Act, e.g., has been amended 129 times since its re-enactment in 1945, due to its flexible amendment rule (Art 44 B-VG), but not for specifically populist, even though sometimes controversial purposes. See also Xenophon Contiades and Alkmene Fotiadou, 'Amendment-Metrics: The Good, the Bad and the Frequently Amended Constitution' in Richard Albert, Xenophon Contiades, and Alkmene Fotiadou (eds.), *The Foundations and Traditions of Constitutional Amendment* (Hart Publishing 2017) 219.

40 Anna Gamper, 'Hierarchiefragen der Verfassungsänderung' in Clemens Jabloner and others (eds.), *Scharfsinn im Recht* (Jan Sramek Verlag 2019) 161, 166–169.

41 Bugarič (n 38) 605; Castillo-Ortiz (n 36) 56–57.

42 Oder (n 38).

that participate in the lawmaking process) represent the people, democracy indeed prevails over all other constitutional principles,[43] without any need even to invoke pre-constitutional concepts such as popular sovereignty or the constituent power of the people.[44] The 'will of the people', as represented by the constitutional lawmaker, legitimizes any kind of constitutional amendment including those that overturn existing constitutional interpretation.

However, perhaps not even the formal hurdles of a constitutional amendment will prevent populist governments (and neither perhaps other governments with respect to their respective aims) from enacting legislation that has direct or indirect impact on constitutional interpretation. In many countries, rules on the interpretation of laws (including the constitution) are entrenched in ordinary or organic laws. Organizational issues, too, such as the appointment or retirement of judges, are not always regulated by constitutions but delegated to subconstitutional legislation, as the Polish case shows most recently; even more so, procedural rules, e.g. on required majorities of judges when they pass a judgment, are hardly ever entrenched in the constitution itself. Even though constitutional silence on the respective issues does not necessarily imply that ordinary or organic laws may regulate these issues in a constitutionally unlimited way, it will nevertheless be much easier to enact such legislation than a constitutional amendment. An ordinary or organic law on constitutional interpretation may be constitutional or not; but it will need a (constitutional) court to, if at all, decide on this question.

But there are also cases where even a constitutional amendment might be challenged and repealed by the constitutional court afterwards. This presupposes a two-layered constitutional structure that enables a court to scrutinize and repeal 'ordinary' constitutional law because a constitutional principle, such as, e.g., the rule of law or fundamental rights, was violated. Even though many constitutions do not expressly provide such a structure, constitutional courts around the world, from the Indian Supreme Court[45] to the Slovak Constitutional Court,[46] increasingly practice a 'basic structure

43 Similarly, Howse (n 1) 646.

44 On these concepts and their relationship, see Corrias (n 4) 14–21. The question here, however, is not whether populists seek to legitimize extra-constitutional action on a pre-constitutional 'will of the people' (such as shown, e.g., by the controversial establishment of the Venezuelan Constituent Assembly in 2017), but how they instrumentalize enacted constitutions.

45 The leading case was *Kesavananda Bharati* SC 23.03.2973, (1973) 4 SCC 225; see also Richard Albert, 'Amending Constitutional Amendment Rules' (2015) 13 International Journal of Constitutional Law 655, 669–670.

46 Constitutional Court of the Slovak Republic Judgment (Nález) of 30 January 2019, PL. ÚS 21/2014-96; Marek Domin, 'A Part of the Constitution Is Unconstitutional, the Slovak Constitutional Court Has Ruled' (IACL-AIDC Blog 6 February 2019) blog-iacl-aidc.org/2019-posts/2019/2/5/a-part-of-the-constitution-is-unconstitutional-the-slovak-constitutional-court-has-ruled accessed 15 October 2019; Simon Drugda, 'Slovak Constitutional Court Strikes Down a Constitutional Amendment' (Blog of the International Journal of Constitutional Law, 25 April 2019) www.iconnectblog.com/2019/04/slovak-constitutional-court-strikes-down-a-constitutional-amendment-but-the-amendment-remains-valid accessed 15 October 2019.

doctrine' according to which constitutional amendments might be found unconstitutional and thus repealed either because certain constitutional amendments are absolutely prohibited due to an explicit or – which may be arguable in case of unrestricted amendment rules – implicit 'eternity clause' or because an entrenched qualified constitutional amendment procedure did not take place.[47]

However, even if, for whatever reason, a national court does not oppose populist measures, an inter- or supranational court, such as the ECtHR or the ECJ, may – this has been shown most recently in the Polish case, where the ECJ found the early compulsory retirement of Polish judges to be contrary to EU law.[48] The ECJ moreover ordered Poland to immediately suspend the application of the national provisions on the powers of the Disciplinary Chamber of the Supreme Court with regard to disciplinary cases concerning judges.[49] But also national courts themselves may find refuge in inter- or supranational law, e.g. by interpreting fundamental rights consistently with inter- or supranational law. In vertical context, courts may thus support each other and prove themselves to be beyond the reach of national populist governments[50] – at least as long as these governments are inclined to heed the judgments of courts at all.

3.4 Escalating or de-escalating populism: the role of courts in constitutional interpretation

Populists claim to be the better democrats and implementers of the 'will of the people' as expressed in elections or plebiscites vis-à-vis diffuse 'elites' to which they often consider courts to belong.[51] Where constitutional or apex courts, at whatever level, oppose populist parties or governments, also by the means of constitutional interpretation,[52] populists will naturally question the independence of courts and their interpretation and invoke the counter-majoritarian

47 See also Tamar Hostovsky Brandes, 'International Law in Domestic Courts in an Era of Populism' (2019) 17 International Journal of Constitutional Law 576, 589–590; Joel Colón-Ríos, 'Introduction: The Forms and Limits of Constitutional Amendments' (2015) 13 International Journal of Constitutional Law 567, 568; (2019) European Journal of Law Reform.

48 ECJ Judgment of 24 June 2019 (Grand Chamber), *European Commission v Republic of Poland*, C-619/18; ECJ Judgment of 5 November 2019 (Grand Chamber), *European Commission v Republic of Poland*, C-192/18.

49 ECJ Order of 8 April 2020, *European Commission v Republic of Poland*, Order of the Court in Case C-791/19 R.

50 Hostovsky Brandes (n 47) 576, 576 ff; Alter (n 7) 262–264 and 268–269.

51 Arato (n 37); Walker (n 4) 520; Bugarič (n 38) 605; Castillo-Ortiz (n 36).

52 See also David Prendergast, 'The Judicial Role in Protecting Democracy from Populism' (2019) 20 German Law Journal 245.

dilemma – that unelected judges govern over and even against the 'will of the people' as represented by the majority in Parliament.[53]

However, and quite apart from populist claims, many national and international apex courts have been confronted with similar criticism regarding their use of interpretation methods in recent years.[54] Not all such criticism is *a priori* populistic or illegitimate. In many states, constitutional interpretation has increasingly become dynamic, to a degree that it can sometimes not be distinguished from constitutional amendment but for formal reasons. This complaint has nothing to do with the kind of antidemocratic 'abusive judicial power'[55] that constitutional courts sometimes exercise – that they rather stick to the governing political power than to the opposition. Constitutional courts should not play the role of political partisans, on *whichever* side. But what is considered problematic here is rather a kind of abusive interpretation where, even despite a liberal purpose, the end cannot always justify the means.

This is the more problematic in cases where the respective constitution – and, analogously, the ECHR or primary EU law – cannot be amended easily (which at the same time stimulates courts to dynamic interpretation), so that it will be difficult to invalidate the prevailing interpretation by an amendment.[56] A spectacular case has recently been the German Federal Constitutional Court's response to a previous judgment of the ECJ[57] criticizing it as 'ultra vires' because of 'objective arbitrariness'.[58]

My final hypothesis is that it might de-escalate populism if courts neither overstretched constitutional interpretation nor their functional claim to

53 See Alexander Mordecai Bickel, *The Least Dangerous Branch* (Yale University Press 1962). The genial argument expressed by Alexander Hamilton in the *Federalist Papers* – namely that even unelected judges manifest a prime democratic quality inasmuch as they defend the constitution which expresses the 'will of the *constitutional* people' against ordinary legislation that just expresses the 'will of the people' – is not part of the populist discourse.

54 Bickel (n 53); Alter (n 7) 249–250; Andrea Pin, 'The Transnational Drivers of Populist Backlash in Europe' [2019] 20 German Law Journal 225, 235; Brian Christopher Jones, 'When Court Criticism Threatens the Rule of Law' (Blog of the International Journal of Constitutional Law, 5 September 2018) http://www.iconnectblog.com/2018/09/when-court-criticism-threatens-the-rule-of-law-a-three-part-test accessed 15 October 2019. With regard to the ECtHR Patricia Popelier, Sarah Lambrecht, and Koen Lemmens (eds.), *Criticism of the European Court of Human Rights* (Intersentia 2016). Jeremy Waldron, 'The Core of the Case Against Judicial Review' (2006) 115 The Yale Law Journal 1346, 1350, Richard Bellamy, *Political Constitutionalism* (Cambridge University Press 2007) 27ff; Alon Harel and Adam Shinar, 'Between Judicial and Legislative Supremacy: A Cautious Defense of Constrained Judicial Review' (2012) 10 International Journal of Constitutional Law 950, 951ff; Paul Craig, 'Political Constitutionalism and the Judicial Role: A Response' (2011) 9 International Journal of Constitutional Law 112, 112 ff.

55 David Landau and Rosalind Dixon, 'Abusive Judicial Review: Courts Against Democracy' (2020) 53 UC Davis Law Review 1313, 1313 ff.

56 See also Pin (n 54) 242.

57 EJC Judgment of 18 December 2018 (Grand Chamber), *Weiss and Others*, C-493/17.

58 German Federal Constitutional Court (BVerfG, Urteil des Zweiten Senats vom 5. Mai 2020 – 2 BvR 859/15, 2 BvR 980/16, 2 BvR 2006/15, 2 BvR 1651/15).

democratic legitimacy as guardians of the constitution.[59] How far legitimate constitutional interpretation reaches may be questionable from case to case, but the entrenchment of written interpretation rules, as pointed out earlier, could be helpful here. Populist complaints that courts behave like undemocratic elites could thus perhaps not be eliminated but at least given no just reason.[60] Even though the constitutional review of laws has an inherently political character that cannot be avoided completely, judges should be what they claim to be: independent, objective and law-oriented. By following the 'political question doctrine' in one way or the other,[61] they contribute to a balanced separation of powers: where one power does not overreach, another power will have less occasion for doing so. Where populist governments enact overreaching measures, however, courts will then have better authority for striking them down. In other words: Neither shall courts themselves exercise 'judicial populism'[62] nor shall they bluntly act as ***political*** antipodes that may interpret constitutions in whatever arbitrary way,[63] only they must oppose a populist government. This does not at all mean that they need to play a generally deferential or weak-form role towards populist governments,[64] but that they may have stronger and more persuasive authority in the long run if they do not believe their interpretive role to be that of the political – not legal – opposition.

3.5 Conclusions

Constitutional comparison shows that a vast majority of written rules on constitutional interpretation are targeted at establishing, maintaining and promoting liberal democracy – especially so in the context of fundamental rights interpretation, but not limited to it. Most of these rules can be found in young Western-style constitutions of states that are not established liberal democracies even though these constitutions strive to make them so. Established liberal democracies rarely entrench such rules in their constitutions, because they rather consider constitutional interpretation to be the domain

59 Similarly, with regard to the ECJ and ECtHR Pin (n 54). Michaela Hailbronner and David Landau, 'Introduction: Constitutional Courts and Populism' (Blog of the International Journal of Constitutional Law, 22 April 2017) www.iconnectblog.com/2017/04/introduction-constitutional-courts-and-populism accessed 15 October 2019; Bilyana Petkova, 'Populism and Judicial Backlash in the United States and Europe' (Blog of the International Journal of Constitutional Law, 30 April 2017) www.iconnectblog.com/2017/04/populism-and-judicial-backlash-in-the-united-states-and-europe accessed 15 October 2019.

60 According to Howse (n 1) 647, the frequency of counter-majoritarian decisions by courts is exaggerated.

61 Loughlin (n 15) 929–930.

62 David Landau, 'Courts and Support Structures' in Erin F. Delaney and Rosalind Dixon (eds), *Comparative Judicial Review* (Edward Elgar Publishing 2018) 226, 233; Meyer and da Rosa de Bustamante (n 38); Oder (n 38).

63 With regard to international law, see Hostovsky Brandes (n 47) 595.

64 See also Prendergast (n 52) 253f.

of independent courts; and non-democratic constitutions do not even pretend to regulate constitutional interpretation by independent courts because they do not provide such courts.

Where written interpretation rules are used in order to amend existing constitutional interpretation, this may be done with a view to disrupt liberal democracy but is not necessarily so. Likewise, the choice of interpretation method, such as originalist, purposive, systematic or dynamic interpretation, does not necessarily manifest a liberal or illiberal understanding of the constitution but primarily shows a preference either for legal clarity and national authenticity or for a more dynamic and open understanding of a living constitution; whether the method turns out in a liberal or illiberal way depends on the constitutional context to which it applies. The importance of written rules of interpretation has so far been underestimated: in my opinion, however, such rules can considerably shape the role that judges play vis-à-vis populist governments – either in a liberal or populist way. Even though constitutional silence on interpretation rules vests judges with more power to decide on constitutional interpretation, this also exposes them to uncertainty and criticism and perhaps even escalates populism in a reactive way. Written interpretive rules could, to some extent, relieve their pressure, even though they are no absolute guarantee of liberalism.

The discourse about the final and authoritative interpreter of the constitution is no specific feature of populist systems but is led also in liberal democracies.[65] While the more general discourse on populist constitutionalism seems to vacillate between the poles of authoritarian-majoritarian democracy[66] and liberal oligarchy, the discourse on constitutional interpretation first and foremost concerns the separation of powers – of powers conceived as communicating and not as isolated vessels.

In- or outside populist systems, courts should be wary to overstep the separation of powers by politicizing constitutional law and its interpretation – because this is not what their independence suggests: they shall not act independently of the constitution, but independent of other state powers and bodies. Only if courts stick faithfully to the constitutional principles on which they feed, can they deprive populist governments of their core – and perhaps only – *constitutional* argument.

65 Mark Tushnet distinguishes strong- and weak-form review by courts along this criterion. See, *inter alia*, Mark Tushnet, 'The Relation Between Political Constitutionalism and Weak-Form Judicial Review' (2013) 14 German Law Journal 2249, 2250.

66 As long as constitutions clearly build on these traditional forms of majoritarian democracy, it is highly hypothetical to supplant them by other forms of democracy some of which, moreover, are in truth not democratic but oligarchic, such as the consideration of 'private interest associations'. Enrique Peruzzotti, 'Post-liberal and Post-populist Democracy' (2019) 4 Chinese Political Science Review 221, 230.

4 Can there be autochthonous methods of constitutional interpretation?

Mark Tushnet

4.1 Introduction

It is common ground among theorists of constitutional interpretation that many logically defensible methods of constitutional interpretation exist. We have labels for these methods: originalism, textualism, living constitutionalism, structural interpretation, and many more. It is also common ground that observation shows that nations vary in the degree to which lawyers and judges within each nation use one or another method.

Note that these methods are transnational in the sense that they are discernibly similar from one to another nation. Originalism in Austria means examining the historical materials associated with the adoption of the Austrian constitution; originalism in India means examining the historical materials associated with the adoption of the Indian constitution. Of course, what those materials are may vary from one to another nation. We may have detailed records of the debates at one nation's constitutional convention but relatively little information about what the public heard about a proposed constitution's terms, and the opposite for another nation – rich information about the information available to the public and almost nothing about what the drafters argued about before presenting their proposal to the public. And of course, we might find different 'schools' of originalism, some emphasizing a specific set of relevant historical materials and others giving priority to a different set. And, further, the degree to which scholars and judges use each school's interpretive method might differ across nations. Yet, with all those qualifications, we can fairly talk about 'originalism' as a method of constitutional interpretation.

I could repeat the preceding exercise for each listed method of interpretation. At the end, we could colour a map of the world's nations using a handful of colours with a few shadings – navy blue, aquamarine, cornflower blue – to show each nation's preferred approach to constitutional interpretation. We might draw an analogy here to the effort in traditional comparative law to identify legal 'families'. And, as with that effort, we might ask, could there be a true outlier, a nation whose 'interpretive colour' differed from the ones used elsewhere on the map or that was not a member of any identifiable legal family? Such a nation would use what I call an autochthonous method of constitutional interpretation.

For my purposes, the term *autochthonous* refers to a phenomenon that (a) is present in one constitutional system but not in others and (b) arises from circumstances unique to the nation in which it occurs, where *unique* is defined to exclude cases in which there are general 'mid-level' similarities in social, economic, and political circumstances across nations. This chapter explores the possibility of autochthonous methods of constitutional interpretation.

At the outset I emphasize that my perspective is a broad, almost jurisprudential one. To distinguish my perspective from others, consider the following: We might observe shades of red and blue scattered around the world, and we might want to ask whether there might be some account given for the existence of these families of constitutional interpretation. So, for example, we might try to determine whether there is something like a distinctive populist method of constitutional interpretation – perhaps newly recognized as an addition to the list of methods.

My concern here is different. I am interested in examining the possibility that somewhere on the map there might be a single blot of a colour not used elsewhere. Again, can there be a truly autochthonous method of constitutional interpretation rather than a local variant on a recognized member of the family of methods?

4.2 Substantive constitutional provisions

I begin by distinguishing three matters of interest: substantive constitutional provisions, interpretations of those provisions, and the methods used to generate those interpretations. Substantive provisions vary among nations: Some nations guarantee social and economic rights, others do not; some nations protect a wide range of such rights, others a smaller set; some nations protect free expression generally, others provide specific protection for artistic expression. Sometimes, though not always, the choices of substantive provisions reflect specific national experiences and in that sense are autochthonous even if the experiences are similar to those elsewhere (where they might or might not have resulted in the inclusion of relevant provisions in the constitution).

For example, on one common account of constitution drafting, drafters should be particularly attentive to the risks their nations distinctively face – potential military coups, for example, or overreaching chief executives – and draft constitutional provisions directed to those risks. Because risks vary from place to place and from time to time, risk-related provisions will vary according to national experience.

A striking example is provided in the South African constitution. Many nations limit the time that a person can be held after arrest but before presentation to a judicial officer. Often these provisions state that the person must appear before a judge within a reasonable period. Not so in South Africa. Here is its constitution's provision on the matter:

> (1) Everyone who is arrested for allegedly committing an offence has the right— … (d) to be brought before a court as soon as reasonably

> possible, but not later than— (i) 48 hours after the arrest; or (ii) the end of the first court day after the expiry of the 48 hours, if the 48 hours expire outside ordinary court hours or on a day which is not an ordinary court day.[1]

It seems clear that the South African provision reflects the distinctive national experience of detentions under apartheid.

This South African provision can be seen as a species of the genus 'provisions dealing with pretrial detentions'. Consider the possibility of a constitutional provision at best loosely related to others in national constitutions – the 'unique' provision. Ecuador's 2008 constitution contains several such provisions, almost all of them resulting from the constitution drafters' desire to create a populist constitution as described in the constitution's elaborate preamble. Its Chapter Five established the 'Transparency and Social Control Branch of Government'. The branch includes the comptroller general and the human rights ombudsman office. These and other components resemble those in other constitutions. The Council for Public Participation and Control, in contrast, is unusual. Its role is basically to oversee the other components of the branch, and its selection method is usual: The National Electoral Council is to 'organize' a 'competitive and merit-based public examination process' for choosing from 'candidacies proposed by social organizations and the citizenry'.[2]

We can see this provision in two ways. It might be the local species of the genus, 'selection mechanisms for independent bodies' – the Ecuadorian analogue of judicial selection commissions. Or it might be a unique and innovative development – to pursue the metaphor, an example of speciation or the separating of a new species from prior ones. On the latter view, the provision might be autochthonous.

Using the word *innovative* to describe such provisions suggests that we can have a sense that something new – and for the moment autochthonous – might diffuse and then lose its autochthonous character. Again, Ecuador provides an example. Its 2008 constitution contains a chapter with four articles describing the 'rights of nature', the first of which asserts that 'Nature … has the right to integral respect for its existence and for the maintenance and regeneration of tis life cycles, structure, functions, and evolution processes'.[3] Scholars interested in the constitutional and nature see this as either a crystallization of inchoate ideas rattling around in other constitutional systems, or as foreshadowing a coming general recognition of ecological rights.[4]

In summary, many substantive constitutional provisions are at most nationally distinctive versions of provisions generically common in constitutions. That generic relationship counsels against treating them as completely

1 Constitution of South Africa, Art. 35 (1) (d).

2 Constitution of Ecuador, Art. 207.

3 Constitution of Ecuador, Art. 71.

4 Cf. Erin Daly, 'Constitutional Protection for Environmental Rights: The Benefits of Environmental Process' (2012) 17 International Journal of Peace Studies 71.

autochthonous. Some provisions, though, may be unique to their environments. If they then spread – populate other lands, so to speak – they might lose their nationally distinctive character and become generic.

4.3 Interpretations of substantive provisions

Interpretations of identical substantive provisions also vary, though here the case is complicated by questions of translation and contextual understanding. Consider a constitutional provision protecting individual privacy. We know that constitutions adopting such a provision – using exactly the same terms, whether in a common language (English in the United States and its subnational constitutions, French in France and Francophone Africa) or in translations that all agree are linguistically identical – can be interpreted to reach different results in different nations.

The reason is straightforward. I use the doctrine of proportionality as the vehicle for my explanation, but many other examples might be adduced. Suppose the proportionality analysis reaches the stage of proportionality as such (or *strictu sensu*, as it is sometimes put). A statute promoting some social goal will be unconstitutionally disproportionate if its intrusion on the constitutionally protected value – here, privacy – is not justified by the extent to which it advances the social goal. But, of course, the degree to which privacy is valued varies from nation to nation. So, a statute might be unconstitutionally disproportionate in a nation that places a high constitutional value on privacy but constitutionally proportionate in a nation that, while recognizing a constitutional right to privacy, places a smaller weight on it (enough smaller to shift the balance with respect to whether the statute advances the social goal enough to outweigh the intrusion on privacy).[5]

An imperfect example of this phenomenon is found in the Alaska Supreme Court's 1975 decision that the state's constitutional guarantee of a right to privacy gave Alaskans a right to possess small amounts of marijuana in their homes for personal use – a holding not reproduced anywhere else in the United States. A concurring opinion by Justice Boochever noted,

> Since the citizens of Alaska, with their strong emphasis on individual liberty, enacted an amendment to the Alaska Constitution expressly providing for a right to privacy not found in the United States Constitution, it can only be concluded that that right is broader in scope than that of the Federal Constitution.[6]

5 It is my understanding that the Alaska state constitution has been interpreted to give greater weight to privacy than has the US national constitution.

6 Tate v Ravin, 537 P2d 494, 512-13 (Alaska 1975) (Boochever, J, concurring). The example is imperfect because the constitution of Alaska contains an express provision guaranteeing a right to privacy, whereas the US Constitution's guarantee is non-textual (or is grounded in constitutional provisions that do not refer specifically to privacy).

National political and social cultures determine the weight given to at least some constitutional values. For that reason there can be varying substantive constitutional interpretations of identical provisions, grounded in national characteristics – autochthonous substantive interpretations. We might qualify this conclusion by challenging the premise that the substantive provisions are identical.

When comparing interpretations of assertedly identical provisions written in different languages, we must be attentive to the possibility that the provisions are not linguistically identical. The US Constitution provides, 'Congress shall make no law … abridging the freedom of speech, or of the press'. The French Constitution incorporates two provisions of the 1789 Declaration of Human and Civil Rights:

> Nul ne doit être inquiété pour ses opinions, même religieuses, pourvu que leur manifestation ne trouble pas l'ordre public établi par la loi', and 'La libre communication des pensées et des opinions est un des droits les plus précieux de l'homme: tout citoyen peut donc parler, écrire, imprimer librement, sauf à répondre de l'abus de cette liberté dans les cas déterminés par la loi.

A standard translation of those provisions is:

> No one may be disturbed on account of his opinions, even religious ones, as long as the manifestation of such opinions does not interfere with the established Law and Order,

and

> The free communication of ideas and of opinions is one of the most precious rights of man. Any citizen may therefore speak, write and publish freely, except what is tantamount to the abuse of this liberty in the cases determined by Law.

Putting aside all the *other* words in these provisions, does *freedom* in the US Constitution mean the same thing as *librement* in the French?

Even apart from issues of translation, we might worry that context matters *within* a single language. As noted above, the Alaskan constitution values privacy more than the US Constitution does, and – I believe – it does so because Alaskans see themselves as the inheritors of a tradition of rugged frontier individualism. We might say that the historical conditions of Alaskan constitutionalism give the word *privacy* a distinctive meaning, different from the word's meaning in the continental United States.

That example illustrates a more general possibility. On some accounts of word- and phrase-meaning, such meanings are inextricably bound up with the entire social world within which the words are uttered (or, in the present context, written). If these accounts are correct, *all* substantive constitutional interpretations are autochthonous. Even if one nation expressly and intentionally borrows a constitutional provision from another country with a common language, the provision's meaning will diverge from its meaning in the original nation.

If this is so, coming up with examples is close to impossible, and I cannot defend the one that follows except by an appeal to my sense of things. The example is the 'clear and present danger' test for determining when a constitution permits regulation of speech that the government says increases the risk of law-breaking. The phrase was introduced to US constitutional law by Justice Oliver Wendell Holmes in 1919,[7] restated in 1951,[8] and restated again in 1969.[9] In 1951, Chief Justice Fred Vinson 'interpreted the phrase' to mean that courts 'must ask whether the gravity of the 'evil', discounted by its improbability, justifies such invasion of free speech as is necessary to avoid the danger'.[10] In 1969 the Court explained that the phrase identified circumstances where advocacy of law violation 'is directed to inciting or producing imminent lawless action and is likely to incite or produce such action'.[11] Courts around the world have 'adopted' the clear-and-present danger test, but they vary widely in the meanings they actually give that test. The US Supreme Court's 1969 formulation, in particular, is not widely followed.[12] So: 'freedom of expression' comes to mean 'clear and present danger', but what *that* means varies from nation to nation.

There is a sense in which this analysis transforms the question at hand – Can nations interpret *identical* constitutional provisions differently? – into the prior one – Can nations have different constitutional provisions? And, just as the answer to the latter question is obviously yes, so should the answer to the transformed question be the same.

These qualifications do not undermine my basic point, though. Either the substantive provisions are autochthonous – 'privacy indexed to Alaska' and 'privacy-indexed-to-the-rest-of-the-United-States' – or the interpretations of the provisions are autochthonous – 'clear-and-present-danger-indexed-to-the-United-States' and 'clear-and-present-danger-indexed-to-Australia'. Once again, we see the possibility of autochthony, here autochthony in constitutional interpretation at the level of specific provisions.

7 Schenck v United States, 249 US 47 (1919).

8 Dennis v United States, 341 US 494 (1951).

9 Brandenburg v Ohio, 395 US 444 (1969).

10 341 US at 510.

11 395 US at 447.

12 For a now-dated comparison between the United States and Canada on this question, see Kent Greenawalt, 'Free Speech in Canada and the United States' (1992) 55 Law & Contemporary Problems 5, at 13–15, which on my reading suggests quite tentatively that Canada's Supreme Court would temper the stringency of the *Brandenburg* version of the clear-and-present-danger test.

4.4 Methods of constitutional interpretation

Is the case different for *methods* of constitutional interpretation? I began this chapter by observing that constitutional theorists in the United States and elsewhere have developed lists of interpretive methods: originalism (with many variants), traditionalism, living constitutionalism (in Canada, 'living tree' interpretation), interpretation with reference to universal moral and political truths, and more. For the United States, Philip Bobbitt has called these 'modalities' of constitutional interpretation, and one modality is especially important in the present context. This is the modality Bobbitt calls, somewhat misleadingly, 'ethical' interpretation, by which he means interpretation with reference to what is described as a nation's ethos or normative self-understanding.[13]

The ethical modality is important here because it rules out one obvious possibility for autochthonous interpretive methods – interpretation in light of the distinctive characteristics of the nation's people. The Preamble to Ireland's 1937 Constitution makes explicit reference to that nation's specific national history and the religious composition of its (then) people.[14] Interpreting a constitutional provision – say, a guarantee that the state will not deprive people of life or liberty without due process of law – in light of the Irish Preamble might lead to Ireland-specific results (as it did with respect to abortion until the constitution was amended) but would not deploy an Ireland-specific modality of interpretation. Rather, it would deploy the universally available ethical modality. To revert to a previous formulation, it would be 'ethical-modality-indexed-to-Ireland', not 'Irish interpretation (in a modality unavailable elsewhere)'.

Something similar might be said about constitutional interpretation that takes the controversial idea of 'Hungarian identity' into account. Much of that identity is laid out in the 2011 constitution's preamble. The contrast with Ireland is instructive. In 1937 the description of Irish identity was not controversial within Ireland. By the twenty-first century the people of Ireland understood that national identity there had changed, and interpreting the constitution with an eye to the *1937* identity was no longer possible. That specific form of the ethical modality had become unavailable. In Hungary, the 2011 description of national identity was controversial from the outset. As I argue later, a modality's availability depends upon agreement within the legal culture that it is available. This might make might the ethical modality unavailable in Hungary.

Though the idea to which he refers is important, Bobbitt's term *ethical* is misleading because it might be confused with another modality of interpretation.

13 Philip Bobbitt, *Constitutional Fate: Theory of the Constitution* (OUP 1982). For Bobbitt, the core message of an 'ethical' interpretation is: 'That's simply not who we are as a people' or, conversely, 'This is who we are as a people'.

14 Similar references are not uncommon in other nation's preambles. For an overview, see Wim Voermans et al, *Constitutional Preambles: A Comparative Analysis* (Edward Elgar 2017).

Call it *philosophical*: constitutional provisions are interpreted with reference to the best available philosophical understanding of the concepts identified by their terms.[15] Of course, people will disagree about what that understanding might be. It might even be the case that disagreements will map systematically on to geography: we might find that a survey would show that a majority of jurists from Western Europe understand the word *equality* in one way, while a majority from Southeast Asia understand it differently. But, the philosophical modality of interpretation is universal rather than autochthonous, just as Bobbitt's ethical modality is: The outcomes might differ, but the modality of interpretation is the same everywhere.

So far, then, we do not have an account in which there can be autochthonous modalities of constitutional interpretation. Bobbitt's work provides the basis for such an account, though. He argues that in the United States the list of interpretive modalities available at any moment is limited.[16] This opens up the possibility of truly autochthonous interpretive methods. Consider the possibility that examining all the interpretive modalities we find in the world leads us to develop a 'set' of modalities consisting of N elements. If each nation uses only a subset of that set – if, for example, the United States does not use 'living tree' interpretation – and if each nation's subset differs from every other nation's (or perhaps if the sets fall into families, with each family different from the others), we might describe interpretive methods as autochthonous: The nation has a distinctive approach to constitutional interpretation, and we might then seek an explanation for why this nation chooses one subset of interpretive methods, that nation another.

This conclusion might be made even more plausible if we supplement Bobbitt's analysis with one offered by Richard Fallon.[17] According to Fallon, US interpretive methodology ranks the interpretive modalities, with originalism as the first, others following. The possibility of ranking modalities makes it even more plausible that nations would differ in interpretive methods. So, for example, the US approach might say, 'Follow the original understanding unless doing so would have disastrous contemporary effects', and the Canadian approach might say, 'Choose the interpretation that best fits contemporary circumstances – 'living tree' interpretation – unless that interpretation is flatly inconsistent with the semantic meaning of relevant constitutional provisions'. Again, we might seek explanations in national experience for the different approaches.

Note that the argument based on Bobbitt's work depends upon the assumption that the modalities available within a nation are limited to a subset

15 Here I refer to Ronald Dworkin's account of constitutional interpretation. See, e.g., Ronald Dworkin, *Freedom's Law: The Moral Reading of the American Constitution* (Harvard University Press 1997). That book's subtitle refers only to the US Constitution, but Dworkin's body of work taken as a whole seems to me to suggest quite strongly that he believed that the 'moral reading' approach should be taken by every constitutional court.

16 Bobbitt (n 13) 6, 8.

17 Richard Fallon, 'A Constructivist Coherence Theory of Constitutional Interpretation' (1987) 100 Harvard Law Review 1189.

of all possible modalities. Of course, within any temporal period – short or long – we will find only some modalities deployed – no more than 'p' of the N possible ones. That might occur, though, only because the need for using a 'new' modality has not yet arisen. A truly autochthonous interpretation is not possible if interpretation everywhere can draw any element from the set of N modalities as needed, though it will appear at any moment that when closely analysed, every nation's interpretive method is autochthonous.

We have reached this point: Bobbitt claims that the modalities available within the United States at any moment are limited. If so, the United States might have an autochthonous method of constitutional interpretation. And, unless there is some reason to think that the United States is special with respect to having a limited set of available modalities, so might every other nation. The question then is, are the modalities of interpretation in the United States (and probably elsewhere) actually limited?

Imagine that a US-based lawyer makes an argument that the US Constitution, properly interpreted, protects a defendant's right to engage in some practice mandated by her religion because – and this is the key point – a specific Bible verse clearly indicates that secular authorities lack the power to prohibit the practice.[18] Other lawyers and all judges would reply that, whatever its merits as an interpretation of the Bible, the argument was not a *legal* argument. One might contrast this with an argument made to an Egyptian court that some constitutional interpretation was correct because it was supported by Koranic verses. In light of the provision in Egypt's constitution that 'The principles of Islamic Sharia are the main source of legislation' (in one translation), this would be a legal argument.

To oversimplify: theology is an available modality of interpretation in Egypt, but not in the United States. The reason is not that the two nation's constitutions themselves identify all the available modalities of interpretation. Nothing in the US Constitution – or in most other national constitutions – prescribes how the document is to be interpreted: Originalism in the United States and 'living tree' interpretation in Canada are imposed on the documents from the outside, so to speak. So too with religious arguments: They are excluded in the United States for reasons unconnected to the US Constitution's text.

The reason for the availability and unavailability of modalities of interpretation lies in national legal culture. And national legal culture is the product of the way lawyers are educated and socialized.[19] At any specific moment lawyers will recognize some arguments as legal, others as 'not legal'. Such recognition can vary from nation to nation, and so – again at any particular moment – national

18 In the 1940s lawyers for Jehovah's Witnesses made such arguments in presenting their cases to the US Supreme Court. See e.g. Appellants' Brief, Cantwell v. Connecticut [310 US 296], No. 632, Oct. Term 1939, p 14 (the challenged statute 'deprives [the defendant] of his liberty to worship ALMIGHTY GOD according to the God-given mandates recorded in Holy Writ'). The brief cited 24 cases and an equal number of Bible verses.

19 For a useful introduction to the role of socialization in creating legal cultures, see Theunis Roux, *The Politics of Principle: The First South African Constitutional Court, 1995–2005* (Cambridge University Press 2013).

methods of constitutional interpretation might be autochthonous. We can examine legal education and socialization in specific nations to explain why some arguments are accepted as legal and others not.[20] And, as before, national legal cultures are not set in stone. Innovations in legal education – including contact among lawyers and legal educators working in different traditions – can induce gradual changes in national legal cultures.[21]

One question lingers. Recall my earlier metaphor of a map with several basic colours, each of which came in several shades. We have reached the point where it is possible to see many nations each of which uses its own set of modalities, some of which other nations use, and each of which has its own ranking of modalities. Are these going to appear on the map as shades of a (quite muddy) single colour – blends with different proportions of red, green, and blue for each nation – or as clearly distinctive colours? Of course we will not be in a position to answer that question without doing a sort of research that, as far as I know, has not been done. I can report, though, my personal sense of things based upon my understanding of methods of constitutional interpretation in the United States, Australia, and Germany: They seem to me different enough to appear as different colours on the map.[22]

4.5 Conclusion

I conclude, then, that there might be distinctive national methods of constitutional interpretation. Constitutional interpretation in European populist regimes might be distinctive – not in terms of substantive interpretations of specific constitutional provisions (of course, that might be so), but in terms of the methods of constitutional interpretation that are deployed. Such distinctiveness would have to be rooted in distinctions among national legal cultures. I admit that I am quite sceptical about the possibility that relevant distinctions exist among those specific cultures as compared with the legal cultures in other parts of Europe, and so am sceptical about possible claims that there is a special way of interpreting constitutions in European populist regimes. But, at least as I have analysed the issue, the possibility that there is such a special way cannot be ruled out.

20 An important example might be the rather strong sense among Australian lawyers that the argument, 'This interpretation would better advance social welfare' – a pragmatic argument of a sort quite common in the United States – is not really a legal argument.

21 The importance of legal culture might be shown by 'failed' innovations, efforts by jurists to import other approaches into their nation's legal culture that nonetheless do not stick. The short life of the so-called 'Mason revolution' in Australian constitutional law might be an example. See Theunis Roux, 'Reinterpreting "the Mason Court Revolution": An Historical Institutionalist Account of Judge-Driven Constitutional Transformation in Australia' (2015) 43 Federal Law Review 1.

22 I find the episode of the Mason Revolution in Australia quite instructive: During that period Australian methods of interpretation began to include hues similar to those dominant in the United States, but afterwards Australia reverted to a set of interpretive methods quite different from that used in the United States.

Part II

Constitutional interpretation and populism in Europe

5 Formalism and judicial self-restraint as tools against populism?

Considerations regarding recent developments of the Austrian Constitutional Court

Konrad Lachmayer

5.1 Introduction

Populism is not a new phenomenon of the last decade in Austria but can be traced back to the 1990s. The developments of the last 30 years have challenged the Austrian constitutional order in many ways, but they also have affected the Austrian Constitutional Court (hereinafter ACC). The Austrian Constitutional Court – celebrating its 100th anniversary in 2020 – is one of the oldest centralized and specialized constitutional courts in the world.[1] Until the 1970s the Court was renowned as a formalist and restrained Court, but has become more activist – especially with regard to human rights – since the 1980s. The interrelation of populist movements and constitutional interpretation has not so far been analysed in a general approach, but examined only with regard to concrete case law.

The following study brings together the different perspectives on the topic over the last few decades and proposes the following hypotheses. First, the Austrian Constitutional Court's methodological approach has changed over time, but these changes do not relate to populism. Second, the Court has shifted in the last ten years from a rights-promoting approach to a rights-protecting approach and once again has become more self-restrained. Third, the Constitutional Court was confronted with different waves of populism. Fourth, the Court maintained its overall methodological approach when it was confronted with populism.

Regarding the analysis of these hypotheses, the study will first focus on the development of populism in Austria. Discussing the question of what can be understood by populism in the Austrian context, the analysis focuses on the rise of the populist Freedom Party in Austria and follows the traces of populism to the New People's Party (since 2017). In a second step, the different approaches adopted by the courts towards populism will be examined

1 See Anna Gamper, 'Constitutional Borrowing from Austria? Einflüsse des B-VG auf ausländische Verfassungen' (2020) Zeitschrift für Öffentliches Recht 99.

and applied to the Constitutional Court's methodological approaches and its reaction to populism. In a third and final step, conclusions will be drawn.

5.2 Populism in Austria

5.2.1 Populism – what kind of populism?

The term populism is highly contested in international scholarship. In a general sense populism is understood as a political programme that 'claims to champion the common person, usually by favourable contrast with a real or perceived elite or establishment'.[2] This understanding, however, creates only a superficial grasp of the concept of populism. While it is not possible to deal with the complex questions of the concept of populism in this article, certain clarifications will be made, and the underlying understanding of populism regarding the following analysis will be presented.

It is important to consider the different understandings of the term populism in the English and the German language. Populism in German is understood as 'opportunistic, popular, often demagogic politics, which aims to gain the favor of the masses (with regard to elections) by dramatizing the political situation'.[3] The German understanding, thus, is much more general and more vague. It includes a much broader group of political movements. The English discussion refers to a much more elaborate concept of populism, which – as mentioned previously – claims to represent the people against an elite in an undemocratic manner.[4] Furthermore, this rhetoric might lead to measures against the ideas of constitutionalism.

A famous discussion on the term populism is presented by Jan-Werner Müller.[5] He argues that populism relates mainly to a claim to be the sole representatives of the people. Other groups (political parties) are understood as illegitimate. Populists claim to represent the (true) people. For him the element of the elite is not crucial; the core element is the anti-pluralist approach of populists.[6] Andres Arato criticizes Müller's perspective because it lacks the element of the 'embodiment of leadership'. According to Arato, populism also includes a 'name and will and even body of a single leader', who identifies the will of the people with the will of the group and avoids the possibility of division.[7]

2 https://www.britannica.com/topic/populism accessed 10 January 2021.

3 See https://www.duden.de/rechtschreibung/Populismus accessed 10 January 2021: 'von Opportunismus geprägte, volksnahe, oft demagogische Politik, die das Ziel hat, durch Dramatisierung der politischen Lage die Gunst der Massen (im Hinblick auf Wahlen) zu gewinnen'.

4 See Cas Mudde and Cristóbal Rovira Kaltwasser, *Populism: A Very Short Introduction* (Oxford University Press 2017) 9: 'Populism has three core concepts: the people, the elite, and the general will'.

5 Jan-Werner Müller, *What Is Populism?* (Penguin 2017).

6 Ibid.

7 Andrew Arato, 'Populism, Constitutional Courts, and Civil Society', in Christine Landfried (ed.), *Judicial Power: How Constitutional Courts Affect Political Transformations* (Cambridge University Press 2019) 318, 326.

In this chapter the following elements are used to identify populism, although it does not seem that all elements have to be represented with the same intensity. The first element of populism is the claim to represent 'the People'; this includes an exclusionary second element against 'the Others', which can refer to different groups, especially minorities. The third element is a combination of the first and second elements, referring to the claim to be protecting the traditional population from the others (especially foreigners). The role and embodiment of a single leader serves as a fourth element. Further elements, which seem to be less essential, concern a form of nationalism, which opposes international cooperation, shows a preference for direct democratic approaches and the narrative of conducting a fight against the elite.

When it comes to populism in Austria, the focus lies on the rises and falls of the Austrian Freedom Party since 1986 (see the next sub-section). Beyond this familiar right-wing-populist narrative, the realignment of the conservative party by Sebastian Kurz (since 2017) also has to be analysed from a populist perspective.

5.2.2 *The Austrian Freedom Party and the rise of populism in Austria*[8]

5.2.2.1 *Jörg Haider and the Austrian Freedom Party (1986–2000)*

Populism in Austria is deeply linked to Jörg Haider's takeover of the Freedom Party in 1986. His xenophobic, right-wing-populist approach, which also included statements in praise of or trivializing the Nazi regime, led to growing success at the election booths in the 1990s. This critical approach towards the government also included an attack on the privileges of the two 'big' parties (the Social Democrats and the conservative People's Party), who formed coalition governments from 1986 to 2000. In 1989, Haider was elected state governor in Carinthia but lost his post because of a trivializing statement he made about the Nazi regime in 1991.[9] In 1999, however, he was re-elected as state governor by a much larger majority. In the meantime, he had been a member of Parliament and, as such, the leader of the largest opposition party. By criticizing the deficiencies of the grand coalition government, he gained increasing political importance.[10] The Freedom Party also became known for its xenophobic and

8 This chapter is based on Konrad Lachmayer, 'Questioning the Basic Values I – Austria and Jörg Haider' in András Jakab and Dimitry Kochenov (eds.), *The Enforcement of EU Law and Values: Ensuring Member States' Compliance* (Oxford University Press 2017) 436–455.

9 Berger, *Kurze Geschichte Österreichs im 20. Jahrhundert* (2nd edn., Facultas Verlags und Buchhandels AG 2008) 408–411.

10 Ruth Picker, Brigitte Salfinger, and Eva Zeglovits, 'Aufstieg und Fall der FPÖ aus der Perspektive der Empirischen Wahlforschung: Eine Langzeitanalyse (1986–2004)' (2004) 33 Österreichische Zeitschrift für Politikwissenschaft 263, 264.

racist election campaigns.[11] Any real and explicit rejection of extreme right-wing political thought was absent.[12] On the contrary, certain FPÖ politicians, including Jörg Haider himself, made use of references to National Socialism.[13] Moreover, Haider attracted attention with the use of defamatory political tactics and his authoritarian political concepts (e.g. the establishment of a 'Third Republic').[14] During the decline of the grand coalition government and political growth of Haider's Freedom Party, Austria joined the EU in 1995 after a referendum in June 1994 (66.6 per cent majority).[15]

Haider transformed the Freedom Party into a right-wing-populist party, fulfilling all the criteria mentioned as characteristics of a populist movement. In accordance with the broadest understanding of the term, the Freedom Party used demagogic politics 'to gain the favor of the masses … by dramatizing the political situation'.[16] Moreover, the Freedom Party claimed to represent 'the People'; this included an exclusionary approach against 'the Others', which especially referred to foreigners but also to ethnic minorities in Austria (like the Slovenian minority in Carinthia).[17] The claim to be protecting the traditional population played a crucial role, which contained an anti-EU nationalistic approach as well. Haider clearly symbolized the charismatic leader who had authority, and he established an authoritarian approach within the party. The Freedom Party regularly claimed there was a need for more direct democratic approaches (which they ignored when this did not benefit them[18]). The fight against the governmental elite formed a crucial part of their political narrative. In conclusion, the Freedom Party is the Austrian prototype of a right-wing-populist party, internationally understood as far-right extremists for good reason, because a clear distinction from national-socialist thinking was never realized (although many affirmations have been made[19]).

11 Haider also exploited opportunities to sue journalists and academics for libel. Because the ordinary courts did not consider freedom of expression properly, he was actually successful in drawing people into long court proceedings. See Alfred J. Noll, 'Die Freiheit der Wissenschaft im Lichte der Strafjustiz' (2000) 29 Österreichische Zeitschrift für Politikwissenschaft 381; Alfred J. Noll, 'Die Arbeit der Strafjustiz im Lichte der Wissenschaft' (2001) 29 Österreichische Zeitschrift für Politikwissenschaft 233.

12 Franziska Marquart, 'Rechtspopulismus im Wandel. Wahlplakate der FPÖ von 1978–2008' (2013) 42 Österreichische Zeitschrift für Politikwissenschaft 353.

13 Andreas Peham, 'Die zwei Seiten des Gemeinschaftsdünkels. Zum antisemitischen Gehalt freiheitlicher Identitätspolitik im Wandel' (2010) 39 Österreichische Zeitschrift für Politikwissenschaft 467.

14 http://www.zeit.de/2000/07/200007.assheuer_haider_.xml accessed 10 January 2021.

15 Stefan Griller, 'Verfassungsfragen der österreichischen EU-Mitgliedschaft' (1995) Zeitschrift für Rechtsvergleichung 89, 100, 107.

16 See https://www.duden.de/rechtschreibung/Populismus accessed 10 January 2021.

17 See Section 5.3.2.

18 See https://www.diepresse.com/5374405/der-arger-der-fpo-mit-dem-volk accessed 10 January 2021.

19 https://www.wienerzeitung.at/nachrichten/politik/oesterreich/2003897-Strache-Identitaere-sind-Verein-mit-dem-FPOe-nie-etwas-zu-tun-hatte.html accessed 10 January 2021.

5.2.2.2 *The European scandal: the Freedom Party in Austrian government – part I (2000–2006)*

The coalition government between the People's Party and the right-wing, populist Freedom Party was viewed domestically as a political trick by the conservatives, but it was never understood as a real threat to Austrian democracy as a whole.[20] Various negative reactions from civil society groups followed, such as a civil society movement which demonstrated against the coalition government every Thursday. The demonstrations continued for more than two years, starting with several thousand participants in 2000 and declining to around 100 participants. The President of the Austrian Republic, Thomas Klestil, was also not impressed by the formation of the government coalition and expressed his concern at the inauguration ceremony.[21]

The international perception of the Austrian political shift was much more dramatic and the reaction far greater than in Austria itself. While Austrians perceived Haider's party as a right-wing populist party,[22] the international media understood Haider as belonging to the far-right,[23] which might be true for some parts of the party base but which was definitely an inadequate description of the Freedom Party's members in government.

EU member states increasingly began to react to the developments in the Austrian government and instigated certain diplomatic measures (EU 14's sanctions against Austria).[24] The labelling of these diplomatic measures as EU 'sanctions' against Austria can be considered a political success of the Austrian government.[25] The Austrian government was thereby able to make

20 In contrast to the Jobbik Party in Hungary today, Haider's party did not have a similar agenda. The Freedom Party did not begin to organize paramilitary groups in Austria or regularly refer to Nazi imagery, nor did it openly argue in favour of abolishing democracy. However, this should not disguise the fact that the Freedom Party repeatedly used xenophobic rhetoric in its politics, sympathized with the Nazi past and had far-right supporters and politicians in its party base as well as authoritarian political ideas.

21 Manfried Welan, 'Regierungssystem unter Druck? Die gewendete Republik' in Anton Pelinka, Fritz Plasser, and Wolfgang Meixner (eds.), *Die Zukunft der österreichischen Demokratie* (Signum Verlag 2000) 335–360.

22 Anton Pelinka, 'Die FPÖ in der vergleichenden Parteienforschung. Zur typologischen Einordnung der Freiheitlichen Partei Österreichs' (2002) 31 Österreichische Zeitschrift für Politikwissenschaft 281.

23 http://www.theguardian.com/world/2000/feb/04/austria.ianblack accessed 10 January 2021. See also the analysis by Christoph Bärenreuter, Stephan Hofer, and Andreas Obermaier, 'Zur Außenwahrnehmung der FPÖ: Der Mediendiskurs in Frankreich, Israel und Schweden über die Nationalratswahlen und die Regierungsbildungen in den Jahren 1999/2000 und 2002/2003' (2004) 33 Österreichische Zeitschrift für Politikwissenschaft 327.

24 See Bojan Bugarič, 'Protecting Democracy Inside the EU: On Article 7 TEU and the Hungarian Turn to Authoritarianism', in Carlos Closa and Dimitry Kochenov (eds.), *Reinforcing the Rule of Law Oversight in the European Union* (Cambridge University Press 2016).

25 Rosa Winkler-Hermaden, 'Als Österreich der Buhmann der EU war' (21 January 2010) *Der Standard*, https://www.derstandard.at/story/1263705581215/eu-sanktionen-als-oesterreich-der-buhmann-der-eu-war accessed 10 January 2021.

political capital out of the European measures by declaring them European 'aggressions' against Austria and pointing to the lack of understanding of the Austrian situation.

The coalition government between the conservative party and the Freedom Party lasted from 2000 to 2006. In 2002 the Freedom Party split, and Heinz-Christian Strache became the new leader of the Freedom Party while Haider's part of the party ('Alliance for the Future of Austria') stayed in government. In 2006, a grand coalition government between the Social Democrats and the People's Party ended the populist experiment.

Haider and his Freedom Party, as well as his Alliance for the Future of Austria Party, had another impact on the Austrian state, which posed an even greater threat to the rule of law. The Haider System managed to undermine the country at its foundations without any significant visible effect between 2000 and 2006, but the dramatic results of his influence are more evident today. Haider's *modus operandi* as state governor, along with that of some members of the government (including the Minister of Finance until 2002), was based on corruption.[26] Particularly after the end of the participation of Haider's party in government in 2006, the number of corruption scandals was enormous and could not be compared to anything which had come before.

The biggest scandal, which could also have affected the European Monetary Union, was the so-called Hypo Scandal,[27] regarding the former state bank of Carinthia.[28] Other corruption scandals involved the website of the Minister of Finance,[29] governmental real-estate projects (the BUWOG Scandal – privatization of apartments owned by the government),[30] and the Telekom Scandal (involving illegal funding of political parties).[31]

In conclusion, the involvement of the populist Freedom Party in government led to an intense conflict with the Austrian Constitutional Court regarding minority rights and to manifold corruption scandals. While in the 1990s the Freedom Party claimed to be fighting against the privileges of the elite, the party proved to be the first to use governmental privileges for their own interests.

After Haider's death in 2008, Haider's Alliance for the Future of Austria became unimportant, but the Freedom Party again increased their vote in elections, which led to a new coalition government of the conservative party and the Freedom Party in 2017 under Chancellor Sebastian Kurz.

26 See https://www.derstandard.at/story/1342947561584/steuerberater-birnbacher-erweitert-gestaendnis accessed 10 January 2021.

27 See http://diepresse.com/home/wirtschaft/economist/4610315/Hypo_Versagen-auf-allen-Linien accessed 10 January 2021.

28 Haider used this bank as his private slush fund to finance several prestigious projects and to finance his state party.

29 http://derstandard.at/1777793/Grasser-Homepage-ueber-220000-Euro-wert---Gerichtsverfahren-moeglich accessed 10 January 2021.

30 https://www.trend.at/skandale/grasser/affaere-wie-karl-heinz-grasser-joerg-haider-buwog-deal-268641 accessed 10 January 2021.

31 Oliver Rathkolb, *Die paradoxe Republik. Österreich 1945–2015* (Paul Zsolnay 2015) 148–155.

5.2.3 Recent development: the Freedom Party in Austrian government – part II (2017–2019)

After the migration crisis 2015, with more than one million refugees traveling through Austria and about 100,000 refugees applying for asylum, the xenophobic political climate in Austria affected the overall political situation and led to another involvement of the reinvigorated Freedom Party in a coalition government in 2017 with the 'new' conservative party under Chancellor Kurz. This involvement of the Freedom Party led to another series of political and legal scandals.

Before the Ibiza Scandal changed the Austrian political situation in 2019, an intelligence agency affair ('BVT-Affäre') dominated the political landscape.[32] Soon after the formation of the coalition government, the then new Minister of the Interior, Mr. Kickl from the Freedom Party, decided to acquire political control over the domestic intelligence agency. The general secretary of the Minister of the Interior orchestrated a house search in the office space of the Federal Office for the Protection of the Constitution and Counterterrorism. This office is the central unit of the domestic intelligence agency and part of the Ministry of the Interior itself. The ministerial cabinet organized the decisive witnesses for the public prosecutor's office, and an artificially created deadline led to rushed action. The house search was executed by a street crimes unit, which would not have been the regular police unit employed for this particular house search, and involved a police officer who was active in the Freedom Party. The reasons for this house search seemed unclear, and the Court of Appeal in Vienna subsequently declared the house search unlawful, because a regular administrative assistant proceeding would have been sufficient to gain the relevant information.[33]

The ostensible reasons did not relate to information regarding far-right extremist activities in Austria; however, the house search led to the confiscation of a significant amount of information about far-right extremists. Political speculations by opposition parties included the suspicion that the Minister was interested in the level of information of the intelligence service on far-right extremists in Austria. Moreover, the preliminary suspension of the head of the domestic intelligence agency failed, because the Federal Administrative Court annulled the suspension because of a lack of evidence for the use of this disciplinary measure. A parliamentary investigation uncovered a highly unprofessional procedure by the Ministry of Interior with unclear aims. The international reputation of the Austrian intelligence service suffered significantly because of the access of

32 See Gregor Heißl and Konrad Lachmayer, 'Zur Leistungsfähigkeit der Gewaltenteilung in der BVT-Affäre. Chronologie und rechtsstaatliche Analyse der BVT-Affäre und ihrer Folgen' (2020) Zeitschrift für öffentliches Recht 531–559.

33 See press release by the Court of Appeal of Vienna, 28 August 2018.

the right-wing populist Freedom Party to sensitive international intelligence.[34] The Austrian Constitutional Court supported the parliamentary investigation by arguing in a formal case that the Minister of the Interior was obliged to hand over all the internal documents of the general secretary of the Ministry to the Parliament, which the Ministry at first refused to do.[35]

The very same Minister of the Interior – Mr. Kickl – questioned the European Convention on Human Rights in the context of asylum law in 2018. He stated that 'law has to follow politics and not politics the law'.[36] He received harsh criticism for this statement not only from law professors and civil society but also from the Minister of Justice and the President of the Republic. It was, however, a significant break of a taboo in that fundamental rights were questioned by a member of the government. Moreover, both leading and minor party members of the Freedom Party have, on a regular basis, made very public xenophobic, racist or Nazi statements. The Freedom Party always tried to create the impression of an immediate reaction to, and non-tolerance of these statements, but in many cases party officials stayed in office or statements were played down.[37]

In conclusion, the involvement of the Freedom Party in government in each case (2000–2002, 2002–2006, 2017–2019) led to significant rule of law violations. The Austrian Constitutional Court maintained rule of law standards, especially rights protection. In 2019 the Austrian Constitutional Court annulled the statutory possibilities of installing spy software on private IT infrastructure or mobile phones,[38] which was enacted in 2018 and was a signature project of the Minister of the Interior, Mr. Kickl. The Constitutional Court declared the statutory provision as disproportionate and unconstitutional, because of a lack of effective legal protection and thus a violation of privacy rights.[39] The Court

34 https://www.washingtonpost.com/world/national-security/austrias-far-right-government-ordered-a-raid-on-its-own-intelligence-service-now-allies-are-freezing-the-country-out/2018/08/17/d20090fc-9985-11e8-b55e-5002300ef004_story.html?noredirect=on accessed 10 January 2021.

35 Austrian Constitutional Court 14 September 2019, UA 1/2018.

36 https://www.diepresse.com/5566984/asyl-recht-muss-politik-folgen-nicht-politik-dem-recht accessed 10 January 2021.

37 In this political atmosphere on Friday, 17 May 2019, 'German media published video footage ("Ibiza Video") showing *Heinz Christian Strache*, the Vice Chancellor and chairman of the so-called "Freedom Party" (FPÖ) at that time, in a meeting with supposed Russian oligarchs. In the video, *Strache* lays out a plan to manipulate voters through media takeovers and sketches possibilities of rigging procurement procedures. The publication of the video footage led to the resignation from all offices of the Vice Chancellor on the following day' (Ibiza Scandal). See Konrad Lachmayer and Lukas Wieser, 'Entering into New Constitutional Territory in Austria. From a Conservative Minority Government to a Transitional Expert Government' (3 June 2019) https://verfassungsblog.de/entering-into-new-constitutional-territory-in-austria/, DOI: https://doi.org/10.17176/20190603-115423-0 accessed 10 January 2021.

38 Austrian Constitutional Court 11 December 2019, G72/2019 ua (G72-74/2019-48, G181-182/2019-18).

39 Ibid.

referred to the case law of the European Court of Human Rights, the European Court of Justice and the German Constitutional Court.[40]

5.3 The Kurz Governments

5.3.1 Kurz I (2017–2019)

The grand coalition government between the Social Democrats and the People's Party collapsed when the (conservative) Minister of Foreign Affairs, Mr. Kurz, took over the People's Party.[41] The following elections led to a significant increase in the People's Party's seats in Parliament (compared with the 2017 elections) and to a coalition government between the 'new' People's Party led by Chancellor Kurz and the Freedom Party. While the populist approach of the Freedom Party was already known, the new approach of Kurz's reorganized People's Party had (and still has) populist tendencies, as well; these could be observed in many initiatives of the Kurz government (covered in this section). The first Kurz government collapsed, which led to the dissolution of Parliament (initiated by Kurz) in the wake of the Ibiza Scandal. The following transitional government, also led by Kurz, lost the confidence of Parliament and was dismissed.

The reorganization of the People's Party in 2017 proved to be successful. This reorganization led to an authoritarian inner-party approach, which transferred significant power to the party leader Kurz. The party was completely reshaped towards the name, will and body of Sebastian Kurz as single leader. One of the reasons for the success was a changed approach towards refugees with the People's Party taking over the positions of the Freedom Party; this was combined with a newly adopted critical approach towards the EU. Over the last 20 years, Austrian legislation in migration law has grown ever more restrictive. The Aliens Police Act 2005 represented a major turn towards a security-based understanding of migration in Austria.[42] Between 2005 and 2018, the Aliens Police Act 2005 was amended 23 times, with five amendments occurring between 2017 and 2018. The Asylum Act 2005 has been amended 17 times since 2005 and 5 times from 2017 to 2019. These amendments contained adjustments making it more complicated to apply for asylum or to stay in Austria.

The Kurz Government further introduced the 'gold plating' argument in the context of the implementation of EU law in Austria. The term 'gold plating' refers to 'unnecessary' rules of member states, which go beyond a

40 See Konrad Lachmayer, 'Rechtsstaatliche Grenzen polizeilicher Überwachungsbefugnisse. Anmerkungen zum Erk des VfGH 11.12.2019, G 72-74/2019 ua', in Gerhard Baumgartner (ed.), *Jahrbuch Öffentliches Recht* (Neuer Wissenschaftlicher Verlag 2020) 105–127.

41 https://www.diepresse.com/5217803/die-ovp-gibt-sebastian-kurz-alle-macht accessed 10 January 2021.

42 In 2005, a coalition of the conservative People's Party and the Freedom Party (2000–2006) was already following a policy agenda which was hostile to foreigners.

European (minimum) standard. This argument prevents the domestic legislator to act in any case in which EU law already exists and national law would make businesses more expensive (e.g. by applying higher labour law standards).[43] The Kurz government adopted this lobbyist argument to argue that EU law should be implemented only in a minimum way, without the national Parliament having the possibility to add further content. However, this political strategy did not liberate businesses but did take away political leeway for legislative policy from Parliament.

The first Kurz Government (2017–2019) changed the role of the weekly ministerial council, which serves as a decision-making body of the government. While the media presentations given after the weekly ministerial council have changed regularly over the last ten years (presentation by the chancellor alone, additionally the vice-chancellor or other members of government), Kurz introduced a governmental spokesperson, which had not existed before. This was part of a new form of governmental 'message control', which aims to prevent differences between members of the government becoming public. Thus, the media is presented only with prepared concepts and not the ad hoc personal statements of ministers.

The Austrian government also initiated a new legislative act to accelerate large infrastructure projects (Location Development Act).[44] The limiting of the duration of administrative procedures to a time frame of 12 months creates a structural problem regarding the Environmental Impact Assessment Directive. Moreover, deficiencies in legal protection were created. The Location Development Act negatively affects the procedural rights of local initiatives and NGOs. Projects of 'special public interest' are prioritized at the expense of environmental protection. Local initiatives and NGOs are prevented from participating and raising critical issues by the measures taken to streamline procedures (e.g. by the possibility to restrict pleading times and topics or the obligation to bear costs caused by a 'culpably delayed submission').[45] Another statutory amendment regarding the Environmental Impact Assessment Act concerned environmental NGOs. Environmental NGOs are involved in the impact assessment process as party to the administrative procedure. The 2018 amendment[46] introduced a novel requirement for the participation of NGOs in administrative procedures (a minimum of 100 members). It is not clear as of this writing whether this 'minimum membership' requirement is compatible with EU or international law. Moreover, NGOs must prove that these requirements are met every three years. NGOs rightly voiced concerns about

43 https://www.eesc.europa.eu/sites/default/files/resources/docs/qe-01-14-863-en-n.pdf accessed 10 January 2021.

44 https://www.derstandard.at/story/2000110172899/eu-kommission-zerpflueckt-oesterreichisches-standortentwicklungsgesetz accessed 10 January 2021.

45 https://www.derstandard.at/story/2000091945947/regierung-boxt-standortgesetz-durch accessed 10 January 2021.

46 Federal Law Gazette I 80/2018.

these kinds of 'Hungarian circumstances'.[47] While the first draft of the amendment still obliged NGOs to provide the names of at least 100 members to the authority, criticism in the context of data protection concerns (GDPR) led to a change, with NGOs having to prove the fulfilment of the minimum-member requirement only to a lawyer or a notary.[48]

In conclusion, the Austrian People's Party under its party leader Sebastian Kurz contains populist elements. The focus on the person of Kurz as a charismatic leader is significant. The 'new conservative party' represents its party leader. Furthermore, the party has adopted a law and order approach towards refugees. After losing the vote of confidence in parliament, Kurz declared in front of party supporters that 'Today Parliament has decided, but in the end [at the elections in September 2019] the people decide'. Even though the movement approach of the new conservative People's Party exhibits clear populist tendencies, the party has not been employing the claim to be the exclusive representatives of 'the people' as a whole. Rather, it is claiming to offer the best solution for the people (which is a regular claim in any democracy). However, Kurz's new People's Party exhibits clear authoritarian tendencies. Examples are the course of action chosen by Kurz in his takeover of the party, the (partly informal) re-structuring of the government or the implementation of message control within the government.

5.3.2 Kurz II (2020–)

After the turbulences of the Ibiza Scandal,[49] the elections in September 2019 brought a new version[50] of a coalition government between the conservative People's Party and the Green Party. Some elements in this coalition government still relate to the exclusive concept of the new conservative People's Party regarding refugees. In the context of migration, the Chancellor declared he would continue his right-wing approach, which he established while in government with the Freedom Party. The Green Party not only accepted this announcement, but also the possibility contained in the coalition agreement that the conservative party may – in the case of another migration crisis like 2015 – look for other majorities in parliament (with the Freedom Party as the most likely ally) to introduce severe migration measures.

More recently, the Ministry of Interior planned to reorganize the provision of legal advice for asylum seekers. In May 2019, during the last days of the first Kurz Government, Parliament approved the establishment of a federal

47 https://kurier.at/politik/inland/ngos-beklagen-frontalangriff-auf-umweltschutz-durch-regierung/400136198 accessed 10 January 2021.

48 See Federal Law Gazette I 80/2018.

49 The Ibiza Scandal led to the dissolution of the coalition government between the People's Party and the Freedom Party, the vote of no-confidence against Kurz and the subsequent dissolution of Parliament.

50 A coalition between these two parties had not existed on a federal level before.

agency[51] to take over the provision of legal advice from NGOs. This federal agency would organize primary care, legal advice and return counselling for asylum seekers. In a 'law and order' policy, the perspectives and possibilities for refugees and migrants, who have come to Austria over the last few years, would be limited to a minimum, preferably resulting in deportation after an efficient asylum procedure. These legislative measures have created tension with EU secondary law regarding legal advice for asylum seekers.[52]

The overall complexity of the Austrian constitutional design and the existing institutions provide a certain level of resilience, but the limitations of this resistance can be clearly observed. Further developments will depend on the new Kurz II government, consisting of a dominant conservative party, but also of a Green Party with a completely different political agenda. The coalition agreement illustrates these tensions, including populist measures concerning refugees as well as reform projects to safeguard the rule of law (e.g. support and strengthening of the judiciary). The Covid-19 crisis has led to further constitutional challenges, which cannot be discussed in detail here.[53]

5.4 Changing approaches of the Austrian Constitutional Court

5.4.1 Judicial approaches towards populism

International constitutional scholarship debates the appropriate role of the judiciary in times of populism. The international debate in comparative constitutional studies seems to agree that (constitutional) courts play a decisive role in times of populism, but that they cannot on their own protect the constitution from authoritarian developments by governments.[54] Populism implies anti-pluralist and anti-democratic claims, which have to be addressed

51 Bundesgesetz über die Errichtung der Bundesagentur für Betreuungs – und Unterstützungsleistungen Gesellschaft mit beschränkter Haftung (BBU-Errichtungsgesetz – BBU-G), Federal Law Gazette I 53/2019.

52 Richtlinie 2013/33/EU (Aufnahmerichtlinie), Art 8, 12, 19, 20, 21, Richtlinie 2013/32/EU (Asylverfahrensrichtlinie), Art 27 Verordnung (EU) Nr. 604/2013 (Dublin III).

53 See for a first analysis Alexander Somek, 'Is the Constitution Law for the Court Only? A Reply to Sebastian Kurz' Verfassungsblog (16 April 2020) at: https://verfassungsblog.de/is-the-constitution-law-for-the-court-only/ accessed 10 January 2021; Konrad Lachmayer, 'Austria: Rule of Law Lacking in Times of Crisis' Verfassungsblog (28 April 2020) at: https://verfassungsblog.de/rule-of-law-lacking-in-times-of-crisis/ accessed 10 January 2021; Kevin Fredy Hinterberger, 'Österreich setzt das Asylrecht aus,' Verfassungsblog (26 April 2020) at: https://verfassungsblog.de/oesterreich-setzt-das-asylrecht-aus/ accessed 10 January 2021.

54 See e.g. Yaniv Roznai, 'Who Will Save the Redheads? Towards an Anti-Bully Theory of Judicial Review and Protection of Democracy' (2020) 29 William & Mary Bill of Rights Journal; András Jakab, 'What Can Constitutional Law Do Against the Erosion of Democracy and the Rule of Law? On the Interconnectedness of the Protection of Democracy and the Rule of Law' (2019) *MPIL Research Paper Series* No. 2019-15.

by constitutional courts. Different approaches can be followed by constitutional/supreme courts, as Yaniv Roznai suggests:[55]

(1) Courts could behave in an activist way to stop further anti-constitutional developments;[56]
(2) Courts could maintain their own approach (as before);
(3) Courts could restrain themselves and try to play for time.

From an Austrian perspective, this chapter will illustrate how the case law of the Austrian Constitutional Court has changed in the last ten years from an activist court to a more restrained court, which acts as the guardian of the constitution, without further developing constitutional rights and principles in new directions. When the Austrian Constitutional Court was already confronted with populism twenty years ago, the Court reacted in an activist way and promoted its rights-based agenda (1).

The character of the Court has changed, but this change was induced not by populism but much more by other factors. Although these factors have not yet been analysed academically, the generational change of judges might be one relevant aspect. The overall change of the Court also had an impact on dealing with the increasing populism in the federal government between 2017 and 2019.

The Austrian Constitutional Court's approach changed from a 'rights-promoting activist' Court (1) to a 'protecting the constitution' Court which maintained its own approach (2). In its 'new' approach, the Constitutional Court has now become much more a guardian of the constitution and its existing case law. In still-existing rights-promoting cases the Court usually refers to the case law of the CJEU or the ECtHR as legitimation for promoting rights but does not develop its own strategy to develop new rights and principles.

5.4.2 Promoting Rights in a European Context (1970–2008)[57]

While the Austrian Constitutional Court was renowned for its formalistic, positivistic and self-restrained case law after World War II, the Court's jurisdiction shifted towards more judicial activism in the 1970s. Inspired by the German Constitutional Court and its constitutional reasoning, the Austrian constitutional court used the concept of rights to develop its own

55 See Roznai (n 54), who prefers to 'stand firm' by following the 'business as usual' approach.

56 See Jakab (n 54). Roznai (n 54) criticizes the approach and believes that it makes things even worse.

57 See with regard to this chapter a former version by the author: Konrad Lachmayer, 'The Austrian Constitutional Court' in András Jakab, Arthur Dyevre, and Giulio Itzcovich (eds.), *Comparative Constitutional Reasoning* (Cambridge University Press 2017) 75–114.

possibilities of substantive review.[58] The most prominent case law refers to the right to equality, which was used as a constitutional basis for the judicial establishment of a principle of reasonability[59] and a principle of the protection of legitimate expectations.[60]

The function and the self-understanding of the Court have changed. The Court has not abandoned the old approach completely but has developed its own mix of judicial restraint, focusing on the meaning of words and historical approaches on the one hand, and judicial activism promoting rights protection and teleological reasoning on the other. The fragmented structure of the Austrian human rights system in the Constitution provides many different sources for the Constitutional Court. The Constitutional Court uses a fundamental rights catalogue from 1867,[61] different post-war treaties (St. Germain 1919, Vienna 1955),[62] the ECHR and other international treaties,[63] further constitutional provisions (e.g. data protection)[64] and finally, since 2012, the EU Charter of Fundamental Rights.[65] Influenced by the ECtHR and the German Constitutional Court, the application of the proportionality test has proved to be most important when dealing with human rights questions by the Austrian Constitutional Court.

The Constitutional Court in particular used the principle of equality to develop new principles and rights.[66] Thus, this principle played a major role in the judicial activism of the Austrian Constitutional Court. The core of the principle of equality refers to the right of equal treatment before the law (Art. 7 Austrian Constitution). The Austrian Constitutional Court has derived a whole set of principles and rights from Art. 7 of the Austrian Constitution since the 1970s. This includes a non-discrimination principle, a principle of prohibition of arbitrariness, a principle of reasonability, a principle of the protection of legitimate expectations, a principle of tax capacity (ability-to-pay principle), an equal treatment of men and women principle, a principle of system coherence, etc. These developments can be linked to the change of the Court towards a more substantive, value-based and active court.

58 See Konrad Lachmayer, 'Eine Sprache, zwei Rechtskulturen: deutsches und österreichisches Verfassungsrechtsdenken' in Uwe Kischel (ed.), *Der Einfluss des deutschen Verfassungsrechtsdenkens in der Welt: Bedeutung, Grenzen, Zukunftsperspektiven* (Mohr Siebeck Verlag 2014) 65–91.

59 VfSlg (Official Collection of Case Law of the Austrian Constitutional Court) 10.043/1984.

60 VfSlg 11.309/1987.

61 Manfred Stelzer, *The Constitution of the Republic of Austria. A Contextual Analysis* (Hart 2011) 209.

62 Ibid., 211–212.

63 See e.g. the International Convention on the Elimination of All Forms of Racial Discrimination, adopted and opened for signature and ratification by General Assembly resolution 2106 (XX) of 21 December 1965 entry into force 4 January 1969.

64 See Sec. 1 Data Protection Act.

65 See VfSlg 19.632/2012.

66 Stelzer (n 61) 242–244.

The Austrian Constitutional Court, in comparison with the German Constitutional Court, still follows an unemotional, prosaic style with relatively short reasoning. Although inspired by the German approach towards EU law, the Austrian Constitutional Court has developed an open-minded attitude towards EU law, trying to implement the EU's legal thinking into Austrian constitutional law. The last 25 years mainly reflect the adaption of the Constitutional Court to EU constitutional law.[67] This development – combined with an increasing relevance of the case law of the ECtHR in Strasbourg – has led to a further strengthening of a rights-and-principle-based approach towards constitutional law. In the 1990s, the Austrian Constitutional Court started to foster its constitutional reasoning based on the rule of law principle and the democratic principle.[68] This again led to an opening in the understanding of the Austrian Constitution not only regarding human rights, but also concerning state organization. The introduction of administrative courts of first instance in 2014 is an impressive result of these changes of the Austrian Constitution and the constitutional reasoning of the Constitutional Court.

5.4.3 The Slovenian Minority Case Law

When it comes to the methodological approach regarding populism, the Carinthian minorities case about road traffic signs illustrates the activist, rights-promoting approach of the Austrian Constitutional Court.[69] The Court did actively fight against populist approaches at that time. In 2001, the Court reached a new decision with regard to bilingual road signs in Carinthia (concerning the Slovenian minority).[70] The case considered the re-evaluation of the (existing) 25 per cent rule (which was lowered by the Austrian Constitutional Court to 10 per cent on the basis of the Treaty of Vienna

67 VfSlg 14.390/1995; VfSlg 14.863/1997; VfSlg 14.886/1997; VfSlg 15.427/2000; VfSlg 17.967/2006; VfSlg 19.499/2011; VfSlg 19.632/2012.

68 See e.g. Martin Hiesel, 'Die Rechtsstaatsjudikatur des Verfassungsgerichtshofes' (1999) Österreichische Juristenzeitung 522; Martin Hiesel, 'Die Entfaltung der Rechtsstaatsjudikatur des Verfassungsgerichtshofs' (2009) Österreichische Juristenzeitung 111; Martin Hiesel, 'Entwicklungen der Rechtsstaatsjudikatur des Verfassungsgerichtshofs' (2016) Österreichische Juristenzeitung 205; see also Harald Eberhard and Konrad Lachmayer, 'Rule of Law in Austria' in *Understandings of the Rule of Law in Various Legal Orders of the World*, Rule of Law Wiki 2011, http://wikis.fu-berlin.de/display/SBprojectrol/Austria accessed 10 January 2021.

69 This section is based on Lachmayer (n 8).

70 Gerhart Holzinger, 'Die Rechte der Volksgruppen in der Rechtsprechung des Verfassungsgerichtshofes' in Bernd-Christian Funk et al. (eds.), *Der Rechtsstaat vor neuen Herausforderungen. Festschrift Adamovich* (Verlag Österreich 2002) 193; Joseph Marko, 'System des österreichischen Volksgruppenrechts und Minderheitenschutzes', in Gregor Heißl (eds.), *Handbuch Menschenrechte* (Facultas Verlagsgesellschaft 2009) 421, 432–435.

from 1955, which does not specify a percentage).[71] The rule regarded the percentage that a minority would have to represent in a population to require the erection of bilingual signs. Using newly elaborated reasoning, the Court argued that it was necessary from the perspective of international law and constitutional minority rights to erect bilingual road signs in more than 200 municipalities.[72]

Jörg Haider, as state governor of Carinthia and leader of the Freedom Party,[73] started a populist campaign against this judgment, not only breaking the law but also attacking the Constitutional Court, whose authority had never before been politically questioned in the Second Republic in such a manner.[74] Haider savagely attacked the President of the Constitutional Court, Ludwig Adamovich, publicly.[75] The Constitutional Court actually reviewed the possibility of starting impeachment proceedings against its own President,[76] not to concede anything to Haider, but rather to create a forum to formally reject Haider's accusations. The ACC thus openly started to oppose the populist attack on the Court, held firm and enabled the strengthening of the protection of minority rights.

Haider toyed with enforcing the judgment using various legal arguments, such as rearranging a village's signage and arguing that the signs were therefore not affected by the judgment, or erecting very small signs in the Slovenian language.[77] This resulted in an extensive body of case law for the Constitutional Court, initiated by the representatives of the Slovenian minority in Carinthia and the Austrian Ombudsman.[78] Haider's activities were politically supported, at least to a certain extent, by ministers in the

71 Art 7 (3) Treaty of Vienna 1955: 'In the administrative and judicial districts of Carinthia, Burgenland and Styria, where there are Slovene, Croat or mixed populations, the Slovene or Croat language shall be accepted as an official language in addition to German. *In such districts topographical terminology and inscriptions shall be in the Slovene or Croat language as well as in German*' (emphasis added).

72 Austrian Constitutional Court, 13 December 2001, VfSlg 16.404/2001; see Michaela Salamun, 'Minority Rights of the Slovene Minority in Carinthia: Placement of Bilingual Signs for Municipal Units (Ortschaften) with 10 Per Cent (Previously 25 Per Cent) Minority Population' (2008) Vienna Journal on International Constitutional Law 135.

73 https://www.diepresse.com/647029/chronologie-der-ortstafel-streit-seit-1955 accessed 10 January 2021.

74 Anna Bender and Konrad Lachmayer, 'Kampf ums Recht: Minderheitenschutz, Rechtsstaat und Verfassungsgerichtshof' in A. Masát, E. Bos et al. (eds.), *Der Donauraum in Europa* (Nomos Verlagsgesellschaft 2013) 336, 340–341.

75 Albert Otti and Michael Karsten Schulze, 'Die Gewalten auf Konfrontationskurs? Eine Fallstudie über das Verhältnis von VfGH und Regierung in den Anfängen der Wende' (2004) 33 Österreichische Zeitschrift für Politikwissenschaft 67, 72–75.

76 VfSlg 16.408/2002.

77 Bernd-Christian Funk, 'Kärntner Ortstafelkonflikt – Zulässigkeit einer Volksbefragung?' (2006) *migraLex* 74.

78 Valerie Leskovar, 'Rights of Minorities and Place Name Signs' (2008) Vienna Journal on International Constitutional Law 141; Alexander Klingenbrunner, 'Bilingual Topography: Differences between German and Slovenian Place Names in Size Are Unconstitutional' (2008) Vienna Journal on International Constitutional Law 146.

Federal Government, who were members of the Freedom Party. Moreover, the Minister of Justice at the time was a member of the Freedom Party and could prohibit any measures initiated by public prosecutors; the Minister for Transport, who could also have been involved in the installation of bilingual road signs, was also a member of the Freedom Party. Haider never implemented the judgment of the Constitutional Court before his death in 2008.

The case of the bilingual road signs clearly showed that the ACC was not only willing to uphold its authority but also to step up towards a more progressive form of rights promotion in times of populism. The Court used judicial activism to extend the scope of minority rights and fostered its approach by establishing a long-lasting case law in this regard. Its open confrontation did create challenges to the Court's authority as the Carinthian governor refused to comply, but the Court held its position and extended its case law until a political compromise was found and the Constitution was amended in 2011.

5.4.4 Protecting Rights in a European Context (2008–2020)

In the last ten years, the Austrian Constitutional Court has changed its general approach to constitutional review. The times of judicial activism seem to have passed, and a more restrained period has begun. The statistics show that the Court has become less activist. In the last few years the Court has reduced the numbers of cases in which it declared a statutory provision as unconstitutional. An important argument of the Constitutional Court is the 'great leeway for legislative policy by the parliament', which can be qualified as a domestic version of the margin of appreciation doctrine of the ECtHR. The Court gave back more political decision-making power to the government. As mentioned earlier, this change in the Court's methodological approach already started before the next wave of populism in Austria and is not linked to populism. The more restrained approach has also affected the Court's way of dealing with populism since 2017.

Although a more general tendency towards judicial restraint can be observed, significant highlights in the case law in the last ten years illustrate that the Court is still the guardian of human rights. Although not actively promoting them, the protection of human rights is still an important part of its case law. Important judgments over the last ten years have often been linked to developments in human rights on a European level. The Austrian Constitutional Court has thus implemented the case law of the ECtHR and the CJEU. This case law refers, for example, to the equality of LGBT persons, including same-sex marriage,[79] the adoption of children by same-sex

79 VfSlg 20.225/2017; Christa Pail, 'Austrian Constitutional Court. Somewhere under the Rainbow: Marriage Equality and the Role of the Austrian Constitutional Court' (2018) Vienna Journal on International Constitutional Law 225.

couples[80] and the recognition of a third gender.[81] The innovative integration of the EU Charter of Fundamental Rights in the constitutional rights adjudication in 2012 is an example of the strengthening of the Court's power (with regard to other apex courts in Austria) and was less the pursuit of a rights-promoting agenda, although it still retained this effect to a certain extent.[82] The Court thus still continues to protect fundamental rights today.[83]

5.4.5 *Surveillance Case Law*

The grand coalition government in power after 2006 tried to avoid implementing the EU Data Retention Directive.[84] The Government remained hesitant until 2011, when Austria had already been punished by the CJEU for missing the implementation deadline for this kind of surveillance directive. Finally, the bill was drafted by the Ministry of Technology in cooperation with a human rights institute to strengthen the constitutional rights elements in the Austrian implementation. The state of Carinthia, as well as human rights activists, immediately initiated proceedings at the Constitutional Court as soon as the implementing act entered into force. The Constitutional Court initiated preliminary proceedings in the CJEU, where an Irish case was already pending.[85]

After the judgment of the CJEU in April 2014, the Constitutional Court ruled in June 2014 on the (un)constitutionality of the Austrian statutory provisions implementing the EU Directive. The Court declared the relevant domestic statutory provisions to be unconstitutional and thus null and void. The Austrian Constitutional Court took over the argumentation of the CJEU.[86]

After ten years of attempts by the Ministry of Interior, the Kurz I government initiated a new surveillance package on the statutory level, which

80 VfSlg 19.942/2014; Iris Murer, 'Exclusion of Registered Partners from Adoption Rights Found to Be Discriminatory' (2015) Vienna Journal on International Constitutional Law 281.

81 VfSlg 20.266/2018.

82 VfSlg 19.632/2012; Gisela Kristoferitsch, 'The Charter of Fundamental Rights of the European Union to be treated like Constitutional Law' (2013) 7 Vienna Journal on International Constitutional Law 88.

83 See recent case law in Chapter IV.

84 See in more detail Konrad Lachmayer, 'The Constitution of Austria in International Constitutional Networks: Pluralism, Dialogues and Diversity' in Anneli Albi and Samo Bardutzky (eds.), *National Constitutions in European and Global Governance: Democracy, Rights, the Rule of Law* (T.M.C. Asser Press 2019) 1271, 1293–1295.

85 See CJEU Case C-189/09 Commission and Council v. Austria [2010] ECR I-00099; Joined cases C-293/12 and C-594/12 Digital Rights Ireland and Seitlinger and Others [2014] ECLI:EU:C:2014:238; VfSlg. 19.702/2012.

86 VfSlg 19.892/2014; Andreas Lehner, 'Data Retention: A Violation of the Right to Data Protection. Strengthening the Judicial Review System in Austria' 8 (2014) Vienna Journal on International Constitutional Law, 445–457.

included intrusive software in personal computers and mobile phones as well as police access to traffic data ('Bundestrojaner', state spyware).[87] Parliament enacted these measures in 2018, and the Austrian Constitutional Court declared the relevant provisions unconstitutional, especially regarding Art. 8 ECHR.[88] Regarding the relevant argumentation, the Constitutional Court referred to the case law of the ECtHR and its own judgment in the Data Retention Case, which was mainly influenced by the CJEU. Although the Court also referred to the German Constitutional Court, the Austrian Constitutional Court was not willing to go one step further to establish a separate right of confidentiality and integrity of IT systems as the German Constitutional Court did.[89]

The surveillance cases of the Austrian Constitutional Court showed that the Court is still willing to protect human rights by declaring the surveillance measures of a populist government unconstitutional. The Court, however, developed existing case law further and was willing to integrate European case law into the Austrian constitutional landscape.

5.5 Conclusion – The Austrian Constitutional Court maintains its own approach

When looking back on the overall tendencies of the last few years, the Austrian Constitutional Court has confirmed the approach adopted over the last ten years; while protecting rights in a European context, the Court has clearly shifted in a more restrained direction.

On the one hand, the Court has held firm in its rights-protecting case law in crucial cases. At the end of 2019 the Constitutional Court declared crucial projects of the Kurz I government, such as stronger state surveillance or fewer social benefits for refugees, to be unconstitutional. Austria offers recognized refugees' different forms of social benefits including a guaranteed minimum income. The states (*Länder*) have the legislative competence to regulate these social benefits. The legislative developments of the last few years – especially in conservative states or states where the Freedom Party participates in the state government – have led to amendments of statutory acts to restrict social benefits, particularly regarding recognized refugees. As a consequence, the CJEU,[90] as well as the Austrian Constitutional Court,[91] declared certain provisions to be contrary to EU law, or unconstitutional.

87 See, with regard to further details, Lachmayer (n 40).

88 Austrian Constitutional Court 11.12.2019, G 72-74/2019 ua.

89 German Constitutional Court 1 BvR 370/07, 1 BvR 595/07.

90 https://www.diepresse.com/5533648/eugh-kippt-kurzung-der-mindestsicherung-fur-asylberechtigte-in-oberosterreich accessed 10 January 2021.

91 VfSlg 20.244/2018, 20.297/2018, 20.300/2018.

On the other hand, a trend towards judicial restraint in the ACC's case law can also be observed. In 2016 the ACC decided[92] in a remarkably formalistic decision against the stronger involvement of environmental issues in constitutional law. In the so-called third runway (of the Vienna airport) decision, the ACC declared that international law concerning climate change must not be considered in the approval of economically significant decisions regarding the establishment of aviation facilities. In 2019, the Constitutional Court qualified the reform of the social security organizations regarding a crucial point of legitimacy (enabling the conservative party to politically influence the Austrian health care system) as constitutional. The Court even extended existing case law regarding the undemocratic composition of self-governing bodies.[93]

In conclusion, although the Austrian Constitutional Court is much more activist than 50 years ago,[94] it has become more formalistic and judicially restrained in the last 10–15 years. This, however, cannot be linked to the populist movements of the last few decades. While acting in an activist way 20 years ago in general and with regard to populist developments, the Court now acts with more restraint in general, but also with regard to populist legislation and law enforcement. Thus, the Court maintains its own approach regarding populism. Although the overall methodological approach is changing over the decades – which might be related to the personal composition of the Court – this does not mean that the Court is adopting its own methodology to react to populism. In that regard the Court's approach corresponds to the 'business-as-usual' model described by Yaniv Roznai.[95]

With regard to human rights, the Court can also be identified as a transformer[96] of the case law of the CJEU and ECtHR. By doing so, the Court keeps its function of protecting human rights and still creates an activist element. While the Court promoted human rights in a more activist way 20–30 years ago, it still remains as a protector of human rights in accordance with still increasing European standards.

The upcoming challenges of the Covid-19 crisis are diverse and have the potential to give populism new strength. We will see if the Court's approach will be successful in defending democracy and protecting the rights of citizens. The first judgments confirm that the Court also maintains its own approach to the Covid-19 crisis.[97]

92 VfSlg 20.185/2017.

93 VfSlg 20.361/2019.

94 Harald Eberhard, 'Judicial activism und judicial self restraint in der Judikatur des VfGH', in Erwin Bernat et al. (eds.), *Festschrift Christian Kopetzki* (Manz 2019) 141, 150.

95 Roznai (n 54).

96 Eberhard (n 94) 141, 150.

97 Austrian Constitutional Court, 14 July 2020, G 202/2020, V 408/2020, V 411/2020, V 363/2020.

6 The Czech Constitutional Court in times of populism

From judicial activism to judicial self-restraint

Zdeněk Kühn

6.1 The legal design of the Czech Constitutional Court and the rise of populism in Czech politics

The Czech Constitutional Court (CCC) is one of the strongest constitutional tribunals anywhere in the world. Its design is framed after the German model of the Federal Constitutional Court. It combines, on the one hand, classical constitutional review (review of the constitutionality of legislation, both concrete, initiated by general courts or the parties, and abstract, initiated by legislators), and on the other hand, a review of the constitutionality of decisions made by public authorities, including general courts (constitutional complaints).

This makes the CCC not only the only Czech court capable of annulling legislation because of its unconstitutionality, but also a sort of 'super-supreme' court, standing *in fact* above the two Czech supreme courts (Supreme Court and Supreme Administrative Court). Although the two supreme courts technically have a final say on the interpretation of the law, the CCC has a final say on the issue of whether or not that interpretation is constitutional. This provides two different avenues for the CCC. Firstly, it has a comfortable way with which it can dispose of the majority of constitutional complaints (by simply saying that the case does not have a constitutional significance and the CCC has no jurisdiction on interpreting the 'ordinary' or 'simple' law). In this way approximately 95% of constitutional complaints could be resolved. Secondly, there is always the possibility that the CCC would pick up the case and proclaim it to be of constitutional importance. In this way, the CCC is able to confirm or modify the case law of the general courts. What is a constitutional or an unconstitutional interpretation of 'ordinary' laws is, after all, ambiguous and provides a substantial leeway for the justices of the CCC to pick up those cases they want to decide on.[1]

1 Interestingly, this is exactly the reason why the law on the South African Constitutional Court which originally enjoyed similar powers was amended and the difference between the issue of lawfulness (the domain of ordinary courts) and constitutionality (the domain of the constitutional court) was abolished. See Christa Rautenbach and Lourens du Plessis, 'Constitutional Court of South Africa' in András Jakab, Arthur Dyevre, and Giulio Itzcovich (eds.), *Comparative Constitutional Reasoning* (Cambridge University Press 2017) 560.

In this chapter, I intend to subject the CCC to an analysis in view of the transformations it has undergone over the three decades of its existence. My aim will be, in particular, to examine to what extent there has been continuity or discontinuity in its decision-making, taking into account an essential institutional issue which the CCC has faced since the very beginning of its existence. The 15 justices of the CCC are appointed by the President of the Czech Republic, subject to the consent of the Senate, for ten years (renewable). Consequently, the constitutional foundations of the CCC already encompass a significant element of discontinuity: the 'ten-year' personnel settings of the court. That is why a major proportion of the constitutional judges is replaced at ten-year intervals (1993, 2003, 2013, 2023, etc.).

As a result of this unfortunately conceived ten-year period, which prevented a gradual replacement of the justices – one-third of the court every three years, for example – the CCC has been subject to regular 'personnel earthquakes' throughout its existence. Moreover, literally every President of the Republic 'models' the Constitutional Court 'to his liking' at the beginning of his mandate. In this regard, the Czech situation differs dramatically from its American archetype. While the latter is also characterized by the co-operation between the Senate and the President, justices are appointed for an indefinite term in the United States. The incumbent U.S. President thus usually gets to appoint two, exceptionally three, justices out of the total number of nine during his one or two terms in presidential office.

One possible way of maintaining at least some continuity is to have a justice re-appointed, but this is basically unheard of in comparative terms as this would impair the judge's independence towards the end of his/her mandate. Nonetheless, both President Klaus and Zeman used this option – three justices were thus serving a second term in office during the 'second' CCC (2003–2013) and two justices during the 'third' CCC (2013–2023, including the Chief Justice).

Moreover, this unfortunate design seems to make the court particularly vulnerable to a rapidly changing political climate and fully dependent on the political ideology of the President of the Republic, and these circumstances can be only partially controlled by the Senate. Between 1993 and 2020, the political landscape of the Czech Republic has changed significantly. The strategies and the nature of presidential appointments have differed, depending on the president in question.

Initially, the first ten years of the Court were defined by the Presidency of Václav Havel (1993–2003). President Havel appointed all justices within a few months (most in 1993, with two in 1994), having little trouble persuading parliamentarians to approve his nominees. In fact, in the early 1990s nominations of justices to the CCC took place beyond public attention because only a few people then realized the potentially enormous political impact of the CCC. Moreover, one should not forget the consensus of liberal constitutionalism (and, economically speaking, neoliberalism and a minimal state) which prevailed among the elites of the post-communist transitions in the 1990s.[2] The CCC emphasized the primacy of an individual over the state.[3] There was a wide consensus that the new democratic constitutions should restrain the parliamentary majority and the executive branch and ensure adherence to the state's basic law through its counter-majoritarian functions.

In contrast, conservative President Klaus (2003–2013) was very sceptical of a strong judiciary. Elected to the Presidency by the Parliament after the 'champion' of Czech liberals, Havel, Klaus tried to change the course of the CCC. So, he adopted a different strategy; he tried to undermine the court by sending people of mediocre quality to the bench. Indeed, some of his nominees were so awkward, to say the least, that many of them were rejected by the Senate. A very painful process followed, when the Court had a number of vacancies and for some time was even unable to sit in full court.[4]

Although President Klaus was a premature messenger of the subsequent Czech populist policies of the 2010s, his effective strength was undermined by the fact that during much of his presidency the Czech political system remained relatively stable. It was only in the second decade of this century that cracks appeared in the system and new populist parties emerged. That is why the only lasting impact President Klaus had on the CCC was that he opened the bench to a much more diverse judicial body. And despite the President's strong belief in judicial self-restraint, it was 'his' judges who took the Court to a peak of judicial activism (as we will see later in this chapter).

Yet another scenario is that of President Miloš Zeman. In 2013 he was a retired politician (a former Prime Minister of the Social Democratic government from 1998 to 2002) who was elected to the presidential office by running an openly nationalist (anti-German) and xenophobic campaign in the very first direct election of the President in Czech history. In 2018 he was re-elected, this time running a populist anti-refugee campaign. According to many, he was able to shift the Czech political system to an unprecedented level of populism.[5] The end of the classical Czech political system and the rise of new populism was confirmed by the electoral victory of Andrej Babiš (a billionaire and a leader of the ANO movement) to the House of Representatives, who formed his cabinet in 2017 with the silent approval of the Czech Communist Party.

Interestingly, the impact of this political storm on the CCC was very limited. There are several reasons for this. First, the Senate, the upper house of

2 Adam Sulikowski, 'Government of Judges and Neoliberal Ideology' in Rafał Mańko, Cosmin Sebastian Cercel, and Adam Sulikowski (eds.), *Law and Critique in Central Europe: Questioning the Past, Resisting the Present* (Counterpress 2016) 16–31.

3 For example, Judgment of 18 October 1995, no. Pl. ÚS 26/94.

4 In English, see J. Kühn and J. Kysela 'Nomination of Constitutional Justices in Post-Communist Countries: Trial, Error, Conflict in the Czech Republic' (2006) 2 European Constitutional Law Review 183.

5 Vladimír Naxera and Petr Krčál, '"This is a Controlled Invasion": The Czech President Miloš Zeman's Populist Perception of Islam and Immigration as Security Threats' (2018) 12 Journal of Nationalism, Memory and Language Politics 192–215.

the legislature, is more resistant to the populist factions than the House of Representatives. This is due to the different electoral systems operating in the two chambers: senators are elected on the basis of the majoritarian system, representatives through a system of proportional representation. The majoritarian system (the winner takes all) effectively reduces political radicalism in the Senate. Even though the House is a much more powerful body, the Senate has effective veto power over the President's choices for the CCC. The Senate can also block any constitutional amendments or changes.

The second reason is accidental and relates to the originally close relations between the President and the Chief Justice of the CCC. Even though President Zeman was able to create the new Court in 2013 to his liking, he voluntarily delegated the selection of new judges to the team of legal experts (the chief judges of both the Supreme and the Supreme Administrative Courts, the Prosecutor General, and especially the Chief Justice, whom the President reappointed to the CCC in 2013). Thanks to his friendly relations with the Constitutional Court's Chief Justice, Rychetský (in office since 2003), the President consulted on most of his nominations in advance with the Chief Justice at the beginning of the President's mandate (2013 and 2014).

It appears that many justices appointed in 2013 and 2014 have been the choices of the Chief Justice rather than the President. The Chief Justice preferred legal wisdom over political ideology. It was only when the President realized that the CCC was not functioning in the way he would like that he interrupted his consultations with the Chief Justice. The President made the few remaining nominations after 2016 according to his own political tastes, trying to find nominees who would deliver his political (populist) message. But in this he faced a hostile Senate which refused one of his nominees in Spring 2019.[6]

As I have said, there has been little methodological or doctrinal impact on the Court's activity in the last ten years which could be plausibly called the impact of political populism. However, I will argue there is at least one such instance of this. In this chapter I intend to pay particular attention to the degree of activism of the 'first' CCC in 1993–2003 and the 'second' and the 'third' CCC in 2003–2013 and post 2013, respectively. I will do so with regard to the two most important functions of the CCC – its reviewing of the constitutionality of legislation (both general and specific) and its reviewing of the constitutionality of judicial decisions (proceedings on constitutional complaints). My argument will be that rising populism has affected the level of judicial activism vis-à-vis the legislature. Populist policies stress that it is the legislature which makes the law, and the Court should not try to change the people's will. Moreover, this is also a natural reaction to

6 The nomination was that of Aleš Gerloch, Professor of the Law School in Prague. Professor Gerloch was criticized by some senators for being too close to the President, for being his political ally or even for being virtually his puppet. Gerloch received only 19 out of 64 votes cast, and his nomination failed. See 'Senate Rejects Ales Gerloch's Nomination to Constitutional Court' Prague Daily Monitor, 21 March 2019.

the overtly activist Court at the end of the first decade of this century (see later in this chapter). In this regard, the 'third' CCC is historically the most self-restrained tribunal since 1989. In contrast, the level of activism of the CCC vis-à-vis the general judiciary has remained pretty stable throughout the Court's existence.

The concepts of judicial activism and self-restraint should therefore be defined at this point. I generally understand judicial self-restraint as a strategy on the part of a judge who tends to accept decisions made by other actors when in doubt in hard cases,[7] whether this relates to laws enacted by the legislature or judicial decisions made by general courts. In this regard, a judge exercising self-restraint will usually give priority to values embraced by those who adopted the decision under review, over his/her own values.[8]

6.2 The two decades of expansion of the powers of the Constitutional Court and the decade of slow retreat

The institutional position of the CCC has been markedly strengthened by its own decision-making in the first two decades of its existence (1993–2012). This case law has undoubtedly made it the strongest constitutional tribunal in Europe, at least on paper. The first three judgements, made by the CCC appointed by President Havel (the CCC in 1993–2003), reinforced its position vis-à-vis the general courts. The fourth and fifth judgements were decided by the court composed of judges appointed by the second president, Klaus (2003–2013). The fourth (and partially also the third) improved its standing in relation to the legislature and the constitutional legislature. Finally, in its fifth judgement, the CCC clearly marked its status over the Court of Justice of the European Union.

The first two judgements were the least disputable in terms of jurisprudence. The first judgement, already adopted during the first year of the CCC's work, excluded any possible existence of a decentralized (diffuse) review of the constitutionality of legislation. The High Court of Prague claimed its power to set aside the legislation adopted by the 'undemocratic' legislature during the communist era (1948–1989). Such an interpretation was possible under the 1991 Charter of Fundamental Rights and Freedoms.[9] However, the CCC rebuffed any attempt to take away part of its exclusive powers. The Czech Constitution (cf. Article 95, which established the duty of the general court to

7 I stress that these must be hard cases of the application of law where there is no consensus in the relevant legal community as to the correct interpretation of the law.

8 It is possible, of course, that a judge will adopt the strategy of self-restraint only because he/she actually agrees with the values behind the object under review, whether it is a law or a court decision. But if a judge can be seen to exercise self-restraint over the longer term, certain conclusions can already be inferred from his/her decisions because it does not seem likely that such a judge would agree with all or most of the acts being reviewed in terms of the values behind them.

9 It makes little sense to protect laws adopted by a non-democratic legislator on equal terms to laws enacted by a parliament genuinely constituted based on the people's will.

present the law to the CCC if the general court was of the opinion that the law is unconstitutional) 'must be understood as a general clause which lays down, without any exceptions, the procedure for assessment of all cases where the courts reach the conclusion that a law is in conflict with constitutional law'.[10]

The second significant extension of the powers of the CCC followed from its judgement of 2001, when the CCC claimed for itself, beyond the scope of what was explicitly stated by the law, the power to determine the unconstitutionality of laws that have already been repealed in the meantime.[11] The CCC reasoned that otherwise there would be no protection whatsoever against unconstitutional laws which had been applied in a case and then later abolished. But it failed to give any consideration whatsoever to the option that equivalent protection could also be provided by the general judiciary.

If the first two judgements did not provoke any scholarly debate,[12] this was not so with the third judgement. Here the CCC expanded the notion of the 'constitutional order' to include international treaties on 'human rights'. The CCC expanded the concept despite the fact that the constitution provided an exhaustive list of what counts as part of the 'constitutional order' (which is essentially the constitution, the Charter of Fundamental Rights and Freedoms and few other constitutional laws) and no international treaties are on that list. This judgement met with strong criticism from scholars who argued that the CCC cannot simply expand the constitution itself. These scholars criticized the idea that according to this novel reading, the CCC is not only involved in interpreting the constitution but also enjoys the ultimate power to say what counts as the constitution.[13] This judgement, too, is intertwined with scepticism towards general courts and their ability to protect international commitments against the legislature.[14]

Seven years later, the CCC strengthened its position towards the constitutional legislature.[15] The case was about the power of the CCC to annul part of the constitution. In this case the CCC annulled the constitutional law which shortened the term of the lower house of the parliament. Acting on the constitutional complaint of one member of parliament (Mr Melčák), the CCC stressed that the constitution provides for a term of four years of the House of Representatives, which is why this general rule cannot be

10 Judgement of 23 June 1994, No. Pl. ÚS 35/94.

11 Judgement of 10 January 2001, No. Pl. ÚS 33/2000.

12 In contrast, the CCC itself was divided in the second case (Pl. ÚS 33/2000) and as many as six constitutional justices wrote their dissenting opinions with regard to such an arrogation of powers.

13 Unlike the previous judgement, this judgement was adopted unanimously. See Judgement of 25 June 2002, File No. Pl. ÚS 36/01.

14 For criticism of the judgement, see Jan Filip, 'Nález č. 403/2002 Sb. jako rukavice hozená ústavodárci Ústavním soudem' (2002) Právní zpravodaj 12–15; or Zdeněnek Kühn and Jan Kysela, 'Je ústavou vždy to, co Ústavní soud řekne, že ústava je? (Euronovela Ústavy ve světle překvapivého nálezu Ústavního soudu)' (2002) 10 Časopis pro právní vědu a praxi 199–214.

15 Judgement File No. Pl. ÚS 27/09 of 10 September 2009 (so-called *Melčák* case).

violated by a specific law. The CCC seemed to be saying that 'ad hoc' laws (created for a particular purpose) are in conflict with the 'substantive core' of the constitution. The very concept of 'constitutional laws contrary to the Constitution' is in no way exceptional from a comparative point of view. As a matter of fact, the CCC already embraced this idea in its very first judgement enacted in 1994. But the exercise of the constitutional tribunal's competence to annul a constitutional law on the grounds of its conflict with the 'substantive core' of the constitution remains mostly a matter of theory across Europe.[16] Indeed, it was precisely the exercise of this very power to annul constitutional laws which was so questionable in the *Melčák* case.

Similarly awkward was the 2012 judgement of the CCC, where a ruling of the EU Court of Justice was declared *ultra vires* – the very first time something like this had happened in European history.[17] The existence of this power is broadly shared among European courts.[18] But what is surprising about the judgement of the CCC is the incredible lightness of the argumentation on the basis of which the constitutional court declared the given ruling of the Court of Justice null and void. The EU Court fell victim to the internal struggle over the interpretation of the Czech constitution between the CCC and the Supreme Administrative Court, in which the Court of Justice acted only as an intermediary, being invited to decide the case via preliminary reference.[19]

However, the 2012 case also marked the zenith of the judicial expansion of the powers of the CCC. Already the 2009 'unconstitutional constitutional law case' (or *Melčák* case) had provoked very heavy political criticism of the CCC, for 'running too wild' and being completely unrestrained. At the same time, and this was typical of the first two decades of the existence of the Czech state governed by the rule of law (and the then still-prevailing notions of liberal constitutionalism), political voices suggesting that this judgement should be ignored were in the minority. In substance, the entire political elite, despite gnashing their teeth, accepted the *Melčák* judgement.[20]

16 Comparative arguments referring to the case law of the Austrian Constitutional Court can be quite confusing for many reasons. Cf. in this regard: Kieran Williams, 'When a Constitutional Amendment Violates the "Substantive Core": the Czech Constitutional Court's September 2009 Early Elections Decision' (2011) 36 Review of Central and East European Law 33–51.

17 Judgement File No. Pl. ÚS 5/12 of 31 January 2012 (*Slovak Pensions XVII*).

18 See a recent German Judgement of 5 May 2020, 2 BvR 859/15, 2 BvR 980/16, 2 BvR 2006/15, 2 BvR 1651/15, relating to the powers of European Central Bank.

19 See Zdeněk Kühn, 'Ultra Vires Review and the Demise of Constitutional Pluralism: the Czecho-Slovak Pension Saga, and the Dangers of State Courts' Defiance of EU Law' (2016) 23 Maastricht Journal of European and Comparative Law 185–194.

20 The then-incumbent head of the Czech Social Democratic Party, Jiří Paroubek, and President Václav Klaus expressed the strongest opposition. Paroubek described the judgement as unconstitutional (Jiří Paroubek, 'Respekt, či překročení pravomocí? Politiky verdikt soudu rozdělil' iDNES.cz, 10 September 2009). The President of the Republic Václav Klaus even called for a major restriction of the Constitutional Court's powers. (Václav Klaus, 'Ústavní soud vědomě prohlubuje krizi, je třeba mu určit nové pravomoce' iDNES.cz, 10 September 2009. However, even President Klaus did not ask that the judgement be ignored at that time.

The second decade of this century brought a new wave of populism into Czech politics. Populism is linked to a deep scepticism about strong constitutional courts which might easily turn into an unrestrained 'government of judges' or judicial supremacy. The justices of the CCC were obviously sensitive to this development. It was already the 'second' court which hit the brakes and stopped an unrestrictive extension of its powers. Some of its decisions are questionable and obviously not in line with the earlier case law.

For instance, facing the dilemma of highly questionable amnesty at the end of the term of the second President of the Republic, Václav Klaus, the CCC proclaimed that the act of a president regarding an amnesty is not subject to a constitutional review[21] (making a clear deviation from the previous case law which had systematically expanded the powers of the court). Furthermore, within a few weeks the CCC refused to deal with the impeachment of the same President because his term of office had expired, despite the fact that the text of the constitution seemed to indicate such an action was possible.[22]

The new ('third') court appointed by the third President, Zeman, continued on this newly opened path of judicial self-restraint. The peak of this case law came with the coronavirus pandemic and the state of emergency imposed all over the country in March–April 2020. The CCC held (faced with strong dissenting opinions) that the declaration of a state of emergency is not justiciable, which is why it could not be challenged before the CCC. And this was not all. The subsequent acts of the government (such as the ban on entry and exit from the country, etc.) are not only beyond constitutional review; they are also beyond the judicial review of the administrative judiciary, the CCC concluded.[23]

The original extremely broad conception of the Court's powers and the subsequent strong and visible limitation of the same powers is just part of the story of the overall political climate. The robust narratives of constitutional liberalism of the 1990s are all but dead. The CCC has not faced similar challenges to its Hungarian or Polish counterparts. However, its judges were able to see that the original idealist conceptions of judicial activism do not fit the age of the great crisis of European liberalism and a new wave of populism.

So far, we have seen the trends. Let us now move to consider the actual numbers relating to the constitutional review of legislation.

6.3 Review of the constitutionality of legislation

In the period from 1993 to the summer of 2003, the 'first' CCC (justices appointed by President Havel) annulled – at least partly – a total of 64 laws (acts of parliament), of which almost one half (26) were annulled on the basis of applications filed by political institutional applicants (i.e. groups of Deputies or Senators of the Parliament, the President of the Republic). From

21 Judgement of 5 March 2013, no. Pl. ÚS 4/13.
22 Judgement of 27 March 2013, no. Pl. ÚS 17/13
23 Judgement of 22 April 2020, no. Pl. ÚS 8/20 (*State of emergency I*).

February 2004[24] to March 2013, the 'second' CCC (justices appointed by President Klaus) annulled a comparable number of laws, a total of 60 laws or their provisions. But only fewer than a third (17) were annulled following applications by political actors. And between April 2013 and June 2020 (the current court, composed of justices appointed by President Zeman), the 'third' CCC annulled only 33 laws (15 laws in the proceedings initiated by political actors).

The Constitutional Court's activities over the course of the first two decades thus appear – at first glance – to exhibit a relative continuity. But this impression does not survive closer scrutiny, primarily because one half (13) of the annulling judgements rendered on the basis of applications from political actors were issued by the 'first' Constitutional Court during the last two and a half years of its work. This highly activist stage began with its judgement regarding a change in the electoral system in January 2001 – probably the most important judgement of the first Constitutional Court in terms of its political impact.[25] Before 2001, the court had issued such judgements only twice a year on average; this changed fundamentally in the period from January 2001 to the summer of 2003. A major part of these judgements was accumulated in a period basically connected with the era of the 'opposition agreement' (on the formation of the Government). A substantial part of these judgements was linked to applications filed by the President of the Republic. The 'second' Constitutional Court thus followed on, in its work in relation to the legislature, from the activist constitutional tribunal operating from 2001 to 2003.

This conclusion does not seem to be supported by statistics. However, we should not neglect one markedly different aspect of the work carried out by the 'second' Constitutional Court. The President of the Republic almost completely disappeared from the ranks of applicants for the annulment of laws.[26] In some of the key cases, President Václav Klaus tended to assume the position of 'defendant' before the constitutional tribunal, rather than being an active applicant. In contrast, President Havel was behind seven at least partially successful applications for the annulment of a law or part of a

24 In the late summer of 2003, the number of constitutional judges decreased below the minimum limit, enabling the court's Plenum to decide on the constitutionality of laws.

25 Judgement of 24 January 2001, no. Pl. ÚS 42/2000. In this case, the CCC rebuffed the attempt of two leading political parties of that time to shift the electoral laws towards majoritarian voting, despite the explicit provision of the constitution which held that the elections to the House of Representatives (unlike the elections to the Senate) are based on proportional representation.

26 Over ten years of his mandate, President Klaus filed a single application with the Constitutional Court for annulling a part of the law. And this was rather a curiosity. Indeed, the President sought annulment of a part of the Judiciary Act, according to which the Supreme Court consists of its President and Vice-President (i.e. not, as the Constitution states, Vice-Presidents in the plural). President Klaus thus wanted to address a certain personal issue connected with a person he wanted to install as a second deputy chief justice. After the Judiciary Act was amended, the CCC discontinued the proceedings. See the resolution of 7 October 2008, File No. Pl. ÚS 17/07.

law during the term in office of the 'first' Constitutional Court. Eight applications filed by Václav Havel were rejected by the 'second' Constitutional Court in April 2004,[27] and two of his applications were unsuccessful before the 'first' tribunal.[28]

If we omit from the statistics ten applications filed by President Havel and one by President Klaus, we will be able to see several peaks in the activities of the Deputies and Senators. During the first three years, the Constitutional Court dealt with a total of 24 applications filed by a group of Deputies and annulled the legislation in 8 cases. At that time, the newly established constitutional tribunal was used, especially by left-wing Deputies, often represented by renowned leftist lawyers. The right-wing CCC of the 1990s was openly hostile to leftist arguments at that the time. This contributed to a significant decrease in the number of applications in the following four years (1996–1999). In total, Deputies and Senators filed only eight applications over these four years. Only one of them was eventually granted.

A sudden change then occurred in 2000, during the third year of the 'opposition agreement' (a *de facto* coalition between the socialists and the conservatives, which was loathed by the liberals who still controlled much of the mainstream media discourse). A total of 21 privileged applications were filed by the Deputies and Senators from 2000 to 2002, and the CCC granted almost one half of them (9). Together with a further four applications made by President Havel, which were successful, the period from 2000 to 2002 was thus the era of the greatest judicial activism, at least in numbers (the Constitutional Court satisfied 13 out of 25 applications filed by Deputies, Senators or the President of the Republic).

In view of the preceding, I consider the first eight years of work by the Constitutional Court an era of relative self-restraint towards the legislature.[29] The judgements which are the most significant for understanding the philosophy of the first CCC are those in which the court dismissed the application – the Unlawfulness of the Communist Regime Act, and both judgements regarding the 'Lustration Act'.[30]

The situation began changing only in 2001, in response to certain constitutional excesses by the parliamentary majority. In 2001–2002, the CCC granted more than one half of the applications. But the success rate started

27 Judgement of 30 June 2004, No. Pl. ÚS 23/02.

28 Judgement of 29 November 1993, File No. Pl. ÚS 41/93, Judgement of 7 June 1995, File No. Pl. ÚS 4/95, No. 168/1995 Coll.

29 This is also noted by Radoslav Procházka in his comparison of constitutional tribunals in the Czech Republic, Hungary, Poland and Slovakia in the 1990s. See Radoslav Procházka, *Mission Accomplished: On Founding Constitutional Adjudication* (Central European University Press 2002).

30 Paradoxically, both judgements regarding the Lustration Act are among the successful applications in my list. However, only a marginal detail was granted within these applications. The substance of these two judgements lies in the dismissal of the key part of each application.

dropping again in 2003.[31] In contrast with the media image of the Constitutional Court as a litigator for political issues, the number of applications made by Deputies and Senators for the annulment of a law has been decreasing, approximately since 2007. Another significant drop in the success rate came after 2014, when the 'third' CCC started to adopt an even more restrained policy towards the legislature. Sensing the overall political atmosphere and a new rising consensus that law should be made by politicians in the parliament, not by judges in their chambers, the CCC voluntarily left the arena.

6.4 Activism of the Constitutional Court in relation to the general judiciary (constitutional complaints)

The second aspect I chose for the purposes of this analysis is the issue of the continuity or discontinuity of the Constitutional Court's case law in matters of constitutional complaints. In my opinion, the basic doctrines followed by the Constitutional Court in matters of constitutional complaints were already formed during the first decade of its existence. Nonetheless, statistics show that, compared to the first decade, the number of judgements annulling decisions of the common courts doubled between 2003 and 2012. We can see, specifically, that the CCC annulled approximately 1,030 judgements of the ordinary courts between 1993 and March 2003, approximately 1,800 were annulled by the second CCC (April 2003–March 2013) and approximately 1,400 by the third CCC (April 2014–June 2020).

The number of annulling judgements thus does not decrease with the knowledge of case law of the CCC. Quite the contrary, it has been rising. The number of judgements of general courts annulled by the CCC is immune to the increasing judicial self-restraint towards the legislature. The explanation seems to me to be clear: the rising populism restrains the CCC with regards to the legislature, but the same logic of judicial self-restraint does not apply to the general judiciary. At the same time this proves that the self-understanding of the CCC remains judicial: the CCC identifies itself primarily as a judicial body. Therefore, the CCC's role is close to something I would call a 'super-supreme' court.

From the doctrinal point of view this self-understanding is questionable, but it remains the reality. It is also an interesting example that the formally Kelsenian model of centralized constitutional review in the Czech Republic is applied in a substantively non-Kelsenian way. Hans Kelsen never anticipated (and would not have been in favour of) an activist constitutional judiciary, such as those which appeared in Europe after World War II. His model was based on the constitutional court as the guardian of the constitution in cases where a breach of constitutional provisions was clear and evident. Kelsen did not envision a constitutional tribunal which would intrude into individual cases decided by ordinary judges; individual cases were within the

31 Of course, my statistics do not include some key judgements of the Constitutional Court, e.g. in the *Melčák* case, which was formally a constitutional complaint.

competence of ordinary judges, and constitutional justices were empowered solely to determine the constitutionality of general norms – not of individual judicial decisions.[32]

This Czech Court's novel self-understanding is also reflected in the constant increase in the number of constitutional complaints. Their numbers are growing – basically every year. While only fewer than 500 constitutional complaints were filed in 1993, their number already exceeded 1,200 two years later, 2,000 in 1998 and 3,000 in 2000. In 2011, the number of constitutional complaints stopped just short of 4,000. In 2012 over 4,900 constitutional complaints were filed, which has been so far the record number in the history of the CCC. Since 2013 the number has remained relatively stable, at around 4,000 complaints annually.

The CCC is thus becoming a victim of its own success, as the first decade of its existence undoubtedly contributed to the cultivation of Czech justice and legal discourse in general.[33] At the same time, however, the CCC is being pushed into a role that does not belong to it – that of some sort of super-review court, eventually assessing the correctness and fairness of each individual decision made by general courts.

This approach brings a clear risk, however. The constitutional courts in the wider region did their best to centralize constitutional review of the legislation, and they limited the power of ordinary courts in this respect. The constitutional courts insisted that they alone have the power to review the constitutionality of the legislation.[34] In doing so, they deprived the general judiciary of its most effective power to resist any legislation which would be in sharp conflict with the rule of law. Having an ultimate say in the review of the decisions of the general judiciary might have helped the overall transformation of the Czech judiciary.[35] On the other hand, for any rising authoritarians it is much easier to take control of the constitutional tribunal with its few judges than to take over an entire judicial system (cf. Hungary or Poland).[36] To sum up, the Czech system could provide a welcome tool for controlling the decentralized judicial decision-making of ordinary (general) courts within one single body comprised of a few judges who have been ideologically scrutinized through political appointments (unlike the much less ideologically predictable echelons of ordinary judges).

32 On the description of Kelsen's model of constitutional judiciary as implemented in 1920 in Austria and Czechoslovakia, see in English Hans Kelsen, 'Judicial Review of Legislation. A Comparative Study of the Austrian and the American Constitution' (1942) 4 The Journal of Politics 183–200.

33 Cf. on this generally Zdeněk Kühn, *The Judiciary in Central and Eastern Europe: Mechanical Jurisprudence in Transformation?* (Brill 2011).

34 Wojciech Sadurski, *Rights before Courts: A Study of Constitutional Courts in Postcommunist States of Central and Eastern Europe* (2nd edition, Springer 2014) 35.

35 See on this for a positive account, Kühn (n 33), chapter 5.

36 Wojciech Sadurski, *Poland's Constitutional Breakdown* (Oxford University Press 2019).

6.5 The personal homogeneity of the first Constitutional Court and the heterogeneity of the second and third court?

The statistics also indicate one further difference between the three decades of the CCC. The first CCC showed a relatively significant right wing – and, in its decisions regarding values, also an anti-communist – ethos. The relatively homogeneous composition of the court and the uniform profiles of the judges can explain why dissenting opinions were expressed only with regard to 73 judgements issued during the first decade of the CCC, whether they were genuine, directed against the operative part, or concurring, i.e. disagreeing with the reasoning.

In contrast, a more balanced representation of various values among judges, including left-wing opinions, within the CCC after 2003, led to a doubling of the number of dissenting opinions (such opinions were issued with regard to a total of 135 judgements by the second CCC between 2003 and 2013 and in 114 cases by the third CCC between 2013 and 2020). The composition of the second and third CCC was substantially more varied in terms of values; its judges not only belong to various political streams but also maintain a wide variety of methodological approaches to the law. The case of the (un)constitutionality of the Institute for the Study of Totalitarian Regimes Act can serve as an example of such conflicts of opinions and values.[37] The arguments and dissenting opinions in this case are all the more remarkable when compared with the case of the 'Lustration', involving a similar conflict of ethical principles and values. Indeed, there were practically no dissenting opinions with respect to the latter case in 2002.[38]

However, the diversity in the composition of the 'second' and 'third' Constitutional Court has also had other, more negative repercussions. The different personalities and ideologies of the individual judges have been manifested in the dramatically different decision-making of individual judges in matters of constitutional complaints. But the simple statistics become even more remarkable if we exclude pre-adjudicated cases, where judges have no real margin for considerations. These are typically cases that follow a prior precedent and are thus, in substance, only a matter of mechanically repeating what has already been stated numerous times (a chamber could make a different decision only if the given question were presented to the Plenum with a view to changing the legal opinion). If these cases are disregarded, we can see that the success rates vary dramatically for individual judges. For instance, while Eliška Wagnerová has been the most forthcoming as judge-rapporteur of the second Court, Vladimír Kůrka stands on the opposite pole as he, in

37 Judgement of 13 March 2008, File No. Pl. ÚS 25/07 (N 56/48 SbNU 791; 160/2008 Coll.).

38 See Judgement File No. Pl. ÚS 9/01 of 5 December 2001 (N 192/24 SbNU 419; 35/2002 Coll.)

fact, has made no contribution at all to the creation of case law concerning constitutional complaints.[39]

There were no such high discrepancies in the first CCC. At the same time, such differences can impair the citizens' trust in the CCC as a single institution. However, there is no simple way of resolving the problem.[40]

6.6 Conclusions

The Czech system of constitutional review has so far been resistant to the rising populism. The reasons for this are partly institutional and partly purely haphazard. The institutional reasons lie in a unique model of judicial appointments to the constitutional court which takes inspiration from the United States (the President appoints subject to the consent of the Senate). This model (especially the Senate which has traditionally been sceptical of Czech Presidents and their attempts to expand their power) has made it difficult for populist presidents since 2003 to appoint judges of their ideology who would be subservient to the demands of the rulers.

Additionally, the second (2003–2013) and the third President (elected in 2013) were not able or even willing to create a court which would reflect their own political agenda. This meant that the judicial personnel were formed on the basis of their merits and not just their political ideology. Interestingly, the only president who created an ideologically homogenous court was Václav Havel in the early 1990s. His court was robustly anti-communist, politically liberal and economically neoliberal.

This does not mean that nothing has changed over the three decades of the Constitutional Court's existence. The Czech political system has changed dramatically, the classical political parties have faded, and new populist movements have taken their place. Even the current Czech President, Miloš Zeman, a classic politician of the 1990s (Prime Minister for the Social Democrats), shifted his political ideology and started to act as a populist. The dramatic political change has left a lasting impact on the judicial behaviour of judges of the CCC. The majority of judges have started to emphasize judicial self-restraint vis-à-vis the legislature. On the other hand, they continue to be very active with regards to the decision-making of the ordinary judiciary. This attitude and the existing institutional settings present a sort of ticking time bomb in the Czech constitutional system. If any other future Czech President were to be more successful in creating a tribunal full of servile judges, the takeover of the independent judicial system could be a very rapid one.

39 Cf., in this respect, an extraordinarily interesting thesis by Ondřej Kadlec, *Metodologie interpretace práva v judikatuře Ústavního soudu ČR* (Charles University, Faculty of Law 2013).

40 In this respect, see Zdeněk Kühn, 'Konzistence judikatury jako problém právní kultury' in Jan Kysela (ed.), *Zákon o Ústavním soudu po třinácti letech* (Eurolex Bohemia 2006) 106ff.

7 Popular initiatives, populism and the Croatian Constitutional Court

Djordje Gardasevic

7.1 Introduction

Unlike states that have been experiencing a populism agenda which derives from actors already in office, I believe there are two major reasons that explain the fact that in Croatia populist claims against constitutionalism have to be searched for in players acting outside of regular government.[1] The first reason for my claim is the lack, since 2000, of clear and solid parliamentary supermajorities, which over time has inevitably led to the need to create coalition governments. Consequently, in Croatia there has been no clear-cut case of governments taking over other constitutional institutions. Additionally, until the 2013 accession, Croatia was heavily engaged in preparations to join the EU, a task which also included adjustments to the European legal system. This made it quite difficult for a populist agenda to prevail within the institutions themselves. The second – and, for my purposes, more important – reason underlying my opening claim is that in Croatia there exists quite an easy method for organizing popular referendum initiatives.[2] Here I side, quite generally, with Carlo Ruzza, who states that

1 In their recent research dealing with differences between populism in an ideational sense and populism as a political communication style in the Croatian case, two prominent Croatian authors also, except for two cases, have focused on populism as emerging primarily from politicians acting outside of the state government. See Marijana Grbeša and Berto Šalaj, 'Textual Analysis: An Inclusive Approach in Croatia' in: Kirk A. Hawkins, Ryan E. Carlin, Levente Littvay, and Cristobal Rovira Kaltwasser (eds.), *The Ideational Approach to Populism: Concept, Theory, and Analysis* (Routledge 2018) 67–89.

2 Here I point to an observation made by Gianfranco Pasquino who states that 'the search for the conditions that give rise to the emergence of populism must continue' and, from the methodological point of view, links this, among other things, to the issue of 'the ways by which government by the people is exercised (through representational institutions or through popular initiatives and referendums?)'. Gianfranco Pasquino, 'Populism and Democracy' in D. Albertazzi and D. McDonnell (eds.) *Twenty-First Century Populism: The Spectre of Western European Democracy* (Palgrave Macmillan 2008) 19. On the other hand, appeals to popular initiatives and referendums have been integral parts of the populist agenda for a long time. For such an observation in reference to American developments in populist politics, see Camila Vergara, 'Crisis Government: The Populist as Plebeian Dictator' in Amit Ron and Majia Nadesan (eds.) *Mapping Populism: Approaches and Methods* (Taylor and Francis 2020) 212; Ronald Formisano, 'Populist Movements in US History: Progressive and Reactionary' in Bridget María Chesterton, York Norman, and

'one can often identify populist undertones in the now recurrent calls for greater public deliberation at local levels, and other forms of political participation by non-state actors, such as promoting referenda, which incorporate the actors of protest politics', and 'foster participation by social movements in decision-making'.[3]

From the substantive point of view, the Croatian Constitution allows nearly everything to be decided by a referendum. Apart from constitutional amendments, this includes proposals on bills, proposals on any other issue considered important for the independence, unity and existence of the Republic of Croatia or, even more extensively, proposals on any other issue within the parliament's competence.[4] Procedurally speaking, since the constitutional revision of 2000, referendums in Croatia may also be called through a popular initiative, if requested by at least 10 percent of all the voters in the State. Moreover, since 2010, a positive referendum vote is deemed successful if it is supported by a mere majority of those who actually participated in voting.[5] In addition, according to the strict letter of the Constitution, in the case of a popular initiative the Parliament must call a referendum. The only way to stop this is if the Constitutional Court decides that the question proposed to be put to a referendum vote is not in accordance with the Constitution or that procedural requirements for the call were not met.[6]

It is thus not a surprise that in recent years, such a fertile ground has triggered a series of popular initiatives.[7] Although, with the exception of the 2013 marriage referendum, they were all blocked either by the Constitutional Court or by the subsequent actions of other state bodies

Gary Marotta (eds.) *Transformations of Populism in Europe and the Americas: History and Recent Tendencies* (Bloomsbury 2016) 136–149. For a general argument that direct democracy can actually cure some of the problems created by populist parties and governments, see John G. Matsusaka, *Let the People Rule – How Direct Democracy Can Meet the Populist Challenge* (Princeton University Press 2020). For a completely different view, construing 'a defense of representative government' which may 'help to dampen the seductive appeal of the populist rhetoric promoting the expanded use of initiatives and referenda', see for instance: John Haskell, *Direct Democracy of Representative Government? Dispelling the Populist Myth* (Westview Press 2001).

3 Carlo Ruzza, 'Populism, Migration, and Xenophobia in Europe' in Carlos de la Torre (ed.), *Routledge Handbook of Global Populism* (Routledge 2019) 204.

4 Article 87 of the Croatian Constitution.

5 It is certain that such an extremely low threshold favors pursuance of 'majoritarianism' as one of the key dimensions of the 'populist constitutionalism' concept. Paul Blokker, 'Populist Constitutionalism' in Carlos de la Torre (ed.), *Routledge Handbook of Global Populism* (Routledge 2019) 113–128. See also Manuel Anselmi, *Populism: An Introduction* (Routledge 2018) 87–90.

6 Article 95 of the Constitutional Law on the Constitutional Court. However, notice the different, deferring view, that the Croatian Constitutional Court took in that respect in the last two cases I describe here (the 2018 Initiatives on the electoral system and the Istanbul Convention).

7 For a similar observation that direct democracy should not be discounted in analyses of populism, because relevant research shows that 'the public is eager to participate in deciding important issues', see Matsusaka (n 2) 61.

(Parliament and the Government),[8] I believe that specific Croatian constitutional arrangements regulating direct decision-making seem to present an almost perfect framework for populists of various sorts. The Croatian example of the popular referendum initiative in this context functions well because the initiative is constitutionalized, it transgresses the boundaries of an advisory institution, and it may be used to decide on a quite extensive range of issues. In this way, as Paul Taggart notes, it well may be a 'useful lightning rod for attracting attention' and 'building up support' for populist movements, used as 'a critique of the lack of participation in representative democracy or as an institutional mechanism to add to representative democracy to make it more participatory'. Popular initiative thus 'may embody a populist impulse'.[9]

My aim here is not to present different and varying definitions of populism, but rather to show its connection to referendums and the relevant practice of the Croatian Constitutional Court in this regard. This indeed is a difficult task. There exist significant theoretical differences both as to which particular direct decision-making institution is most linked to promoting populist ideas (referendums in general, plebiscites or, maybe, popular initiatives in the strict sense) and also as to whether referendums are a constitutive element of definitions of populism. Thus, for instance, Cathérine Colliot-Thélène argues that populist movements

> certainly show a strong preference for the referendum, rather than for the votes of the elected assemblies, but the referendum is part of the panoply of instruments of modern democracies. And governments that are usually not suspected of being populist also resort to referenda, often with plebiscitary intentions.[10]

On the other hand, my focus here is neither on populist presidents nor on populist political parties or governments already in power. It is certainly well known that all these actors play an inevitable role in theoretical discussions on populism, and it has already been clearly noted that referendums, along with

8 Here one may notice that the Croatian experience with referendums so far generally conforms to the evaluation which David Butler and Austin Ranney made already in 1994: 'in the few polities with both government-controlled referendums and popular initiatives, referendum measures referred to the voters by governments have generally succeeded more than measures placed on the ballot by popular initiatives'. David Butler and Austin Ranney, 'Theory' in David Butler and Austin Ranney (eds.), *Referendums Around the World – the Growing Use of Direct Democracy* (The AEI Press 1994) 20.

9 Paul Taggart, *Populism* (Open University Press 2000) 103–105. On the other hand, from the rhetorical point of view, popular initiatives may serve the goal that Jan-Werner Müller well captures in the following words: 'The danger comes, in other words, from within the democratic world – the political actors posing the danger speak the language of democratic values'. Jan-Werner Müller, *What Is Populism* (University of Pennsylvania Press 2016) 6.

10 Cathérine Colliot-Thélène, 'Populism as a Conceptual Problem' in Gregor Fitzi, Jürgen Mackert, and Bryan S. Turner (eds.), *Populism and the Crisis of Democracy, Volume 1: Concepts and Theory* (Routledge 2019) 18.

other strategies, are used by populist governments to 'weaken the remaining checks and balances' inherent in a modern constitutional state.[11] Or, as Steven Levitsky and James Loxton note, in their conflicts with the 'traditional elite' presidents often use referenda to 'circumvent Congress and convoke a constituent assembly aimed at "re-founding" the institutional order'.[12] On the other hand, Ángel Rivero claims that direct democracy, which means 'the people's will', is characteristic of new European populism, where 'the vast majority of European populist parties, either from the right or from the left, are strong supporters of referenda (or, to be more precise, of plebiscites) as the paramount democratic institution'.[13]

In this contribution, I will rather focus on bottom-up popular referendum initiatives, since they are typical of the Croatian case. In addition, here I find support from Paris Aslanidis whose research on bottom-up populist social movements suggests that 'populism is not the exclusive domain of political parties and their leaders'. He stresses, instead, that populism must also be analyzed as a transformation of 'grassroots populism into an institutionalized force', a process in which a 'mode of articulation' of social grievances leads to a 'collective action frame' that 'aims at triggering a cognitive process that transforms discontent into action'.[14]

7.2 Popular initiative as the means of fostering populist claims

So far, popular initiatives in Croatia have addressed a wide range of issues: the status of members of military in proceedings related to alleged war crimes, Croatia joining NATO, state borders with Slovenia, amendments to the Labor Law, the constitutional definition of marriage, the official use

11 Gregor Fitzi, 'Introduction: Political Populism as a Symptom of the Great Transformation of Democracy' in Gregor Fitzi, Jürgen Mackert, and Bryan S. Turner (eds.), *Populism and the Crisis of Democracy, Volume 2: Politics, Social Movements and Extremism* (Routledge 2019) 6. For the same argument, and several examples of European states for this purpose, see also: Klaus Bachmann, 'The Role of Populist Parties and Movements in Transitions to Hybrid Regimes in Europe' in Gregor Fitzi, Jürgen Mackert, and Bryan S. Turner (eds.), *Populism and the Crisis of Democracy, Volume 2: Politics, Social Movements and Extremism* (Routledge 2019) 121–136. For Latin American experiences, see, for instance: Carlos de la Torre, 'The Contested Meanings of Populist Revolutions in Latin America' in Bridget María Chesterton, York Norman, and Gary Marotta (eds.), *Transformations of Populism in Europe and the Americas: History and Recent Tendencies* (Bloomsbury 2016) 330–344.

12 Steven Levitsky and James Loxton, 'Populism and Competitive Authoritarianism in Latin America' in Carlos de la Torre (ed.) *Routledge Handbook of Global Populism* (Routledge 2019) 337.

13 Ángel Rivero, 'Populism and Democracy in Europe' in Carlos de la Torre (ed.) *Routledge Handbook of Global Populism* (Routledge 2019) 286.

14 Paris Aslanidis, 'Populism and Social Movements' in Cristobal Rovira Kaltwasser, Paul A. Taggart, Paulina Ochoa Espejo, and Pierre Ostiguy (eds.) *The Oxford Handbook of Populism* (Oxford University Press 2017) 305–325. Although Aslanidis's analysis is further directed to transformations vis-à-vis political parties, I find these general elements very inspiring for my own approach to popular referendum initiatives.

of minority languages, the process of privatization, the prohibition on the 'outsourcing' of technical services in the public sector and the prohibition on the handing over of certain highways under concessions, two proposals on adopting new constitutional rules for parliamentary elections, constitutional requirements for popular initiatives themselves, denouncing the Istanbul Convention and amendments to the law regulating pensions.[15]

One additional point here also concerns the Croatian practice as related specifically to constitutional referendums. Since 1990, the Croatian Constitution has been amended five times in total, four times in the Parliament and once through a referendum (the 2013 'Marriage Referendum'). However, quite strikingly, popular constitutional referendum initiatives in Croatia have been far more frequent than this one successful example might suggest. In fact, apart from the 2013 case, to date there have been four more such initiatives, all of them within the last six years.[16] This growing use of popular initiatives thus might affirm what Cass Mudde and Cristóbal Rovira Kaltwasser state, i.e. that 'populists-in-opposition tend to call for more transparency and the implementation of more democracy', including referendums, in order to 'break the alleged stranglehold of the elite'.[17] Moreover, of these five popular constitutional initiatives, three have dealt with some sort of identity issue (the position of gender minorities in the case of marriage; the argument that the Istanbul Convention is primarily about introducing a gender ideology; the rights of national minorities). Four initiatives were substantively addressed against political 'elites' as such or their specific actions (the only exception here being, arguably, the 2013 marriage referendum). This, I believe, attests to the seriousness of the whole situation.

The populist note generally inherent in such specifically constitutional initiatives is clearly visible. To paraphrase Benjamin Krämer, they can be seen as instances in which the 'will of the people has to be registered once and for all' and a referendum thus becomes a 'redemptive act that brings an issue to a final decision and a lesson, or even punishment, for elites'.[18] This, it seems,

15 For a more extensive view on the Croatian popular referendum initiatives, see Djordje Gardasevic, 'Constitutional Interpretations of Direct Democracy in Croatia' (2015) 12 Iustinianus Primus Law Review 1–50.

16 Here, I exclude the 2019 proposal of the candidate running in presidential elections because this case never came about, although it represents a serious attempt which must not be underrated.

17 Cass Mudde and Cristóbal Rovira Kaltwasser, *Populism: A Very Short Introduction* (Oxford University Press 2017) 93. See also the claim by Paul Blokker that 'Populists call for making popular sovereignty a reality, which in constitutional terms means the creation of a more direct relation between the people and the constitutional complex of norms and values'. Blokker (n 5) 116.

18 Benjamin Krämer, 'Populist and Non-Populist Media: Their Paradoxical Role in the Development and Diffusion of a Right-Wing Ideology' in Reinhard Heinisch, Christina Holtz-Bacha, and Oscar Mazzoleni (eds.), *Political Populism: A Handbook, Volume 3 of International Studies on Populism* (Nomos 2017) 414. In my view, constitutional popular initiatives are thus very good at performing the task of creating of what Paul Blokker identifies as 'a durable majority'. Blokker (n 5).

also goes along with Jan-Werner Müller's observation that 'while populists often call for referenda, such exercises are not about initiating open-ended processes of democratic will-formation among citizens'. He rather stresses the following: 'Populists simply wish to be confirmed in what they have already determined the will of the real people to be. Populism is not a path to more participation in politics'.[19] Moreover, in constitutional referendum initiatives that have addressed the restructuring of the parliamentary electoral system, one may also, as Saskia P. Ruth and Kirk A. Hawkins claim, confirm the populist striving to 'value the seal of popular approval that only a formally open, competitive election can provide', and favoring, at the same time, 'direct participatory mechanisms such as recall, initiative and referenda – including those that can be initiated by citizens'.[20]

In the remaining part of this chapter, I will focus on the interpretative approaches of the Croatian Constitutional Court in several referendum cases which I believe are important for understanding my opening claim that in Croatia populist claims against constitutionalism have to be searched for in players acting outside of regular government. I also suggest that the analysis focuses on constitutional referendums, although, in order to get a wider picture of the Court's interpretative tools, I will also add some observations on other relevant initiatives, as they have been addressed by the Court in previous years.

The early case of the 2010 referendum on the Labor Law presents an opening example because it was the first instance in which the Court had to formally deal with the case of a popular initiative. Factually, a number of trade unions had started an initiative for a referendum on the rejection of the governmental proposal to amend the Labor Act and thus prevent restrictions on workers' benefits. However, once the initiative had collected enough signatures, the Government withdrew its amendment from the parliamentary procedure. This fact, in the view of the Court, meant that the referendum could not be called, because the referendum question itself was found to be technically connected to the governmental bill. Therefore, in quite a simple ruling, the Court actually proclaimed the Government to be the master of the procedure it had itself started in the first place.[21] However, confronted with some more difficult challenges that emerged a few years later, the Court abandoned this strict procedural reading of the Constitution and, in the two following cases, instead opted to invoke both the 'heavy' concept of 'constitutional identity' and a strict type of proportionality analysis.[22]

19 Müller (n 9) 102. This particular conclusion by Müller fits the 'Marriage' type of referendum I describe in the next section, but not popular initiatives aiming to reconstruct the parliamentary electoral rules.

20 Saskia P. Ruth and Kirk A. Hawkins, 'Populism and Democratic Representation in Latin America' in Reinhard Heinisch, Christina Holtz-Bacha, and Oscar Mazzoleni (eds.), *Political Populism: A Handbook, Volume 3 of International Studies on Populism* (Nomos 2017) 260.

21 Decision of the Constitutional Court U-VIIR-4696/2010, 20 October 2010.

22 I have previously offered an extensive analysis and critic of these two cases in Gardasevic (n 15).

7.3 The game becomes serious: the introduction of the constitutional identity concept

The central place in this era undoubtedly belongs to the 2013 'Marriage Referendum' which, as I said before, has so far been the only example of a popular constitutional referendum initiative to have actually succeeded.[23] The path to amending the Constitution, however, was initially marked by an attempt by the Parliament to qualify the expectedly successful referendum simply as the first step in the whole procedure. Therefore, the idea was to finish the amendment process through a subsequent parliamentary ratification – or, to express it better, rejection – because the governing majority at the time strongly opposed the whole plan for a new constitutional definition of marriage. This approach was resolutely rejected by the Court which specified that the Constitution contained two independent constitutional amendment procedures: one to be carried out by the Parliament[24] and another through a constitutional referendum.[25] Thus, the Court concluded that a decision made directly by the people on a referendum has a constitutive character and results in an immediate transformation of the constitutional text, taking legal effect on the actual day a referendum is held.[26] The interpretive tools the Court applied here were twofold. On one hand, it relied on a linguistic interpretation of two different and separate constitutional norms regulating constitutional amendments. On the other, it offered a systemic approach by which the Constitution should be read comprehensively, in accordance with the highest values of the constitutional order which themselves serve as the grounds for interpretation of the Constitution.

This systemic approach is visible in the following passage of the said in *Warning*:

> The Constitution should be read as a whole. It cannot be approached in such a way that from a unity of relationships which are constituted by it one particular provision is taken out and then interpreted separately and mechanically, independently from all other values which are protected by the Constitution. The Constitution possesses an internal unity and the meaning of a particular part of it is related to all other provisions. If seen in its unity, the Constitution reflects particular comprehensive principles and fundamental decisions according to which all its other individual

23 I believe that the examples of the 'Marriage Referendum', as well as those pertaining to the mandates of the parliamentary representatives of national minorities and the Istanbul Convention I describe later in this chapter, may well fit into a description of a populist agenda as essentially being opposed to pluralism in general and more specifically to 'procedures that ensure, most notably, minority rights'. For this claim, see Agnes Akkerman, Cas Mudde, and Andrej Zaslove, 'How Populist Are the People? Measuring Populist Attitudes in Voters' (2014) 47 Comparative Political Studies 1327. This is also in line with Jan-Werner Müller's general claims on populism as being inherently anti-pluralist and, as a form of identity politics, aiming at exclusive representation. Müller (n 9).

24 Chapter IX of the Constitution.

25 Article 87 of the Constitution.

26 Constitutional Court, Warning U-VIIR-5292/2013, 28 October 2013.

> provisions must be interpreted. Therefore, none of the constitutional provisions may be taken out of context and interpreted independently. In other words, each particular constitutional provision must always be interpreted in accordance with the highest values of the constitutional order which constitute the basis for interpreting the Constitution.[27]

To this general statement, the Court added that the highest values, in combination with the constitutional provision guaranteeing that the people shall exercise the sovereign powers through the election of representatives and through direct decision-making,[28] constitute the concept of the 'Croatian Constitutional Identity'. In practical terms, this meant that the Parliament did not have the power to substantively interfere with the direct expression of the will of voters. The main issue in this case, however, arose a few days later when the Court issued its second interpretation. The Statement made by the Court[29] merits attention in three points. Firstly, the Court rejected that the referendum question was contrary to both international[30] and domestic law.[31] Secondly, it reasoned that constitutional provisions regulating referendums meant that 'a constitutional referendum may be called in order to introduce some changes in the state constitutional order', and that this was also 'in accordance with the legal purpose of popular initiatives, which may be summarized in the following formula: to change something already existing in the legal order or to include in the legal order something new'. From that point of view, the Court further argued that the introduction of an existing definition from a law into the Constitution could not be accepted as such a 'novelty'. Most notably, relying on the Venice Commission's statements[32] that 'systemic constitutionalisation of legal institutes in a democratic society' was unacceptable due to the fact that it would undermine democratic principles of checks and balances and the separation of powers, the Court concluded that this was an imperative to be obeyed in cases of both referendums and parliamentary enacted constitutional amendments.[33] Clearly, the Court thus introduced the theory of 'unconstitutional constitutional amendments'.

27 The highest values of the constitutional order are presented in Article 3 of the Constitution.

28 Article 1, para 3 of the Constitution.

29 Constitutional Court, Statement on the Popular Constitutional Referendum on the Definition of Marriage, SuS-1/2013, 14 November 2013.

30 In short, the Court here analysed the case in terms of Article 9 of the EU Charter of Fundamental Rights and articles 8, 12 and 14 of the European Convention on Human Rights.

31 Here, the Court invoked various provisions of the Family Law, the Law on Same-Sex Unions and the Law on the Prohibition of Discrimination.

32 *Opinion on the Fourth Amendment to the Fundamental Law of Hungary*, Venice Commission, Opinion 720/2013, CDL-AD(2013)012, Strasbourg, 17 June 2013.

33 However, in the end, the Court somewhat relaxed its standing by claiming that there could be some exceptions to the prohibition on the incorporation of strictly legal institutes in the Constitution. Those exceptions, however, should be justified on the basis of their connection to deeply embedded social and cultural characteristics of the society (*Schalk and Kopf v. Austria* case).

The Statement marked a significant change in the practice of the Court because in previous cases it had explicitly argued that it had only the power to review the formal constitutionality of constitutional amendments. The same position was taken in doctrine.[34] Thirdly, the Court also provided an additional theory of its own constitutional review powers by reasoning that even in the absence of a proper parliamentary motion to examine popular referendum initiatives,[35] it could nonetheless, for that purpose, rely upon its general control powers.[36] This new systemic interpretation of the Court's powers is best captured in its following words:

> On the basis of Article 125 al. 9 of the Constitution and Articles 2 par. 1 and 87 al. 2 of the Constitutional Law, the Constitutional Court possesses the general constitutional duty to guarantee respect for the Constitution and to supervise the constitutionality of a state referendum, right up until the formal end of the referendum procedure. Accordingly, after the Croatian parliament decides to call a referendum on the basis of a popular constitutional initiative, without having previously acted upon the Article 95 par. 1 of the Constitutional Law, the Constitutional Court does not lose its general powers of control over the constitutionality of such a referendum. However, taking into account the constitution-making power of the Croatian parliament as the highest law-making and representative body in the State, the Constitutional Court assesses that it can use general control powers in such a situation only exceptionally, when it determines that there exists such a formal or substantial unconstitutionality of a referendum question or such a grave procedural error that it threatens to undermine the structural features of the Croatian constitutional state, and its constitutional identity, including the highest values of the constitutional order of the Republic of Croatia (Articles 1 and 3 of the Constitution). Primary protection of these values does not exclude the power of the constitution-maker to expressly exclude some other issues from the range of permitted referendum questions.

34 Jasna Omejec, 'Kontrola ustavnosti ustavnih normi (ustavnih amandmana i ustavnih zakona' (2010) Godišnjak Akademije pravnih znanosti Hrvatske 21 22 and 25 26.

35 According to the strict letter of Article 95 of the Constitutional Law on the Constitutional Court, the Court can review the constitutionality of popular referendum initiatives only if requested by the Parliament.

36 Article 125 al. 9 of the Constitution gives the Court the power to 'Supervise the constitutionality and legality of elections and national referendums, and decide on the electoral disputes which are not within the jurisdiction of courts'. Moreover, Article 2 par. 1 of the Constitutional Law prescribes that the Court 'guarantees respect for and application of the Constitution and bases its actions on the provisions of the Constitution and Constitutional Law on the Constitutional Court' while its Article 87 al. 2 empowers it to 'supervise the constitutionality and legality of a state referendum'.

7.4 Proportionality in action

The second case that marked a significant turn in the Court's approach to referendums came with the 2014 popular initiative that sought to change the Constitutional Law on the Rights of National Minorities.[37] The idea was to prescribe that in territories of local self-government, state administration and judicial units, the official use of a national minority language and script could be implemented only if members of a national minority made up at least half of the population in such units.[38]

The opening words of the Constitutional Court's reasoning in this case revealed several important standpoints.[39] Firstly, that the Constitution was not value-neutral, but that it defined the Republic of Croatia as a democratic state based on national equality, respect for human rights and rule of law principles, all of which must be realized without discrimination. Secondly, that democracy based on the rule of law and protection of human rights represents the only political model recognized by the Constitution. Thirdly, that pluralism, as a central feature of a democratic society, requires respect for diversities and particular identities, as well as dialogue and a search for balance which negates any abuse of a dominant position. Fourthly, that languages and scripts of national minorities must be qualified as universal and constant values which determine the identity of the Croatian constitutional state. Fifthly, that, consequently, any raising of the threshold required to activate the collective rights of minorities must be rationally justified exclusively on reasons which emerge from the democratic society based on the rule of law and protection of human rights. And sixthly, that the raising of the threshold must have a clearly expressed legitimate aim in the public interest, as well as that it must be necessary in a democratic society or 'strictly proportional' to this legitimate aim.

As a result of the application of this scheme, the Court declared the referendum unconstitutional because it lacked a rational basis and a legitimate aim to be pursued with the legal change sought. The Court also found that the initiative was principally undertaken because of the

> factual circumstances related to the Serbian national minority

and

> the legal obligation to secure official use of language and script on the basis of … the Constitutional Law on the Rights of National Minorities, for that minority, in a number of municipalities and towns, including the

37 For an additional analysis of this particular case, see also Jurij Toplak and Djordje Gardasevic, 'Concepts of National and Constitutional Identity in Croatian Constitutional Law' (2017) 42 Review of Central and East European Law 263–293.

38 In the existing version of the law, this threshold was settled at one-third of the whole population in local units.

39 Decision of the Constitutional Court U-VIIR-4640/2014, 12 August 2014.

town of Vukovar, would cease to exist with the proposed increase of the threshold.

This, in the Court's view, meant that

> in the proposed referendum question, considering its content and the way it was formulated, in a legal sense there exists a concealed aim which, as such, cannot be assessed as a legitimate one.

Finally, the Court explicitly also stated that

> to require a call for a referendum with the message that the Cyrillic alphabet in the town of Vukovar was 'seen as a symbol of suffering' is a deeply disturbing act which attacks an alphabet as a universal civilization heritage of a mankind that determines the very identity of the Croatian constitutional state. From that message emerges an irrationality which must be pointed out.

7.5 Back to the linguistic approach

Contrary to those two examples, which showed the Constitutional Court's willingness to undertake sophisticated and thorough analyses of popular referendum initiatives, the following case seems to mark the return to a more rudimentary type of analysis.

The 2014 referendum initiative on the electoral system came as the first major initiative to amend constitutional rules regulating elections. Technically, the initiative proposed the following: to prescribe that election of parliamentary representatives is to be done through the proportional system; to introduce preferential votes; to establish that electoral units conform to regional territorial units in which at least 20 representatives are elected; to lower the election threshold to 3 percent or 2 percent of votes in electoral units; to prohibit coalition lists of two or more political parties; to introduce a right to vote by electronic means. The Court declared that not enough signatures were collected, and this effectively stopped the referendum. In substance, the central issue in this case was linked to the interpretation of Article 87 of the Constitution, which prescribes that a popular referendum initiative can be accepted only if it has been supported by 'ten percent of all the voters in the Republic of Croatia'. For the Court, the phrase 'in the Republic of Croatia' had a strict territorial meaning and, therefore, the only relevant element to calculate what actually represented 10 percent of all the voters was the voters' legal place of residence.[40] Consequently, the Court concluded that 10 percent should be calculated from the total number of only those Croatian voters who reside within the territory of the State. This

40 Decision of the Constitutional Court U-VIIR-7346/2014, 10 December 2014.

condition was not in this case fulfilled. To this core holding, however, the Court added two more interpretations. In the first, it established that a right to vote on a referendum belonged to voters, regardless of exactly where they would be permanently or temporarily residing at the time the referendum was held. The diaspora was thus clearly included in this scenario. This rule was interpreted directly from Article 45 of the Constitution, which generally regulates the right to vote. In the second interpretation, the Court determined that a right to give their signature in support of a particular popular initiative belonged to every eligible Croatian citizen, regardless of their permanent residence. The only condition thereof was that such voters gave their signatures only within the proper territory of the Republic of Croatia. This also meant that diplomatic-consular offices of the State in other countries were thus excluded from the concept of territory. The decisive element for such a construction of the rule was, again, the territorial principle embodied in the formulation of Article 87 of the Croatian Constitution.

As can be seen, the interpretation of the Court in its entirety actually introduced the 'triple' categorization of voters: those who can generally vote on a referendum, those who can give their signatures in support of particular initiatives and those who must be included in the calculation of the 10 percent requirement. Such an outcome, however, is quite problematic for a number of reasons. First, by insisting on the 'territorial' element of the norm, the interpretation described actually results in an unacceptable division of voters constitutionally entitled to participate in political decision-making. Second, there is no plausible reason to pursue the 'territorial' element at the expense of a more comprehensive and teleological approach in conformity with the Court's general position that the Constitution should always be read as a whole. Third, the Court's triple scheme ends up in a completely unacceptable result that in the *same referendum the same voters* may participate in *different roles.*

7.6 Systemic interpretation in play

In 2015, however, the Court again switched to a more demonstrative way of systemic interpretation of the Constitution with two initiatives addressing the austerity measures.[41] These two cases include the initiative to enact laws to prohibit the 'outsourcing' of technical services in the public sector and to prohibit transfer of certain highways under concession. The interpretation of the Court in those two cases remained on the same general footing, and I will thus here describe only the first case.[42] As a response to the government's

41 For an additional description of those cases, see Djordje Gardasevic, 'Croatian Constitutional Adjudication in Times of Stress' in Zoltán Szente and Fruzsina Gárdos-Orosz (eds.), *New Challenges to Constitutional Adjudication in Europe – a Comparative Perspective* (Routledge 2018) 27–44.

42 One notable difference, however, came when, in the second case, the Court explicitly incorporated entrepreneurial and market freedoms into the concept of the 'Identity of the Croatian Constitutional State'. Decision of the Constitutional Court U-VIIR-1158/2015, 21 April 2015.

'outsourcing' plan, several trade unions organized an initiative not only to prohibit it by a new law, but also to secure that complementary and non-basic services in the public sector are carried out only by those employed in that sector.

This time, the Court insisted upon the delimitation between the 'exclusive' constitutional powers of representative state bodies and the direct decision-making powers of the people.[43] For that purpose, it argued that the entirety of the Constitution implied that the Government had 'the exclusive constitutional power and obligation to propose the state budget and the annual accounts', while the Croatian Parliament 'had the exclusive constitutional power and obligation to adopt the state budget'.[44] In addition, it stressed that the Government was constitutionally empowered 'to direct and control the operation of the state administration, to direct the performance and development of the public services, and to take care of the economic development of the country'.[45] In a more comprehensive way, the Court further stated that 'direct democracy is, by the Constitution, permissible and legitimate, but is not the primary and ordinary way of deciding on the regulation of economic, legal and political relations in the Republic of Croatia'. Consequently, it reasoned that laws may not be subject to a referendum vote if they are not in accordance with the legal system as a whole or when they are directed to regulating issues that fall within the exclusive competence of the bodies of representative democracy.

Scrutinizing the proposed law, the Court found that general bans contained in it qualified as 'blanket' prohibitions, which 'may lead to automatic and non-selective limitation or repeal of a possibility of changes without which there can be no progress in the implementation of necessary economic, social, political and administrative reforms'. In the Court's interpretation, those bans, seen as 'permanent measures', would prevent the Parliament and the Government from pursuing their constitutional responsibilities in the future. It also declared that the bans 'prevent changes in the organization of optimal labor law models … in terms of the economic capabilities of the State'. Additionally, the Court stated that the bans directly influenced the

> functionality of the State and the budget framework in processes of economic, social, political and administrative reforms for which – according to the Constitution – bodies of representative democracy, and not the Organizational Committee (of a popular initiative – note Dj. G.) … bear full responsibility.

All this meant that the proposed law was contrary to the Croatian legal system as a whole. Finally, the Court concluded that the 'exclusive powers' of the representative state bodies were infringed because the blanket prohibitions would 'restrict the Government and the Parliament in framing the state

43 Decision of the Constitutional Court U-VIIR-1159/2015, 8 April 2015.

44 Articles 113/2, 81/3 and 91 of the Constitution.

45 Article 113/6–8 of the Constitution.

budget' whose task is to define salaries and other remunerations for those employed in the public sector. Clearly, such an interpretation of the Court is wrong, at least because it erred in qualifying the proposed law, which can easily be changed afterwards in an ordinary parliamentary procedure, as a permanent ban.

7.7 The story continues: recent failed attempts

In 2018 two separate popular constitutional initiatives were organized in order to, respectively, denounce the Istanbul Convention and once again try to redefine rules for parliamentary elections. In both cases, the Constitutional Court deferred to the Parliament and the Government which found that not enough signatures for calling a referendum had been collected.

The Court's approach in these cases was obviously wrong because it had a clear jurisdiction to verify any lack of the required number of signatures itself. Be that as it may, however, it seems that those two cases might have been a great opportunity for the Court to present its own interpretation on the constitutionality of the said initiatives. I will try to offer here my own view of the possible outcomes thereof.

In the case of the Istanbul Convention, the organizers of the initiative firstly proposed that voters in a referendum should decide on whether to denounce the already ratified document. However, once they realized that the attempt could fail on the basis of the theory of the exclusive powers of the Parliament, which the Court introduced in the 'austerity' referendum cases, the Initiative supplemented the action with a proposal to amend the Constitution itself. For that purpose, the new amendment would allow that international treaties may formally be denounced in a referendum as well as in the Parliament. My strong hypothesis here, based on the previous case law of the Court, is that this would also fail. In fact, I guess that the Court, had it properly examined the merits of the case, would have relied on two arguments. The first would have been some explanation that the Initiative, despite its proclamation that it wished generally to regulate the reach of referendums in relation to international treaties, actually aimed at denouncing just one of them. And even though that, possibly, might not suffice to meet the element of the 'concealed aim' I have already described in the context of the referendum on national minorities' languages, the second argument would surely have been made. Concretely, that the Initiative in fact tried to pursue a purely political, and not a constitutional aim.[46]

The second 2018 Initiative, named 'The People Decides', sought to amend the Constitution again in reference to parliamentary electoral rules. In its most delicate part, the initiative wanted to redefine the mandate of national minorities' parliamentary representatives (NMPRs), who hold reserved parliamentary seats and are elected in a special electoral unit, in order to exclude them

46 Decision of the Constitutional Court U-I-3597/2010, 29 July 2011.

from voting on two crucial issues: confidence in the government and adoption of the state budget.[47] The Initiative based its action upon three principal arguments. First, that NMPRs are elected by a significantly smaller number of votes than other representatives and that they therefore lack legitimacy for participating in crucial decision-making. Second, that NMPRs should primarily represent the specific interests of minorities and not those of the general population. And third, that the NMPRs' mandates should be limited because of the 'frequent practice of undisguised political trading' with minority representatives in processes involving the creation of government and the adoption of the country's budget. I believe that the Court, had it taken the case into consideration, would have easily rejected all three arguments.

As for the argument based on the lack of legitimacy, it is clear that the smaller number of votes required for the election of NMPRs is simply a natural consequence of the definition of minorities as such, and that the whole NMPRs model in Croatia is a special expression of the affirmative action approach. This may be confirmed by the classical definition of minority given by Francesco Capotorti, by the Preamble of the Croatian Constitution and the Croatian Constitutional Law on the Rights of National Minorities. Furthermore, the secondary claim of the Initiative here was that national minorities in Croatia vote in general electoral units rather than in their special unit. However, statistically this statement is only valid for some minorities. This fact obviously makes the whole argument arbitrary and discriminatory. In other words, even if one supports the idea that, on account of their abstention from voting in the special electoral unit, national minorities should be deprived of the right to participate in deciding on the state budget and confidence in the government, this could, at most, only apply to some minorities; the Initiative's proposition regarding the restrictions on minority parliamentary mandates, however, extends to all national minorities. As for the Initiative's argument based on the nature of the minority parliamentary mandate, i.e. that the NMPRs should (primarily) represent the interests of minorities who elected them, the underlying reasoning thereof was that the minority representatives, because of the way in which and the purpose for which they are elected, have a special and not a general political mandate. Here, again, the case law of the Court for a long time held that, as an expression of popular sovereignty, parliamentary representatives in Croatia represent the interests of the people as a whole and not just of those voters who elected them.[48] And as for the third Initiative's argument, based on the claim regarding 'political trading', it may be said that any claim as to the existence of abusive

47 The analysis pertaining to the 'People Decides' referendum proposal is partly taken from the paper which I presented jointly with Prof. Jurij Toplak from the Faculty of Law, University of Maribor (Slovenia) at the 2019 Association for the Study of Nationalities World Convention, held at Columbia University, 2–4 May 2019. However, this previous paper, written under the title 'National Minorities' Rights Redesigned by Referendum Means: the 2018 Croatian Case', has not been published.

48 Decision of the Constitutional Court U-I-732/1998, 12 April 2001; Decision of the Constitutional Court U-I-3789/2003, 8 December 2010.

conduct by parliamentary representatives should be solved by applying individual criminal law measures and not by redesigning the political model of the country.[49] Similar answers to this particular argument may also be found in the case law of the Croatian Constitutional Court.[50]

7.8 Conclusion

I have tried here to show how the Croatian Constitutional Court has dealt with popular referendum initiatives both in general, and in the context of some populist claims they pursued. My attention was focused on the interpretive approaches the Court used for that purpose. Let me now offer some final remarks.

As can be seen, the approaches adopted varied significantly from case to case. The procedural reading of the Constitution which opened the whole series with the Labor Law case was replaced with the 'heavy' concept of 'constitutional identity' and the strict type of proportionality analysis in the 'Marriage referendum' and the referendum on minority rights. Taking into account the growing seriousness those initiatives presented, this might have been expected even though some significant differences between them can be observed. Whereas in the latter case the Court mainly applied the proportionality approach it usually uses when dealing with the constitutionality of restrictions of fundamental rights, in the former it not only relied on the new concept of 'constitutional identity' but also took an opportunity to extend its own powers of review. I have elsewhere argued that this might have been primarily because the Court wanted to strengthen its own position vis-à-vis other branches, rather than to solve the particular case at hand.[51] In that context, one may also notice the role of the *Warning* the Court first issued in the case, but even more its invocation of the Venice Commission report from the Hungarian case, not to mention the construction of the 'unconstitutional constitutional amendment' doctrine, applicable, in the Court's view, in cases of constitutional amendments enacted both by referendum and by Parliament. Interestingly, in the 2014 initiative on the electoral system the Court opted for a more robust linguistic approach which ended up in a curious division of the political community entitled to participate in different stages of referendum proceedings. In the two 2015 initiatives addressing the economic policy of the state, the Court again switched, this time in favor of a systemic reading of the Constitution and implied restrictions on referendum decision-making. However, the whole approach erred in proclaiming the proposed legal 'bans' as being permanent measures, which, as such, they simply could not have been.

49 In other words, strict requirements of criminal law demand precise evidence related to particular individuals and their conduct. Therefore, a general proposal to solve the problem by redesigning the whole system not only suffers from discrimination concerns, but also points to a possible criticism that it contains a 'concealed aim', as I have described before.

50 Decision of the Constitutional Court, U-I-3789/2003, 8 December 2010.

51 Gardasevic (n 15).

One must, however, notice that the 'constitutional identity' element appeared this time as well, when the Court incorporated into it entrepreneurial and market freedoms. Finally, in the two 2018 initiatives the Court simply deferred to the findings of political branches of government that not enough signatures required for calling the referendums had been collected, even though it had a clear constitutional mandate to take over.

Bearing all this in mind, one can conclude: that the Constitutional Court's interpretation methods *were* affected by cases emerging from popular initiatives; that there exists *no unified interpretive approach* to those initiatives; and that such diversity in interpretation, with the exception of the 'Marriage referendum', ended up in blocking all popular initiatives undertaken in the observed period. On the other hand, the Court *did construe some* 'precedents' which filled out the field of popular initiative referendum law and should be taken into account, if at least some type of a principled approach is expected, in future cases. That populist claims in this context still do appear in Croatian society is clearly visible in the last two initiatives organized in 2018. Certainly, the game is far from over.

8 Constitutional identity as a populist notion?

The Council of State and the forging of the Greek constitutional identity through the crisis

Apostolos Vlachogiannis

8.1 Introduction

Populism and constitutional identity are both two relatively vague notions presently in fashion. As of late, they have inspired numerous discussions and theoretical debates.[1] In the current European context, they have been associated initially with the recent economic crisis and lately increasingly with the migration/refugee 'crisis'. Correspondingly, European integration, in the sense of a leitmotiv, has been a common denominator and target of both populist waves.[2] This, in fact, could be a first sign that these two concepts are more or less intertwined and can be associated with each other in the current political context. Before explicitly spelling out and elaborating this idea, it is first necessary to go through the main predicates of each concept.

Whereas the exact meaning and the identifying marks of populism are still debated,[3] there is no doubt that right-wing exclusionary populism is on the rise across Europe.[4] This vogue has significant repercussions in constitutional theory as well. It has been argued that a populist constitutional theory

1 Suffice it to mention the extensive literature on both concepts. For an overview of populism, see Cristóbal Rovira Kaltwasser and others (eds.), *The Oxford Handbook of Populism* (Oxford University Press 2017). On the notion of constitutional identity, mention could be made to the following books: Christian Calliess and Gerhard van der Schyff, *Constitutional Identity in a Europe of Multilevel Constitutionalism* (Cambridge University Press 2019); Elke Cloots, *National Identity in EU Law* (Oxford University Press 2015); François-Xavier Millet, *L'Union européenne et l'identité constitutionnelle de l'Etat membre* (LGDJ-Lextenso 2013); Alejandro Saiz Arnaiz and Carina Alcoberro Llivina (eds.), *National Constitutional Identity and European Integration* (Intersentia 2013); Laurence Burgorgue-Larsen (ed.), *L'identité constitutionnelle saisie par les juges en Europe* (Pedone 2011).

2 European integration is particularly the target of what Paul Blokker calls 'transnational populism'. Paul Blokker 'Varieties of Populist Constitutionalism: The Transnational Dimension' (2019) 20 German Law Journal 332, 346–347.

3 Cas Mudde calls populism an 'essentially contested concept'. Cas Mudde, 'Populism: An Ideational Approach' in Kaltwasser and others (n 1) 27.

4 Cas Mudde and Cristóbal Rovira Kaltwasser, 'Exclusionary vs. Inclusionary Populism: Comparing Contemporary Europe and Latin America' (2013) 48 Government and Opposition 147–148.

advances three basic claims: 'one claim concerns the nature of constituent power, a second one regards the scope of popular sovereignty and a third claim relates to what constitutional identity entails'.[5] More correctly, populist constitutionalism is most often perceived as a threat to liberal democracy.[6] It attacks the separation of powers, agitating in favour of the 'liberation' of the people from the burdensome effect of checks and balances.[7] It also tries to forcefully undermine the legitimacy of the status quo and the 'establishment' in order to shake off the influence of the governing or technocratic elites. The ultimate goal is to impose the will of the true People, viewed as a uniform and monolithic whole.[8]

On the other hand, the notion of constitutional identity has been a constant reference in the jurisprudence of most national constitutional courts during the past decade.[9] Starting from the renowned declarations of the French *Conseil constitutionnel*[10] and the German *Bunvesverfassungsgericht* (hereafter: BVerfG),[11] through the Italian,[12] Czech[13] and Hungarian Constitutional Courts[14] – just to mention a few – constitutional identity appears to be a palimpsest mirroring the deepest desires of national constitutionalism. It has been mainly used by national courts as a counter-limit to European integration, a way to undermine the principle of the primacy of European Union law[15] and eventually to protest against the new European economic governance.[16]

In the current debate about populism and the need to combat it, courts play a double role: that of the victim of populism and that of the possible obstacle to populism. Indeed, the accrued power that judges possess in modern

5 Luigi Corrias, 'Populism in a Constitutional Key: Constituent Power, Popular Sovereignty and Constitutional Identity' (2016) 12 European Constitutional Law Review 6, 8.

6 See Stefan Rummens, 'Populism as a Threat to Liberal Democracy' in Kaltwasser and others (n 1), as well as Jan-Werner Müller, *What Is Populism* (University of Pennsylvania Press 2016) 68.

7 Blokker (n 2) 333.

8 Cristóbal Rovira Kaltwasser, 'Populism and the Question of How to Respond to It' in Kaltwasser and others (n 1) 490.

9 Pietro Faraguna, 'Constitutional Identity in the EU – a Shield or a Sword?' (2017) 18 German Law Journal 1617, 1630–1631.

10 Décision no. 92-308 DC du 9 avril 1992 (Maastricht I); décision no. 2006-540 DC du 27 juillet 2006 (Loi relative au droit d'auteur et aux droits voisins dans la société de l'information), para 6.

11 BVerfG, Judgment of the Second Senate of 30 June 2009 – 2 BvE 2/08 (Lisbon Treaty).

12 Corte Cost., 26 gennaio 2017, n. 24, Foro it. 2017, II, 394 (It.).

13 Czech Constitutional Court, Case Pl. ÚS 5/12 Slovak Pensions XVII, 31 January 2012.

14 Decision 22/2016 (XII. 5.) of the Hungarian Constitutional Court.

15 Understood this way, constitutional identity is used as a 'hard shield' to limit further integration. Faraguna (n 9) 1629.

16 For a short overview of the developments in the Economic Union during the years of the crisis summed up by the term 'new European economic governance', see Kaarlo Tuori, *European Constitutionalism* (Cambridge University Press 2015) 195.

constitutional democracies and the ensuing judicialization of public affairs[17] are sometimes presented as a source of discontent, which could account for the rise of populism and the emergence of the bipolar scheme: judicial elite v. the people.[18] Most often, courts are therefore portrayed as the victim of populism. At the same time, judicial intervention is usually described as an antidote to populism or as a means of defence against it.[19] In other words, according to the dominant narrative, courts stand, axiomatically and under almost any circumstances, in contrast to populism, either as its target or as its counterpart. However – and herein lies a paradox – we need to ask ourselves if it is true that within a specific context courts could also succumb to the sirens of populism and claim to be the true representative of the people and last bastion of hope in times of an intense crisis of representation. Would it then be pertinent to speak about 'judicial populist constitutionalism'? What happens, furthermore, when a court flirting with populism and communitarian constitutional ideals and values[20] gets hold of the ambiguous notion of constitutional identity and twists it into a populist notion? Is it even possible that the two are compatible or attracted to each other?

I will argue in this chapter that this in fact has been the case in Greece. In some recent instances, the Greek Council of State (hereafter: CoS) has advanced ideas which echo, if they are not inspired by, communitarian and ethno-nationalist approaches to constitutionalism[21] and which are indeed very suggestive of exclusionary right-wing populist tendencies.[22] Meanwhile, in one of its relevant judgments, explicit reference is made to the notion of constitutional identity. The notion condenses, in the eyes of the Court, the eternal and inalterable hard-wired features of Greek self-identity extracted from the text of the Constitution and enjoying the status of constitutional principles.

What makes things stranger and even more interesting is the fact that Greece has not been one of the 'usual suspects', in the sense that it has not been classified as a populist regime, despite the development of strong populist tendencies during the years of the crisis (*grosso modo* 2010–2018); nor can the Council of State, a court renowned for its independence and liberalism for

17 What Ran Hirschl calls 'juristocracy' in his book *Towards Juristocracy: The Origins and Consequences of the New Constitutionalism* (Harvard University Press 2007).

18 Andrea Pin, 'The Transnational Drivers of Populist Backlash in Europe: The Role of Courts' (2019) 20 German Law Journal 225, 227.

19 David Prendergast, 'The Judicial Role in Protecting Democracy from Populism' (2019) 20 German Law Journal 245, 261. Tushnet criticizes this belief by pointing to the fact that 'treating efforts to transform the courts as a strong point against populism … may often be a defense of a failed status'. Mark Tushnet, 'Varieties of Populism' (2019) 20 German Law Journal 382, 385.

20 As per the communitarian view of the Constitution, see Camil Ungureanu, 'The European Constitution-Making and the Question of Religion' (2007) EUI Working Papers No. 2007/01, 3–4 https://cadmus.eui.eu/handle/1814/6663 accessed 19 April 2020.

21 Blokker (n 2) 339–340.

22 For the distinction between exclusionary and inclusionary populism, see Mudde and Kaltwasser (n 4) 167–168.

the greater part of its century-long existence,[23] be considered to have been 'captured' by the government. Having said that, the Supreme Administrative Court has played an active role in the past few years during the economic crisis, which has set the stage for its gradual immersion into populist ideas.

Within the context of the crisis, the Court initially adopted what could be schematically called an anti-populist agenda. Following its emblematic judgment on the constitutionality of the first bailout agreement signed by Greece,[24] many other leading cases showed deference to the political branches. The Court placed its 'affirmative stamp of legitimacy'[25] on extremely painful policy choices, which were made to the discontent of a large part of the population. This is why, at this first phase, its attitude towards the crisis has been described as submissive.[26] Gradually, however, as the crisis went on and the policies designed to tackle it embraced even more fields and became more intrusive, the Court's stance began to change. At a second stage, submission gave way to reaction.[27] From that point on, the Court changed its attitude. Following several judgments that blocked particularly anti-popular measures, such as pension and salary cuts,[28] and undergoing a change of leadership as well, the Court appeared in the forefront of the political scene as a guardian of the interests of the people. It thus increasingly claimed the role of the true voice of the people and defender of its eternal consistence and long-lasting values, as opposed to the ephemeral character of the crisis. Given that in the economic field, the ruling elites, the legislature and political parties appeared powerless to impose the will and defend the interests of the People, the Court had to step in and fill the representational void. Its independence was the necessary precondition, so that it would not succumb to the factual pressure of any passing crisis. By taking advantage of its institutional privilege, it would be able to stand up against Europe or the Troika, foreigners or any other 'foe', and thus delineate a space that could be neither invaded nor squeezed by the dictates of 'outsiders'. Its foundational 'populist' judgments appeared in fact during times of widespread populism within Greek society and served as a

23 The Council of State was established as a judicial organ in 1929 with the explicit aim to serve as the basic guarantor of the principle of the rule of law, according to the famous words of its creator Eleftherios Venizelos. Since then, it possesses and frequently exercises the power of judicial review of legislative acts, a power guaranteed even in times of the eclipse of democratic institutions, such as the dictatorship of 1967–1974.

24 CoS Plen 668/2012.

25 This is the famous expression that Charles Black used with regard to the Supreme Court's role in legitimating the New Deal. Charles Black, *The People and the Court: Judicial Review in a Democracy* (The Macmillan Company 1960) 64.

26 Xenophon Contiades and Alkmene Fotiadou, 'On Resilience of Constitutions. What Makes Constitutions Resistant to External Shocks?' (2015) 9 International Constitutional Law Journal 3, 16.

27 Apostolos Vlachogiannis, 'From Submission to Reaction: The Greek Courts' Stance on the Financial Crisis' in Zoltán Szente and Fruszina Gárdos-Orosz (eds.), *New Challenges to Constitutional Adjudication in Europe: A Comparative Perspective* (Routledge 2018).

28 CoS Plen 2192/2014 (declaring the salary cuts of army and police officers unconstitutional); CoS Plen 2287–2290/2015 (declaring pension cuts unconstitutional).

reminder that even when the State is perceived to be financially or otherwise subdued, it is the Court's responsibility to speak for the People and the Nation and defend the primordial components of its identity.

Three sets of cases illustrate this point: those dealing with the law determining the conditions of granting nationality to aliens, those regarding Sunday work and those related to the teaching of religion in schools. The first part of the chapter will explore the relevant case law in order to outline its main features and examine its contribution in the forging of a protean Greek constitutional identity through the crisis. The second part will try to explain how exactly the notion of constitutional identity is shaped (and twisted or abused) in order to serve populist tendencies. The last part will attempt to draw some lessons from the Greek case regarding the relation of courts, European integration and populism.

8.2 The forging of the Greek constitutional identity through the crisis

The notion of constitutional identity has not been a complete stranger to the jurisprudence of the CoS, even before the crisis. In fact, in one of the few cases originating from Greece where the Court of Justice of the European Union (CJUE) was presented with the opportunity to elaborate and shed light on this cryptic notion, it was thanks to the initiative of the CoS.[29] In the so-called 'main shareholder' case, the CoS had to rule on the conformity of the recently amended Article 14, para 9 of the Constitution regulating the ownership, financial standing and means of financing of the media with Council Directive 93/37/EEC.[30] While the first judgment on this case seemed to be an act of defiance against European Union law,[31] the final judgment exploited the method of interpreting the national Constitution 'in light of the European Union law' and thus avoided a potential conflict.[32] In the meantime, after a request for a preliminary judgment,[33] the Advocate General Maduro had presented his thoughts on the possible (mis)uses of the notion of constitutional identity as the following:

> If respect for the constitutional identity of the Member States can thus constitute a legitimate interest which, in principle, justifies a restriction of the obligations imposed by Community law, it can all the more be relied upon by a Member State to justify its assessment of constitutional

29 Case C-213/07 *Michaniki AE v Ethniko Symvoulio Radiotileorasis and Ypourgos Epikrateias* [2008] I-09999 (*Michaniki*).

30 Council Directive 93/37/EEC of 14 June 1993 concerning the coordination of procedures for the award of public works contracts [1993] OJ L199/54 (Directive 93/37), as amended by European Parliament and Council Directive 97/52/EC of 13 October 1997 [1997] OJ L328/1.

31 CoS 3242/2004 (4th Chamber), especially para 18.

32 CoS Plen 3470/2011.

33 CoS Plen 3670/2006.

> measures which must supplement Community legislation in order to ensure observance, on its territory, of the principles and rules laid down by or underlying that legislation. It is, nevertheless, necessary to point out that that respect owed to the constitutional identity of the Member States cannot be understood as an absolute obligation to defer to all national constitutional rules. Were that the case, national constitutions could become instruments allowing Member States to avoid Community law in given fields. … Furthermore, it could lead to discrimination between Member States based on the contents of their respective national constitutions. Just as Community law takes the national constitutional identity of the Member States into consideration, national constitutional law must be adapted to the requirements of the Community legal order.[34]

What is noteworthy, in view of this judicial saga, is the fact that the CoS did not mention or make use of the notion of constitutional identity, even though it obviously had the chance. It would have been a clear-cut evocation pointing to the debated subject of the primacy of EU law and its relation with national constitutions. This is, in fact, how the notion has been mainly put to use by other national constitutional courts, such as the German or the French one, especially after the ratification of EU Treaties.[35] However, the CoS did not choose to do so and follow the same path. Instead, it decided to delve into the notion of constitutional identity in a radically different context and background, with a view to defending a dissimilar set of values.

The case law of the CoS relating to the notion of constitutional identity emerged in the context of the crisis and contains primarily three Plenary Session judgments pertaining to three thorny societal issues: nationality, Sunday laws and compulsory religious education. All these judgments received widespread publicity and have had considerable impact on public opinion. Before examining them, it would be useful to cite the constitutional provisions serving as their main legal basis:

> Art 1 para 3: All powers derive from the People and exist for the People and the Nation; they shall be exercised as specified by the Constitution.
>
> Art 3 para 1: The prevailing religion in Greece is that of the Eastern Orthodox Church of Christ.
>
> Art 16 para 2: Education constitutes a basic mission for the State and shall aim at the moral, intellectual, professional and physical training of Greeks, the development of national and religious consciousness and at their formation as free and responsible citizens.[36]

34 *Michaniki* (n 29), Opinion of AG Maduro, para 31.

35 See n 10 and n 11.

36 Official translation in English of the Greek Constitution https://www.hellenicparliament.gr/UserFiles/f3c70a23-7696-49db-9148-f24dce6a27c8/001-156%20aggliko.pdf accessed 19 April 2020.

As a general outline, all three sets of judgments employ highly creative and loose methods of interpretation of the constitutional text. By these means, they succeed in offering a coherent – at least from the point of view of the majority of the Court – set of metaphysical values and principles that form the blueprint of the Greek constitutional identity. The two judgments on nationality (4th Chamber and Plenary Session[37]) establish the constitutional obligation to defend and preserve the ethnic character of the State; whereas the two judgments on Sunday work (Suspension Committee and Plenary Session[38]) and the two on religious education (both Plenary Session[39]) present the Greek Orthodox religion as a central component of Greek constitutional identity. As the Court openly admits, the common denominator of these judgments is safeguarding the ethnic and religious character of the Greek State; a concept which translates the ethnic and religious unity of the Greek People into legal/constitutional terms.[40]

The first two judgments on nationality invalidated sections of law 3838/2010 (Nationality Act) which reformed, in a progressive way, the conditions required for granting nationality to second-generation immigrants born or raised in Greece. The Chamber judgment was bold in its formulation of the constitutional obligation to preserve the continuity of the Nation throughout the centuries and to prevent its disintegration through massive naturalizations.[41] The Court stressed the importance over time of *jus sanguinis* laws in the Greek legal order and the need for those who seek citizenship to prove that they have *a genuine individual link* to the Greek nation. In its own words, Greek nationality law should not:

> allow foreign people to enter the popular community (people) without having an essential genuine link with it – especially by prescribing massive naturalizations – in a way that the composite element of the State (people) and its supreme organ (people-electoral body) would be constituted arbitrarily and in the end, the notion of the Nation would be disintegrated.[42]

By contrast, the Plenary Session judgment played down the 'blood rhetoric',[43] all the while staying faithful to a romantic approach to the Nation[44]

37 CoS 350/2011 (4th Chamb); CoS Plen 460/2013.

38 CoS Susp Com 307/2014; CoS Plen 100/2017.

39 CoS Plen 660/2018; CoS Plen 1749/2019.

40 In this sense, the approach of the CoS has striking analogies to Central and Eastern European populism. For the latter, see Gábor Halmai, 'Populism, Authoritarianism and Constitutionalism' (2019) 20 German Law Journal 269, 307.

41 CoS 350/2011 (4th Chamb), para 9.

42 Ibid., paras 10 and 13.

43 Giorgos Katrougalos, 'Ethnos, laos kai dikaiomata stin apofasi StE Ol 460/2013' (2013) 1 Theoria kai Praxi Dioikitikou Dikaiou 31, 32.

44 Ioannis Koutsoukos, 'I ithageneia, to Ethnos kai to kratos dikaiou' (2011) Efimerida Dioikitikou Dikaiou 77–78.

and a subsequently phobic approach to the phenomenon of migrant integration.[45] It declared in a similar vein to the Chamber judgment, and even more emphatically:

> the minimum condition and limit of relevant legislative provisions for the granting of Greek nationality is the existence of a genuine link of the foreigner to the Greek State and Greek society, which are not spineless organisms and ephemeral creations, but represent unity over time with a specific cultural background, a community with relatively stable mores and customs, a common language with a long tradition, elements that are bequeathed from generation to generation with the help of smaller community entities (family) and organized state entities (education).[46]

What is interesting from an interpretative point of view is the fact that both majority opinions compile every concrete reference to the word 'Nation' in the constitutional text, however related to the case at hand, in order to deduce a highly abstract constitutional principle. By means of this holistic approach, which could also be treated as an interpretative manoeuvre, the Court imposed on the legislature a very high level of scrutiny, contrary to the established interpretation of the Article 4 para 3[47] drafters' intention.[48] As a consequence, the judge becomes the *porte-parole* of the Nation,[49] the voice of national consciousness and the main defender of its continuity throughout the centuries, in spite of the troubles of history. Additionally, on this occasion, the CoS invoked, for the first time ever, the notion of constitutional identity in the Plenary Session judgment of 2013. It is worth highlighting the fact that the Court avoided evoking the notion of constitution identity when confronted with issues of national sovereignty and the constitutionality of the bailout agreements signed with the Troika.[50] It had recourse to the notion only when dealing with issues of nationality. Concretely, it stated that

> the Greek State was established and continues to exist as a national state with a specific history and this character is guaranteed by art. 1 para 3 of the Constitution in force.

Immediately after this, it pointed to the fact that the Greek State

45 Panagiotis Mantzoufas, *Oikonomiki krisi kai to Syntagma* (Sakkoulas 2014) 198–199.

46 CoS Plen 460/2013, para 6.

47 All persons possessing the qualifications for citizenship as specified by law are Greek citizens. Withdrawal of Greek citizenship shall be permitted only in case of voluntary acquisition of another citizenship or of undertaking service contrary to national interests in a foreign country, under the conditions and procedures more specifically provided by law.

48 Christos Papastylianos, 'Ta syntagmatika oria tou nomotheti os pros tin ktisi tis ithageneias kai ta politika dikaiomata ton allodapon' (2011) Efimerida Dioikitikou Dikaiou 71.

49 Koutsoukos (n 44) 83.

50 Cf CoS Plen 668/2012.

> is integrated in a supranational community of Nation-states with similar constitutional traditions (European Union) which according to article 4 paragraph 2 of the Treaty on European Union respects their national identity, inherent in their fundamental structures, political and constitutional.[51]

By means of this citation, it also insinuated and subtly put forward the argument that the ethnic character of the State is not a Greek peculiarity, but instead a common element of the European constitutional tradition.

In the Sunday law judgment, the Court invalidated, in plenary session, on formal grounds (unconstitutional delegation of powers) a ministerial decision regulating commerce on Sundays.[52] Beforehand, it had granted interim measures suspending the implementation of the ministerial decision, on the grounds that the plaintiffs' right to leisure and its common enjoyment with their family during the common Sunday holiday, as well as their right to exercise their religion, would be severely and irreparably injured.[53]

Although the plenary session reasoning omits any reference to free exercise of religion, the perceived violation of this right appears to have strongly motivated the judgment. As the subsequent judgments on religious education confirm, there is in fact a strong religious justification of the decision. The Court refers to a BVerfG judgment protecting the status of Sunday as a religious holiday,[54] and the Suspension Committee judgment explicitly mentions free exercise of religion as a justifying ground of the judgment.[55] It is not without relevance that both were hailed as landmark judgments by commentators, for the reason, among others, that they safeguarded the exercise of religious rights.[56] Significantly enough, this measure was also part of the bailout agreement signed with the Troika,[57] hence it constitutes a point of contact (or of breach) between the economic crisis and constitutional identity. It marks an attempt to limit the predominant effects of economic considerations in policy making and to favour non-material/spiritual ones.[58]

What is, however, implicitly stated in the Sunday law judgment becomes manifest in the following two Plenary Session judgments about the teaching

51 CoS Plen 460/2013, para 6.

52 CoS Plen 100/2017.

53 CoS Susp Com 307/2014, para 7.

54 BverfG – BvR 2857 and 2858/07 – 1.12.2009, especially chap B, II (cited by CoS Plen 100/2017, para 10).

55 CoS Susp Com 307/2014, para 7.

56 Panos Lazaratos, 'I Kyriaki os syntagmatiki arhi' (2014) Theoria kai Praxi Dioikitikou Dikaiou 862; Panos Lazaratos, 'To dikaioma ston elefthero hrono tis Kyriakis' (2017) Theoria kai Praxi Dioikitikou Dikaiou 307.

57 Law 4254/2014, which contains the delegation clause, was voted in order to implement law 4046/2012 ratifying the second bailout agreement between Greece and its lenders (Memorandum II). It is in fact entitled 'Measures to Support the Greek Economy Within the Framework of the Implementation of Law 4046/2012 and Other Provisions'.

58 Spyros Vlahopoulos, 'I zoi den einai mono oikonomia – To dikaioma sti sylllogiki evdomadiaia argia' [in Greek] (2017) Theoria kai Praxi Dioikitikou Dikaiou 313.

of religion in schools. The issue of religion has always been a very heated subject, stirring debate and sowing conflict within Greek society.[59] In the past, state practice in the realm of religion had led the European Court of Human Rights (ECtHR) to issue several judgments ruling against Greece for violation of the European Convention on Human Rights (ECHR) and in particular Article 9.[60] That said, especially in the past two decades, the CoS has been a principal force for promoting religious tolerance. Against this background, we have witnessed, nonetheless, retrogression during the years of the crisis.

In the path-breaking judgment of 2018, the CoS reactivated the 'prevailing religion' clause of Article 3 of the Constitution, which had previously lain dormant. Notwithstanding the dominant interpretation of the clause, which insists that it is a purely declaratory clause,[61] it yields full normative power to it. It evokes as a further argument the phrase of the Preamble of the Constitution which states: 'In the name of the Holy and Consubstantial and Indivisible Trinity'. The invocation of the Preamble as a guiding principle of constitutional interpretation recalls the 'aspirational interpretation' of the Preamble of the US Constitution preached by Justice Brennan.[62] In our case, however, the 'transformative purpose of the text'[63] has been turned on its head, in order to justify not the extension but the restriction of fundamental rights, despite the Court's own rhetoric. Using this twist, the Court then reads these religious references into the 'religious consciousness' clause of Article 16, para 2 and draws the logical conclusions. More precisely, the Court is adamant when declaring that according to its systematic and holistic interpretation of the text, there is a constitutional obligation of the legislature to safeguard and develop not just the religious consciousness of children, in abstract terms, but concretely their Greek Orthodox consciousness. This obligation is linked to the uncontested fact that the Greek state is extremely religiously homogenous. Therefore, parents and their children have a right to be taught their religion in school. This right is further

59 We should bear in mind that according to Weiler's classification, Greece constitutes one pole of the pendulum regarding Church-State relations in Europe, the other being France, the most fervent proponent of State religious neutrality. Joseph Weiler, *Un'Europa Cristiana. Un saggio esplorativo* (2nd ed. Biblioteca Univ Rizzoli 2003) 70–73, cited by Ungureanu (n 20) 5.

60 See for instance *Kokkinakis v Greece* (1993) Series A no 263; *Thlimmenos v Greece* 1997-IV 2000; more recently, *Papageorgiou and Others v Greece* App no 4762/18 and 6140/18 (ECtHR, 31 October 2019). Yannakopoulos argues more precisely that religion has served in the past as a counter-limit to the application of the ECtHR. Constantin Yannakopoulos, *I epidrasi tou dikaiou tis Evropaikis Enosis ston dikastiko elegho tis syntagmatikotitas ton nomon* (Sakkoulas 2013) 415.

61 Giorgos Stavropoulos, 'To mathima ton thriskeftikon ypo to fos tis prosfatis 660/2018 apofasis tou Symvouliou tis Epikrateias' (2018) Theoria kai Praxi Dioikitikou Dikaiou 358.

62 William J. Brennan, 'The Constitution of the United States: Contemporary Ratification' (1986) 27 South Texas Law Review 433.

63 Ibid. 438.

guaranteed by Article 2 of Protocol No 1 to the ECHR.[64] Lawmakers, as well as the administration, are hence instructed to provide schoolchildren with a complete and elaborate knowledge of the Orthodox dogma and instil in them the moral values and traditions of the Eastern Orthodox Church.[65]

In general, the Court's interpretative approach to the aforementioned clauses is quite anachronistic and revives militant ideas about the relation of Church and State, which more or less lead to the fusion of the two.[66] What is even more surprising is the way that the Court gives new meaning not only to constitutional clauses, but also to articles of the ECHR. Based on the interpretation of the Court, instead of protecting the rights of minorities, the ECHR supposedly guarantees and imposes majoritarian beliefs. Moreover, at some point, which is extremely important, the Court makes a detour and binds all previous judgments together by citing them as a whole: just as the term 'development of national consciousness' means preserving the ethnic character of the State, the term 'development of religious consciousness' means preserving the Orthodox identity of the State.[67] It follows that Greek constitutional identity, as sketched out by the Court, is based on a two-fold constitutional tradition: ethnic and religious. Tradition and identity are blended together, and, at the final stage, constitutional status is attributed to both of them.

8.3 Understanding the Court's use of the notion of constitutional identity

Right after the entry into force of the Lisbon Treaty, and especially during the recent economic crisis, the notion of constitutional identity has been seen as the new means of limiting and certainly, up to a point, challenging European integration. By referring to the dynamics of a notion consecrated by the European Treaties themselves,[68] national constitutional courts have tended to it in order to prevent further loss of national sovereignty. Through the lenses of a conflictual and no longer dialogical approach to the relation of European Union law and national constitutional orders, the demand to respect national constitutional identity has become the trademark of a

64 No person shall be denied the right to education. In the exercise of any functions which it assumes in relation to education and to teaching, the State shall respect the right of parents to ensure such education and teaching in conformity with their own religious and philosophical convictions.

65 CoS Plen 660/2018, para 14.

66 Stavropoulos (n 61) 359.

67 CoS Plen 660/2018, para 14.

68 Article 4 (2) TEU: The Union shall respect the equality of Member States before the Treaties as well as their national identities, inherent in their fundamental structures, political and constitutional, inclusive of regional and local self-government. It shall respect their essential State functions, including ensuring the territorial integrity of the State, maintaining law and order and safeguarding national security. In particular, national security remains the sole responsibility of each Member State.

jurisprudence of doubt towards more integration. In this light, the widespread use of the notion marks the rise of a new form of 'judicial constitutional patriotism'.[69]

The notion of constitutional identity lends itself, nevertheless, to various interpretations. The BVerfG proceeds in a dogmatic construction of the notion which corresponds, according to its reasoning, to the essence of national sovereignty and the core elements of the theory of State.[70] However, when the CoS evokes the notion, it does not consider the eternity clause of the Greek Constitution,[71] as its German counterpart does, nor the common founding constitutional principles of all member states. By contrast, it focuses on identity as difference, i.e. a condensation of constitutionally protected national particularities.[72] It is all about constitutional selfness and distinguishing it from the homogenizing effect of European integration and/or globalization. Let us be reminded here that the French *Conseil Constitutionnel* has also indirectly interpreted the notion of constitutional identity in a similar vein. The official commentary of the Constitutional Treaty for Europe decision[73] has cited in particular the principle of *laïcité* as an example of a principle not subject to European interference. Such an interference would indeed amount to running contrary to a principle 'inherent in the constitutional order of France'.[74]

It is obvious that the sights of the Court are set on the past and on the traditions of the country, understood as pre-political components of national selfhood. Its approach is based on what we could qualify, recalling and paraphrasing Walter Benjamin, as a strand of constitutional historicism. By contrast to progressivism, as well as redemptivism, constitutional historicism requires looking backwards in order to find meaning. It seeks faith in the values and practices developed in the past and grants priority to intergenerational consensus.[75] As a result, these values and ideals are truly important in the present and for the future. Their preservation is in fact of critical importance for the

69 In a sense completely different than the constitutional patriotism preached by Müller. See Jan-Werner Müller, *Constitutional patriotism* (Princeton University Press 2007).

70 Monica Claes and Jan-Herman Reestman, 'The Protection of National Constitutional Identity and the Limits of European Integration at the Occasion of the Gauweiler Case' (2015) 16 German Law Journal 917, 923-27. This could in fact mean that the BVerfG protects not only the identity of the German State, but, in theory, the identity of any member state.

71 Contained in art 110 para 1 of the Constitution.

72 For a more detailed analysis of the distinction between constitutional identity as difference and constitutional identity despite difference (i.e. the approach adopted by the BVerfG), see Faraguna (n 9) 1622.

73 Décision no. 2004-505 DC du 19 novembre 2004 (Traité établissant une Constitution pour l'Europe). For the commentary of the decision, see https://www.conseil-constitutionnel.fr/sites/default/files/as/root/bank_mm/decisions/2004505dc/ccc_2004505dc.pdf accessed 25 April 2020.

74 Décision no. 2006-540 DC du 27 juillet 2006 (n 10), para 6.

75 For Benjamin's notion of historicism, see Walter Benjamin, *Über den Begriff der Geschichte* in *Gesammelte Schriften*, vol. I-2 (Suhrkamp 1980) 702. For the notion of constitutional historicism, inspired by Benjamin, see Amy Kapzcynski, 'Historicism, Progress, and the Redemptive Constitution' (2005) 26 Cardozo Law Review 1041, 1044–1045.

subsistence of the Nation in question. When they are under threat, either from globalization or European technocrats or migrants, the Court considers it to be its duty to act and protect what keeps the People together, what makes the People unique. By guaranteeing these values and ideals, the Court feels that it is guaranteeing a future to the Nation. Constitutional identity is no longer a purely legal notion, but, more importantly, it is an expression of the true self of the Nation and no less than an existential condition for its survival. These would indeed be considered things worth protecting and fighting for. From this point of view, it follows that tradition and constitutional identity are considered to be something more than an account of the past: they enjoy normative status and therefore *ought* to be preserved.[76]

To see matters clearly, the judgment on nationality adopts a nativist approach and constitutes a form of 'judicial activism in the service of the Nation under conditions of economic crisis'.[77] The link between economic and migration/refugee crisis perceived as common threats against the ethnic character of the State underlies the reasoning of the judgment. Equally, preserving the religious identity of the State is associated with the ideal of religious homogeneity, which could be under threat by recent migration/refugee flows. These arguments have been advanced by countries such as Hungary[78] and Poland[79] and constitute a topos of right-wing populist rhetoric.[80] Extending this point, it could be argued that the Court has treated religion and its own understanding of Church-State relations as an integral part of the 'material Constitution', viewed as an 'ordering force standing in internal relation with the formal constitutional settlement'.[81] In light of this view, whatever the written provisions' true meaning, the protection of religion should always be a driving force of constitutional interpretation.

It follows from this that the CoS embraces a version of constitutional identity linked to populism. It is by no accident that the former President of the CoS, who presided during most of these judgments, made the point, in a statement to the press, that the Court should be in touch with public

76 Corrias (n 5) 23.

77 Mantzoufas (n 45) 198–199.

78 Suffice it to cite a statement by Prime Minister Viktor Orbán on February 2017: 'I find the preservation of ethnic homogeneity very important'. Cited by Gabor Halmai, 'Abuse of Constitutional Identity. The Hungarian Constitutional Court on Interpretation of Article E) (2) of the Fundamental Law' (2018) 43 Review of Central and East European Law 23, 36.

79 Regarding the argument of ethnic homogeneity, see the remarks made by Poland, contained in the observations of the Court, in Joined Cases C-643 and C-647/15 *Slovak Republic et al v Council of the European Union* [2017] ECLI:EU:C:2017:631, para 302. For a broader view of the approach of the Polish Government on this matter, see also The Chancellery of the Prime Minister, *White Paper on the Reform of the Polish Judiciary*, Warsaw, 7 March 2018, especially paras 169–176 https://www.premier.gov.pl/files/files/white_paper_en_full.pdf accessed 19 April 2020.

80 Blokker (n 2) 340.

81 Marco Goldoni and Michael A. Wilkinson, 'The Material Constitution' (2018) 81 MLR 567, 595.

opinion when deciding hard cases. He specifically said in front of journalists that:

> [the case at hand] is important and equally important cases are pending before the Court and there are [cases dealing with] salaries, pensions; there is the crisis of Greek society. Our duty as judges is to stay in touch with Greek society. We have to stand united in order to face the great challenges.[82]

This statement provoked the ire of his predecessor as President of the CoS, who retorted in a predictable anti-populist judicial style that a judge must never be influenced by circumstances which shape public opinion at a specific moment of time.[83]

Populism and constitutional identity are hence intertwined in the Court's rhetoric. Identity becomes a slogan used in a populist exclusionary fashion to stress what makes the 'true Greek people' different from others, i.e. national conscience and adherence to the Greek Orthodox Christian dogma. Accordingly, it comes to no surprise that the Court sees itself as the original and true voice of the Greek nation. What is even more crucial is the fact that this case law, which revives decades-old doctrinal debates and concepts, materializes within the context of the economic crisis and what is perceived by parts of the electorate to be a 'loss of sovereignty' as a result of the financial aid programs and the engagements accompanying them. In fact, these judgments could also be understood and explained as a form of resistance to the emerging new European economic governance and its technocratic asphyxiation of member states' vital political space in the field of economic and fiscal policy.

Through this instrumental and deeply ideological use of the notion of constitutional identity, which has striking analogies with the use of self-identity by the Hungarian Constitutional Court,[84] the CoS supposedly strikes back at the Troika and European institutions, at Greece's lenders and all perceived 'foes' of the Nation, establishing a direct line of contact with the silent mass of the population, the People itself. Through its unavoidable vagueness, the

82 'Aixmes Sakellariou kai yposhcscis Tsipra, meta ton "seismo" sto StE' *Kathimerini* (Athens, 6 October 2016) https://www.kathimerini.gr/877891/article/epikairothta/politikh/aixmes-sakellarioy-kai-yposxeseis-tsipra-meta-to-seismo-sto-ste accessed 19 April 2020.

83 Konstantinos Zoulas, 'Pikrammenos: O dikastis den epireazetai apo ti sygkyria' *Kathimerini* (Athens, 14 October 2016) https://www.kathimerini.gr/879131/article/epikairothta/ellada/pikrammenos-o-dikasths-den-ephreazetai-apo-th-sygkyria accessed 19 April 2020.

84 See Decision 22/2016. (XII. 5.) of the Hungarian Constitutional Court. See also the amended Section (4) of Article R of the Hungarian Constitution, which states that 'The protection of the constitutional identity and Christian culture of Hungary shall be an obligation of every organ of the State'.

notion of constitutional identity turns into a populist notion and shows its inherently explosive content.[85]

8.4 Lessons to be drawn from the Greek experience

It is now time to ask ourselves what lessons can be drawn from the Greek judicial experience regarding the convergence of populism and constitutional identity. First of all, I think that it has been shown so far that courts are not, axiomatically, immune to populism and cannot in all circumstances be treated as the definite stronghold against populism. The idea of a populist court is not a contradiction *per se*. Let us remind ourselves here of the Supreme Court Justice William O. Douglas (of Western origin and a fervent New Dealer) who, paraphrasing the Preamble of the US Constitution, chose as the title of one his books the following: *We the Judges*.[86] There should be no doubt that courts have an important role to play when democracy and rule of law are under threat. It is their duty to defend liberal democracy through their power of judicial review exercised in a John Hart Ely vein of representation-reinforcing theory.[87] They can indeed provide, up to a certain point and at the initial stages, a check on governments who, speaking in the name of the 'People', seek to silence any dissenters. However, when populism gains ground, there is a need for a more comprehensive institutional strategy in order to combat it. It would be futile and even dangerous to mistakenly believe that courts can win the war singlehandedly. Most of all, we have to bear in mind that populism needs to be primarily combatted politically, not judicially. Otherwise, the populist propaganda pointing to the elites as a barrier against the execution of the will of the People tends to become a self-fulfilling prophecy.

Secondly, populist constitutionalism is usually associated with constituent power and often pursues the creation of a new Constitution.[88] However, a populist leader or government need not necessarily put into play the constituent power. Instead, courts 'tainted' by populist rhetoric can easily instrumentalize the Constitution, reshape existing concepts, twist the meaning of constitutional provisions and create new constitutional principles in order to back or further a populist agenda. Conceptual instruments such as general will, popular and national sovereignty, nation and religion are most of the time already contained in the constitutional text or underlie it. The meaning of these clauses is produced under the guise of 'interpretation'. What courts

85 Daniel Kelemen and Laurent Pech, 'Why autocrats love constitutional identity and constitutional pluralism: Lessons from Hungary and Poland' (2018) RECONNECT Working Paper No. 2 – September 2018, 5–6 and 9–10 https://www.reconnect-europe.eu/wp-content/uploads/2018/10/RECONNECT-WorkingPaper2-Kelemen-Pech-LP-KO.pdf accessed 19 April 2020.

86 William O. Douglas, *We the Judges: Studies in American and Indian Constitutional Law from Marshall to Mukherjea* (Doubleday & Company Inc 1956).

87 Prendergast (n 19) 246–247. See also John H. Ely, *Democracy and Distrust: A Theory of Judicial Review* (Harvard University Press 1980).

88 Corrias (n 5) 8.

really do, when 'searching' for their hidden meaning, is to create constitutional constructions that flesh out and implement the constitutional text and its underlying principles.[89] An illiberal reading is often more than enough to produce the desired outcome. The interpretation by the CoS of Article 2 of Protocol No 1 to the ECHR regarding the right to education and the respect of parents' religious and philosophical convictions suffices to prove the point.

Last but not least, in the case of Greece, populist reaction and the subsequent evocation of the notion of constitutional identity were initially fuelled by the economic crisis. The main target was undoubtedly surveillance mechanisms established by the European institutions and linked to financial assistance programs; indirectly, the target was also European integration in the economic and fiscal field. However, things have changed and now the main cause of reaction seems to be the migration/refugee issue. What is even more troubling is that European integration in the field of asylum policy, external border control and relocation/integration policy concerning refugees can still remain a target for populists. A possible deadlock and resistance to relevant European policies is already at play.[90] Combining communitarian ideals, voluntaristic conceptions of national and popular sovereignty as well as denouncement of Brussels' technocratic government is a cocktail that has seduced even national constitutional courts – though one has to say in more elaborate form – let alone parts of the electorate. One could venture to say that the notion of national or constitutional identity, originating from the European Treaties themselves, will be used more and more in this direction in the immediate future.

8.5 Epilogue

During the past few years, the CoS has elaborated through several judgments a protean conception of the Greek constitutional identity. The notion was shaped under very stressful circumstances for the country and seemingly as a reaction to a variety of different perceived threats to the existence of the Nation. This has allowed for the notion of constitutional identity to be entangled with the widespread populist tendencies within the exact same period. In this light, the 'affair' between populism and constitutional identity in Greece, through the medium of the courts, could in fact be regarded as a passing product of the crisis.

Indeed, after almost a decade, the period of the crisis seems to be over both for the country and the Court. In fact, it can be argued that the Greek CoS, luckily enough, after a short ambivalent period, has shied away from populism. All the judgments commented on in this chapter, on nationality, Sunday laws and religious education, appear in many respects distanced in time, a parenthesis soon to be forgotten. The dynamic of the Court is now

89 Jack Balkin, *Living Originalism* (Harvard University Press 2011) 14–15.

90 See, for instance, the recent ECJ judgment on refugee relocation. Joined Cases C-715/17, C-718/17 and C-719/17 *European Commission v Republic of Poland and Others* [2020] ECLI:EU:C:2020:257.

different, and it hardly seems possible that the notion of constitutional identity will be further developed in this direction in the near future.

Having said that, although this may well be the case as far as the general outline of the course of the Court is concerned, caution is still necessary. The Court's relevant case law has not been reversed;[91] for the most part, it is still standing and has even been reaffirmed so as to become settled, as the recent decision in 2019 about the teaching of religion in schools shows. As a consequence, the notion of constitutional identity has been engraved in the Greek constitutional order and can be reactivated when the circumstances change and a similar representational void to the one produced during the past years of the economic crisis emerges.

This is why the CoS needs to intervene and produce a brand-new conception of the notion of constitutional identity. Hopefully, the Court will go on and elaborate a different understanding of this contested notion that will replace the introverted one sketched out in this chapter. Along this direction, it has to create an identity-less phobic towards modern-day challenges and more open to liberal ideals and to European integration. Through this path, it should be guided by Article 28 of the Constitution and especially its interpretative declaration,[92] which, according to its dominant interpretation, serves as a 'portal' through which EU goals are integrated into the national legal order.[93] Otherwise, the relic of a constitutional identity stressing religious and ethnic particularities might come to haunt us again in the future.

91 The only exception to the rule being the Sunday law judgments, which could be qualified as the 'weakest link' of the constitutional identity jurisprudence. In judgment 18/2019, the 4th Chamber of the CoS implicitly, though not expressly, reversed its previous judgments and ruled in favour of the constitutionality of a new ministerial decision, which essentially had the same content as the previous one, but which, in the Court's opinion, was better documented, hence justified. In his concurring opinion, the Chamber's President asked for the explicit reversal of the Sunday laws precedent on the ground that such a limitation of the legislature's power conveys a paternalistic approach which would be incompatible with the liberal character of the Constitution (para 12).

92 Article 28 constitutes the foundation for the participation of the country in the European integration process.

93 Lina Papadopoulou, *National Constitution and Community Law: The Question of Primacy* (A.N. Sakkoulas 2009) 443–446, where also all relevant citations to other writers can be found.

9 Constitutional interpretation under the new Fundamental Law of Hungary

Fruzsina Gárdos-Orosz

9.1 Introduction

Hungary is categorized as a Member State of the European Union that is ruled by a populist Government.[1] The Hungarian Government is qualified as populist because according to the scholarship of political science, many elements of the definition of populism fit with the Hungarian political system. Furthermore, the Government has a two thirds constitution-making majority in the Parliament; therefore, the constitutionalism in Hungary since 2010 has been formed and transformed by the ruling political majority. As political goals can easily be transformed into constitutional changes and the constitutional environment adapts to the ruling political agenda immediately, the scholarly criteria of so-called populist constitutionalism can be clearly observed and studied in Hungary.

Zoltán Szente, in the introductory chapter of this book, identifies the elements of populist constitutionalism in the negative and in the positive sense, based upon a wide review of the literature in law and in political science. He describes how these elements can be found to different extents in different countries, but in the legal and political science scholarship, these characteristics appear to be basic elements of the concept of populist constitutionalism. The elements are the following: (1) a criticism of the separation of law and politics, stating that populists reject the restriction of political power by legal norms, and they reject the politically neutral conception of law in liberal democracy because it undermines the representation of the national interest; and (2) anti-elitism, the juxtaposition of the virtuous people and the corrupt elite and reference to a united people (nation, community) as opposed to a privileged cosmopolitan elite (with international organizations or EU institutions, NGOs included) that protects the rights of LGBTQ communities or immigrants, alternative churches or other minorities that do not represent

1 For example, Andrew Arato, 'How We Got Here? Transition Failures, Their Causes and the Populist Interest in the Constitution' (2019) 45 Philosophy and Social Criticism 1108; Bojan Bugarič, 'The Two Faces of Populism: Between Authoritarian and Democratic Populism' (2019) 20 German Law Journal 392, 393; Bojan Bugarič, Alenka Kuhelj, 'Varieties of Populism in Europe: Is the Rule of Law in Danger?' (2018) 10 Hague Journal on the Rule of Law 22; Manuel Anselmi, *Populism. An Introduction* (Routledge 2018) 87.

the majority interest.[2] Anti-institutionalism, anti-pluralism, and anti-liberalism are the next components that Szente identifies in the literature,[3] together with the logic that public interest and the general will of the people should take precedence over individual and particular interests.

Among the positive criteria of populist constitutionalism, Szente identifies popular sovereignty first. The populist interpretation of constituent power puts the rule of the people above the rule of law, a 'collective subject' moulded by tradition, common suffering and destiny receives greater competence in direct decision making. Populist constitutionalism can be characterized by the absolutization of the majority principle, as long as the populist parties have won the election. This majoritarian conception of democracy regards electoral empowerment as an expression of the will of the people and, on that basis, rejects the constitutional restriction of power.[4] The instrumentalization of the law means, in regimes like Hungary, that the constitution can provide an effective toolbox for preserving power and breaking down checks and balances while the formalities of the rule of law are observed; therefore, these populist regimes are characterized by active constitution-making, as far as this is possible for them.[5]

My examination is based on this scholarly observation which has been explained in detail in the introduction to this book, and I presume here the very convincing results of the previous examinations claiming that in Hungary, most of these attributes of populism are typical of the exercise of power.[6] Without, therefore, making any further contribution to this discussion on populism and constitutionalism in Hungary, I accept that Hungary is classified by an overwhelming majority of populism scholars as a populist country governed by a populist government with all those constitutional aspirations.[7] Furthermore, given that in Hungary, the Fidesz-KDNP party coalition led by Viktor Orbán won the two thirds constitution-making majority in the Parliament in the 2010, 2014 and 2018 general parliamentary elections, the Government majority in Parliament can therefore change the Constitution, and so Hungary is a litmus paper to examine the operation of populist constitutionalism.

I will thus examine in this chapter whether this new populist constitutional system which has developed in Hungary since 2010 gives a different role or rule to constitutional interpretation, i.e. to the procedure that gives final

2 See Szente, Chapter 1 in this volume.

3 Ibid.

4 Ibid.

5 Ibid.

6 For example, Paul Blokker, 'Populist Counter-Constitutionalism, Conservatism, and Legal Fundamentalism' (2019) 15 European Constitutional Law Review 519, 543; David Landau, 'Abusive Constitutionalism' (2013) 47 UC Davis Law Review 213.

7 For example, Gábor Attila Tóth, 'Constitutional Markers of Authoritarianism' (2019) 11 Hague Journal on the Rule of Law 37–61; Gábor Halmai, 'Populism, Authoritarianism and Constitutionalism' (2019) 20 German Law Journal 296–313. Tímea Drinóczi and Agnieszka Bień-Kacała, 'Illiberal Constitutionalism: The Case of Hungary and Poland' (2019) 20 German Law Journal 1141, 1148.

meaning to the words of the constitution. My next question is, if I answer the previous question in the positive, whether the new methods of interpretation are relevant or not in general in the jurisprudence of the Constitutional Court (hereinafter Court or CC) and especially in the argumentation of those judicial decisions that are favourable to the aforementioned populist agenda.

The first part of this chapter describes the constitutional context relevant to our topic. I will argue that although there are new constitutional requirements of interpretation prescribed in the constitutional text, these are rather neutral with regard to the populist constitutional agenda. If they are not neutral, for example, the reference to the achievements of the historical constitution or to the Preamble, the so-called National Avowal, they have not had a significant impact on the general constitutional interpretation so far. On the other hand, non-usual use of the classical interpretative methods or substantive new concepts have appeared in the case law of the Hungarian Constitutional Court independently of the constitutional interpretative requirements, to serve the basis of a *ratio decidendi* that favours the aforementioned populist elements of the new constitutional agenda.

My conclusion will focus on the role of the prescribed compulsory interpretative methods in the substantive constitutional change in populist constitutionalism. The change proposed by the two thirds populist political majority in Parliament in the form of a new Fundamental Law and several constitutional amendments is advanced by the decisions of the Constitutional Court, but the cause of this new deferential approach cannot be reduced to the usage of the partly new text and the new methods of interpretation introduced by the Fundamental Law. Although in some cases the new methods appear in the constitutional jurisprudence, there is no close connection between the introduction of the new interpretative requirements into the constitutional text and the constitutional jurisprudence favourable in many cases to the populist agenda, as I will explain here.

9.2 The new methods of constitutional interpretation

9.2.1 The Constitutional Court

'*Clientelism*, *state capture*, and the "*Gleichschaltung*" of certain social systems (putting them under direct political control), which are also characteristic of populist governments, require the use of legal instruments' – observes Szente in the introductory chapter, describing one characteristic of populist constitutionalism identified by the populism literature. Hungarian legal scholarship often argues that the Constitutional Court was captured after 2010, because legal and constitutional changes had a great effect on the Constitutional Court after 2010.[8]

8 Fruzsina Gárdos-Orosz, 'Challenges to Constitutional Adjudication in Hungary since 2010' in Martin Belov (ed.), *The Role of Courts in Contemporary Legal Orders* (Eleven Publishing 2019) 321.

The Hungarian Constitutional Court was established on 1 January 1990, right after the democratic transition of 1989–1990. In the period after 1990, and in the years following the democratic change of regime, the Constitutional Court, perhaps justifiably open to criticism for its activism,[9] took on a significant role in forming the new constitutional democracy in Hungary after communism.[10] The new constitution of Hungary – the Fundamental Law – entered into force on 1 January 2012 and replaced the previous Constitution[11] that had been revised completely in 1989–1990. The Fidesz-KDNP party coalition, having gained a two-thirds constitution-making majority at the 2010 general elections, envisaged a new role for the Constitutional Court. The new regulation had been adopted in several steps, starting as early as in 2010 with the increase in the number of judges from 11 to 15 (the new members being elected by the new Government majority in Parliament) and the restriction on the competence to review legislation on public finance (occurring well after the 2008 financial crisis). The aim of the transformation, according to the official reasoning of the Act on the Constitutional Court, was to give more emphasis to the protection of fundamental rights in individual judicial cases by the introduction of the German-type constitutional complaint and, on the other hand, to abolish the possibility of *actio popularis*, by which procedure anyone could turn to the Constitutional Court without any particular interest in order to initiate the annulment of a piece of legislation deemed unconstitutional. There were significant scholarly concerns that by these changes the constitution-making majority was reconsidering the central role of this institution in maintaining the rule of law and liberal democracy in Hungary by effectively reviewing the legislative and the government branches.[12] Although the Constitutional Court, which is structurally separated from the Judiciary, still has the power to annul laws, some of its decisions were overridden by constitutional amendments in the 2010–2013 period, and the number of constitutional review procedures has significantly decreased following the new regulation, because, pursuant to Article 24 of the Fundamental Law, although the Constitutional Court is the principal organ for the protection of the Fundamental Law, it only reviews laws following a proposal by the Government, one-fourth of the Members of the National Assembly, the President of the *Kúria* (the supreme court), the Prosecutor General or the Commissioner for Fundamental Rights, and according to Article 37 Section (4) of the Fundamental Law, it generally cannot review public finance legislation.

9 Zoltán Szente, 'The Interpretative Practice of the Hungarian Constitutional Court: A Critical View' (2013) 14 German Law Journal 186.

10 Attila Vincze, Péter Csuhány, Pál Sonnevend, András Jakab, 'Az Alkotmánybíróság' in András Jakab (ed.), *Az alkotmány kommentárja* (Századvéd 2009) 239–264.

11 Act XX of 1949 on the Constitution.

12 Gábor Halmai, 'Dismantling Constitutional Review in Hungary' (2019) Rivista de diritti comparati 18.

9.2.2 The collection of the principles and methods of constitutional interpretation laid down in the Fundamental Law

Unlike the old Constitution (of 1949/1989), the Fundamental Law of 2011 defines the major methods of constitutional interpretation. The relevant guidance is scattered around the constitutional text without any hierarchy of the different interpretive principles to be used.[13]

Article N Section (1) declares that Hungary enforces 'the principle of balanced, transparent and sustainable budget management', while Section (3) makes respect for this principle the duty of – among others – the Constitutional Court.

According to Article R Section (3), the provisions of the Fundamental Law must be interpreted (a) 'in accordance with their purposes', (b) 'with the Avowal of National Faith', and (c) 'with the achievements of our historical constitution'. Section (4) of the same Article states that 'the protection of the constitutional identity and the Christian culture of Hungary shall be an obligation of every organ of the State'.

In Article I (3), the Fundamental Law further codified the basic rule of interpretation for conflicts involving fundamental rights:

> The rules for fundamental rights and obligations shall be laid down in an Act. A fundamental right may only be restricted to allow the effective use of another fundamental right or to protect a constitutional value, to the extent absolutely necessary, proportionate to the objective pursued and with full respect for the essential content of that fundamental right.

It was not only the imposition of binding interpretative principles and methods which emerged as a constitutional means to influence the jurisdiction of the Constitutional Court, but also the provision of the Fourth Amendment to the Fundamental Law in March 2013, repealing (loosening the legal effect of) all Constitutional Court rulings made prior to the entry into force of the new Fundamental Law in 2012. The goal of this amendment was clearly to compel the Constitutional Court to change its jurisprudence, adapting it to the values of the Fundamental Law.

Furthermore, according to Article 28 of the Fundamental Law:

> In the course of the application of law, courts shall interpret the text of laws primarily in accordance with their purposes and with the Fundamental Law. The purposes of the laws should be defined primarily in accordance with the preamble of the law and the official reasoning given to the law in the procedure of adaptation or the amendments. When interpreting the Fundamental Law or laws, it shall be presumed that

13 Tímea Drinóczi, Nóra Chronowski, and Miklós Kocsis, 'What Questions of Interpretation May Be Raised by the New Hungarian Constitution?' (2012) 1 Vienna Journal on International Constitutional Law 41–64.

they serve moral and economic purposes which are in accordance with common sense and the public good.

In other words, in the course of the constitutional review of judicial decisions, the Constitutional Court checks whether the court properly considered the objective purpose of the legal norms it had to apply in the specific case. This 'objective purpose' was first understood by the Constitutional Court as the social aim that the lawmaker wanted to achieve by the legal act, rather than the subjective and original intent of those who took part in the lawmaking process; but later, by the Seventh Amendment to the Fundamental Law in 2018, the text changed, and the constitution-making majority made it clear that this purpose is understood according to the legislator's intention.

Due to the fact that there are a variety of different methods of constitutional interpretation in theory, the Fundamental Law cannot give a closed list of the methods. It contains only a list of the preferred interpretative methods that must be taken into consideration for the decision.

9.3 A new populist set of the methods of interpretation, or the reformulation of the classical methods?

In this part, I will briefly list the methods that became important and recognizable in the jurisprudence of the Hungarian Constitutional Court following the democratic transition.[14] I will match these methods with the new regulations listed earlier from the Fundamental Law in order to understand the nature of the new constitutional requirements. Then, I will assess whether the methods prescribed in the Fundamental Law are theoretically favourable for a regime that builds populist constitutionalism or are fairly neutral as regards these goals.

(a) Pure textualism is often referred to as the plain meaning method. The plain meaning rule is not an explicit requirement of the constitutional text, but this method is favourable for the present constitutional order in Hungary as the text of the Fundamental Law was formulated in 2011 by the same political majority as the ruling one in 2020 and has already been amended eight times. It is the leading method of interpretation in the Hungarian constitutional jurisprudence, and the plain meaning of the constitutional text is always referred to in the decisions of the Constitutional Court as a starting point of the argumentation.

(b) The originalist interpretation seeks to find the original intent of the constitution makers reflected by the text.

Article R refers to the achievements of the historical constitution as a compulsory reference point for interpretation. As it does in the United States,

14 András Jakab, *Comparative Constitutional Reasoning* (Cambridge University Press 2017); Szente (n. 9) 186.

originalism leads the court back to the constitutional values of the past, and the reference to the achievements of the historical constitution could play a similar role in Hungarian jurisprudence through the requirement to adjust the present text to historical constitutional achievements. It emphasizes the long history of constitutional values in Hungary, and this approach is present in Hungary through the mention made of the achievements of the historical constitution. This approach to constitutional interpretation is favourable for populists for two reasons. One is mentioned by Graber, who notes in this book that the old values and understandings of constitutionalism are always more conservative and traditionalist than a progressive understanding of the text that is not bound by the past. Second, traditionalism, by emphasizing common values and traditions, is always a nation-building element in populist constitutionalism, as I mentioned earlier. Accepting that the achievements of the historical constitution are constitutional values which are regarded in the light of certain theories and non-positivist legal approaches as the roots of the present legal order, this view serves the goals of populist constitutional politics by leading judges towards meanings based on a common, traditional, naturally less open, less progressive and less inclusive understanding of the law.

(c) The teleological (purposive) interpretation wishes to discover the goal, the aim of the rule, the *ratio legis*. This emerges in Article R of the Fundamental Law, when the requirement is that constitutional provisions should be interpreted in accordance with their purposes. We would think that this provision alone would give a wide margin of appreciation to the Constitutional Court, but the next sentence in Section (4) about the protection of constitutional identity and Christian culture restricts this freedom to define the purpose of the rule.

(d) A pragmatic interpretation occurs when the judge takes into consideration the social, economic, technological, political, etc., effects of the decision. Article N of the Fundamental Law requires all state organs to act with respect for the financial goals of the state, although this provision does not have a great relevance, as according to Article 37 Section (4), the Constitutional Court cannot review controversies related to public finance legislation. Still, if the Constitutional Court must observe the financial goals of the state, the necessity of the pragmatic approach to the constitutional interpretation becomes a requirement, which might lead to judicial deference towards the populist political majority in specific cases.

(e) Contextual interpretation is when the constitutional text is understood in the entire context of the constitution, taking into consideration the other related provisions of the text. The integrity of the constitutional text is a keyword in this method. Article R of the Fundamental Law requires the broad contextual interpretation explicitly, in the strict sense, and implicitly, in the broad sense. In the strict sense, it requires that the Preamble of the Fundamental Law, should be considered when interpreting the other provisions of the text. This is a requirement of the coherent interpretation of the constitutional text which includes the preamble, i.e. the long National Avowal with the values of the political majority contained within it. In the broad sense, I argue that when a contextual analysis is carried out on the Fundamental Law, it is not restricted to the Constitution itself but the historical constitution and Christian culture should be taken into account as the entire context of the Fundamental Law. This understanding of the requirement of contextual interpretation is favourable for the populist agenda that I summarized in the introduction, because it helps to create an interpretation which is in line with the values of populist constitutionalism: the uniform values of the family, common tradition, a work-based society, Christian values, etc.

(f) The moral interpretation is based on the assumption that there is a political philosophy behind the constitutional text which is able to lead the judge to the right understanding of the norm. This political philosophy is based on the morals of the community in constitutional populism. The necessity of the moral understanding is also present in the text of the Fundamental Law, when, for example, in Article R, the Fundamental Law requires respect for constitutional identity. Respect for constitutional identity, as the notion is not previously defined in the constitutional text or elsewhere, does not have a legal (although it does have a political) meaning at the moment of the adoption; therefore, there is a textual window to allow the political philosophy of the constitution-making majority to become one of the tools of interpretation.

In sum, my assumption is that although these methods of interpretation certainly differ with regard to the room they leave for judicial discretion, all these alterations to or specifications of the classical interpretative methods, as codified in the text of the Fundamental Law, can be used in a favourable way for populism, to back up changes in the constitutional rules and principles. I argue that what is new is not only the fact that certain compulsory methods of interpretation are defined in the constitutional text, but that this collection of interpretations is a populist toolkit designed by the constitution-making two-thirds majority to help the transformation of the constitutional values, not only through the constitutional text but also through new interpretation.

My next question is whether these methods do, in fact, have a significant relevance in the jurisprudence of the Constitutional Court, or whether the changes in the constitutional jurisprudence that have been indicated in several scholarly works since 2010 can rather be attributed to substantive innovations or weak argumentations in the jurisprudence.

9.4 The use of binding interpretative methods in constitutional jurisprudence

9.4.1 The application of the new methods of interpretation

My first question is whether the new methods of interpretation have been used at all by the Constitutional Court, and if so, how often and in which cases they were used. Although the constitution makers tried to impose limits on the freedom of the Constitutional Court to interpret the Fundamental Law independently from the majority will, at first this was not clearly successful. After the new constitution entered into effect, the Constitutional Court declared in 2012 that the Court may continue to use arguments in its decisions which had also been made before the entry into force of the Fundamental Law, if the Fundamental Law contains the same or similar provisions for the case compared to those of the previous Constitution.[15] When in 2013 the Fourth Amendment *expressis verbis* declared the repeal of all Constitutional Court rulings made before 2012, the Court appeared to maintain its earlier position, saying that the Court must hereto justify in more detail if it wishes to use arguments contained in its pre-2012 decisions. This means that the Constitutional Court simply refused openly to ignore its earlier decisions, and practice also shows that it refers to its previous judgments in many cases, or it refers to a new judgment that has confirmed the previous jurisprudence.

As to the use of the specific interpretative method, its significant impact on the Constitutional Court's jurisprudence cannot be demonstrated or proved. At first sight, as I described earlier, the constitutional command to respect the achievements of the historical constitution has had the greatest impact on constitutional interpretation, because it appears in a significant number of cases in the jurisprudence, unlike the other requirements.[16] However, in fact, the Constitutional Court often used merely formal statements referring to the historical constitution when reasoning its decisions.[17] The Court has not yet developed a doctrinally sound method or theory of how to take into account the achievements of the historical constitution.[18] Its interpretative practice is consistent only in the sense that a legal norm may not be invalidated solely on the basis of Article R (3); however, in reality, the references to the historical constitution are usually merely decorations of the reasoning of the Court's rulings.[19] Although the constitutional provision for respecting the achievements of the historical constitution is certainly flexible enough to be used in almost any reasoning, it is less useful when it comes to provide compelling arguments for definite interpretation results.

The content of the unwritten, historical constitution was inherently ever-changing, and there is no guidance to determine which period or state of the historical constitution the new constitution should take as its reference point. The Fundamental Law only records that the self-determination of the Hungarian state was lost on 19 March 1944, when Nazi Germany occupied

15 Decision 22/2012. (V. 11.) of the Constitutional Court.

16 Zoltán Szente, 'A 2011. évi Alaptörvény és a történeti alkotmány összekapcsolásának mítosza' (2019) *Közjogi Szemle* 1–8.

17 Szente (n 9); Gábor Attila Tóth 'Historicism or Art Nouveau: A Comment on Zoltán Szente, The Interpretative practice of the Hungarian Constitutional Court, a Critical View' (2013) German Law Journal 615–626.

18 Imre Vörös, 'A történeti alkotmány az Alkotmánybíróság gyakorlatában' (2016) Közjogi Szemle 46. Ádám Rixer, 'Hungary's Fundamental Law and the Concept of the Historical Constituiton' (2013) 4 European Journal of European History of Law 8.

19 Szente (n 15) 5.

the country. Presumably, this date is the endpoint of the historical constitution. However, because of the wartime regulations or the anti-Jewish laws that were in force in 1944, this state of the historical constitution can hardly be assumed or followed. In reality, the Constitutional Court occasionally selects certain rules or customs of historical Hungarian public law, i.e. it considers the historical constitution as a sort of menu.[20]

As in Hungarian legal traditions, the preambles of legal norms, such as the National Avowal, did not have normative power, making the constitutional preamble a sub-principle of interpretation represents a real innovation. Given that this preamble contains very abstract values, solemn phrases and historical references, its real effect on the case law is fairly limited.

Furthermore, although the Fundamental Law has certainly assigned a preeminent role to the purposive interpretation in Article R when exploring the meaning of the constitutional text, this intention hardly prevails in practice. The Constitutional Court only rarely uses this reasoning, and hardly ever refers to this guidance of the Fundamental Law. The intention of revealing the purpose can be concluded, at most, from the fact that in certain cases the Court asks for the lawmaker's position. However, this is a contingent rather than a well-founded practice, as the role and methodology of using purposive interpretation is completely unclear in Hungarian constitutional jurisprudence.[21]

As to Article N imposing the obligation on the Court to take into account budgetary considerations, this suffers from some deficiencies. Not only is its content unclear and obscure, but it is questionable which constitutional requirements should be preferred if the issue of constitutionality is confronted with economic rationality (such as a balanced budget). However, it would be an extremely difficult task to use this interpretative guideline, anyway, as the scope for constitutional review of public finance legislation is grievously restricted. Since 2011, the Constitutional Court has been able to review and annul laws relating to public finance only if they violate the right to life and human dignity; the right to the protection of personal data; freedom of thought, conscience and religion; and the rights related to Hungarian citizenship. In effect, the Court may not review any budgetary law, so, in the absence of the relevant power, it would hardly be able to enforce budgetary considerations in the course of constitutional interpretation, and it has not yet done so in jurisprudence.

In sum, although the new methods certainly aimed at changing the jurisprudence of the Constitutional Court, these requirements appeared to be quite weak and uncertain when they come to creating substantive changes in the interpretative mindset. However, substantive changes can be detected, as I will highlight in the next section. The notion of human dignity and the notion of constitutional identity, for example, have become substantive interpretative tool concepts that have influenced the jurisprudence of the

20 Szente (n 15) 6.
21 Szente (n 9).

Constitutional Court in some cases, and a doctrinally confused interpretation, a mix of the classical methods of interpretation, has also led to deferential decisions that favour the populist constitutional agenda.

9.4.2 Cases advancing populist constitutionalism (favouring the populist agenda) and the use of the new methods of interpretation in these specific cases

In the introductory chapter to this book, Szente identifies secondary characteristics of constitutional populism, following the populism literature. These secondary characteristics that follow from the primary goals of political constitutionalism have a recognizable legal nature besides from the political one. The following can be highlighted: the development of *constitutional identity (a)*, *legal borrowings (b)* to appear to be similar to liberal constitutional democracies to increase legitimacy and adopting a defensive stance in relation to international and EU law, *reference to crisis management (c)* as a source of legitimacy to implement new measures which differ from the former rule of law requirements, *restriction of certain fundamental rights (d)*, as well as the *intolerance of or discrimination against certain minorities (e)*. This usually affects political rights, especially freedom of expression.

I will discuss five cases in this section, one for each characteristic, and examine whether the favourable decision for the political agenda produces new approaches to the interpretation of the constitution.[22]

(a) In Decision 22/2016 (XII. 5.) the interpretation of the Fundamental Law had been requested from the Court by the ombudsman. As explained in the motion, the concrete constitutional issue was related to the European Union Council Decision (EU) 2015/1601 of 22 September 2015 on migration, but the ombudsman initiated the authoritative interpretation of Article E of the Fundamental Law related to the accession to and cooperation with the EU. In this decision, the Constitutional Court developed the notion of constitutional identity which was not present in any domestic legal text at that time. The case was decided at a moment when the Government had already failed to get through a constitutional amendment with similar content, because in those months it did not have the two-thirds majority in Parliament, and an attempt to incorporate such a rule by a referendum had also failed.[23] National populism aims at protecting national approaches to sensitive questions such as migration, and these countries are against the EU

22 We discuss these cases and other related issues in greater detail in Eszter Bodnár-Fruzsina Gárdos-Orosz and Zoltán Pozsár-Szentmiklósy, *Hungary*, in Richard Albert, David Landau, Pietro Faraguna, and Simon Drugda (eds.), *2019 Global Review of Constitutional Law* (ICONnect-Clough Center 2020) 166–171, (2019) 138–142, (2018) 231–258, (2017) 77–81. Some case summaries here are based on these texts.

23 Zoltán Szente, 'The Controversial Anti-Migrant Referendum in Hungary, Invalid' Vervassungsblog https://constitutional-change.com/tag/invalid-referendum/.

elites if the protection of the people demands; furthermore, anti-pluralism in society and therefore an anti-migrant policy is also typical of the Hungarian regime, therefore the legal and constitutional reflection of this approach can best be concentrated in the notion of constitutional identity.

The Constitutional Court stated that the EU provides adequate protection for fundamental rights. The Constitutional Court, however, cannot set aside the protection of domestic fundamental rights, and it must grant that the joint exercise of competences with the EU would not result in a violation of human dignity as protected by the Hungarian Fundamental Law, or the essential content of other fundamental rights. The Court set two main limitations in the context of the question regarding the legal acts of the Union that extend beyond the jointly exercised competences. Firstly, the joint exercise of a competence cannot violate Hungary's sovereignty; secondly, it cannot lead to the violation of its constitutional identity. The Constitutional Court emphasized that the protection of constitutional identity should take the form of a constitutional dialogue based on the principles of equality and collegiality, implemented with mutual respect for each other.

I argue that this new substantive concept of constitutional identity was developed in line with national populist political goals,[24] because it serves as a basis for a protective national constitutionalism against the EU or international legislation, which is considered to be elitist, internationalist, pluralist, liberal and pro-migration, according to existing political communications. A proof of this argument is that as soon as the Government in Parliament regained its two-thirds constitution-amending majority, Parliament added the notion of constitutional identity to the text of the Fundamental Law in Article R, with the Seventh Amendment to the Fundamental Law.

Within the reasoning of the Court, the reference to the National Avowal is solely decorative, and the historical constitution is also not part of the specific argumentation:

> The Constitutional Court of Hungary interprets the concept of constitutional identity as Hungary's self-identity and it unfolds the content of this concept from case to case, on the basis of the whole Fundamental Law and certain provisions thereof, in accordance with the National Avowal and the achievements of our historical constitution – as required by Article R (3) of the Fundamental Law.

Instead of a convincing reasoning of this decision the Court opens up an uncertain, case-by-case interpretation of a central substantive concept related to the interpretation of all the other provisions of the Fundamental Law.

24 Gábor Halmai, 'Abuse of Constitutional Identity. The Hungarian Constitutional Court on Interpretation of Article E) (2) of the Fundamental Law' (2018) Review of Central and East European Law; Nóra Chronowski and Attila Vincze, 'Önazonosság és európai integráció' (2017) Jogtudományi Közlöny 117–131.

The new substantive concepts of possibly transformative value in this decision do not have identifiable legal content, which might logically lead to a deferential judicial approach, not just in this but in future decisions.

(b) Constitutional borrowings can be demonstrated by the so-called CEU and NGO cases.[25] In Hungary, some NGOs and the Central European University are acknowledged as elements of the elite of the 1989 democratic transition, observing the values of liberal constitutionalism based on individualism, internationalism and pluralism. The legislative amendments that were to be reviewed by the Court in constitutional complaint and ex post constitutional review procedures were voted by the Government majority in Parliament to implement unfavourable measures to stop or obstruct the activity of these institutions in Hungary.

The Constitutional Court did not decide on the sensitive cases. The Court could not initiate a preliminary ruling procedure before the European Court of Justice because the case was primarily national, but with reference to the necessity of dialogue, it suspended both procedures until the decision of the ECJ was completed, in which Hungary was sued by the Commission in an infringement procedure for the same rules.

The Venice Commission related to the NGO regulation amendment criticized several points of the regulation because, while on paper certain provisions requiring transparency of foreign funding may appear to be in line with European standards, the context surrounding the adoption of the relevant law, and specifically a virulent campaign by some state authorities against civil society organizations receiving foreign funding, portraying them as acting against the interests of Hungarian society, may render such provisions problematic.[26] The Amendment of the National Tertiary Education Act was also criticized not only in Hungary, but by the Council of Europe Parliamentary Assembly and the Venice Commission.[27]

In the Constitutional Court decisions on the suspensions, the dissenting opinions warned of the implausible argumentation of basing a domestic decision on EU law grounds with reference to the 'dialogue' – a borrowed approach from the jurisprudence of other European constitutional courts. The problem here is that the Hungarian case was very different in nature from other cases in which preliminary reference appeared to be a good tool and the reasoning of the decision was developed using the borrowed concept to exempt the legislative majority from an unavoidable, unfavourable constitutional decision.

25 Decisions 3198/2018. (VI. 21.) and 3199/2018. (VI. 21.) of the Constitutional Court.

26 Hungary – Opinion on the Draft Law on the Transparency of Organisations Receiving Support from Abroad. http://www.venice.coe.int/webforms/documents/?pdf=CDL-AD(2017)015-e.

27 Hungary – Opinion on Act XXV of 4 April 2017 on the Amendment of Act CCIV of 2011 on National Tertiary Education. http://www.venice.coe.int/webforms/documents/?pdf=CDL-AD(2017)022-e.

(c) Good examples of the reference to the crisis situation to strengthen populist intentions with constitutional argumentation are the decisions of the Constitutional Court related to credit crisis jurisprudence. The decisions conformed to government policy and accepted the constitutionality of the extraordinary measures that were introduced to interfere with contractual relationships to help debtors in foreign currency loan related cases. The legislative decision and its communication were extremely anti-elitist, against financial institutions and foreign elites and at the same time very protective of the people: the only true representative of the people – the Government majority – helped in this troubling situation, according to the reasoning of the legislative acts introduced.

The Act that the Parliament adopted to put an end to the deepest credit crunch crisis in Hungary in 2011 regulated two areas: the declaration that exchange rate margins are null and void in contracts and that unilateral amendments to contracts are unfair. For financial institutions to rebut the presumption of unfairness, the Act created a very specific and rigorous order of procedure.[28] In its relevant ruling,[29] the Court created unconventional and unusual standards with regard to retroactive effect, fair trial rights and the right to property in Hungarian constitutional law as a reaction to the Government's crisis argument, but did not refer to its duty to apply the new methods of interpretation and so come to a new interpretative result regarding certain constitutional provisions.[30] In another decision on the same issue,[31] the Constitutional Court highlighted, for example, that the global financial crisis of 2008–2009 rendered the debtor's right to freedom of action and self-determination meaningless, which

> undermined their right to human dignity as well ... This is unacceptable, because human dignity shall be inviolable (Article 2 of the Fundamental Law), and shall be the primary obligation of the State to protect these rights (Article 1 (1) of the Fundamental Law).

This surprising interpretation of the material basis of the general freedom of action understood as human dignity in order to back up the invasive legislative provisions with a conclusive argument, was challenged by many within the Constitutional Court in concurring or dissenting opinions. The unconventional interpretation which made human dignity a trump card, however,

28 See, on the detailed analyses of the law and this decision, Fruzsina Gárdos-Orosz, 'Constitutional Justice in Credit Crisis' 66 Südosteuropa (2018) 94–118.

29 Decision 34/2014 (XII. 4) of the Constitutional Court.

30 Gárdos-Orosz (n 25) 101.

31 Decision 2/2015 (II. 2.) of the Constitutional Court.

has had a precedent effect,[32] not necessarily in line with the former concept of human dignity,[33] but rather as a substantive concept of the interpretation of the other constitutional provisions. It seems that in a 'crisis situation' (when large numbers of people face a challenging situation), the constitutional limits of the state's intervention by way of legislation changes due to this ultimate duty to respect and protect human dignity, as Article 2 of the Fundamental Law was understood this way. In this case there was no reference to new methods of interpretation, but still the Court arrived at a new substantive understanding of human dignity in relation to Article M on consumer protection. In the decision, there is one sole reference to Article R as a tool for interpretation to back up this meaning of Article M, where the Court states that according to the National Avowal, 'We hold that we have a general duty to help the vulnerable and the poor'.

(d) The new balance of fundamental rights can also be seen in other decisions. This approach to freedom of expression expressly stated in Article IX of the Fundamental Law in relation to the protection of human dignity was further reinforced by the Constitutional Court jurisprudence in a significant case of freedom of assembly. Freedom of expression is the basis of freedom of assembly, and human dignity is the basis of the protection of privacy and the home in human rights doctrine. In the case that I refer to in order to demonstrate the judicial change in freedom of assembly rights, these rights were restricted in order that the protection of privacy and home would prevail in certain situations. This approach is in line with the textual change in the position of freedom of expression.

Freedom of assembly was regulated in Hungary by an act adopted in 1989 as a huge step in the democratic transition process. According to the very liberal regulation, the previously existing ban on assembly is possible in only two cases: if, according to the police, it seriously endangers the proper functioning of the representative state institutions or courts, or if the circulation of the traffic cannot be secured by another route. In its decision, however, the Court established a different balance between these rights.[34] It held that the police acted lawfully and constitutionally when it used a new, non-codified reason for the prior interdiction in relation to a demonstration in front of the home of the prime minister (the reason was the assumed violation of the privacy of the inhabitants of the neighbouring district). The CC also

32 Kinga Zakariás, *Az emberi méltóság* (Pázmány Press 2019) especially 68–97; Gergely Deli and István Kukorelli, 'Az emberi méltóság alapjoga Magyarországon' (2015) 70 Jogtudományi Közlöny 337–347; Kinga Zkariás, Márk Várszegi, Existenzminimum und würdiges Leben – die Menschenwürde als Grundlage des Sozialstaates: Eine ungarisch-deutsche Rechtsvergleichung, in Christian Schubel, Stephan Kirste, Peter-Christian Müller-Graff, Oliver Diggelmann, and Ulrich Hufeld (eds.), *Jahrbuch für Vergleichende Staats- und Rechtswissenschaften – 2018/2019* (Nomos 2020) 57–99.

33 Catherine Dupré, *The Age of Dignity: Human Rights and Constitutionalism in Europe* (Hart Publishing 2015) 82–112.

34 Decision 13/2016 (VII. 18.) of the Constitutional Court.

argued that there was an unconstitutional omission, meaning that the Parliament should amend the act on the freedom of assembly in order to regulate cases in which freedom of assembly and the right to privacy embedded in human dignity are in conflict. In this case human dignity served also as a substantive tool of interpretation to give a changed meaning to the right to privacy against the right to assembly.

I argue that this reinterpretation of human dignity is becoming a substantive tool concept in interpretation in order to strengthen the new approach of the Fundamental Law to human rights protection. We have the impression that in this new approach included in the Fundamental Law by the populist majority, a human being is protected together with his/her dignity, in that this dignity is defined in constitutional jurisprudence by attributing certain specific qualities to a human being, which qualities should be protected as the inviolable human dignity (very strongly against other conflicting rights) in jurisprudence: these qualities are the home, the privacy of the family, a certain degree of welfare, exemption from hate speech, qualities that appear in the aforementioned cases and also in populist political communication, the textual emphasis on Christian culture and the illiberal goals of populist constitutionalism as described in the introduction. There was no reference to the new methods of interpretation in this case, although the meaning changed, despite the unchanged text.

(e) The decision 2/2019. (III. 5.) of the Constitutional Court is related to the anti-migration, anti-pluralism, anti-diversity policy of the state that attempts to create a homogeneous society. The Seventh Amendment implemented a new condition for granting asylum: those persons shall not be entitled to asylum who arrived in the territory of Hungary through any country where they were not persecuted or directly threatened with persecution.

The Government requested the abstract interpretation of this provision of the Fundamental Law – especially that of the new provision related to asylum – in the light of the Seventh Amendment. The motive behind this was the dispute between the Government and the European Commission on the compliance of the new Hungarian regulation on asylum (including the Seventh Amendment) with EU Law.

The Constitutional Court declared here (going completely against its own earlier standpoint in the CEU case) that the interpretation of the Fundamental Law cannot be derogated by any interpretation by another organ – addressing this implicitly to the institutions of the EU. Regarding the new provision of the Fundamental Law on the right to asylum, the Constitutional Court reached a controversial conclusion with a completely eclectic interpretation. According to this, the contextual interpretation of this provision against the textual interpretation means that in these cases, the right to asylum does not function as a fundamental subjective right, but respecting the principle of non-refoulement the asylum seeker should be subject to regulation by the statutes of the Hungarian state. The reasoning of this case was striking because it is quite rare – especially in the case of a very new amendment – that the Constitutional Court does not interpret it according to the plain meaning method, and in this case the reasoning clearly served the Government's interest to take a step back in order to try to conform with EU requirements in response to a conflict which was not desired at that moment.

9.5 Conclusions

In spite of the fact that the Constitutional Court is the authentic interpreter of the constitutional text, and it is bound by the methods defined in the Fundamental Law, the body has, in principle, considerable room for manoeuvre, since the constitution maker did not establish a hierarchy of the different interpretative methods, which are very different in their (legal) nature and did not lay down an exclusive list.

Some scholars argue that the jurisprudence of the Constitutional Court has significantly changed in the last few years and these changes have been favourable to the Government populist majority. I have proved in this chapter that there certainly are Constitutional Court decisions that favour the political agenda which is qualified as populist, but in these decisions the new methods of interpretation prescribed in the text of the Fundamental Law do not have much relevance. Although each of these methods of interpretation could help to develop a new philosophy of argumentation, this has not happened yet. When the Constitutional Court refers to these new methods, the reference is usually an ornament to the decision, and in those cases favourable to the Government, the new interpretative methods do not acquire a significant role, either. Decisions favourable to populism use an eclectic method of interpretation and an eclectic set of classical methods and new substantive concepts, such as constitutional identity or human dignity.

If the substantive change of the jurisprudence and of the attitude of the Constitutional Court are not due primarily to the new text of the Fundamental Law, and furthermore, to the different set of methods of interpretation, even if this latter might be favourably used to support the realization of the populist constitutional goals, the judicial behaviour can rather be attributed to the voluntary engagement in the creative process of building populist constitutionalism.

10 The populist reforms in Italy and the instrument of the constitutionally conforming interpretation

*Gianmario Demuro and Riccardo Montaldo**

10.1 Could the Italian context be defined as populist?

A first question to be analysed for the purposes of this chapter is whether the Italian polity can be defined as effectively populist, based on the definition of populism elaborated by the most relevant literature on the subject and by the conceptualisation of this book.[1]

In this regard, a first element emerging from this analysis is the difficulty of identifying a 'typical' populism, as an ideology or political current, since populisms are in fact characterised by their approach to politics and their communicative style, which in particular exploits modern communication technologies.[2] In fact, each populist party and leader tends to present, in its own communications, a Manichean division of society into homogeneous groups,[3] dividing the 'pure' people from the corrupt elites, particularly the parliamentary ones, emphasising the need for a leader. A leader who immediately interprets the people's will and protects it from all that is different from the people themselves, be it intermediary bodies and entities, international organisations such as the European Union, or the financial market, but also and above from all the individuals that stand out from the majority: immigrants, Muslims, Jews, Roma, and so on.[4]

There is indeed a clear correlation between populism, xenophobia and racism: populisms overestimate, in their programs and communications, the theme of migration and foreigners, indicating them in particular as risk factors for the cultural values of the 'people'.[5]

A further element common to all populisms is also represented by the use of various media to their advantage, and in particular new media, which allow

* Although the present contribution is the result of a joint work and reflection, paragraphs 10.1 and 10.4 should be ascribed to Gianmario Demuro, while the paragraphs 10.2 and 10.3 should be ascribed to Riccardo Montaldo.

1 See Zoltán Szente, Chapter 1 in this volume.

2 Ilvo Diamanti and Marc Lazar, *Popolocrazia. La metamorfosi delle nostre democrazie* (Laterza 2018), 6–7.

3 Moreno Mancosu, 'Populism, Emotionalized Blame Attribution and Selective Exposure in Social Media. A Comparative Analysis of Italy and UK' (2018) 1 Comunicazione politica, 76; Yves Mény and Yves Surel, *Populismo e democrazia* (Il Mulino 2000), 66.

4 Carlo Fusaro, 'L'ascesa del populismo in Europa. Italia, la terra promessa' (2019) forumcostituzionale.it, 26 August 2019, 2.

5 Mény and Surel (n 3) 192–193.

populist leaders to communicate directly with the electorate and exploit new technologies to obtain the greatest consensus possible,[6] exploiting a communication style based on simple messages and characterised by a strong emotional charge.[7]

Finally, all populisms present the common trait, derived from the aversion to the establishment, of the promotion of mechanisms of direct democracy, which in particular exploit new technologies, as the only solution to effectively give a voice to the people.[8]

Having defined the common traits of populism, it can be said that Italy is not only a context characterised by the presence of several political movements that could be defined as populist, but that it has also been at the forefront of the development of contemporary populism[9] and has therefore constituted a context in which populism has been able to develop and prevail quite easily,[10] and this even before the period covered by this study, relating to the period in which the majority was composed of the two populist parties of *Movimento5Stelle* and *Lega*. Italy indeed witnessed the unprecedented success in the 2013 parliamentary elections of the populist party *Movimento5Stelle* (which received 25% of the votes), a social movement created around a network and revolving around an online platform that is opaque and controlled by a private individual. Moreover, the 2018 elections resulted in the union between the *Movimento* and the right-wing populism of the *Lega*, with which a parliamentary majority was formed until August 2019.[11]

The roots of current Italian populism can be found in the crisis of the parties of the early 1990s,[12] in particular thanks to the birth of new parties such as Silvio Berlusconi's *Forza Italia*, a party that already embodied all the typical aspects of current populisms, starting from the use of the media, which replaced the parties themselves as a tool for mobilising public opinion.[13] However, as observed by Fusaro,[14] neither *Forza Italia* nor leaders of parties born in the same period (in particular Antonio di Pietro and Umberto Bossi) can be defined as fully populist,[15] since they accepted dialogue with opposing political forces and recognised the role of the European Union

6 Fusaro (n 4) 3–4; Mancosu (n 3) 75.

7 Diamanti and Lazar (n 2) 24; Mancosu (n 3), 76.

8 Yves Mény, *Popolo ma non troppo. Il malinteso democratico* (Il Mulino 2019), 90.

9 Fusaro (n 4) 6.

10 Diamanti and Lazar (n 2) 11–12.

11 Fusaro (n 4) 7.

12 As noted by Mény (n 8) 158–159, the early 1990s showed an increase in populism in every context, probably due to the collapse of the Soviet bloc. Fusaro (n 4) 7. As a phenomenon, the increase of populism was, however, not fully understood and was minimised as a particular kind of right-wing extremism, and therefore there was a failure to analyse it correctly and to deal with it.

13 Mény and Surel (n 3) 111.

14 Fusaro (n 4) 7–8.

15 Diamanti and Lazar (n 2) 11–12 argue instead that *Forza Italia*, *Lega Nord* and *Italia dei Valori* represent examples of real populism, in particular defining Di Pietro's party as a 'justicialist populism'.

and the importance of international obligations. Yet, according to the same author,[16] it was precisely the use of populist forms of communication on the part of those representing the institutions that constituted a key element in the development in the following years – and in particular after the economic crisis of 2008[17] – of the modern parties, which are openly and proudly populist. It might, in fact, be remembered that the current President of the Italian Council of Ministers, i.e. Prime Minister Giuseppe Conte, has clearly stated on more than one occasion that he is proudly populist.[18]

The *Lega* and the *Movimento5Stelle* undoubtedly stand out among the Italian populist parties, being characterised by the typical elements of traditional populism, in particular the aversion to the parliamentary and European elites and, in the specific case of the *Lega*, to the migratory phenomenon as a problem of security and as an injury to the integrity of the 'Italian people', which must be protected from the 'other' represented by migrants;[19] it is also the main theme, as will be seen, of the *decreti sicurezza*. To these 'traditional' elements is then added, in the case of both parties, the constant use of the web as a direct communication tool, so much so that some authors talk of '*webpopulism*'.[20] For these reasons, it is therefore possible to affirm, as previously noted, that the Italian context is without doubt characterised by the strong presence of populism(s), according to the elements defining such phenomena.[21]

Nevertheless, even though this is an undeniable trend, it is also true that Italy cannot be defined as a 'populist regime', since there has never been a political movement or party, however openly and self-declaredly populist it might be, which has been able to move outside constitutional boundaries and to affect their foundation.[22] In this regard, it is particularly interesting to see how this capacity for resistance of the Italian constitutional order has been particularly put to the test by the parliamentary majority composed by the *Lega* and *Movimento5Stelle*, through two proposals for constitutional reform, both concerning the strengthening of direct democracy processes at the expense of the parliamentary one, and both markedly populist, with the

16 Fusaro (n 4) 8.

17 A typical reason for the birth of populist movements, as noted by Diamanti and Lazar (n 2) 31 ff. and Mény and Surel (n 3) 111.

18 Mény (n 8) 182.

19 Diamanti and Lazar (n 2) 17.

20 Ibid. 119.

21 Ibid.

22 An example that may be recalled is Judgment No. 262 of 2009, where the *Corte Costituzionale* declared the unconstitutionality of Law No. 124 of 2008, introduced by the will of the then President of the Council, Silvio Berlusconi, in order to grant to the four highest political offices (i.e. President of the Republic, President of the Council, President of the Senate and President of the Deputies' Chamber) a substantial immunity from criminal proceedings, through their suspension for the duration of the mandate. This was initiated with the aim, in theory, of protecting these offices from damage to the exercise of their functions deriving from a long judicial procedure, which in any case has no constitutional basis (Judgment No. 262, §§ 7.33 and 8) and which had in fact the aim of suspending various proceedings, which had just started, against Silvio Berlusconi himself.

intention of subverting the democratic representative system in favour of a populist model of the state.

The first reform, which has been definitively approved by the Italian Parliament,[23] concerns the reduction in the number of the members of Parliament, bringing it down from 945 (630 deputies and 315 senators) to 600 (400 deputies and 200 senators). As argued by scholars such as Algostino,[24] the reform should be considered markedly populist since, although justified by the (typically populist) argument that it reduces the numbers of the parliamentary elite and the excessive costs of politics, it actually undermines the spaces of representation and the opportunities for dialogue between the majority and the minority, which represent the true fulcrum of a pluralist democracy. As a result of this serious wound to minority political forces, the reform would therefore lead to an authoritarian state, where only the majority is recognised.

As regards the second reform proposal, which is still under discussion and must be read together with the previous one for its effects on the representative system,[25] it aims to strengthen the instrument of the popular law initiative, envisaged from Article 71, second paragraph, of the Italian Constitution, stating that '[t]he people may initiate legislation by proposing a bill drawn up in sections and signed by at least fifty-thousand voters'.

The reform proposal aims to strengthen this instrument by introducing a 'deliberative' or 'propositional' referendum, which would be called for if a law initiative is not approved by the Parliament within 18 months, or if it is approved with substantial changes. As with the previous reform, this also hides, behind the intent to strengthen direct democracy and therefore the will of the people, a clearly populist and authoritarian intent. This is mainly due to the role that the reform attributes to the committee of the promoters of the law initiative: they can indeed renounce the referendum, acting as the only negotiators with the Parliament,[26] thus becoming subjects within the political debate,[27] even though they have no representative function as regards the electorate nor any political responsibility towards it.[28] The reform would therefore

23 With a very wide approval, coming from 553 members out of the 600 total voters of the Chamber of Deputies, and moreover following the change in the majority of the Government, confirming that now the communication tools and populist propaganda are well established, even in parties that are not considered populist.

24 Alessandra Algostino, Perché ridurre il numero dei parlamentari è contro la democrazia (2019) forumcostituzionale.it, 30 September 2019, 8.

25 Enzo Cheli (2019), Intervento alla Tavola Rotonda AIC, 'Iniziativa legislativa e referendum, le proposte di revisione costituzionale', (2019) 1–2 Osservatorio Costituzionale, 181; Massimo Luciani, Intervento alla Tavola Rotonda AIC, 'Iniziativa legislative e referendum, le proposte di revisione costituzionale' (2019) 1–2 Osservatorio Costituzionale, 200.

26 Luciani (n 26) 206.

27 Giulio M. Salerno, Intervento alla Tavola Rotonda AIC, 'Iniziativa legislative e referendum, le proposte di revisione costituzionale' (2019) 1–2 Osservatorio Costituzionale 226.

28 Michele Belletti, 'I rischi di sbilanciamento e di contrapposizione tra democrazia partecipativa e democrazia rappresentativa nel ddl AS n. 1089, di riforma costituzionale, recante Disposizioni in materia di iniziativa legislativa popolare e di referendum' (2019) federalismi.it, 22 May 2019 7ff.

essentially introduce a sort of extra-parliamentary elite,[29] capable of distorting the function of the referendum, complementary to the representative dynamics, attributing to it instead a power of opposition and subversion of the parliamentary will.[30] This therefore transforms the promoting committee into an alternative legislator,[31] which could well exploit the new technologies, exactly as populist movements do, to exploit and further accentuate the plebiscite nature that every call for a referendum naturally possesses.[32]

Like the previous constitutional reform, therefore, the one relating to the strengthening of the popular law initiative also shows a clear subversive tendency of the current representative and parliamentary order, thus further confirming that the Italian context is characterised by the presence of strong populist movements and political parties.

A very evident tendency, which is further demonstrated in the normative acts introduced by the majority *Movimento5Stelle-Lega*, in particular, is the aforementioned '*decreti sicurezza*'.

10.2 The so-called '*decreti sicurezza*' and the containment of illegal migrants

Proceeding to the analysis of the two decrees, these are the Law Decree no. 113 of 2018, or '*Security and immigration decree*', and the Decree no. 53 of 2019, containing '*Urgent provisions regarding public order and security*', also known as '*Security Decree* bis'.

The importance of these provisions for the present analysis is justified by their markedly populist imprint, which allows us, as will be seen in the rest of this contribution, to analyse their impact on the constitutional order and its ability to react to them, in particular by means of the common judges and the Constitutional Court.

29 Pasquale Pasquino, 'Popolo o élite? Il referendum propositivo e la retorica della democrazia diretta' (2019) lacostituzione.info, 23 April 2019.

30 Ida Angela Nicotra, 'Referendum propositivo e democrazia rappresentativa: alla ricerca di una sintesi' (2019) federalismi.it, 22 May 2019, 8.

31 Pasquino (n 30).

32 Adele Anzon Demmig, 'L'iniziativa legislativa popolare "indiretta" (c.d. referendum propositivo) nel progetto di legge costituzionale in itinere' (2019) forumcostituzionale.it, 22 March 2019, 2–3; Antonino Spadaro, Su alcuni rischi, forse mortali, della democrazia costituzionale contemporanea. Prime considerazioni (2017) 1 Rivista AIC 9.

Moreover, there are further problems, which the reform proposal does not consider, in delegating the solution to a future implementation law. One of the most significant problems is the lack of regulation on the relationships that could emerge not only among several popular law proposals on the same subject, but also between the popular law proposals and those of parliamentary or governmental initiative, which could, in theory, remain ineffective (Ugo de Siervo, Intervento alla Tavola Rotonda AIC, 'Iniziativa legislativa e referendum, le proposte di revisione costituzionale' (2019) 1–2 Osservatorio Costituzionale 236–238). This creates the potential for the atrophy of parliamentary activity on the matters which are subjects of popular initiative(s), which on the contrary would have the certainty of leading to a legislative text, albeit with minimal modifications: a fast track, in essence, to which no other law proposal has access. Belletti (n 29) 6.

Indeed, as can be clearly seen from the title of the first decree, these provisions actually represent two markedly populist measures, in particular in terms of the xenophobic and racist character that distinguishes populist movements, especially if expressed by right- and extreme-right-wing parties. In fact, defining 'security and immigration' as goals of the decree, it clearly recalls the *topos* of the foreigner as the main cause of public safety problems in the country.[33]

A *topos*, a goal that is in clear contrast to the personalist principle expressed by the Italian Constitution in Article 2,[34] which, read together with the ample right of asylum recognised in Article 10, paragraph 3, and the opening to the international community in name of the values of peace and justice according to Article 11, would impose a very different treatment of the foreigner, who should be considered as a person, and who should be entitled – just like any citizen – to universal and intangible rights. The two latter provisions indeed state, respectively, that:

> A foreigner who is denied the effective exercise of the democratic liberties guaranteed by the Italian Constitution in his or her own country has the right of asylum in the territory of the Italian Republic, in accordance with the conditions established by law;

And that:

> Italy rejects war as an instrument of aggression against the freedom of other peoples and as a means for the settlement of international disputes.
>
> Italy agrees, on conditions of equality with other States, to the limitations of sovereignty that may be necessary to a world order ensuring peace and justice among the Nations.
>
> Italy promotes and encourages international organisations having such ends.

Beyond the obvious doubts regarding the legitimacy of the use of the instrument of the emergency decree, unjustified both by the absence of the requirements of necessity and urgency and by the heterogeneity of the content,[35] both decrees in fact present numerous provisions that go against these principles, limiting the protection of rights not only to irregular immigrants, but also to asylum seekers.

33 Alessandra Algostino, 'Il decreto "sicurezza e immigrazione" (decreto legge n. 113 del 2018): estinzione del diritto di asilo, repressione del dissenso e diseguaglianza' (2018) 2 Costituzionalismo.it 173.

34 According to the personalist principle, expressed in Article 2 of the Italian Constitution, there is an ontological priority of the human being with respect to the State, and the latter has a constitutional obligation to grant the development, in every aspect, of the personality of each individual (Anna Maria Poggi, *Per un 'diverso' Stato sociale. La parabola del diritto all'istruzione nel nostro Paese* (Il Mulino 2019) 75ff. The text of Article 2 states, in its first paragraph, that 'The Republic recognises and guarantees the inviolable rights of the person, as an individual and in the social groups where human personality is expressed'.

35 Algostino (n 34) 168–170.

In particular, the first Law Decree substantially eliminated the residence permit for humanitarian reasons, limiting it to a few specific cases, while extending the hypothesis of a limitation of personal freedom to foreigners, both by prolonging the time of detention in the reception centres for foreigners awaiting forced repatriation, which could reach 180 days, and by providing that asylum seekers could be detained for identification purposes, for the same number of days: a treatment that is hardly compatible with the right to asylum recognised by the Constitution. The decree also shows a clear populist tendency in its provisions aimed at suppressing dissent and punishing social hardship, for example by tightening the penalties for road blockades and illegal occupation of buildings.

The 'safety bis' decree represents a reinforcement of the previous one, containing provisions for combating illegal immigration, and for strengthening the effectiveness of administrative action in support of security policies. Among these, in order to emphasise the populist and xenophobic nature of the provision, the one that stands out the most is the attribution to the Ministry of the Interior, as national authority for public security, of the power to limit or prohibit the entry, transit or docking of ships in territorial waters for reasons of order and public safety, with the provision of sanctions between ten and fifty thousand euros for the commanders of any ships that do not respect the prohibitions imposed. This is a provision which is clearly adopted in order to limit the intervention of the various NGOs operating in the Mediterranean dedicated to the rescue of migrants, and which also represents a clear consequence of the numerous interventions of the former Minister of the Interior, Matteo Salvini, aimed at preventing them from entering and docking on Italian territory.

10.3 The application of the constitutionally conforming interpretation

The two Security Decrees therefore undoubtedly constitute an example of a clearly populist-inspired measure, characterised in particular by a xenophobic and foreigner-hostile inspiration, and aimed at suppressing dissent and minorities' right to expression, which features various elements of doubtful legitimacy on the constitutional level.

Therefore, the discussions to reform and mitigate the scope of these measures, recently launched after the change in the Government majority, and which must be monitored in the future, must be undoubtedly deemed as positive. Pending such reforms, in order to proceed in the analysis outlined in the previous paragraph – that is, to understand whether or not these markedly populist provisions can stand up to the examination of the Italian constitutional order – it is necessary to question whether the common judges have sufficient tools to limit the negative effects of the two decrees, or whether instead recourse to the Constitutional Court is needed.

The answer to this question is positive, and it resides in the interpretative tool of the so-called '*constitutionally conforming interpretation*'[36] or '*adjust-*

36 Giusi Sorrenti, *L'interpretazione conforme a Costituzione* (Giuffrè 2006).

ing interpretation',[37] that is, the duty of all common judges to apply the provisions of the law even though these present some doubts regarding constitutional legitimacy, and overcoming such doubts by means, specifically, of an interpretation that allows a reading of it according to the Constitution. This mechanism, developed primarily by Italian constitutional jurisprudence in order to maintain the declaration of constitutional illegitimacy as a last resort, thus making it possible to 'save' the provision if it is possible to interpret it in accordance with the Constitution, subsequently developed as a real '*doctrine of conforming interpretation*', which directly concerns the common judge and his/her role as interpreter of the law.

It seems appropriate to briefly outline the development of the doctrine of conforming interpretation in the Italian constitutional context, which can be divided into three time phases.[38]

The first phase, between 1956 and the first half of the 1970s, saw the Italian Constitutional Court exclusively adopt the role of 'conforming interpreter' of the constitutional charter. This was done, on the one hand, in order to eliminate from the legal system or adapt to it the old legislation enacted prior to the Constitution and which conflicted with its provisions; and on the other hand, because the common judges had not yet developed sufficient constitutional sensitivity.

The second phase started in 1965, in the years in which another interpretative doctrine was itself affirmed, that is, the 'living law' doctrine, according to which the text of the provision should not represent the sole basis of the interpretation of the Court, but instead that the judges should also consider the way in which the provision is mainly interpreted.[39] The Court would therefore not have to declare a rule illegitimate if the prevailing interpretation is in accordance with the Constitution.[40]

37 Alessandro Pace, 'I limiti dell'interpretazione "adeguatrice"' (1963) Giurisprudenza Costituzionale.

38 For a more detailed analysis of the historical evolution of conforming interpretation in the Italian constitutional context, please refer to Giuseppe Laneve, 'L'interpretazione conforme a Costituzione: problemi e prospettive di un sistema diffuso di applicazione costituzionale all'interno di un sindacato (che resta) accentrato' (2011) federalismi.it, 7 September 2011, 14ff.

39 This process started, in particular, with Judgments No. 11 and 52 of 1965.

40 Although, as pointed out by Martinuzzi (Alessandro Martinuzzi, 'Il ritorno senz'armi su un vecchio campo di battaglia: nota alle sentt. nn. 1 e 3 del 2015 della Corte costituzionale' (2015) forumcostituzionale.it, 13 March 2015, 9), living law can, on the contrary, represent an obstacle to conforming interpretation, if the interpretation of living law proves to be contrary to the constitutional dictate; this is also the opinion of the Constitutional Court, as was well established in Judgment No. 350 of 1997, § 2. One critic of such evolution of conforming interpretation, Ruotolo (2011, 11), recalls the position of Pace (Alessandro Pace, 'Identità o differenza tra la questione di costituzionalità della norma e la questione di costituzionalità dell'interpretazione?' (1965) Giurisprudenza Costituzionale 1656), who observed instead that the Constitutional Court should always declare the illegitimacy of a norm, even if only one of the possible interpretations is unconstitutional. Therefore, in the words of Pace, 'unless a binding interpretation, in a sense in accordance with the Constitution, can be given, the acts must, in actual doubt as to their legitimacy, be declared unconstitutional'; Pace (n 38) 1073.

The third and final phase started in the second half of the 1990s and is distinguished by a clear favouring of the conforming interpretation made by the common judges, as can be clearly seen in a 2000 decision where the Court declared that all judges should consider,

> as the pre-eminent hermeneutic canon, the principle of constitutional supremacy. This requires the interpreter to opt, among as many abstract solutions that are possible, for the one that makes the provision in accordance with the Constitution.[41]

Despite this, as Napoli observed,[42] the presence of an interpretation that may lead to a result that does not comply with the constitutional provisions always allows the judge to raise a question of legitimacy before the Constitutional Court.

The efficacy of this interpretative tool, used in order to limit the scope of the Security Decrees, has emerged in particular in some recent rulings of the Courts of Bologna, Genova and Firenze, all of which relate to the interpretation of Article 13 of the first Security Decree, regarding enrolment in the population register. With regards to this, Article 13 of the Decree in fact provides that a residence permit does not constitute a title of registration. This has led several public offices to deny the requests for enrolment presented by several foreign applicants, including an asylum seeker who appealed to the aforementioned Courts to challenge these decisions.

In particular, the Court of Bologna, acting similarly to what was done in a previous judgment of the Court of Firenze (RG 361/2019, 18 March 2019), and in a subsequent one by the Court of Genova (RG 2365/2019, 22 May 2019), imposed, in its decision of 22 May 2019, that the asylum seeker's application for registration should be accepted, based on a conforming interpretation of the aforementioned provision, representing the first case of this kind as regards the Security Decree. In fact, as justified in the sentence, such a provision does not entail a general prohibition on foreigners enrolling on the register, which would represent a clear violation of the equality and non-discrimination principle and would therefore impose a declaration of unconstitutionality on the part of the Constitutional Court. On the contrary, such a violation was not found in the contested provision by the aforementioned courts, who could therefore interpret them in accordance with the Constitution, understanding them in the sense that the residence permit must not (and cannot) be considered as the sole requirement for entry in the population registry, since, as also evidenced by the courts, this has never been the case. Enrolment in the registry depends on several factors, which are assessed by the public offices: these do include the residence permit in the case of foreign applicants, which

41 Judgment No. 113 of 2000, § 3.

42 Cristina Napoli, 'A proposito della lingua italiana nelle Università (sentenza n. 42 del 2017) l'opportunità dell'intervento della Corte attenua l'onere di interpretazione conforme?' (2017) 2 Quaderni Costituzionali 367, commenting on Judgment No. 42 of 2017.

is therefore subject to evaluation, but does not represent, in any case, a determining factor, as underlined by the Court of Bologna itself.

The provision can be interpreted in this sense in the light of the context in which it is placed, above all the constitutional one, in consideration above all of the protection of fundamental rights, for which there can be no discrimination between citizens and foreigners. The enrolment on the population registers, in fact, despite being the result of a mere anagraphic identification, is in particular a necessary requirement for access to various rights: school enrolment, signing of an employment contract, determination of revenue values for access to social benefits, etc.

An interesting question, which must be examined, is whether the judges have correctly used the instrument of the conforming interpretation, or if instead it was necessary to appeal to the Constitutional Court.

The first limitation of the conforming interpretation is naturally represented by the wording of the provision: the judge cannot transgress it, move in a substantial way to disapply it or find a meaning that is not there. This does not mean that the judge must stop at the literal criterion, since systematic (and constitutional) interpretation is possible, and indeed necessary: from this perspective, a conforming interpretation is almost a kind of logical-systematic interpretation. The judge should raise an issue of constitutional legitimacy only when the provision has an unambiguous wording, from which an interpretation conforming to the Constitution cannot be derived. In this respect – which also pertains to the duty of conforming interpretation as a requirement of admissibility for raising a question of constitutional legitimacy – it is appropriate to consider how constitutional jurisprudence has evolved with respect to Judgment No. 356 of 1996. In this judgment, the Constitutional Court indeed stated that the provision is illegitimate only when it is impossible to give a constitutional interpretation, while more recent decisions[43] consider the duty sufficiently respected if a conforming interpretation is difficult or improbable. Considering this, it seems that the decision of the Court of Bologna has complied with this criterion, as the provision of the Security Decree may not be interpreted as unequivocal, so as not to allow a systematic and conforming interpretation.

A second limitation, particularly problematic, is then represented by the so-called 'living law'. That is, when facing an unconstitutional interpretation of a provision, which has been consolidated within the jurisprudence even if the provision allows a conforming interpretation, the judge is free to follow the latter with, however, a high risk that the decision will be annulled at the subsequent level of judgment. The question of 'living law' presents problems even in a case in which the judge deems it necessary to appeal to the Constitutional Court, which would face a difficult alternative: declare the illegitimacy of the provision, ignoring the possible conforming interpretation;

43 Such as Judgment No. 42 of 2017.

or reject the appeal with an interpretative sentence, which would, however, conflict with the consolidated interpretation.[44]

Even in this respect, however, the decision of the Court of Bologna, as well as the other decisions mentioned, does not present such issues, as no unconstitutional case law has yet been consolidated, and indeed, given the similar rulings of the Courts of Firenze and Genova, an opposite tendency seems to be affirming itself.

This seems, in fact, to be confirmed, as recalled by Chinaglia,[45] by the numerous court orders that followed the ones issued by the Courts of Bologna, Genova and Firenze.[46] The same author[47] nevertheless recalls the presence, of some court orders in the opposite direction as well,[48] with which a question of constitutional legitimacy was raised before the Constitutional Court, therefore expressing the belief, contrary to the currently prevailing interpretation, that the conforming interpretation does not represent a sufficient instrument for the protection of human rights, guaranteed by the Constitution and violated by the Law Decree, in particular on the basis of the observation, common to all court orders, that the intent of the legislator cannot be ignored by the interpreter. Therefore, given the aforementioned objectives of the Decree, which are openly populist and in contrast with the constitutional dictate, the only possible interpretation would be to consider the provisions of the decree as illegitimate, thus justifying the appeal to the Constitutional Court.[49]

It will therefore be of extreme interest, in the near future, to observe whether the Constitutional Court will follow the orientation of the conforming interpretation, or if it instead will deem a more incisive intervention more appropriate, declaring the contested provisions of the Security Decree unconstitutional.

44 As well emphasised by the Constitutional Court in the aforementioned Judgment No. 350 del 1997, § 2, if a provision has assumed in the 'living law' such an established unconstitutional interpretation, it is necessary that it is submitted to a judgment of constitutional legitimacy, given that the provision 'lives in such a rooted way in the legal order that it is hard to assume a change in the system without the intervention of the legislator or [of the] Court'. In this regard, please also refer to Martinuzzi (n 41) 9, and Ruotolo (M. Ruotolo, 'Quando il giudice deve "fare da sé"', in questionegiustizia.it, 22 ottobre 2018).

45 Francesca Chinaglia, 'Aspettando la Corte Costituzionale: gli orientamenti della giurisprudenza di merito sul divieto di iscrizione anagrafica del richiedente asilo' (2020) forumcostituzionale.it, 5 March 2020, 9.

46 In particular, the Author recalls the Court orders from: Prato (RG 1183/2019, 28 May 2019), Lecce (RG 5330/2019, 4 July 2019), Cagliari (RG 4521/2019,31 July 2019), Parma (RG 2379/2019, 2 August 2019), Catania (RG 12686/2019, 1 November 2019), Rome (RG 62244/2019, 25 November 2019), Bergamo (RG 8772/2019, 14 January 2020).

47 Chinaglia (n 46) 9.

48 Referring in particular to the court orders of the Courts of Ancona (RG 3081/2019, 29 July 2019), Milano (RG 14134/2019, 1 August 2019) and Salerno (RG 145, 153, 158 and 159/2019, 9 August 2019).

49 It is interesting to note that, despite considering the instrument of conforming interpretation insufficient to solve the issues deriving from the Security Decree, none of the court orders includes indications on interpretation methods that could instead represent a valid solution.

10.4 The (missing) intervention of the Constitutional Court on the Security Decrees

Before coming to the conclusions of this contribution, it should be noted that not only the common judges but also the Constitutional Court had the opportunity to deal with the legitimacy of the Security Decrees.

In fact, following the introduction of the first decree, eight Italian regions filed appeals against it to the Constitutional Court, complaining of an injury to their competences, procedural defects in the approval of the decree and above all – from a point of view which is particularly relevant for the topic discussed in this contribution, regarding the protection of individual rights – also in regard to the fulfilment of international obligations.[50] This relevance emerges even more when considering the fact that, among the objects of the appeal pertaining to individual rights, there was also the issue, examined by the Courts of Bologna, Genova and Firenze, of the enrolment of foreigners in the population registries. The applicant regions, in particular, stressed that the provision was a violation of the duty of protection of foreigners imposed in the aforementioned Article 10 of the Constitution, as well as the principle of equality, expressed by Article 3,[51] as the contested provision created an unreasonable discrimination between citizens and foreigners, who were also regularly resident in the territory thanks to their residence permit.[52]

This last profile, that of the protection of human rights, falls in particular within the doctrine of '*ridondanza*' (redundancy), that is to say the recourse by the Regions to parameters other than those of competence, in the event that a state regulation, in this case that of the Security Decree, still leads to an injury in the regional spheres of competence. That of redundancy, or 'indirect injury of competence',[53] represents a doctrine that has emerged since 1960,[54] as an exception to the general principle for constitutional appeals brought by Regions, expressed by the second paragraph of Article 127 of the Italian Constitution, which establishes that

> a Region may question the constitutional legitimacy of a State or regional law or measure having the force of law before the Constitutional Court

50 Diletta Tega, 'I ricorsi regionali contro il decreto sicurezza: la ridondanza dalla difesa delle competenze allo scontro sui diritti' (2019) 2 Quaderni Costituzionali 413.

51 Which indeed states that 'All citizens have equal social dignity and are equal before the law, without distinction of sex, race, language, religion, political opinion, personal and social conditions' and, at § 2, that 'It is the duty of the Republic to remove those obstacles of an economic or social nature which constrain the freedom and equality of citizens, thereby impeding the full development of the human person and the effective participation of all workers in the political, economic and social organisation of the country'.

52 Tega (n 51) 414.

53 Carlo Padula, 'Aggiornamenti in tema di ridondanza' (2019) 3 Le Regioni 762.

54 Starting from Judgment No. 32, where the Constitutional Court affirmed for the first time that Regions may lament the illegitimacy of provisions not related to their competence if these competences are still harmed by such provisions. See Padula (n 54) 739.

within sixty days from its publication, when it deems that said law or measure infringes upon its competence.

Thus, through the redundancy doctrine, a literal interpretation of this constitutional provision is avoided, allowing a wider range to regional appeals.

Over the years, however, there has been considerable uncertainty regarding the conditions of admissibility of regional appeals motivated by such a doctrine,[55] which in recent times has pushed the Constitutional Court to give it a better understanding,[56] in particular by defining the limits of appeals motivated by redundancy, defining a framework favourable for regional appeals.[57]

And it is in this context of reorganisation that Judgment No. 194 of 2019 fits in, with which the Constitutional Court has ruled on the appeals of the Regions against the first Security Decree, declaring them, however, inadmissible. In fact, the Court denied the applicability of the redundancy, first of all in consideration of the generality of the appeals, and because of their failure to indicate the regional competences that were assumed to have been violated,[58] and probably also in response to the reconstruction carried out in the appeal of the Piemonte Region,[59] according to which the regional appeal should instead always be admissible, for any type of defect of constitutionality, regardless of considerations on competences.[60]

Beyond the specific arguments on the appropriateness of using redundancy as a parameter for the regional appeal, however, the Court has failed to pronounce itself, even incidentally, on the matters covered by the appeal, without offering any indication in this regard.[61] In particular, as regards the provision relating to the enrolment of foreigners in public registries, the Court affirmed that it could not pronounce itself, in the absence of a consolidated application practice,[62] reserving the evaluation of the appealed provision to any future appeal. This motivation did not, however, convince Rauti,[63] who claimed that the mere hypothesis of the violation should have prompted the Court to rule on the matter, providing an interpretation of the provision that could resolve its doubts regarding constitutionality, and guiding the future decisions of the common judges.

55 Emanuele Rossi, 'Il fine meritevole giustifica l'utilizzo elastico dei mezzi: la Corte e la "ridondanza"' (2012) 1 Giurisprudenza Costituzionale, 300.

56 Starting from Judgment No. 5 of 2018.

57 Padula (n 54) 759.

58 § 5.4 of the Judgment.

59 § 30 of the appeal of the Piemonte Region, available at https://www.regione.piemonte.it.

60 Padula (n 54) 761.

61 Alessio Rauti, 'Il decreto sicurezza di fronte alla Consulta. L'importanza (e le incertezze) della sentenza n. 194 del 2019' (2020) forumcostituzionale.it, 29 February 2020, 13.

62 § 7.8 of the Judgment.

63 Rauti (n 62) 21, 23.

10.5 Conclusions

In conclusion, in the light of the analysis carried out in this chapter, it clearly emerges that Italy represents a context characterised by a strong presence of populist political forces, which can be also defined as a populist system. Such populism is also clearly affirmed and established in the normative production and in the recent constitutional reform proposals that put the very parliamentary representative system at risk.

However, responding to the central question of this work – that is, whether the Italian context presents sufficient jurisprudential tools to counter these phenomena, or instead it is necessary to introduce new ones – it can be affirmed with certainty that the instrument of constitutionally compliant interpretation constitutes an effective and sufficient means for each judge. This instrument indeed allows the judiciary, as seen in the recent cases presented before the Courts of Bologna, Firenze and Genova, to directly apply constitutional principles and values, thus exercising a kind of judicial review power to contest a clearly populist provision[64] which has discriminatory and racist intent, limiting its meaning within the boundaries imposed by the constitutionally guaranteed rights and freedoms.

These conclusions are further strengthened in consideration of Judgment No. 194 of the Italian Constitutional Court, which, as seen in the last paragraph of this contribution, did not take this important opportunity to take a concrete position on the populist measures included in the first Security Decree.

In other words, it appears that the Constitution contains in itself and in its fundamental principles all the elements necessary to counter the populist phenomenon through the decision of common judges, and the instrument of constitutionally conforming interpretation is the means available to each judge to give these principles concrete implementation.

64 On the topic of judicial review, please refer to Gianmario Demuro, *Costituzionalismo europeo e tutela multilivello dei diritti. Lezioni* (Giappichelli 2009).

11 Whatever works

Constitutional interpretation in Poland in times of populism

Wojciech Brzozowski

11.1 Introduction

The anatomy of constitutional populism is a matter of ultimate concern to so many public law scholars these days that even approaching this topic requires a great deal of boldness. With so many existing contributions on the democratic retrogression, how can one hope to shed a new light on the issue? Yet, when I was asked to prepare the Polish chapter to this volume on constitutional interpretation in times of populism, I thought to myself that the experience of Poland in this respect was, sadly but truly, unique and worth sharing.

The aim of this chapter is to find the answer to a classic Shakespearean question: is there a method in their madness? This time, however, the issue is not the political or legal technology of coming to power and holding on to it, so successfully deployed by the populist movements in Central Europe and elsewhere. In this respect, we know very well that there actually *is* a method in their madness – which, by the way, is not really madness after all, but rather a meticulous master plan – and that the populists tend to take pages from the same playbook, whoever may have written it first. They do indeed follow a very similar pattern when dealing with any constraints on state power and eliminating any checks upon the political branches of government, or limiting the rights of the political opposition and anyone who is not satisfied with the populist rule. We know this very well; in Poland, we know this all too well.

In fact, the question is much more demanding this time. Does constitutional populism bring any new quality, good or bad, to the art of legal interpretation? Has it developed any entirely new theories, doctrines or methods of interpretation which could be seen as a contribution to the legal science, or even as an alternative to the art of legal interpretation as we know it?

It is high time these questions received proper answers. For some time now, I could not help noticing the growing consternation among many Western scholars over their sense that they have failed to fully understand this phenomenon and have possibly missed something important from the recent developments in global constitutionalism. Such anxiety is only occasionally revealed in conference papers but is likely to spread rapidly in the *conversations de couloir*. Let me voice these doubts: Is this some new emerging theory which has not yet received sufficient attention but is inevitably going to transform contemporary constitutionalism? Isn't it our responsibility to comprehend it at all cost, even if we do not like what we learn? And when we understand the true nature of it, will it be possible to tame populist constitutionalism, like a wild animal which may not know how to behave with people but ultimately shares the same basic needs and instincts? In other words, and less metaphorically, can the populist interpretation be understood, and should legal science come to terms with it? In academia, this is inevitably the right approach to any emerging issue. Many great minds have been making attempts at understanding the contribution that populism brings to constitutional studies.[1]

In this chapter, I will not seek any general explanations which would hold true for any populist regime. I am not even sure if such explanations actually exist. Instead, I intend to add the missing puzzle piece to help the readers see the bigger picture – my puzzle piece depicting the Polish experience against the bigger picture of illiberal constitutionalism, as far as constitutional interpretation is concerned. I will start with some preliminary comments regarding the methodology and the criteria for assessment in order to ensure a sounder footing for the study (Section 11.2). Subsequently, I will examine four aspects of recent constitutional practice which should be helpful in determining what is specific about constitutional interpretation in Poland in times of populism (Section 11.3). Then I will proceed to explore the potential reasons for adopting this specific approach (Section 11.4). In the last part, I will attempt to answer if populist constitutionalism can be seen as 'new constitutionalism' (Section 11.5).

11.2 Preliminaries

Before turning to the main argument, some preliminary comments need to be made.

First, in this study I will overlook the scholarly discussion on the nature of political populism, its definitions and empirical models, or the discontent that fuels it. Populism has often been described as a chameleonic concept, swiftly adjusting to popular demand but lacking any core values. For the purposes of this study, it suffices to resort to Bojan Bugarič's laconic observation that populism's distinctive features are 'the prioritization of popular sovereignty, direct democracy, and a strong emphasis on anti-elitism'.[2] Neither will I reflect on the question of whether the political regime installed in Poland in

1 For a critical analysis of these attempts, see Kriszta Kovács and Gábor Attila Tóth, 'The Age of Constitutional Barbarism' (*Verfassungsblog*, 7 September 2019) www.verfassungsblog.de/the-age-of-constitutional-barbarism accessed 14 April 2020 (citing Armin von Bogdandy and Mark Tushnet).

2 Bojan Bugarič, 'Central Europe's Descent into Autocracy: A Constitutional Analysis of Authoritarian Populism' (2019) 15 European Constitutional Law Review 597, 598.

2015 should be classified as populist. Instead, I will assume that it is such a regime, which to many, myself included, seems far from any doubt or dispute. I do not see any necessity to elaborate further on what has been so convincingly proven by other scholars.[3]

Second, it needs to be remembered that constitutional interpretation is not the exclusive domain of the constitutional courts, or of any courts at all, for that matter. It must not be reduced to judicial interpretation of the constitution. There is an established tendency to assume that it is the courts' understanding of national constitutions that reveals their ultimate meaning and that the intellectual process of reaching this understanding needs to be subjected to some consistent interpretive methodology, even if the boundaries between revealing the meaning and creating it are often unclear.[4] Yet, this is true only as long as the courts, and especially the constitutional court, have the last word in constitutional disputes. This is not necessarily the case with political regimes which question the rule of law and are drifting away from democracy, and certainly not the case of Poland.

It needs to be remembered that the populist revolution relied greatly on constitutional arguments and interpretations put forward by the political branches of government and by their committed supporters – interpretations which were proposed and enforced precisely against the judges and the courts. This is particularly evident with regard to the initial phase of the populist rule in Poland, when the independent institutions such as courts were trying to defend the established interpretive tradition from the populist attack. In this phase, they were typically neutralized and destroyed by means of non-judicial interpretation of the constitution promoted by the legislative and executive branches of government.[5] Only after the constitutional

3 See, notably, Wojciech Sadurski, *Poland's Constitutional Breakdown* (Oxford University Press 2019) 20–27. However, it has also been argued that most of the common characteristics of real populism are either not practiced in authoritarian populist regimes or, at best, they serve only as rhetoric; see Gábor Halmai, 'Populism, Authoritarianism and Constitutionalism' (2019) 20 German Law Journal 296, 313.

4 Jeffrey Goldsworthy, 'Constitutional Interpretation' in Michel Rosenfeld and András Sajó (eds.), *The Oxford Handbook of Comparative Constitutional Law* (Oxford University Press 2012) 690.

5 Sadurski (n 3) 61–79. On the technique of 'neutralization' or 'disablement' of the constitutional court, see Lech Garlicki, 'Constitutional Court and Politics: The Polish Crisis' in Christine Landfried (ed.), *Judicial Power: How Constitutional Courts Affect Political Transformations* (Cambridge University Press 2019) 159. See also Marcin Stębelski, 'Parliament versus Constitutional Court – Selected Issues Pertaining to the Constitutional Dispute in Poland' in Marcel Szabó, Petra Lea Láncos, and Réka Varga (eds.), *Hungarian Yearbook of International Law and European Law 2016* (Eleven International Publishing 2017); Mirosław Granat, 'Constitutional Judiciary in Crisis: The Case of Poland' in Zoltán Szente and Fruzsina Gárdos-Orosz (eds.), *New Challenges to Constitutional Adjudication in Europe: A Comparative Perspective* (Routledge 2018); Adam Krzywoń, 'La crisis constitucional en Polonia (2015–2017): como cuestionar el sistema del equilibrio constitucional en dos años' (2018) 41 Teoría y Realidad Constitucional 359.

court had been taken over, did it start speaking the populist language.[6] In brief, both constitutional adjudication and constitutional practice should be considered when exploring the populist contribution to constitutional theory.

Third, when asking whether new tools and methods have been developed, one should always confront rhetoric with real life. Admittedly, studying the speeches of the populist leaders, such as Viktor Orbán's widely commented panegyric on illiberal democracy,[7] can be a great help in demystifying political intentions and guessing what the future may bring, but declared political intentions do not need to be reflected in the adopted legal measures. While speeches are supposed to be politically attractive, legal measures are meant to be effective, and it is not always easy to reconcile these two qualities.[8] This is why I will not limit myself to the official populist agenda, which usually stresses the need to bring the law back to the people, to restore national sovereignty or to eliminate foreign influence from the decision-making process. In the end, it is the hidden agenda and the legal arguments that matter, not the oratory skills which paved the way for the populists to take power.

Last, I will rely on three criteria in assessing whether the populist approach to constitutional interpretation opens a new chapter in constitutional theory, and these are: novelty, consistency and theoretical soundness.

By novelty I mean that an approach should be genuinely fresh and unique. Any doctrine (or a method or tool) which proposes only minor corrections to the pre-existing doctrines (methods, tools) is not new within this sense; neither is any doctrine which rejects the previous constitutional rules simply because they were allegedly being applied by morally corrupt people who acted in bad will or served foreign masters, or cared only for their private interests.

The consistency of the approach means that actions required or justified by such an approach should demonstrate commitment to some coherent abstract principles. These principles should not just serve some one-time strategy but ought to remain relatively stable over time; this condition should not be exceedingly difficult to meet, as populist regimes have emerged recently and have not had much time to evolve.

6 Sadurski (n 3) 79–84; Wojciech Brzozowski, 'Can the Constitutional Court Accelerate Democratic Backsliding? Lessons from the Polish Experience' in Martin Belov (ed.), *The Role of Courts in Contemporary Legal Orders* (Eleven International Publishing 2019).

7 Prime Minister Viktor Orbán's Speech at the 25th Bálványos Summer Free University and Student Camp, 26 July 2014, www.kormany.hu/en/the-prime-minister/the-prime-minister-s-speeches/prime-minister-viktor-orban-s-speech-a-the-25th-balvanyos-summer-free-university-and-student-camp accessed 14 April 2020.

8 It would seem that there was a reason behind Jan-Werner Müller dedicating separate chapters of his brilliant tractate on populism to 'What populists say' and 'What populists do, or populism in power'; Jan-Werner Müller, *What Is Populism?* (University of Pennsylvania Press 2016).

Finally, theoretical soundness implies that the approach should demonstrate a considerable level of cogency, seriousness and completeness, and be amenable to academic description.

11.3 Change or continuity?

Since 2015, which marks the beginning of the constitutional crisis, the struggle over the rule of law in Poland has reached a level of complexity which makes it virtually impossible to do justice to the course of events in a book chapter. Most of them have been captured and explored elsewhere, notably in Wojciech Sadurski's excellent book,[9] but it should be borne in mind that every month brings new developments: the story continues and the decay advances. Or, as the old Polish proverb says, the deeper one goes into the forest, the more trees there are.

This is why I will focus only on four aspects which I consider to be essential for the assessment of how constitutional interpretation works in times of populism in Poland. These four aspects are: (1) the approach to the limits of judicial power, which appears to be the key problem; (2) the preferred methods of constitutional interpretation; (3) the approach to the pre-existing *acquis constitutionnel* (encompassing both earlier findings of the constitutional court and earlier practice) and (4) the approach to international law, and to EU law in particular.

11.3.1 The limits of judicial power

The cornerstone of the populist critique of liberal democracy is the profound distrust of the elites and the judiciary. Anyone who plans to study the history of populism needs to be prepared to go through endless tirades on the excessive power of the courts and about the need to bring the power back to people, which obviously implies taking it away from those who stole it to those who should own it. It comes as no surprise that the role of the villain in this casting has been assigned to independent professional bodies such as the courts, which are repeatedly accused of being undemocratic and exempt from any social control. The righteous owners, from whom the power had been stolen, are of course the ordinary people. This is not to say that these mythical ordinary people can now expect to be suddenly empowered by means of direct democracy, for populist constitutionalism has very little to do with popular constitutionalism.[10] Luckily, the will of the people happens to be embodied in

9 Sadurski (n 3).

10 Ana Micaela Alterio, 'El constitucionalismo popular y el populismo constitucional como categorías constitucionales' in Roberto Gargarella and Roberto Niembro Ortega (eds.), *Constitucionalismo progresista: Retos y perspectivas: Un homenaje a Mark Tushnet* (Universidad Nacional Autónoma de México 2016); Jan-Werner Müller, 'Populism and Constitutionalism' in Cristóbal Rovira Kaltwasser, Paul Taggart, Paulina Ochoa Espejo, and Pierre Ostiguy (eds.), *The Oxford Handbook of Populism* (Oxford University Press 2017).

parliament's vote! And that suggests – if irony is to be abandoned from this moment – that what we are really dealing with here is a power conflict between the political branches of government and the judiciary.

At the early stage of the Polish constitutional crisis, the foundations of the populist legal philosophy were probably best explained by the late Lech Morawski, one of the quasi-judges of the Polish Constitutional Tribunal.[11] His views on the ongoing conflict were presented at a conference held at the University of Oxford,[12] where they sparked a major controversy. In his presentation, Morawski quoted Béla Pokol, a Hungarian constitutional judge, who had been warning about the dangers of the 'juristocratic' system of government.[13] One of Morawski's points was that such a system actually existed in Poland, and having replaced the traditional forms of government, it allowed judges, sometimes by a narrow majority, to decide on legislation and exercise supreme legislative power. The irony of the situation should not escape our attention: someone who considered himself to be a member of a constitutional court, then under attack from an anti-judicial political movement, complained about judges being too powerful when compared with the political branches of government. In the end, Morawski declared: 'the opposition acts as if the Tribunal were the owner of the Constitution and had the exclusive right to decide about its meaning. I strongly reject such a position'.

This bizarre lecture was not a one-time show. Morawski's argument has been recently repeated by Jarosław Kaczyński, the leader of the Polish populists, who claimed that the power of the courts had nothing to do with democracy and that it was a system of government that best served oligarchy.[14] It can be assumed that this is the official doctrine of the ruling party. If taken seriously, this approach should lead to at least three conclusions with regard to constitutional interpretation: (1) that judicial activism is essentially wrong, and judicial restraint is the only right conduct for a judge; (2) that there is no need to develop any new or extraordinary tools for constitutional adjudication; and (3) that the constitutional court must not have the final word in constitutional disputes.

11 The term 'quasi-judges', used interchangeably with 'duplicate judges', is typically used when referring to persons elected to seats in the Polish Constitutional Tribunal which were not vacant at the moment of election. The exact timeline can be found in the Opinion on Amendments to the Act of 25 June 2015 on the Constitutional Tribunal of Poland, adopted by the Venice Commission at its 106th Plenary Session (Venice, 11–12 March 2016), CDL-AD(2016)001; or, in a more thrilling convention, in Sadurski (n 3) 61–70.

12 Lech Morawski, 'The Polish Constitutional Crisis and Institutional Self-Defence', www.trybunal.gov.pl/fileadmin/content/uroczystosci_spotkania_wizyty/2017/2017_05_09_Oxford/Wystapienie_prof._L.Morawskiego_w_Oxfordzie.pdf accessed 14 April 2020.

13 Surprisingly, no reference was made to another famous, and much older, book on judicial empowerment, which proposed the same term: Ran Hirschl, *Towards Juristocracy: The Origins and Consequences of the New Constitutionalism* (Harvard University Press 2007).

14 'Prezes PiS: Władza sądów nie ma nic wspólnego z demokracją', www.wgospodarce.pl/informacje/68088-prezes-pis-wladza-sadow-nie-ma-nic-wspolnego-z-demokracja accessed 14 April 2020.

Ironically, the new Constitutional Tribunal, now entirely deferential to the legislation proposed by the populist government, does not seem to be as restrained in its powers as one could have expected after listening to Morawski's and Kaczyński's speeches.

One of the judicial tools particularly distrusted by the populists was the concept of an interpretative judgment, that is, a judgment in which the Constitutional Tribunal does not invalidate the challenged provision in its entirety but quashes only one of its possible interpretations. The basis for suspicion was that this technique might effectively obscure the difference between constitutional review and constitutional interpretation. Morawski warned during his Oxford speech that

> [t]he Polish Constitution authorizes the Tribunal only to review the compliance of statutes and other normative acts with the Constitution, but not to give interpretative guidelines to courts and other state bodies in the operative parts of its decisions ... By means of interpretative judgements, the Tribunal creates constantly new rules or modifies the content of existing rules.[15]

But if anyone had thought that the new judges would no longer resort to this technique, they could not have been more wrong. It has been pushed to the extreme, because now the Constitutional Court does not simply provide the courts with guidelines for interpretation – it may now give an interpretation so detailed that it replaces the courts in deciding a case.

How is this possible? Obviously, such surprising outbursts of judicial activism may be reserved only for special occasions, such as when the validity of appointments to the Constitutional Court was being questioned before the Supreme Court. Technically, the Supreme Court is not entitled to review parliamentary decisions in personal matters, but in the course of civil proceedings, e.g. in a labour dispute, it can verify whether the person who acts in the name of a legal person, or a state body, has the right to represent it. This happened when the new president of the Constitutional Tribunal submitted her written position to the Supreme Court in an individual case. As the votes of the wrongfully appointed judges affected the appointment of the Tribunal's new president, this gave the Supreme Court a unique opportunity to question the validity of all these appointments.

The populist Constitutional Tribunal instantly realized that it needed to defend itself, and it did so by declaring that the opening provision of the Civil Procedure Code, which merely defines the notion of 'civil matters', was unconstitutional 'insofar as it pertains to evaluating the correctness of the process of electing a judge of the Constitutional Tribunal'.[16] The application which enabled the Tribunal to perform this peculiar review had been conveniently lodged right on time by a group of deputies of the ruling party,

15 Morawski (n 12).

16 CT judgment of 24 October 2017, K 10/17.

and it is noteworthy that it was heard within two months and one week, at an unusual speed. This emergency protocol most likely would not have been approved by Morawski, who had criticized the Tribunal harshly for departing from the chronological order of considering cases.

Another special occasion of this kind arose when the Constitutional Tribunal was expected by the populist party to save one of its leaders from criminal liability for abuse of power. It seemed problematic, and anything but obvious, to find a role for a constitutional court to play so that such a final result could be achieved. Yet, special needs apparently deserve special treatment.

The convict, now back in the political arena, had been sentenced to three years' imprisonment, but before his appeal could be heard, he was pardoned by the President of the Republic. This led to a fundamental question of whether the President can grant pardons at any time, even before the final sentence of the criminal court. This question could have been answered by the Supreme Court, which was about to assess the validity of the pardon. However, shortly before that, the Constitutional Tribunal interfered and found that the provisions of the Criminal Procedure Code, the Code of Procedure Concerning Misdemeanours and the Executive Penal Code 'insofar as they do not render amnesty granted in individual cases as a negative premise for conducting, respectively, criminal proceedings, proceedings on misdemeanours or criminal enforcement proceedings' were unconstitutional.[17] Needless to say, nobody could doubt that this judgment was tailored to one very special figure.

The same pattern was followed in the middle of the political storm which accompanied the attempts to remove the President of the Supreme Court, whose term of office was not about to expire as quickly as the populist party had expected. The Constitutional Tribunal came in handy again, this time setting the ground for political action by declaring that a provision of the Act on the Supreme Court 'insofar as it concerns the rules of procedure for selecting candidates for the position of the First President of the Supreme Court' was unconstitutional.[18] The 'insofar formula' is nothing new to the Tribunal's practice, but the use made of it by the populist judges is truly unusual, as it disguises individual decisions as constitutional review. Now, the Tribunal is abandoning even such a thin disguise: it has recently moved as far as to review the constitutionality of a Supreme Court's judgment, under the pretext that it was in fact a normative act.[19] This has been, arguably, the most flagrant abuse of power in the short history of the populist Tribunal.

It is also a great surprise how open the 'new' judges of the Supreme Court – which is still being packed at the time of writing of this chapter – are to the idea of freezing orders. When such interim measures were being adopted by the 'old' Constitutional Tribunal, in a helpless act of self-defence against the new legislation aimed at paralyzing the constitutional review, the very idea of a

17 CT judgment of 17 July 2018, K 9/17.
18 CT judgment of 24 October 2017, K 3/17.
19 CT judgment of 20 April 2020, U 2/20.

freezing order was bluntly rejected by the populists. Neither the parliament nor the President of the Republic respected the orders, announcing that the Constitutional Tribunal had manipulated the legal order and that it had no right to suspend duly enacted legislation. But it did not take long to see how the interim measures were being used to speed up the packing of the Supreme Court and to cripple the implementation of the recent judgment of the European Court of Justice,[20] which could effectively undermine the populist plan of taking over the judiciary. Freezing orders, originally taken from the civil procedure, now suddenly became part of the populist constitutional toolkit.

One more example: the 'old' Constitutional Tribunal used to be accused of excessive judicial activism, which allegedly amounted to depriving parliament of its power, and of knitting a tight net of constraints which left parliament helpless and unable to make decisions. The populists even invented a name for this: 'impossibilism', meaning that the law, and the constitution in particular, became an obstacle in achieving political goals and carrying out the desired reforms.[21] (In passing, it is hard not to note that this is exactly what the constitution is supposed to be: an obstacle to promoting antidemocratic agendas.) But now that the Constitutional Tribunal has been taken over by the populists, it is being openly used by the political branches of government as a rubber stamp.[22] It is expected to pronounce the constitutionality of measures which are obviously unconstitutional – precisely in order to avoid questioning them and taking them back in future. This clear abuse of the *res judicata* principle is yet another example of how the populist views on the judiciary change depending on the situation.

It is also fascinating to see how deeply convinced the populists have now become that the institution which should have the final word in the constitutional disputes is the Constitutional Tribunal. Whenever the new antidemocratic legislation on the Supreme Court is being criticized and dismissed

20 Joined cases C-585/18, C-624/18 and C-625/18 *AK and Others v Sąd Najwyższy* ECLI:EU:C:2019:982. In this judgment, the ECJ was confronted with the question whether the newly created Disciplinary Chamber of the Supreme Court, whose members had been appointed under circumstances raising legitimate doubts as to the independence and impartiality of the Chamber, offered sufficient guarantees of a fair trial. The ECJ did not answer that question openly but decided that a domestic court which had doubts about another court being independent should assess the matter itself. See Barbara Grabowska-Moroz and Jakub Jaraczewski, 'High Expectations: The CJEU Decision about the Independence of Polish Courts' (*Verfassungsblog*, 19 November 2019) www.verfassungsblog.de/high-expectations accessed 14 April 2020; Michał Krajewski and Michał Ziółkowski, 'The Power of "Appearances"' (*Verfassungsblog*, 26 November 2019) www.verfassungsblog.de/the-power-of-appearances accessed 14 April 2020. Shortly afterwards, one of the 'new' judges at the Supreme Court issued a freezing order aimed at preventing the remaining chambers of the Supreme Court from making such an assessment (SC, decision of 20 January 2020, V CSK 347/19).

21 Sadurski (n 3) 172–173.

22 Tomasz Tadeusz Koncewicz, 'Farewell to the Polish Constitutional Court' (*Verfassungsblog*, 9 July 2016) www.verfassungsblog.de/farewell-to-the-polish-constitutional-court accessed 14 April 2020.

as unconstitutional by legal scholars, the instant reaction of the populists is that until the Constitutional Tribunal has its word and the judgment is passed, any legislation is entitled to the presumption of constitutionality. The populists would have never said this before, when they questioned the legitimacy of the previous Act on the Constitutional Tribunal before its takeover. Apparently, the roles have changed – and a beggar who sits on the throne now speaks like the king.

11.3.2 The preferred methods of constitutional interpretation

It should be expected that the populist approach to legal interpretation, and most of all constitutional interpretation, would be hostile to the idea of departing from the literal meaning of the law. Any such divergence would automatically raise suspicions as to the intention of the interpreter: the plain meaning can be understood by anyone, while considering the purpose or the context of a legal norm introduces an element of uncertainty and requires professional skills. In his Oxford speech, Morawski argued that the law should be as precise as possible and that the constitution must not be interpreted as a living instrument, for it is not the role of the Constitutional Court to create or to change the law.[23]

Rendering the law easily understandable to 'ordinary folks' clearly belongs in the populist basket of slogans, but arguably, there is more to it than mere rhetoric: this praise of literal interpretation is consistent with the more general approach of disregard for the constitution. As Paul Blokker puts it, the populists tend to collapse the distinction between ordinary and constitutional politics and to downplay the constitution's status as a rigid, higher law.[24] Blurring this distinction implies the rejection of the distinctiveness of constitutional interpretation, which by its very nature relies greatly on the judge's reading and requires striking a fair balance between competing principles more often than happens with ordinary legislation. The alternative for the constitutional interpreter is to engage in a technical examination of isolated words and phrases, at the same time neglecting the existing case law and ultimately failing to see the bigger picture.[25]

23 Morawski (n 12).

24 Paul Blokker, 'Populism as a Constitutional Project' (2019) 17 International Journal of Constitutional Law 535, 545.

25 This new approach, of course, does not result from sheer ignorance. It is deliberately aimed at loosening the constitutional constraints, leaving more space for statutory regulation and in this way promoting what has been wittily called 'statutory anti-constitutionalism', i.e. a theoretical legal framework within which an unconstitutional result can be achieved by means of a series of statutory amendments; see Maciej Bernatt and Michał Ziółkowski, 'Statutory Anti-Constitutionalism' (2019) 28 Washington International Law Journal 487. In a much similar vein, Rosalind Dixon and David Landau describe the Polish populist strategy as 'as a combination of subconstitutional legislation and aggressive reinterpretations of the constitution'. See Rosalind Dixon and David Landau, '1989–2019: From Democratic to Abusive Constitutional Borrowing' (2019) 17 International Journal of Constitutional Law 489, 492.

It could be assumed then that the populist approach to constitutional interpretation would be based on textual canons and grammatical interpretation, while, as the Bible says, 'anything else comes from the devil'. With regard to Poland, this intuition has proven to be right on many occasions. Indeed, the populist government quite often appeared to be very principled about holding on to the literal meaning of the constitution, especially when the party launched its assault on the independence of the judiciary.

It suffices to recall two examples from constitutional practice. One of the legal tricks invented by the Polish parliament to facilitate the packing of the Constitutional Tribunal was the introduction of a two-thirds majority requirement for adopting decisions on the unconstitutionality of laws, combined with two more requirements: that of sitting as a full bench for abstract cases and that of a quorum of 13 out of 15 judges. This was obviously supposed to force the Tribunal's president to recognize three persons elected to seats which were not vacant at the moment of the election as legitimate judges. The argument of the government was that the Polish constitution stipulated that the judgments of the Constitutional Tribunal would be made 'by a majority of votes',[26] thus allowing parliament to decide freely, by means of ordinary legislation, whether it should be a simple or qualified majority.[27] A similar attachment to literal interpretation of the constitution was demonstrated as soon as the populist government proceeded to pack the Supreme Court. Justifying the proposed amendment to the Act on the Supreme Court, it was argued that if the constitution stipulated that a statute shall 'establish an age limit beyond which a judge shall proceed to retirement'[28] and no particular age limit was mentioned, it was entirely up to parliament to decide on this matter. Those who insisted that this paragraph needed to be read in light of the principle of judicial independence – and so by no means would the paragraph allow parliament to simply sack all the sitting judges with one vote, by lowering the age of retirement – would be dismissed as legal swindlers. Textual interpretation, entirely oblivious to the constitutional context and to the established interpretive practice, prevailed. The case became widely known as it was brought before the European Court of Justice – and, unsurprisingly, was lost by the Polish government.[29]

Ironically, sometimes textual interpretation stands in your way and impedes your agenda. This may happen when you discover that the President of the Supreme Courts was appointed for a six-year term of office[30] and cannot be simply removed together with other judges. This is where you

26 Cf. Art. 190(5) of the Polish Constitution.

27 The Venice Commission was right to note that the established reading which assumed that this provision required a simple majority had become part of constitutional practice and thus could not be altered by the ordinary legislator; see 'Opinion on Amendments to the Act of 25 June 2015 on the Constitutional Tribunal of Poland, adopted by the Venice Commission at its 106th Plenary Session (Venice, 11–12 March 2016)' paras 81–82.

28 Cf. Art. 180(4) of the Polish Constitution.

29 Case C-192/18 *Commission v Poland* ECLI:EU:C:2019:924.

30 Cf. Art. 183(3) of the Polish Constitution.

start speculating that maybe a six-year term is not really a term but a time limit and that it means 'a maximum of six years', so in fact it can be cut short by parliament if necessary.[31] Or let us take a look at the issue of the publication of the Constitutional Tribunal's judgments by the government. They are required to be immediately published in the official journal,[32] an obligation which was never questioned in the past. Still, when the Tribunal did not conform to the new legislative measures adopted by the populist parliament and declared them unconstitutional, the government refused to publish the judgment on the grounds that it had been issued in breach of the law and that the obligation to publish judgments needed to be seen in light of the Tribunal's constitutional position, thus giving the government the right to assess the procedural compliance of the judgment.[33]

As this shows, the preferred methods of constitutional interpretation change over time, depending on what the populists want to achieve. If a fixed rule turns out to be their ball and chain, they just cut it off. There is hardly any consistency in this approach: rules can be invented, dismissed or reinvented if this is supposed to help achieve the desired interpretive result.

11.3.3 The approach to earlier findings

This should be the real acid test for the 'new' Constitutional Tribunal. If the reason for the populists to come to power was genuinely the treason of the elites, and the constitutional interpretation before 2015 had been corrupt, then the populist rule should open an entirely new chapter in Polish constitutional history. Demonstrating continuity should not even be considered. Why continue something which is illegitimate and morally bankrupt?

The truth appears to be much more complicated. If we remember that the Constitutional Tribunal was taken over by the populist nominees, including those elected to seats already filled at the moment of election, in the last days of December 2016, then it can be assumed that the new era in constitutional adjudication was launched in 2017. Over the years 2017, 2018 and 2019, the Tribunal issued, respectively, 94, 72 and 70 judgments,[34] which constitutes a vast amount of research material. While a small number of these judgments touch upon issues of great importance for the constitutional system,

31 This interpretation was promoted by Jarosław Kaczyński, www.rp.pl/Prawnicy/307279961-Konstytucja-wedlug-prezesa-Kaczynskiego---komentuje-Wojciech-Tumidalski.html accessed 14 April 2020.

32 Cf. Art. 190(2) of the Polish Constitution.

33 See 'Poland – Opinion on the Act on the Constitutional Tribunal, adopted by the Venice Commission at its 108th Plenary Session (Venice, 14–15 October 2016)'.

34 These figures demonstrate a sharp decrease as compared to the previous years, in which the number of judgments always exceeded 100, reaching as high as 188 in 2015 (statistics available at www.ipo.trybunal.gov.pl/ipo accessed 14 April 2020). The reasons are twofold: the apparent rise of distrust in the Tribunal, mirrored in the declining number of submitted motions, and the lack of commitment of the Tribunal itself, which is now deciding fewer cases and holding fewer public hearings than before.

the majority rather belong to the 'business as usual' section in the Tribunal's practice. The change, though, should be visible in the approach both to the landmark cases and to everyday-life cases, for the latter were supposed to be more important for ordinary people.

But as one reads these judgments, it becomes clear that there has been no revolutionary shift with regard to adjudication techniques. The Tribunal still refers to its earlier jurisprudence, and it does so openly; it follows the established patterns concerning the admissibility of applications; it uses the same methods for adjudication, even if sometimes it stretches them to the extreme, as with the case of the 'insofar formula'. It almost gives the impression that this new institution mimics the 'old' Tribunal, so that nobody would realize that the political circumstances and the legal reality are so different now.

However, sometimes upholding the previously established interpretation could jeopardize the plans of the government. Notably, it would have made it impossible for quasi-judges to sit on panels, because the 'old' Constitutional Tribunal refused to recognize them as properly elected ones.[35] It would also have blocked the plan to recast the National Council of the Judiciary, which was to be dissolved in order to be packed with political nominees, for the 'old' Tribunal did not allow such constitutional trickery.[36]

Now this is no longer an obstacle. If the earlier case law stands in its way, the Constitutional Tribunal feels free to simply dismiss it and officially change its views on a particular matter.[37] Should the applicant insist, highlighting inconsistencies in the Court's reasoning, the judges will declare that *they* are the Court now and they know better what the Court meant.[38] Control over constitutional interpretation is indeed a powerful weapon.

11.3.4 The approach to international law and EU law

It is widely known that the populist governments are usually reluctant to accept constraints resulting from international law standards. This is above all simply because constraints are constraints, and the populists do not like them. Another important reason is that the international legal framework has been elaborated and accepted elsewhere, so it is hardly within the populist reach; it may be relatively easy to pack the constitutional court, but not the European Court of Justice. To voice their anger and distrust, the populists 'denounce international law as an undemocratic, elitist project',[39] and whoever stands up for international law standards, such as judicial independence, is at risk of being accused of serving foreign interests.

35 CT judgment of 3 December 2015, K 34/15.

36 CT judgment of 18 July 2007, K 25/07.

37 CT judgment of 20 June 2017, K 5/17. This judgment openly rejected the views expressed in the case K 25/07 (ibid.).

38 CT judgment of 24 October 2017, K 1/17. This judgment modified the argument provided in the case K 34/15 (n 35).

39 Tamara Hostovsky Brandes, 'International Law in Domestic Courts in an Era of Populism' (2019) 17 International Journal of Constitutional Law 576, 580.

This short description, no matter how simplified it may appear, is very true for Poland.[40] One of the excellent examples is the report of the team of experts in constitutional law, some of them self-proclaimed, who were summoned by the speaker of the populist-dominated parliament and asked to deliberate on the constitutional crisis. However, the name of the report, which makes an unclear reference to 'the issues related to the Constitutional Tribunal', is slightly misleading. The document is mostly a polemic with the Venice Commission, which had been very critical of the new Polish legislation regarding the Constitutional Tribunal, and it should be recommended to anyone wishing to understand the populist intellectual framing of the constitutional crisis.[41] The Venice Commission was, inter alia, reproached for 'adopting a paternalistic supervisory attitude' in its dialogue with Poland.[42] The parliamentary experts also asserted that the concept of 'European and international standards' did not imply 'the abolition of respect for constitutional heritage and solutions characteristic for individual Member States',[43] which might suggest that they were attempting to refer to the concept of constitutional identity, but ultimately this was not mentioned in the document. It is right to read this report not really as a reply to the Venice Commission, but rather as a message to the domestic reader, an attempt to depict an international institution that endorses this liberal neutrality of law as a myth.[44]

Needless to say, in the view of the populists, the European Union cannot be trusted either. The preliminary references to the European Court of Justice, especially in matters related to judicial independence, are always treated with suspicion, as they tend to undermine national sovereignty. Any judge making a preliminary reference under Article 267 TFEU risks being prosecuted and subject to disciplinary measures.[45] And who said that Article 267 TFEU was even compatible with the Polish Constitution?[46]

40 As regards the Constitutional Tribunal, not many references to international standards can be found in its case law, as the Tribunal resorts to these standards rather sparingly; this is not a major change, though, as compared with the previous periods.

41 'Report of the Team of Experts on the Issues Related to the Constitutional Tribunal of 15 July 2016', www.sejm.gov.pl/media8.nsf/files/ASEA-ADRKC8/%24File/Report%20of%20the%20Team%20of%20Experts%20on%20the%20Issues%20Related%20to%20the%20Constitutional%20Tribunal.pdf accessed 14 April 2020.

42 Ibid. 22.

43 Ibid. 25.

44 Blokker (n 24) 535.

45 At the time of writing of this chapter, this has been noted by the ECJ, which ordered Poland to immediately suspend the application of the national provisions on the powers of the Disciplinary Chamber of the Supreme Court with regard to disciplinary cases concerning judges. One of the grounds was that, according to the Commission, the new disciplinary regime allowed the right of courts to refer questions for a preliminary ruling to the ECJ to be limited by the possibility of the initiation of disciplinary proceedings (Order of the Court in Case C-791/19 R, 8 April 2020, *Commission v Poland*).

46 The motion challenging the institution of preliminary reference as unconstitutional was filed by the Prosecutor General in 2018 (case no K 7/18). As of end of April 2020, the case has not been examined by the Constitutional Tribunal.

What matters most, though, is that the Polish populists, being hostile to EU bodies and generally distrustful of foreign institutions, have not invented or adopted any clear new doctrine concerning international law. The fact that they disregard certain institutions, such as the Venice Commission, or show little respect for some international treaties, such as the Istanbul Convention,[47] has not translated into any effort aimed at theory-building. The populist response to Europe and the world may be described as different from before, but it is certainly not an alternative to the international legal order as we know it.

11.4 Why cherry picking?

It should be abundantly clear at this point that the populist constitutionalism in Poland may be a new quality, but there is no clear method or doctrine behind it, unless one likes to think that having no theory is a theory in itself – but chaos in theory is not the same as chaos theory. What we are really dealing with is an entirely new *approach* to law, which should not be confused with *theory*.

In my view, this new approach is best described as the cherry-picking model, with the only guiding principle being to use whatever works, whatever promises to help achieve the aims pursued, even at the cost of consistency. If the good old liberal democratic way of thinking happens to justify the constitutional interpretation expected by the political branches of government, the interpreter will most likely resort to the old methods, proudly demonstrating their commitment to legal tradition. Nonetheless, if the desired outcome is unachievable within the pre-established order, they will not hesitate to abandon it.

This new approach to constitutional interpretation is therefore purely instrumental, just like the practical populist approach to constitutional politics as a whole;[48] it is also deeply cynical, considering the political declarations. This strategy may not be pleasingly neat to describe in scholarly terms, and it will most likely leave no trace in the theory of constitutional interpretation, but for those who practice it, it has two major advantages. First, it is highly effective, as it ignores any constraints. Second, it leaves opponents completely helpless, for it is virtually impossible to keep up with somebody who tends to change the rules of the game all the time, or to mix various rules taken from different games.

The reasons to adopt such an approach seem to be fourfold, and I will now proceed to discuss each of them briefly.

47 Council of Europe Convention on preventing and combating violence against women and domestic violence, Istanbul, 11 May 2011. See Katarzyna Sękowska-Kozłowska, 'The Istanbul Convention in Poland: Between the "War on Gender" and Legal Reform' in Johanna Niemi, Lourdes Peroni, and Vladislava Stoyanova (eds.), *International Law and Violence Against Women: Europe and the Istanbul Convention* (Routledge 2020).

48 Blokker (n 24) 552.

11.4.1 Pragmatism

Populism implies pathological pragmatism – every legal mechanism, including constitutional adjudication, is expected to help implement the political agenda. Constitutional interpretation is merely a handy tool for achieving this aim and justifying it in official terms. Populism is sceptical about rules and procedures because these may bring about unexpected results. Accepting rules and following procedures would constitute an act of self-restraint, which is precisely what the populists wish to avoid.

It does not take much to realize that in order to escape this problem, the populists may choose between three paths. First, they may decide to break the rules openly, which, however, is not a popular option, as they care a great deal about the appearances of legality (see Section 11.4.3). Second, they may choose to accept only a minimum set of rules, but if they do, they will still be bound by them. Third, they may accept many rules, some of them contradictory, and just use them as they please, depending on the present need – and this is exactly what they do. Juggling with interpretive methodologies obviously shields the populists from the negative consequences of the constitutional interpretation they promoted the day before, but more importantly, it helps them use the constitution, by means of twisted and corrupted constitutional review, against those who truly defend it. In less pleasant but straightforward terms, if the constitution were a dog, the populists are no longer afraid of being bitten; now they turn the dog on their opponents.

11.4.2 Ideology

It is hard to say whether populist projects around the world are actually driven by any particular ideology, and even harder to determine whether there is one populism or in fact a variety of populisms. As far as Poland is concerned, the ideological motivation does still matter, but in the age of populism it seems to be secondary to the purely political game. In its simplified version, the populist ideology focuses on the fight against many-faced evil – elites, minorities, migrants, foreign influence – and its heralds are reluctant to waste time on abstract discussions on the nature of law. Admittedly, attempts at theoretical insights are being offered, such as Morawski's Oxford speech or the works of Ryszard Legutko, a conservative intellectual and an MEP of the ruling party,[49] but at the end of the day, who reads academic books and conference papers?

Nevertheless, should we wish to dig deeper, interesting explanations can be found. One of these explanations is the unexpected comeback of Carl Schmitt's theory. The thought of Carl Schmitt has been enjoying a revival among public law scholars since they realized that it had quite a lot to say

49 For a summary of Legutko's ideas which served as bases for conservative populism, see Paul Blokker, 'Populist Counter-Constitutionalism, Conservatism, and Legal Fundamentalism' (2019) 15 European Constitutional Law Review 519, 524–30.

that could be applied to the current political reality. There are some who believe that the recent developments in the region, and especially in Poland, can be best described by adopting Schmitt's theoretical framework.[50] Without elaborating on this, it is hard not to note that ruling in the state of exception, decisions emanating from a particular authority, rejecting the idea of negotiation – this is all from Schmitt's political imaginarium.

Has Kaczyński been reading Schmitt, then? Maybe, but there is truth in the common belief that many people who read the right books owe that to their mentors who encouraged them to do so. If we turn to Kaczyński's personal tutors, many would claim that it was one of his academic teachers who shaped his views on law and politics: Stanisław Ehrlich, a committed Marxist and an influential lawyer in the communist era.[51] Indeed, there is a striking resemblance between the political philosophy of Ehrlich and the political agenda of Kaczyński. Rejecting the law as a source of the legitimacy of power; seeing democracy as a battlefield where war is aged between groups with conflicting interests; accepting illegal changes to the system in order to (allegedly) support marginalized groups; calling for establishing a single 'centre of political decision' which would rule the country – it is morbidly fascinating to read how it all came true.

If re-reading Ehrlich is the key to understanding Kaczyński, it becomes even clearer than before that constitutional interpretation cannot be *ars pro arte* and that it should serve the political agenda directly. In the end, it is the social and political context that matters, not abstract principles.

11.4.3 Reputation

As already mentioned, the Polish populists would never admit that they are breaking the law. Their project may be revolutionary in legal terms, but appearances of legality cannot be abandoned. For this reason, the populists need to justify their actions with a 'proper' interpretation of the constitution, and the best way to achieve this is to use the old methods and old techniques, but to twist them to the extreme and possibly adding some new elements. This is how continuity of the legal order can be demonstrated, in a way which is convincing and appealing to so many: by mixing the new with the old. The need to demonstrate continuity shown by true revolutionaries may be surprising at first, yet it cannot be denied: the judgments of the 'new' Constitutional Tribunal resemble the old ones, its earlier case law is still being cited, and the pre-2015 concepts are being used to justify the new order.

The reasons for this are not hard to identify. If the populist project were openly illegal, it would in fact be more vulnerable. At the early stage, such

50 Wojciech Engelking, 'The Political Character of the Judiciary: Schmitt, Kelsen and the Polish Constitutional Tribunal' in Belov (n 6).

51 Dawid Bunikowski, 'The Constitutional Crisis in Poland, Schmittian Questions and Kaczyński's Political and Legal Philosophy' (2018) 26 Journal of Contemporary European Studies 285, 294–296.

conduct would have enabled dedicated state agencies to step in and adopt measures which would end with the dissolution of the political party. Later, the populists would have had difficulty finding followers and supporters in academia and among lawyers, whose support was crucial for some parts of the plan, notably packing the courts, to become reality. The appearance of legality was also useful for the purposes of foreign policy, especially for the game played with the Court of Justice. This is why populists need to have their own lawyers, their own judges, their own parliamentary experts, even their own legal journals. It has been a truly long run. Paul Blokker is right to observe that 'conservative intellectuals and civil society groups have been gathering strength since the early 1990s, have increasingly radicalised and have become significant political forces which mobilise society and provide intellectual support, expertise, and legitimacy to populist projects'.[52] Today, corrupting some of the elites with financial incentives and by promoting them to prestigious offices is the next step and an essential part of this strategy.

Another important factor is the question of future accountability. If the populists are ever removed from power, having a record of blatantly illegal actions would pose a great threat to their personal safety. Yet, with contradictory legal opinions on the conformity of their actions with the constitution, today's major controversy is likely to be reduced in future to a mere dispute between lawyers. Opening the doors to various legal interpretations is, in fact, a method to ensure immunity to the interpreter, and the art of reading the constitution once again appears to be instrumental to political goals.

11.4.4 Rhetoric

One final factor needs to be mentioned: the nature of the populist persuasion and how it affects constitutional interpretation. Referring to the earlier developments and highlighting the alleged similarities has an important rhetorical component which should not be missed – it legitimizes the political narrative about the populist government not exceeding the previously established limits of democratic power.

Psychology lies beyond the scope of this chapter and even more beyond my area of expertise. Still, it is impossible to overlook the fact that this you-did-it-first approach is something very characteristic of the Polish populists, who have a genuine talent for exploiting and abusing the previously applied methods and techniques of constitutional adjudication, or even weaponizing the dogmas of constitutional democracy. This has already happened multiple times with the presumption of the constitutionality of legislation, even if it is deliberately unconstitutional, or with the final effect of judgments of the Constitutional Tribunal, even if the panel was composed of wrongfully appointed judges. How easily these concepts have now been turned against the constitution!

52 Blokker (n 49) 521.

Zooming out further, this is part of another subtle but crucial issue. It has been recently argued that the wave of populism could be seen as a health check for constitutional democracy.[53] The disturbing ease with which populist leaders and their obedient state institutions have been using traditional tools and methods of constitutional interpretation should immediately alert all those who still believe in the constitution to its weaknesses. Kim Lane Scheppele hits the nail on the head when she argues that

> populism has become the obsessive focus of many of us academics precisely because the criticisms of liberal constitutionalism made by the populists hit us where we live. Populists expose the vulnerabilities in the theories that our profession has taken for granted.[54]

The experience of the populist rule highlights the risk of the traditional principles of constitutional interpretation being used to justify blatantly unconstitutional ideas. Some of these principles, such as the unconditional presumption of constitutionality, may need to be revisited.

11.5 Conclusions

This chapter has explored the developments in constitutional interpretation in Poland under populist rule and aimed to provide a convincing conceptual framework for the observed tendencies. I have sought to demonstrate that *populist* constitutionalism is not *new* constitutionalism. It does not propose any new theory or doctrine regarding constitutional interpretation, nor has it developed any new methods of constitutional adjudication. The pre-established methods and tools are still in use, sometimes slightly refashioned, sometimes badly abused, but apparently without any intention of replacing them. So was the dismantling of the constitutional order simply a method to question the credentials of the previous government? It transpires that the only problem with the alleged one-sidedness of constitutional interpretation before the populist era was not the lack of impartiality; quite simply, the side was wrong.

I argue that constitutional interpretation in Poland in times of populism does not have much to do with any theory. It does not make any valuable contribution to global constitutionalism that would need to be studied before it could be accepted as its new current. It is not new, much less consistent, and it could hardly be framed in any academic model or serve to build a new one – even though it certainly deserves to be studied if the myths surrounding it are to be laid to rest!

Instead, what we are dealing with is merely a new approach to constitutional interpretation, based on an interplay between the established tools

53 Oran Doyle, Erik Longo and Andrea Pin, 'Populism: A Health Check for Constitutional Democracy?' (2019) 20 German Law Journal 401.

54 Kim Lane Scheppele, 'The Opportunism of Populists and the Defense of Constitutional Liberalism' (2019) 20 German Law Journal 314, 315.

and methods and new ones. This hybrid approach is purely instrumental and result-oriented: it is all about winning, so if some interpretations are likely to make the player lose the game, why not flip the chess board and change the rules of interpretation? This brutality is not supposed to be an intellectual alternative to democracy – it is a statement per se. Optimistically, it does not necessarily mean that the populist approach to the art of reading the constitution is totally unpredictable. As a matter of fact, it is the exact opposite, for these days most of the rulings of the Constitutional Tribunal can be easily guessed before they are officially announced. All it takes to make the right guess is to know the expectations of the political branches of government.

So in the end, there is a method in their madness. This abusive constitutional interpretation in the Polish populist regime reveals the same pattern as the populist approach to the idea of constitutional borrowing. When Rosalind Dixon and David Landau argue that many Eastern European states have been importing the Western doctrines, designs and concepts 'in superficial, shallow, acontextual, or anti-purposive ways',[55] they could just as well be describing how the Polish Constitution is being read now.

In the opening remarks, I asserted that in this chapter I would refrain from making general statements which would hold true for any populist regimes. Despite many similarities, which are always tempting for those undertaking comparative legal studies, the populist regimes differ in terms of national history and legal culture. It has even been suggested that some of them have been so successful due to specific features of national identity, or even certain widespread psychological tendencies,[56] a bitter interpretation which I find overly fatalistic. The populist regimes also differ with regard to how strong the parliamentary opposition is and who the populist leaders are. As Martin Krygier observed, '[s]ome of these are cynics, some fanatics, some clowns, some perhaps none (or all) of the above'.[57] Here is the Polish puzzle piece, then – let us see how it fits with the other ones.

55 Dixon and Landau (n 25) 489.

56 Tímea Drinóczi and Agnieszka Bień-Kacała, 'Extra-Legal Particularities and Illiberal Constitutionalism – the Case of Hungary and Poland' (2018) 59 Hungarian Journal of Legal Studies 338, 346–50.

57 Martin Krygier, 'The Challenge of Institutionalisation: Post-Communist "Transitions", Populism, and the Rule of Law' (2019) 15 European Constitutional Law Review 544, 562.

12 *Non sequiturs* in constitutional adjudication

Populism or epistemic deficit?

Alexandra Mercescu

12.1 Introduction

One of the core elements of the so-called 'New Constitutionalism' is centred around the idea of an efficient control of the political by the law.[1] In general, judicial review is perceived to be an institution sufficiently apt to successfully fulfil this ambitious task, at least under non-exceptional circumstances, being now advocated even in countries traditionally reluctant to recognize the power of judges to interfere with the imagined legislative will.[2] However, judicial review across legal cultures is not uniform. For some countries, parliamentary sovereignty, while protecting democracy but possibly endangering rights, remains a valid model of constitutionalism. As Jeffrey Goldsworthy notes,

> [t]he constitutional traditions of different countries reflect different views as to which of those dangers is to be feared more, a question that continues to engage legal and political theorists. It is surely possible that the answer varies from one country to another, depending on their different political, social, and cultural circumstances.[3]

Moreover, countries that evaluate differently the priority of threats and prefer therefore to adopt judicial review differ nonetheless in their understanding of the tools, such as proportionality, that are employed to realize the aims of judicial review.[4]

Judicial review is yet to become the universal weapon against the fight of political unruliness. Moreover, it is yet to achieve a configuration which

1 Tamas Győrfi, *Against the New Constitutionalism* (Edward Elgar 2016) 8.

2 Travor Allan, *Constitutional Justice, a Liberal Theory of the Rule of Law* (Oxford University Press 2001).

3 Jeffrey Goldsworthy, 'Homogenizing Constitutions' (2003) 23 Oxford Journal of Legal Studies 483, 505.

4 Jacco Bomhoff, 'Balancing, the Global and the Local: Judicial Balancing as a Problematic Topic in Comparative (Constitutional) Law' (2008) 31 Hastings International & Comparative Law Review 555. For a more comprehensive analysis, see Jacco Bomhoff, *Balancing Constitutional Rights* (Cambridge University Press 2013) 190–234.

dispenses with the interpreter's discretion. It was and continues to be hailed as a mechanism ensuring a fair amount of control over what would otherwise constitute unbridled and therefore dangerous politics. However, as soon as theoreticians realized that, realistically speaking, and crudely put, it is not so much about politicians being constrained by the law but about some people (politicians) being constrained by other people (judges), unsurprisingly, they became preoccupied with finding solutions meant to supposedly render the whole review process more objective, by including interpretative[5] or eternity clauses, for instance, in the fundamental text. Under this ideal, if politics is to be constrained by law, law is to be constrained by language (as if language were to be automatically applied). In any case, for countries that by and large do believe in its benefits, the question arises whether judicial review remains efficient in the face of problematic political agendas such as the recent waves of populism. Does constitutional interpretation differ radically when applied by courts that are more or less overtly endorsing populist regimes? I wish to answer this question by looking in particular at a decision of the Constitutional Court of Romania that has been severely criticized as infringing on the rule of law. Essentially, I will seek to determine whether its language and reasoning are any different from those displayed in the more 'regular' decisions of the Court, but not before discussing the particular background of Romanian politics and constitutionalism.

12.2 Romania's political landscape: populist or not?

From a comparative perspective, unlike Hungary, whose constitutional judges are now to interpret at least in part an overtly non-liberal new constitution,[6] and Poland, whose Constitutional Court 'realizes the politics of the ruling majority', 'effectively desisting from protecting the constitutional order against unconstitutional measures',[7] Romania's constitutionalism has been quite unspectacular. By contrast, when looked at from the perspective of its evolution, it is clear that the recent years have brought some spectacular interventions of the Constitutional

5 See Anna Gamper, 'Constitutional Courts, Constitutional Interpretation, and Subnational Constitutionalism Perspectives on Federalism' (2014) 6 Perspectives on Federalism E-28.

6 Gábor Halmai, 'A Coup Against Constitutional Democracy: The Case of Hungary' in Mark A. Graber, Sanford Levinson, and Mark Tushnet (eds), *Constitutional Democracy in Crisis?* (Oxford University Press 2018); Zoltán Szente, 'The Political Orientation of the Members of the Hungarian Constitutional Court between 2010 and 2014' (2016) 1 Constitutional Studies 123.

7 See Przemysław Tacik, 'Polish Constitutional Identity under the Illiberal Turn' in Alexandra Mercescu (ed.), *Constitutional Identities in Central and Eastern Europe* (Peter Lang 2020), 167. At the date of this writing both countries continue to engage in authoritarian politics as they exploit the emergency related to the Covid-19 pandemic crisis. See Gábor Halmai, 'Don't Be Fooled by Autocrats', (*Verfassungsblog*, 22 April 2020), https://verfassungsblog.de/dont-be-fooled-by-autocrats/ accessed 23 April 2020; Wojciech Sadurski, 'The Polish Presidential Campaign in the Shadow of the Pandemic' (*Verfassungsblog*, 18 March 2020), https://verfassungsblog.de/the-polish-presidential-campaign-in-the-shadow-of-the-pandemic/ accessed 23 March 2020.

Court in the Romanian political life, some of which are highly controversial. Indeed, since the constitutional revision of 2003, when it was granted the power to adjudicate on conflicts of a juridical nature between public authorities, the Court gained great visibility and is now a major player in the organization of the polis,[8] constantly invoked by politicians and extensively covered by the media.

The country has witnessed in recent times a series of political initiatives which were problematic from a rule of law point of view, the most worrisome of which were the attacks on the judiciary.[9] Whether these are to be called populist, however, is a question open to debate. The existing literature speaks in fact to this incertitude regarding labelling. Several authors seem to point to the presence of some signs of illiberalism in Romania as well, but barely take the discussion further and, in any case, it is rather unclear to what extent the disturbing elements are not expressions of institutional failures and impoverished political and civic life typical of the region rather than manifestations of a broader populist agenda. For instance, Silvia Suteu notes that '[i]n countries such as Romania, endemic corruption and weak institutions have long coexisted with populist discourse which may yet develop into populist state capture'.[10] For his part, in 2015, Paul Blokker expressed preoccupation with the direction in which Romania was heading but he did so rather hesitatingly:

> The troublesome Hungarian, and possibly Romanian, developments regarding democracy, constitutionalism and the rule of law call for the attention of the European Union and its Member States.[11]

In the same year, Bugarič relied on the *Nations in Transit* 2012 report – *Fragile Frontier: Democracy's Growing Vulnerability in Central and Southeastern Europe* – to draw some alarming conclusions concerning Romania as well:

> Six of the ten EU member states in the region (Hungary, Bulgaria, the Czech Republic, Lithuania, Romania, and Slovakia) have experienced net declines [in key governance institutions] over the past five years.[12]

8 Paul Blokker, 'The Evolution of Constitutionalism in Post-Communist Countries' in Peter Van Elsuwege and Roman Petrov (eds.), *Post-Soviet Constitutions and Challenges of Regional Integration: Adapting to European and Eurasian Integration Projects* (Routledge 2017) 3.

9 For an overview of this problematic initiatives, see Bianca Selejan-Guţan, 'New Challenges Against the Judiciary in Romania', (*Verfassungsblog*, 22 February 2019) https://verfassungsblog.de/new-challenges-against-the-judiciary-in-romania/ accessed 12 February 2020.

10 Silvia Suteu, 'The Populist Turn in Central and Eastern Europe: Is Deliberative Democracy Part of the Solution?' (2019) 15 European Constitutional Law Review 488.

11 Paul Blokker, 'EU Democratic Oversight and Domestic Deviation from the Rule of Law: Sociological Reflections' in Carlos Closa and Dimitry Kochenov (eds.), *Reinforcing the Rule of Law Oversight in the European Union* (Cambridge University Press 2015).

12 Bojan Bugarič, 'A Crisis of Constitutional Democracy in Post-Communist Europe: "Lands In-between" Democracy and Authoritarianism' (2015) 13 International Journal of Constitutional Law 219, 220.

The author recalled that the international press saw in the new Romanian government's actions to consolidate its power a constitutional crisis amounting to nothing less than a '"quiet coup d'état"'.[13] In fact, as other commentators have underlined, '[i]n Romania, political will to tackle domestic institutional reform has been uneven since 2007', the year of its EU accession.[14] If prior to the accession the pressure to effectively fight endemic corruption was important, the will to reform 'petered out after accession thanks to collusion among much of the political elite, which closed ranks in order to roll back reform'.[15] All in all, four years into the European Union, Romania was displaying a 'mixed record in corruption control and judicial reform'.[16] The last decades have surely registered important progress, especially that Romania continued to be monitored under the Cooperation and Verification Mechanism, but given the various ups and downs of constitutionalism, it is definitively fair to say, even today, that 'gains appear vulnerable to reversal'.[17]

As of the time of my writing, *Partidul Social Democrat* (PSD), the continuator of the communist legacy and the party most associated with ethno-nationalistic and populist discourses, was ousted after it lost a vote of confidence, and while it still retains a majority of seats in Parliament, the threat of populism does not seem nearby.[18] Several interpretations of this state of affairs can be offered. One is to say that, despite scholars' tendencies to read populism into Romanian politics, in fact, populism, as understood by Jan-Werner Müller,[19] never really caught up in Romanian society. Another perspective is to suggest that those populist moments that certainly took place in Romania in recent years have been successfully overcome. Yet another interpretation could point to the inherent populist character of politics, with Romania experiencing, rather inevitably, populist moments every now and then. Given Romania's ethnonationalism, there are reasons to believe that a more or less 'mild' form of populism is a recurring feature of Romanian politics.

12.3 Discourses of constitutionalism in the Romanian context

Undoubtedly, the social imaginary that was being built after the collapse of communism in Romania rested on the notion of legality. As Cosmin Cercel argues:

13 Ibid. 221.

14 Aneta B. Spendzharova and Milada Anna Vachudova, 'Catching Up? Consolidating Liberal Democracy in Bulgaria and Romania after EU Accession' (2012) 35(1) West European Politics 51.

15 Ibid. 41.

16 Ibid. 55.

17 Suteu (n 10) 494.

18 Although the Covid-19 crisis has revealed signs of yet another type of populism, namely penal (or military) populism: Alexandra Mercescu, 'The COVID-19 Crisis in Romania, or on How One Cannot Escape (Bad, Legal) Culture', http://exceptions.eu/2020/05/11/the-covid-19-crisis-in-romania-or-on-how-one-cannot-escape-bad-legal-culture/ 11 May 2020.

19 Jan-Werner Müller, *What Is Populism?* (University of Pennsylvania Press 2016).

> This dispositive of legality was indeed not only the prevailing language of transitional constitutionalism and transitional justice, but also that of the prevalent constitutional theory, spilling later into the ideology of institutional and political actors and even going beyond the formal borders of the polities. In short, it was the politico-legal theory of the lawyers and officials in Central and Eastern Europe determined to break with the past and to pave the way to a new form of constitutional patriotism.[20]

In scholarship as in practice, constitutionalism was understood in a technical manner, through the prism of a hierarchy of laws and as placed exclusively in the hands of the constitutional judiciary who were to act as a neutral arbiter between state powers on the one hand and the state and its citizens on the other. In the first decade after 1989, the language of legal constitutionalism, while present, mattered little in practice insofar as the role of the Constitutional Court was limited even on paper (note that before the 2003 revision, it was possible for the Parliament to override the Court's decisions by a supermajority). With the rise of the Court in the years after 2000, legal constitutionalism became entrenched as the ultimate language for the defence of the rule of law and kept being propagated as such in everyday discourses that presented the Court as the neutral 'guardian of the Constitution'. In law schools, students were (and are still being) taught that while the Constitutional Court constitutes a political body, it does not rank among the different state powers. This has not been without consequences. As Blokker maintains, 'an intrinsic problem of legal constitutionalism in the post-communist transformations has been its tendency to isolate constitutional questions from the wider public',[21] an observation in line with the assessment of Gábor Halmai and Wojciech Sadurski, who also 'argued that legal constitutionalism might have a 'negative effect' in new democracies and might lead to the perpetuation of the problem of both weak political parties and civil society'.[22]

After 2003, in any case, when the Romanian Constitutional Court (RCC) started to consolidate its power, political constitutionalism emphasizing the importance of legislatures over courts did not emerge in scholarship. The latter continued to display its strong 'ideological attachment to the belief in law as foundational for polities … reminiscent of an unavowed, and for that matter, an unarticulated version of legal formalism that ultimately turns around

20 Cosmin Cercel, 'The Destruction of Legal Reason: Lessons from the Past', (2019) 89 Acta Universitatis Lodziensis Folia Iuridica 15, 25.

21 Paul Blokker, 'From Legal to Political Constitutionalism', (*Verfassungsblog*, 4 June 2017) https://verfassungsblog.de/from-legal-to-political-constitutionalism/ accessed 20 January 2020.

22 Gábor Halmai, 'Illiberalism in East-Central Europe', (2019) European University Institute Working Paper 5/2019, https://papers.ssrn.com/sol3/papers.cfm?abstract_id=3486420 accessed 15 March 2020; Wojciech Sadurski, 'Transitional Constitutionalism: Simplistic and Fancy Theories' in Adam Czarnota, Martin Krygier, and Wojciech Sadurski (eds.), *Rethinking the Rule of Law after Communism* (CEU Press 2005) 9–24.

the conundrum of liberal legality in times of crisis'.[23] Political constitutionalism was equally absent from public discourses with a recent exception on the occasion of which one of the newly established parties in Romania (*Uniunea Salvați România* – USR) launched a warning about the need to reconsider the Court's role in the face of what they claimed to be its obvious politicization as a result of a series of cases that involved public authorities.

In addition, the notion of 'constitutional identity' would have had the potential to be a channel through which political constitutionalism could have entered the legal and political stage insofar as it begs the question of who should determine its content, and it allows for an answer in the direction of actors other than the courts. In the Romanian context, however, the notion was rather ignored not only by politicians but also by the courts themselves. Thus, in a 2012 decision, the Romanian Constitutional Court employed, for the first time, the concept of 'constitutional identity' in an argumentation in favour of the president's right and obligation to attend the meetings of the European Union Council.[24] No populist or abusive usage of the notion can be detected (at the time, the President was rather unpopular). On the other hand, it is true that the mention was made in passing; consequently, it is hard to ascertain what exactly the judges wanted to obtain by its use. All in all, scholars deplore the precarious state of the notion in Romanian constitutional case law:

> The constitutional judges used the phrase constitutional identity only formally, in the context of a preamble meant to recapitulate the sharing of competences between the European institutions and the EU member states, by virtue of the basic treaties of the Union. No further reference is made to the Romanian constitutional identity in the Court's argument. Beyond the rhetoric of legal argumentation, nothing makes us believe that the RCC would take seriously the capacity of national constitutional identity to act as a shield/defense.[25]

While legal constitutionalism has never had a serious contender in the Romanian political or academic landscape, the recent waves of protests – the biggest ever since the fall of communism – point to the rise of a new form of constitutionalism in Romanian society, namely civic constitutionalism.[26] Traditionally, Romania was seen as unable to engage its citizens with the language of constitutionalism. Thus, it was first noted that the process of

23 Cercel (n 20) 24.

24 Decision no. 683 of 27 June 2012.

25 Manuel Guțan, 'Identitatea constituțională românească între pozitivism juridic și abordare interdisciplinară' in Raluca Bercea (ed.), *Comparația în științele sociale. Mizele interdisciplinarității* (Universul Juridic 2015) 182.

26 Lucian Bojin and Alexandra Mercescu, 'Protests in Romania: Civil Society, Populism and Civic Constitutionalism' in Alexandra Mercescu (ed.), *Constitutional Identities in Central and Eastern Europe* (Peter Lang 2020). The discussion on the topic of civic constitutionalism is an adapted excerpt from our co-authored text.

constitution-making immediately after the fall of the communist regime consisted in 'the affirmation of the majority's constitutional view, rather than a genuine pluralist dialogue'.[27] Indeed, 'in the early years of Romanian democratic constitutionalism, citizens' formal possibilities and actual capacities for engagement in constitutional politics have been severely limited'.[28] While the 2003 revision did better in this respect, with civic participation contributing to the process, Blokker could still remark in 2012 the following:

> Not only has a weak culture of constitutionalism emerged, but what seems worse is that a constitutional language is distant from societal interaction, and mostly abused for narrow political purposes. Constitutional values seem to fail to inform wider society in terms of a civic and political orientation to constitutional values and public debate on the foundations of Romanian democracy.[29]

For the last five years, however, this paradigm seems to have been changing as a significant part of the population was ready to engage in 'contentious politics' – a process that involves interactions in which actors make claims bearing on other actors' interests, leading to coordinated efforts on behalf of shared interests or programs, in which governments are involved as targets, initiators of claims, or third parties. Contentious politics thus brings together three familiar features of social life: contention, collective action, and politics.[30]

Importantly, on the occasion of the last two protests, people's discontent was not purely a question of policy and ideological preferences but touched upon matters that otherwise could and have been addressed in terms of constitutionality (it was the street's pressure that made the Ombudsman attack the bill before the Constitutional Court). Indeed, as it has been noted by one of the protesters himself: 'the trigger of the # rezist was quite technical, so the protesters had to educate themselves in very niche areas such as justice and public administration'.[31] What is interesting is that many voices among protesters, who were using the rule of law vocabulary, seemed determined to continue to manifest their rage irrespective of the Court's decision. In one particular case, when the decision ran counter to what the people demonstrating would have wanted, they immediately sanctioned the outcome by accusing the Constitutional Court of doing politics (one slogan read: 'the Constitutional Court – PSD's puppet'). In other words, consciously or not,

27 Paul Blokker, 'The Romanian Constitution and Civic Engagement' (2019) 11(3) *Vienna Journal on International Constitutional Law* 437.

28 Ibid.

29 Paul Blokker, 'Romanian Constitutionalism: Form without Content?' (2012), https://ssrn.com/abstract=2146568 accessed 20 January 2020.

30 Charles Tilly and Sidney Tarrow, *Contentious Politics* (Oxford University Press 2015) 7.

31 Cosmin Pojonaru, 'The Unexpected Romanians: Fighting Civic Apathy with Civic Energy' in Ana Adi and Darren Lilleker, *#rezist – Romania's 2017 Anti-Corruption Protests: Causes, Development and Implications* (Quadrigo 2017) 47.

protesters were claiming that they have a role to play in defending the constitutional order, which raises the theoretical questions of popular and civic constitutionalism, as opposed to legal and political constitutionalism (for Mény and Surel, civic or popular constitutionalism would be oxymoronic, for populism should be understood in opposition to constitutionalism, the latter offering a legalistic, procedural or institutional vision of how to best manage the polis).[32]

Were there any signs of a populist constitutionalism in this civic constitutionalism? While some voices accused protesters of being populist in their hostile rhetoric towards the lower classes known to be the supporting base of the ruling party, a closer scrutiny shows that protests were starkly opposed to forms of 'constitutional populism' that

> imply a delegitimization of the pre-existing constitution, which from the populist point of view is part of the enemy sphere of the elite and the status quo, not only aims at the elimination of the foundations of the institutional structure of liberal democracy but also at a new foundation in a hierarchical way, highly dependent on a direct and constant consensus between the leader and the base.[33]

To the contrary, the most recent Romanian protests inscribed themselves from end to end in the logic of liberal democracy. The people's intervention, then, was a move towards correcting liberal democracy gone astray and could hardly be equated with a critique of liberal democracy. Thus, while clearly conveying the message that legal technicalities matter less in times of crisis, the protesters never departed from the constitutional rule of law vocabulary (indeed, the media coverage used the term very frequently during that period), which they openly embraced (Facebook posts being a proof).

12.4 Interpreting the Constitution

Having briefly depicted Romanian constitutionalism, I want to argue that no matter what vision of constitutionalism one wishes to embrace, for constitutional adjudication and thus legal, or rather judicial, constitutionalism to remain credible (alone or alongside other forms of constitutionalism), less formalistic and more open to debate, Constitutional Courts have to be able to boast an important epistemic authority, by which I essentially mean the capacity to do things with language wisely. In particular, I will look at two decisions that could be qualified as populist or at least as problematic from a rule of law point of view. My aim is to see whether there are any significant differences in the language and the reasoning of the Court in these decisions as opposed to the more 'regular' ones, which are usually perceived as purely

32 Yves Mény and Yves Surel, 'The Constitutive Ambiguity of Populism' in Yves Mény and Yves Surel (eds.), *Democracy and the Populist Challenge* (Palgrave 2012) 1–11.

33 Manuel Anselmi, *Populism* (Routledge 2018) 88.

technical interventions, eliciting no special attention from the political point of view. This discussion will further allow me to draw some conclusion on what kind of Constitutional Court the Romanian Court is/should be and what kind of judicial politics it is/should be doing thirty years after the fall of the communist regime.

12.4.1 *Decision no. 358/2018 – a problematic constitutional intervention*

12.4.1.1 *The political background*

I should note from the very start the Romanian context of a bicephalous executive: on the one hand, the elected President, whose prerogatives are rather limited and more honorary, and the Prime Minister and their government, on the other. As presidential and parliamentary elections are held at different times, cohabitation is generally the norm in Romanian politics. Hence, the Government and the President exercise a certain amount of control upon each other.

Under the patronage of the European Union which monitors the progress made by the country, in the last ten years, Romania assumed anti-corruption as one of its main goals, and therefore a series of corresponding measures were implemented. Accordingly, the independence of the judiciary became much stronger than in the aftermath of the Revolution, and prosecutors felt encouraged to go after high-profile politicians who were long suspected of crimes involving public money. The chief of the National Anti-Corruption Prosecuting Office (Laura-Codruța Kövesi, who was recently elected head of the newly formed EU Prosecutor's Office) was soon made into a public hero. She posed a problem to the ruling party, many members of which had already been convicted, were being under investigation or simply hoped that once she was no longer to be in office, they would be able to move on with the type of crony capitalism that kept PSD together as a party for thirty years now.

Speculating on some of the rumours about mass surveillance techniques being used by the secret services to target corrupt officials as well as on a couple of proven instances of abuses by prosecutors, some of which started to feel overconfident under Kövesi's direction, the Minister of Justice initiated a procedure for removing her from office. The President interpreted his constitutional and legal (infra-constitutional) prerogatives in the procedure as decisive and refused to confirm her removal from office upon reception of the proposal from the Minister.

12.4.1.2 *The legal background*

The procedure of removal essentially involves three authorities: the Minister of Justice, the Superior Council of Magistracy (the entity endowed with the responsibility of ensuring judges' and prosecutors' independence) and the President of Romania. While it was clear that the Council plays only a consultative role (it issues a non-binding recommendation, approving of or disapproving of the Minister's proposal of destitution), it was rather unclear who holds more power between the Minister and the President when it comes to having the final say on the chief prosecutor's removal from office. The relevant provisions read as follows:

Art. 132 (1) of the Romanian Constitution:

> The prosecutors carry out their activity in accordance with the principles of legality, impartiality, and hierarchical control under the authority of the Minister of Justice.

Art. 94 (c) of the Romanian Constitution:

> The President of Romania also has the following powers: ... to make appointments to public offices in the conditions defined by the law;

Art. 54 of Law no. 303/2004:

> The President of Romania is to revoke the prosecutors who hold management positions provided in paragraph (1) [namely, the Prosecutor General of the Prosecutor's Office attached to the High Court of Cassation and Justice, his deputy and vice-deputy, the general prosecutor of the National Anticorruption Prosecutor's Office, his deputies, the chief prosecutors of these prosecutors' offices, as well as the chief prosecutor of the Directorate for the Investigation of Organized Crime and Terrorism Offenses and their deputies], at the proposal of the Minister of Justice who can take action ex officio, at the request of the general meeting or, as the case may be, of the general prosecutor of the Prosecutor's Office attached to the High Court of Cassation and Justice or of the general prosecutor of the National Anticorruption Directorate, after the opinion of the Superior Council of Magistracy is issued, for the reasons provided for in art. 51 paragraph (2) that apply accordingly.

Art. 146 (e) of the Romanian Constitution:

> The Constitutional Court has the following functions:
> ... to solve legal disputes of a constitutional nature between public authorities, upon request of the President of Romania, one of the presidents of the two Chambers, the Prime Minister, or of the President of the High Council of the Judiciary.

Against this political and legal background, the conflict between the Minister of Justice and the President was referred to the Constitutional Court (upon request by the Prime Minister). The solution turned on two major technicalities: Does this conflict amount to a legal conflict of a constitutional nature between public authorities and, if so, does Article 54 of Law no. 303/2004 give the President the power to review the Minister's decision only from a procedural point of view or substantially as well (i.e. to appreciate whether the measure is desirable or not)?

12.4.1.3 A formalist result

The court – by a majority of 6–3 – decided for the Minister of Justice in what was a fiercely contested decision.[34] It was considered at best political, if not an outright attack on the rule of law, for it was seen to impinge on the efficacy of the checks and balances system. Essentially, the Court attributed a purely formal role to the President by depriving him of the possibility to oppose himself to the reasons offered by the Minister for the revocation. If the revocation met the formal criteria established by the law (that is, if it was duly signed by the Minister and motivated, irrespective of the quality of the reasons), the President had no other option than to accept the revocation.

It is certain that the texts themselves did not explicitly stipulate how the competences are to be imparted between the two authorities. Realistically speaking, then, any solution would have been a 'political' solution and not a 'technical' one. However, an analysis of the decision from the standpoint of its language and logical (not necessarily legal) reasoning reveals some problematic aspects.

Thus, the text contains several *non sequiturs*. To give just one example, the majority presupposed that when two public authorities are involved in an appointment procedure, only one has a decisional role while the other retains a merely formal position. It then infers that in the case under scrutiny, it must be the person who proposed the measure. But it certainly does not follow from the fact that a procedure of joint appointment is provided for by the law that one entity needs to play only a ceremonial role. Moreover, the Court has repeatedly invoked in its case law the principle of symmetry (and this irrespective of the fact that in one decision it clearly stated that this principle is a principle of private law and has no bearing on public law matters, even less so of a constitutional order[35]). Thus, where the Constitution endows the President with the power to appoint to a public office, it correlatively provides, though implicitly, for the power to dismiss that person. Also, by virtue of the same principle, the Court decided, in its past case law,

34 See for instance Vlad Perju, 'Analiza constituțională a deciziei CCR 358/2018' (2018), https://www.contributors.ro/analiza-constitutionala-a-deciziei-ccr-3582018/ accessed 20 March 2020. Meanwhile, Ms. Kövesi filed a complaint at the European Court of Human Rights and won the case on grounds of infringements of her right to a fair trial and freedom of expression: see Case of *Kövesi v. Romania*, Application no. 3594/19, decided on 5 May 2020. My analysis will not address the failures that the ECtHR itself identified in respect of the procedure concerning Ms. Kövesi before the RCC but will limit itself to a critique from the perspective of the *language* and *interpretative quality* of the Romanian Constitutional Court's decision.

35 Decision no. 731 of 10 July 2012.

that because the Constitution empowers the President to send the statute back for re-examination only once before signing it into law, it empowers him to act accordingly in similar situations. The Court argued that a joint procedure for the execution of a given constitutional measure amounts to a similar situation. This creative case law notwithstanding, the Court decided that the principle of symmetry does not apply to revocation procedures (but only in relation to appointments). 'The hypothesis under examination does not fall within the coordinates of the [above-mentioned] decision', stated the Court, without further explanation of why this would actually be the case. The reasoning of the majority therefore appears *tautological.*

As far as the methods of interpretation are concerned, while the Minister of Justice, as a party to the dispute, invoked the systematic, the teleological and the grammatical method, the Court preferred to appeal to the historical method to which it conferred, unprecedently, a superior place, thus instituting a hierarchy of sorts between the several existing methods of interpretation:

> The Court must identify the will of the original constituent, together with the motivations underlying it, thus resorting to the historical method of interpretation. To the extent that this will is unambiguous and non-susceptible of interpretations, the Court cannot depart from the will of the original constituent, in the sense that it cannot, by means of other methods of interpretation, give a new/different interpretation to the constitutional text in question, because otherwise it would replace the original constituent's will with its own.[36]

Concretely, the judges examined what models of control for prosecutors the constituent power had in view at the time of the adoption of the Constitution. Studying the various proposals that were made, the Court concluded that the prosecutors were, undeniably, placed under the authority of the Minister of Justice. However, the Court fails to indicate why this constitutional arrangement precludes a veto from the part of another authority, in this case, the President of the Republic. As such, the historical method does not directly uphold the outcome of the case.

Moreover, the Court treated its own case law incoherently. Thus, previous decisions that would have sustained the opposite solution were either totally ignored or simply dismissed in a tautological manner (for instance, a number of relevant decisions were favourable to an interpretation according to which the President was bestowed by the Constitution with a power of appreciation in respect to appointments and not with a mere honorary role[37]). The Court also dismissed the arguments based on the increased legitimacy of the

36 Decision no. 358 of 30 May 2018.

37 Decision no. 375 of 6 June 2005; Decision no. 551 of 9 April 2009; Decision no. 683 of 27 June 2012.

President as a result of him/her being elected by universal suffrage, although it seemed ready to accept them elsewhere.[38]

While the result itself is clearly formalist in the sense in which it understands the control exerted by the President upon the Minister of Justice as a control of legality (formal, procedural) and not one of opportunity (substantial), not all the language of the Court is formalist. In fact, the Court uses extensive and creative interpretations to reach this otherwise formalist result. Thus, the Court has constructed the following argument: in the case of appointments of prosecutors, the law requires the Minister of Justice to take into consideration very few criteria (such as the number of years of expertise); therefore, his margin of appreciation in choosing the right person is considerable and has to be checked by the President. By contrast, in the case of revocation, the law constrains the Minister by allowing him to revoke a prosecutor only when multiple, strict, criteria are met. Therefore, there is no need for extra control on the part of the President, for it must be assumed that the law 'controls' to a large extent the procedure. This argument *per se* is not unreasonable. However, I believe one can make, equally reasonably, the precise opposite case. Indeed, the criteria inscribed in the law for revoking a prosecutor are far from being precise to the point of allowing no interpretation at all (be jurists reminded that to read is to interpret[39]). Thus, there is room for the Minister to act politically in deciding to revoke a prosecutor, even though he will be able to cloak his decision in legal jargon. Consequently, it can be argued, without stretching the legal text, that there is an institutional need for the President to control the Minister's decision.

12.4.2 Other constitutional 'mischiefs'

In this sub-section I wish to provide two brief examples to further uphold the view that the Romanian Constitutional Court suffers from an epistemic deficit. In doing so, I want to also emphasize that there are several ways in which this epistemic deficit can manifest itself.

First, in one decision from 2017, the RCC held, in a procedure that was not provided for by the law, that it is necessary for it to 'regulate' the writing of separate and concurrent opinions at the Constitutional Court.[40] Until the Court's extra-legal intervention, the law provided simply that 'the judge who voted against [the majority's solution] can write a separate opinion' without any specification as to the circumstances under which it should be written or the language thereof.[41] Essentially, the Court established that its President has the right to control the content of separate and concurrent opinions, namely to ask for their rewriting if their tone is deemed inappropriate

38 Decision no. 375 of 6 June 2005.

39 For an excursus on reading in law, see Pierre Legrand, 'What Is That, To Read Foreign Law?' (2019) 14 Journal of Comparative Law 290.

40 Decision no. 1 of 12 January 2017.

41 Art. 59 of Law no. 47/1992.

and, if so, to eventually prohibit their publication in the *Official Gazette* and their attachment to the file. The decision triggered fierce criticism. Quite apart from the criticism related to the legality of the procedure and to the idea of silencing separate opinions (whether to have or not dissenting opinions is certainly a question open to debate), what strikes one immediately is the language employed by the majority which lacks a lot to be desired both as judicial reasoning and as language *tout court*.[42] Many of the RCC's decisions, the one discussed here included, reflect a disturbing legal logorrhoea (including repetitions and purportedly exhaustive enumerations) indicative of the judges' formalism. For the purpose of my argument, it is not important, however, that the court ruled *ultra vires*.[43] What is important is that its formalist reasoning and language betrayed a very shallow understanding of the role of separate opinions, something which threatens the epistemic quality of its decisions.

Second, at a time when several Central and Eastern European constitutional courts started to engage with the language of constitutional identity, for better or for worse, the RCC displayed timidity in assuming this language (and not for reasons having to do with the notion being an empty signifier, prone to abuses as it has been shown[44]). As if to acknowledge the rising importance of the notion and thus to formally recognize that the Court adheres to the European constitutionalist vocabulary, the Court mentioned the notion in passing but failed to do anything significantly with it. Thus, the Court signalled its knowledge and understanding of European constitutionalism but refused to participate in building itself in this direction. This attitude might be symptomatic of what Manuel Guţan has called the 'tendential constitutionalism' of Romania – 'a pattern of constitutional development that perpetually mediates between the need to become "European"

42 For instance, awkwardly enough, the Court states that '[t]he separate or concurring opinion is drafted in relation to the constitutional law problem that the decision of the Constitutional Court examines, comprising the logical, inductive or deductive reasoning on which the Constitutional Court judge relies and which it applies in the formation, development and sustaining of its point of view'. For a critique precisely as regards language, also emphasizing the general intellectual paucity of dissident opinions at the RCC, see Valentin Constantin, 'Sterilizarea opiniilor dizidente şi concurente la Curtea Constituţională a României' (*Juridice*, 12 September 2017), https://www.juridice.ro/essentials/1666/sterilizarea-opiniilor-dizidente-si-concurente-la-curtea-constitutionala-a-romaniei accessed 20 January 2020.

43 It is not the first time the Constitutional Court has acted *ultra vires* in a spectacular fashion. In the summer of 2012 during the President's impeachment, one of the Court's judges sent an 'errata' to the *Official Gazette* which 'was inserted retroactively in the ... text ... [thus] changing the original meaning of the holding': Bogdan Iancu, 'Constitutional-Judicial Culture in Romania – Ambivalence or Possibility' in Manuel Guţan and Bianca Selejan Guţan (eds.), *Europeanization and Judicial Culture in Contemporary Democracies* (C.H. Beck 2014) 146.

44 Zoltán Szente, 'The Constitutional Identity Conundrum' in Alexandra Mercescu (ed.), *Constitutional Identities in Central and Eastern Europe* (Peter Lang 2020).

and the need to remain "Romanian"'.[45] Guţan alludes in his work to the limits of the Romanian society in sustaining constitutional transplantation, invoking Romania's ethnonationalist constitutionalism.[46] While this can certainly constitute a valid explanation for Romania's ambivalent relation with Europeanization, I want to also place the reluctance of constitutional judges to approach 'constitutional identity' in particular on their fear of intellectual (political) engagement. Romanian constitutional judges are simply not trained to produce innovative/political reasoning and one can see this in the often-convoluted explanations which leave the reader with a sense of confusion (if not bemusement).

To summarize, a (constitutional) court's ruling is deficient from an epistemic point of view if:

i. its language and reasoning display a poor argumentative quality, whether or not it is pronounced *ultra vires*.[47]
ii. it fails to engage with new arguments/concepts in spite of the legal community's expectations in this regard.

Philosophically speaking, in the first case the Court fails to engage in a dialogue with itself, whereas in the second it eschews dialogue with the others (theoreticians or other professionals from the legal community or judges from other jurisdictions). To say it differently, while the first is a problem of language and reasoning, the second is a problem of a complete lack thereof or of silence.

12.5 Populism or epistemic deficit?

Given the charged political climate in which it was pronounced, the decision analysed in Section 12.4.1 can be deemed populist when judged by its result as it leads to a situation where the checks and balances mechanism is curtailed rather than enhanced. Otherwise, in terms of its formal structure, its legal reasoning and its language, one must say that the court's ruling does not differ fundamentally from other 'regular' (less visible political) decisions. An examination of other, less problematic, case law and even of the two dissenting opinions to the Decision no. 315/2018 reveals the same deficiencies: *non sequiturs*, tautologies, contradictions and selective treatment of case law. To a certain extent, it is fair to say that these elements are present in any

45 Manuel Guţan, 'Tendential Constitutionalism and the Limits of European Constitutional Culture' in Martin Belov (ed.), *Global Constitutionalism and Its Challenges to Westphalian Constitutional Law* (Hart 2018).

46 For an account of Romania as a 'people-nation', see Claude Karnoouh, *Inventarea poporului-naţiune. Cronici din România şi Europa Orientală 1973–2007* (Idea 2007).

47 I am aware of course that 'poor argumentative quality' is not a standard to be objectively established. I will nonetheless seek to explain below what I have in mind, without committing in this text to elaborating on how an epistemically meaningful style of reasoning and writing could be brought about in the Romanian context.

constitutional adjudication. However, their systematic presence in Romanian constitutional adjudication, coupled with attitudes that impair debate, encourage passivity or simply refrain from participating in judicial dialogue (as evidenced by the discussion in Section 12.4.2), is a reason for concern. The Constitutional Court should represent a space of public reason (in the Habermasian sense) that sets the (intelligible) tone of the conversation. This is all the more so in the contemporary world when we no longer imagine the language of the constitution as immutable and expressing some historical truths about one country's identity. Rather, we envisage it as a resource put at the society's disposal in order for it to negotiate an always-in-flux identity. As Oliviero Angeli argues, it seems that there has been 'a shift from interpreting the constitution as part of a grand national narrative of "we the people" to continuously justifying as an object of differing and potentially conflicting views'.[48]

It is a matter of epistemic honesty to admit that:

> irrespective of all denial and all desire … judge[s] wield enormous power, including political power, at the very least in the sense in which judicial decisions reveal discretionary determinations, and therefore value-laden decisions, regarding the regulation or the administration of the polis.[49]

Indeed, as soon as we descend from the macro-level of institutional design (which can or cannot facilitate the judicialization of politics) to the micro-level of a text posited before a panel of judges who need to ascribe meaning to it, discretion creeps in and judges

> might have no alternative than to … use as much information as possible, transform it down the road into legal jargon via the code of the legal (autopoietic) sub-system and hope that it will pass as a convincing, legitimate legal decision in the eyes of their legal and social community.[50]

To put it otherwise, then, as long as judges will be called upon to decide cases (and not necessarily constitutional ones), there will be judicialized politics. In fact, as Martin Shapiro reminds us, 'to a very large degree it is not so

48 Oliviero Angeli, 'Global Constitutionalism and Constitutional Imagination' (2017) 6 Global Constitutionalism 359, 375.

49 Pierre Legrand, 'Adjudication as Grammatication: The Case of French Judicial Politics' in Luís Pereira Coutinho, Massimo La Torre, and Steven Smith, *Judicial Activism: An Interdisciplinary Approach to the American and European Experiences* (Springer 2015) 51.

50 Raluca Bercea and Alexandra Mercescu, 'Ideology Within and Behind the Decisions of European Judges' (2017) 8 Romanian Journal of Comparative Law 149, 185.

much that courts do more [politics] now as that students of politics now see more of what courts do'.[51]

Politics needs not be understood, however, as being exclusively embodied by the daily battles of political life. In his book entitled *The Politics of Dialogue*, Polish sociologist Leszek Koczanowicz convincingly enters a plea for understanding democracy as more than just political institutions. The author does not dismiss the importance of party politics and institutionalized democracy but seeks to supplement them with a view to promoting the universalization of human interactions. Thus, politics, or more specifically political dialogue, should be reconfigured, according to Koczanowicz, as a 'form of life', as 'an exercise in community building'[52] where its primary function lies with understanding, not agreement (compromise). I fully empathize with the author's proposal to embrace the notion of a non-consensual democracy as 'recognition of the impossibility to formulate one, universal viewpoint that extends over our entire society', or as 'an admission of a failure of reason', as Koczanowicz eloquently puts it.[53]

Assessed against this background, law is meritorious to the extent that it lays the ground for infinite human encounters. Nonetheless, the legal realm also strays insofar as it insists that its solutions are neutral, mere expressions of (legal) technique. Therefore, it casts a shadow on how far law can contribute to making the self and the other refine their understanding of themselves and of each other. In fact, the opposite could be the case. In line with Mary Ann Glendon's thesis on the exacerbated proliferation of rights talk,[54] it has been documented that the juridification of society leads people to believe that peers cannot be trusted, for they are presumed to be self-seeking individuals.[55]

Now, if courts are to compete with legislatures for legitimacy as regards rule-making, they already find themselves in a privileged position, for it seems that 'citizens do not expect very much in the way of reasoning from legislatures, at least not as a condition for regarding statutes as binding'.[56] Nonetheless, to the extent that one wishes to respond to concerns related to countermajoritarianism, civil-law courts in particular would be well advised to adopt a more tentative, more dialogical also, less 'apodictic' style,[57] for a deficit of good writing and

51 Martin Shapiro, 'Courts in Authoritarian Regimes' in Tom Ginsburg and Tamir Moustafa (eds.), *Rule by Law: The Politics of Courts in Authoritarian Regimes* (Cambridge University Press 2008) 329.

52 Leszek Koczanowicz, *The Politics of Dialogue* (Edinburgh University Press 2015) 133, 106.

53 Ibid. 162.

54 Mary Ann Glendon, *Rights Talk [:] The Impoverishment of Political Discourse* (The Free Press 1991).

55 Mitchell Callan and Aaron Kay, 'Associations Between Law, Competitiveness, and the Pursuit of Self-Interest' in Jon Hanson (ed.), *Ideology, Psychology, and Law* (Oxford University Press 2012) 193.

56 John Ferejohn, 'Judicializing Politics, Politicizing Law' (2002) 65 Law and Contemporary Problems 41, 54.

57 Pierre Legrand, 'Perspectives du dehors sur le civilisme français' in Nicholas Kasirer (ed.), *Le droit civil, avant tout un style?* (Thémis 2003) 178.

convincing argumentation represents a deficit of democracy and representativeness. As contestable as this might seem to the traditional lawyer, judges should, through their language, give up partially on law's 'mulish seriousness' hailing from the belief that 'law involves nothing less lofty than justice'.[58] This means that courts should strive to become, linguistically speaking, as less authoritative as possible even while sovereignly deciding on law's interpretation.

Law's authoritativeness can refer to at least two distinct aspects in this context. Firstly, it is noteworthy to mention that judicial decisions can hardly depart from 'the forms legated by law's triumphal and monumental history'.[59] As such, at least in the civil-law world, their line of reasoning as well as their style are patently authoritative. In effect, in putting an end to a conflict, judicial decisions, especially in countries where dissenting opinions are unknown or rarely used, provide little room for conceding that other solutions would have been equally valid. Law is there to end the conversation and to do so trenchantly, which, of course, has the obvious merit of avoiding the exhaustion implied in an endless exchange of ideas. However, this also means that law formulates its dictates in terms of right and wrong, often without providing sufficiently compelling explanations.

Secondly, law is authoritative in that not only does it present power as knowledge, but given its exclusionary ethos, it also forces participants to use a very specific set of arguments for the advancement of their cause. Imagine a conflict between neighbours which stays out of court: in trying to settle the dispute, every party can appeal to any type of argument as long as he or she manages to transmit it in an intelligible manner, irrespective of whether or not it is persuasive for the other party. In other words, anything goes: mercy, economic, moral or philosophical considerations, religious arguments, emotions, analogies, metaphors, comparisons, legal rules, compromises. In a court of law, social complexity is inevitably reduced since parties have to refer to legal materials, which lead them to convert the wide range of available reasons into very specific claims. In rejecting other discourses, law refuses to accept, in theory, that its concepts are 'precarious and pragmatic constructions which can be disarticulated and transformed as a result of the agonistic struggle among the adversaries'.[60] Thus, judicial outcomes are framed in terms that seem immutable. The irony lies with the fact that, in practice, open-ended, extra-normative considerations infiltrate the judges' reasoning. These are, however, rarely exposed to the reader as they usually get cloaked in legal jargon, thus contributing towards completing the tranquil picture of an aseptic legal science.

To call for a less authoritarian legal language, then, one acknowledging that law's meaning depends not only on written texts, is to plead for an increase of courts' legitimacy and representativeness. According to Mattias

58 Günter Frankenberg, 'Down by Law: Irony, Seriousness, and Reason' (2011) 12 German Law Journal 300, 301.

59 Cosmin Cercel, *Towards a Jurisprudence of State Communism* (Routledge 2017) 202.

60 Ibid. 33.

Kumm, a court's democratic legitimacy is given by a series of factors: volitional (how participative and transparent the process of judges' nomination is), identitarian (how diverse the people who sit on the Court are), argumentative (to what extent the court fears engagement with more open forms of practical public reasoning) and vicarious (to what extent legislatures can intervene after the court has decided).[61] The Romanian Constitutional Court scores low on all of them (except maybe in respect of the identitarian one – in any case less relevant in a culturally homogenous society as the Romanian one is[62]).

Or the deficit of argumentative representativeness is especially dangerous in times of populism. At the level of rhetoric, when Courts advance weak reasonings in general, populists or other authoritarian-inclined governments can speculate on this. They can argue, for instance, that when Constitutional Courts uphold their cause, the judges are not doing anything different. To see that they are doing something different, we need to rely on epistemic arguments, as analyses of legality will most often prove inconclusive. Or, epistemic arguments risk being equally inconclusive if deficiencies of language and logic are a pervasive feature of mostly all constitutional rulings. What is more, courts themselves might not be aware that by not rigorously framing their arguments, they provide populists with a dangerous legitimizing tool.

As Rosenfeld shows, 'the precise boundaries between legitimate constitutionalization of politics and illegitimate politicization of the Constitution are undoubtedly hard to draw'.[63] I would argue that this becomes especially so in a context such as the Romanian one where the Court is still to improve on its argumentative skills. To use here Rosenfeld's terminology, the Romanian Constitutional Court does not have a problem in doing *judicial politics in form* (its decisions conform to the legal form to the extent that they refer to statutes, precedents, soft law instruments, known methods of interpretation). However, when it comes to its *judicial politics in substance*, it is not as substantial as one might wish.

In his article 'After the Heroes Have Left the Scene', Mark Tushnet emphasizes the importance of 'attending to temporality in studying who sits on Constitutional Courts and what those courts do'.[64] The Romanian context speaks to this importance. As I see it, the Court is still, almost thirty years after its establishment, a first-generation Court that needs to step in to

61 Mattias Kumm, 'On the Representativeness of Constitutional Courts' in Christine Landfried (ed.), *Judicial Power: How Constitutional Courts Affect Political Transformations* (Cambridge University Press 2019) 281–291.

62 Currently, five men and four women sit as justices of the Romanian Constitutional Court, of which one is an ethnic Hungarian.

63 Michel Rosenfeld, 'Judicial Politics versus Ordinary Politics' in Christine Landfried (ed.), *Judicial Power: How Constitutional Courts Affect Political Transformations* (Cambridge University Press 2019) 63.

64 Mark Tushnet, 'After the Heroes Have Left the Scene' in Christine Landfried (ed.), *Judicial Power: How Constitutional Courts Affect Political Transformations* (Cambridge University Press 2019) 293.

allocate authority to institutions. And, indeed, politicians find it useful and are more and more prepared to allocate important work to the Court (as attested by the increasing number of cases resolved under 'the conflict of competences' clause). As the Court finds itself thus legitimized, it might not feel any particular pressure to accrue the quality of its judicial politics. A brief overview of the judges' biographies suffices to show that most of the judges are not well placed to elaborate sophisticated political decisions in judicial terms. Some of the judges' backgrounds are extremely dubious (denoting opportunistic behaviour in the extreme as in the case of a judge who had no career in law but was a politician who throughout his career belonged to no fewer than five political parties). In addition, some of the Court's more theoretical statements reflect a very simplistic understanding of their own role to the point in which one can cast a serious doubt on how much they are aware of their power. For instance, in one decision the Court stated: 'interpretation is not an activity generating legal norms, it is one of explanation'.[65] The case law of the Court is replete with such naïve statements, and though they might be seen as mere theoretical musings with no real impact on the solutions themselves, they do in fact shape the way judges reason and prevent them from putting forth solid rationales as long as the solution is presented as the obvious truth.

This might change when the Court enters its second-generation phase, as it can be expected to want to establish itself as an important game-changer even in the absence of political calls to that effect. This can mean that constitutional judges will start acknowledging at least a certain margin of discretion on their behalf, which in turn will prompt them to better justify their decisions. As Bogdan Iancu argues, '[t]he fact that … the Romanian Constitutional Court does not appear to have acquired the essential features of a credible judicial culture … cautions skepticism towards the possibility of creating or fostering legal culture solely by institutional or normative design'.[66] It should be expected that the composition of the Court will make room in the future for specialists with more serious credentials who have a broader understanding of constitutional matters. Until then, there are at least two reasons for optimism.

The first is that the Court is on the way to assimilating a human-rights discourse which helps it reach progressive decisions even when these are poorly written. If, according to a study conducted in 2005, between 1994 and 2003 the Constitutional Court invoked the texts of the Convention and the case law of the European Court of Human Rights as grounds for about 380 decisions (out of the total of almost 3,000 issued in that time interval), at present, the Constitutional Court invokes them in such a number in just

65 Decision no. 358 of 30 May 2018.
66 Iancu (n 43) 147.

one year.[67] In time, the vocabulary of the ECtHr might force the Court to adopt itself a more value-orientated, public reasoning speech.

The second reason for optimism relates to the fact that it takes little to make the Court more relevant intellectually. For instance, it suffices for the Court to welcome a new member, the 'hero' whom Tushnet speaks about in his aforementioned contribution, to alter the dynamic of the Court altogether. Indeed, a refined jurist has the capacity to steer the Court into a different direction in terms of its discursive style and reasoning, legal and general alike. A judge with the appropriate credentials who approaches the Constitution in a cosmopolitan spirit could force the other judges as well at least to strive to raise to the occasions presented to them.

12.6 Conclusions

At least two sets of conclusions can be drawn, I believe, from this case study. The first are more general and they regard legal interpretation in populist times. The second refer, more specifically, to the Romanian constitutional landscape, which provided me with the background for the more theoretical discussions. The two can be connected through a concept that I advanced in this chapter, namely that of 'epistemic deficit'.

My study revealed that it is possible that those decisions one can recognize as populist, mostly because of their outcome, respect the legal form no less than the more regular decisions do. By 'legal form' I mean the classical legal vocabulary, the legal procedures and the typical methods of interpretation. The result might be contestable but legally speaking – that is, formally speaking – the road taken to reach that result is as legal as those followed in cases whose outcomes are not questionable from a rule of law point of view. Now, what appears as a populist decision can be the result of poor argumentation or plain incompetence rather than of the implementation of a populist agenda consciously weakening constitutional guarantees and control mechanisms. Indeed, in contexts where constitutional adjudication lacks in argumentative quality in general, it becomes even more problematic to draw the line between legitimate judicial politics and illegitimate judicial politics, which is something that populist politicians could speculate in their favour. Under such a scenario, the outcome of the case remains almost the exclusive criterion speaking to the decision's populism.

By contrast, in jurisdictions where the legal community is accustomed to being offered highly refined legal reasonings by the courts, it might become possible to identify populist decisions by an analysis of their language as well. Thus, the epistemic community of lawyers might detect possible differences in the language from the one of the 'good old times'. However, the fact remains that the law alone cannot equip us jurists with all the necessary

67 Tudorel Toader and Marieta Safta, *The Dialogue of Constitutional Judges* (Peter Lang 2016).

evaluative tools for unequivocally determining what counts as democratic backsliding in adjudication. Valid (in the legal sense) decisions might still appear problematic from an interpretative standpoint. Or, a verdict of interpretative 'wrongdoing' on the part of the courts could hardly be pronounced without taking into account considerations (sociological, philosophical, political) that exceed the realm of the law. To use Hart's 'rule of recognition' vocabulary, formally recognized as law, such problematic decisions will not be accepted as intellectually compelling. In this case, the rule of recognition operates, paradoxically, both to recognize and to deny the status of law to the very same ruling.

The case study supports the idea that no method of interpretation is more susceptible than others to being 'hijacked' by the populist or to be put to the use of poor political thought. While the historical method has been privileged by the majority of the Court in the first case examined here, grammatical, systematic and teleological interpretations were all proposed to the judges by one of the party in order to uphold the very problematic outcome that was eventually held by the Court itself. Or those methods of interpretation were not manifestly ill-placed. The Court might have as well founded its decision on any or some of them.

Another conclusion that one can draw from this study is that formalist results (in the Romanian case that I scrutinized here, the attribution to the President of a merely formal role in a given procedure with implications for checks and balances) can be achieved through non-formalist means. While no legal method, not even the grammatical one, is inherently formalistic, some methods appear nonetheless more open-ended than others. Thus, one can easily see why the teleological method is less constraining than the grammatical one, and yet there is no correlation between the method's indeterminacy and the outcome of the case. Central and Eastern European legal cultures are often accused of being too formalistic. However, it is important to retain that the mere use of less formalistic methods like the teleological or the historical one to the detriment of the textualist method, for instance, does not necessarily entail desirable results from a rule of law point of view. Strict methods can lead to creative results and vice versa; namely, creative methods can lead to results that entrench or encourage formalistic thinking and all in all weaken constitutional guarantees.

Coming to the Romanian constitutional order, which I took as a background for my theoretical reflections, I have showed that the Constitutional Court is still a first-generation Court with a problematic composition (in terms of its members' professional trajectories, which affects its representativeness) and an argumentative capacity that leaves a lot to be desired. I called this 'epistemic deficit'. Indeed, before we start any political, philosophical or even legal discussion about a ruling's appropriateness, we have to inquire about a ruling's epistemic quality. Does it reflect bad faith, or simply poor argumentation? A decision might conflict with our political preferences. One can find it too 'socialist', for instance. But it should never be epistemically deficient. The epistemic authority of a constitutional court is not a given. It has to be relentlessly built with each new generation of judges.

Constitutional courts are not insulated from critique. One critique that we hear oftentimes refers to the Court being too politicized. However, as long as constitutional courts exist, they do hold important political power, and one cannot change this. To change this would mean to change language itself, to render it from indeterminate and flexible determinate and still. Now, with power comes responsibility, and the responsibility of constitutional judges takes first and foremost, I have argued, an epistemic form. In other words, one should ask the following question: 'What does one do with the language at his or her disposal?'. There are no correct solutions in the usage of language, but there are certainly authoritarian ways of using language qua judicial language as when the interpreter makes little effort to steer the language towards coherence and persuasiveness. However, epistemic activism should not be taken to mean judicial activism. Courts can be activist while being epistemically dormant. These activist courts that are epistemically 'lazy' entertain the post-political *Zeitgeist* of our time and thus contribute to the accumulation of resentment on the part of those excluded from the process of identity search and eventually to populist claims. A decision of the Constitutional Court cannot generate ideological approval among all the members of a society, but it can and should generate epistemic approval, signalling the writing of a to-be-continued story and the possibility of critique. As the Romanian examples show, when courts display weak epistemic authority and the political environment is fraught with bad intentions (be they populist or other), it becomes hard to say for which values the judiciary stands. It is unsurprising, then, that courts lose their guidance role in the judicial community and, more broadly, in society. If anything, the recent populist attacks on the rule of law reminded us that 'as a minimum, the law is about interpreting texts',[68] that texts are not self-executing and that, therefore, the people who are behind law's curtains (and their background, competences, inclinations, aspirations, political preferences, linguistic abilities, etc.) matter as much as long-standing legal rules, principles and doctrines.

68 Costas Douzinas, 'Law and Justice in Postmodernity' in Steven Connor (ed.), *The Cambridge Companion to Postmodernism* (Cambridge University Press 2006) 200.

13 Constitutional interpretation and populism in contemporary Spain

Francisco Balaguer Callejón

13.1 Introduction

The relationship between populism and constitutional interpretation has various aspects that must be analysed before concluding with the negative response that could be given in the first place regarding the specific interpretation of constitutional jurisdiction in Spain. In reality, one of the essential functions of constitutional jurisdiction is precisely to control the effects that populist movements can bring about,[1] especially when they achieve majorities with government policies that are contrary to the constitution, with a tendency to limit the rights of minorities and opposition or to close down the political process, making it difficult to alternate in power. From this perspective, it could well be said that populism and constitutional interpretation are two basically incompatible terms, especially at the level of constitutional jurisdiction.

Naturally, the definition of what populism is considered to be and also of what is understood by constitution and constitutional interpretation are prior factors that can determine different responses to this radical incompatibility. As regards populism, there is a wide variety of movements of a diverse nature whose classification is not easy, although there have been notable attempts to do so through political science, sociology and constitutional law.[2] Left-wing populisms are not the same as those on the right, national populisms or those with a religious inspiration, those with an ethnic component or those that do not even have a very precise ideological line beyond

1 Cf. David Prendergast, 'The Judicial Role in Protecting Democracy from Populism' (2019) 20 German Law Journal 245–262; cf. also Gilmar Ferreira Mendes, 'Jurisdicción constitucional, democracia en crisis y efectividad de los derechos fundamentales en Brasil' in P. Häberle, F. Balaguer Callejón, I. Sarlet, C. Strapazzon and A. Aguilar (Coords.), *Derechos fundamentales, desarrollo y crisis del constitucionalismo multinivel. Libro Homenaje a Jörg Luther* (Thomson Reuters 2020).

2 Pierre Rosanvallon, *Le Siècle du populisme. Histoire, théorie, critique* (Éditions Le Seuil 2020) Kindle Edition; Mark Tushnet, 'Varieties of Populism' (2019) 20 German Law Journal 382–389; Isaiah Berlin, 'To Define Populism' in *The Isaiah Berlin Virtual Library*; Gábor Halmai, 'Populism, Authoritarianism and Constitutionalism' (2019) 20 German Law Journal 296–313.

questioning the traditional political class or appealing to the people and to plebiscitary democracy.

The analysis carried out here attempts to be essentially constitutional and is based on some very precise theoretical lines that will allow us to point out the problems that populism poses in its essential features and in relation to the constitutional rule of law and normative constitutions. The latter are the constitutional models implemented in Europe as of the end of the Second World War with the new Italian Constitution of 1947 and the German one of 1949, which were followed by other European countries later, including Spain in 1978. This analysis is consistent with the idea of measuring populism in relation to a specific constitutional model and therefore without diluting the analysis in a generalist perspective that can use the names 'constitution' or 'constitutional' to accommodate even populist regimes. Such a perspective denatures the historical meaning of a constitution in the context of modern constitutionalism and the scientific analysis itself and can end up legitimizing profoundly undemocratic political action under the guise of a 'democracy' based on direct appeal to the people, to the nation or to a constitutional identity paradoxically set up by extra-constitutional elements.[3]

The fact that populism has penetrated the constitutional interpretation of some constitutional jurisdictions, as a consequence of the situation of democratic involution in some countries governed by populist or national populist movements, should not be a hindrance to pointing out the radical incompatibility between that constitutional interpretation and the model of the constitutional state in force in Europe. That is what we are going to do here, indicating the reasons for this incompatibility from a constitutional perspective.

In many countries that follow the model of normative constitutions, as is the case of Spain, the articulation of the constitutional jurisdiction is very technical, which makes it relatively impervious to new forms of constitutional interpretation that may arise with the arrival of populist movements. This does not mean that constitutional jurisprudence is itself technically faultless or that it is not subject to political tensions, partisan influences or even to conditions derived from particularly sensitive public opinion, in certain areas, deriving from particularly sensitive public opinion in certain areas.[4]

There are several reasons why, in countries like Spain, the wave of populism may reach, if it does, jurisdictional institutions somewhat later than other state institutions or the centre of political and social debate. Indeed, there are a number of basic antagonisms between the system of constitutional jurisdiction and populist movements that could be explained in

3 Halmai (n 2) 306 et seq.

4 On this matter, I refer the reader to the study I carried out on constitutional jurisprudence in Spain: Francisco Balaguer Callejón, 'Constitutional Courts under Pressure – New Challenges to Constitutional Adjudication: The Case of Spain' in Zoltán Szente and Fruzsina Gárdos-Orosz (eds.), *New Challenges to Constitutional Adjudication in Europe: A Comparative Perspective* (Routledge 2018) 164–184.

relation to the following dichotomies: reason v. will; constitutional democracy v. majority democracy; pluralistic democracy v. plebiscitary democracy; constitutional order v. popular or national sovereignty. Some of these variables (such as majority democracy or popular or national sovereignty) are not totally incompatible with the normative constitution, as we will see, but only partially with some of their temporal and spatial coordinates.[5]

All of these aspects can hinder populist stances from becoming established at the jurisdictional level of constitutional interpretation. However, in the opposite direction, it should be noted that these stances are taking up more and more space in public debate, so that there may be a growing 'diffuse' influence of populism on constitutional interpretation, which ultimately ends up affecting the constitutional jurisdiction in countries where this has not yet happened. This diffuse influence upon constitutional interpretation does not necessarily have to do with specific content or even with techniques of interpretation, but may be related to cultural guidelines and new paradigms that are being introduced in our societies through social networks and applications developed by technological companies.[6] Some trends in particular could be noted. (1) The fragmentation and radicalization of public sphere, which hinder the constitutional purpose of society's overall organization and the articulation of fundamental consensus. (2) A new perception of time requiring immediate responses to political and constitutional problems, which inevitably may also influence the work of constitutional jurisprudence and make difficult long-term planning characteristic of constitutions. (3) The difficulty of articulating an effective guarantee of constitutional rights against technological companies and Internet applications. (4) The configuration of truth in the public space that is currently conditioned by phenomena such as fake news and post-truth, which find an especially favourable environment to spread in social networks. (5) The intervention of global agents and for eign groups in domestic public debate through social networks, which also affects the way in which the constitution is interpreted, because it distorts the internal domestic constitutional interpretation according to external foreign interests.

As we can see, we are dealing with a dialectic in which opposing forces operate, generating tension around the relationship between constitutional interpretation and populism. Some of these forces act against the penetration

5 In other words, the spatial and temporal coordinates defined in the constitutional rule of law in contrast with the legal rule of law. For example, majority democracy is not acceptable at the constituent moment, when a fundamental consensus is required, whereas national or popular sovereignty has no place under the constitutional order, in which all powers must be subject to the constitution. In the previous legal rule of law, however, these coordinates did not exist: the law expressed sovereign power as defined by the majority decision. Francisco Balaguer Callejón, *Fuentes del Derecho* (Tecnos 1991).

6 Francisco Balaguer Callejón, 'Las dos grandes crisis del constitucionalismo frente a la globalización en el siglo XXI' in *Nomos. Le attualitá nel diritto, 2018. Anticipazioni Convegno: Passato, presente e futuro del costituzionalismo e dell'Europa*. http://www.nomos-leattualitaneldiritto.it/wp-content/uploads/2018/09/Balaguer_Costituzionalismo.pdf.

of populism in the interpretation of the constitution, essentially at a jurisdictional level. Others, on the other hand, act in favour of this penetration, albeit still in a diffuse way in many countries, but already generating cultural guidelines and new paradigms that are affecting the constitutional interpretation.

The radical incompatibility between populism and constitution occurs because populism breaks up the constitution's space and time coordinates. Unlike constitutional parties, populist movements want to be both part and whole, constitutive moment and subsequent constitutional periods, suppressing conceptual boundaries and depriving the constitution of its essence and its very meaning. The breakdown of those coordinates is not merely a formal matter because the constitution exists upon those coordinates and ceases to exist if they disappear. When they disappear, jurisdictional control of the ruling majorities is not possible, and the guarantee of fundamental rights is not possible at the constitutional level.

At the core of these space and time coordinates of the constitution is pluralism, the recognition that the people or the nation cannot be anything other than a group of free people who have different approaches to politics and society and who pool their partial truths to build a common constitutional order, to which all submit equally. Therefore, there is not absolute truth or a fundamentalist interpretation of the constitution in favour of a specific group, nor can the people or the nation become instruments to denature the constitution itself.

Populist and nationalist movements concur on a fundamentalist way of understanding truth. The constitutional interpretation by the populist and national populist movements is impregnated with this absolutism, with this perception of the truth as something exclusive that belongs to them, so that they do not need to see the other fragments of the mirror, those belonging to other people and other social sectors, to determine the truth.[7] The constitutional interpretation by the populist and national populist movements is totally conditioned by their prior truth, the people or the nation that they consider superior to the constitution.[8] From this perspective, these movements tend to legitimize themselves directly through the people or the nation. But their interpretation of the will of the people or the nation is not mediated by the constitution itself. Instead, it is presented as a will that the political leaders of these movements know directly and even represent directly.[9]

7 Francisco Balaguer Callejón, 'Interpretación constitucional y populismo' (2020) 33 Revista de Derecho Constitucional Europeo.

8 Because, as Alessandro Morelli indicates, populism does not tolerate any form of limitation of popular sovereignty which it identifies with the political majority. Alessandro Morelli, 'El reduccionismo populista y sus efectos en la representación política y en la jurisdicción' (2019) 31 Revista de Derecho Constitucional Europeo n 31.

9 It could be said that they even 'embody' it through a 'représentation-miroir', through the man-people, the leader who reflects in himself all the members of the people. Rosanvallon (n 2) 50 et seq.

In this way, populisms end up breaking the logic of constitutional state and normative constitutions. By resorting to preconceptions that they place above the constitution, they distort the norms of the constitution and turn it into an inert object, to be manipulated according to their political interests. The interpretation that populist and national populist movements make of the concepts of people and nation disconnects them from their constitutional context by considering them as preconceptions that existed before the constitution and that can be placed above it in the event that those movements consider that there is a conflict with the constitution. In this way, these movements end up breaking up the rationale behind the constitution by appealing to a primary political power that they claim to represent while attributing a partial political ideology to the constitution, incompatible with the idea of wholeness and fundamental consensus that the constitution represents. Through their self-attributed ability to interpret the will of the people exclusively, they also attribute themselves the ability to interpret the constitution exclusively, subordinating it moreover to the will of the people or the nation.

13.2 The political and social context of Spain

The political and social context of Spain has been transformed in a very significant way in recent years. As in other countries, the financial crisis in Spain led to important changes in the political structure, with an end to bipartisanship that had been a constant in national politics. In the electoral processes prior to the separatist crisis in Catalonia, the political system fragmented into four significant national parties: two conservative ones and two progressive ones: PP and Ciudadanos against PSOE and Podemos.

After the outbreak of the separatist crisis in Catalonia, a new reorganization of the political sphere took place, initially with the highly significant growth of Ciudadanos, a party of Catalan origin that has manifested itself since its creation against Catalan nationalism. The last general elections saw the decline of this party and the rise of VOX, which can be considered a populist national party with relations with other parties of this nature in Europe, basically coinciding in their political programmes, despite the diversity of these movements in Europe[10] and what is being promoted by Steve Bannon and the American far right.[11] While the initial transformations in the political system (with the four parties indicated) originated in the financial crisis, those that occurred later have been driven by the separatist crisis in

10 Cf. the report by J.A. Aunión and Ignacio Povedano, published in the newspaper *El País* on 14 June 2020, based on a survey of 50 academics from 20 countries that specialize in studies of populism. Despite this heterogeneity, it places VOX clearly within these national populist or right-wing populist trends: 'Donde se sitúa VOX en la ultraderecha europea', https://elpais.com/internacional/2020-06-13/donde-se-situa-vox-en-la-ultraderecha-europea.html.

11 Interview by Daniel Verdú with Steve Bannon, *El País*, 25 March 2019: https://elpais.com/internacional/2019/03/24/actualidad/1553454729_290547.html.

Catalonia, which has led to a split in the traditional PP vote that had grouped together all the conservative sectors.[12] Part of that vote initially went to Ciudadanos and later to VOX.

At the time of writing (July 2020), Podemos is part of the Government of Spain through a pact with the PSOE and has greatly moderated its speech so that its populist character (since it has been defined as such by specialists in the analysis of populism[13]) is not perceptible in its political performance. Among the conservative parties, VOX clearly ranks among the national populist movements being promoted by the American far right through social networks.[14] Alongside this nationwide populism, one must also take into account the populist movements in Catalonia, in particular the old Convergencia, which has changed its name several times and has clearly leaned towards populism in recent years; as well as CUP, a secessionist movement too, but on the other wing of the political spectrum. In Catalan secessionism the orientation towards populism is not linked to a political ideology that fits neatly into the parameters of other European populist movements (for example, anti-immigration). As we shall see, its affiliation with populist movements has to do with its rejection of constitutional democracy, its contempt for judicial institutions and specifically the constitutional court, and its interpretation of the constitutional order in a populist sense with regard to the structural aspects of the democratic rule of law that we have defined in the Introduction to this chapter.

The fragmentation of the political system has not reached the constitutional jurisdiction because until now its members' appointments have been agreed between the PSOE and the PP. Although the PP has to compete with VOX for an electoral space that it previously monopolized, it cannot be said that it has taken a complete turn towards populism beyond the government of the regional Community of Madrid, where the populist tendency was already traditional and has been reinforced in recent times. As far as this study is concerned, it should be noted that for the moment, no populist movement has managed to promote candidates to the Constitutional Court, nor have they managed to generate a jurisprudential line of interpretation of the constitution that can be defined as populist.

13.3 Populist challenges to constitutional jurisprudence

The fact that populism has not hitherto permeated the jurisprudential interpretation of the constitution in Spain does not imply that the constitutional jurisdiction has not had to face the challenge of populism in some of its rulings. In particular, the long series of rulings related to secessionism in

12 Balaguer Callejón (n 4).

13 Rosanvallon (n 2).

14 Manuel Viejo and Antonio Alonso, 'La estrategia de Vox en redes sociales: ya es el primer partido en Instagram, la plataforma con más jóvenes' *El País*, 16 December 2018. https://elpais.com/politica/2018/12/12/actualidad/1544624671_005462.html.

Catalonia acted precisely to counteract the populist tendencies at the base of some parties that have encouraged action aimed at Catalan independence. They are rulings in which the Constitutional Court has had to interpret the possibilities and limits of the constitution in relation to the proceedings and secessionist postulates.

It should be noted, however, that this has been a problem to which the Constitutional Court itself contributed in a very relevant way through STC 31/2010, as we indicated in a previous work on this subject.[15] Despite this, the Constitutional Court has subsequently assumed a more open position in relation to the procedures that the Catalan secessionists could have activated to reform the Constitution, indicating that the Spanish Constitution may not only be reformed but also even admits its total revision.[16] Therefore, from the constitutional perspective, the secessionists' claims could have followed the constitutional channels through an initiative for constitutional reform promoted by the Autonomous Community region itself, which is provided for in the Spanish Constitution,[17] but paradoxically they have never tried, although they could have done so. Another matter would be the success or failure of such an initiative for reform during its subsequent processing, based on political negotiation between all the parties involved. But what is not constitutionally acceptable to the Constitutional Court is unilateral action contrary to the constitutional order.

The list of pronouncements of the Constitutional Court related to this topic is very long[18] and has not ceased since 2014 to today. In 2014, the

15 Balaguer Callejón (n 4). As indicated previously in that work: 'Constitutional Court Judgment 31/2010, of 28 June, relating to the Statute of Catalonia, declared that just one complete Article of the Statute was unconstitutional together with another three specific paragraphs of Articles or specific clauses that do not affect relevant legal issues related to the reform. However, its political impact was very negative as it unnecessarily affected questions of identity and because of the circumstances under which the pronouncement of the Constitutional Court was made ... STC 31/2010, in relation to the Statute of Catalonia, has fostered a large drive towards pro-independence positions and an evolution towards these positions on the part of the main nationalist party, which has been the governing party throughout almost the entire existence of the Autonomous Region. The motives are not just in the judgment; they are also related to the challenge to the Statute by the Partido Popular, despite no claim being lodged by the same party against the Statute of Andalusia, which contains a large number of similar articles to that of Catalonia. The many types of incidents suffered by the process before the Constitutional Court (challenges of judges, leaks of draft judgments, etc.) contributed to generating a growing feeling of discontent in a large part of Catalonian society in relation to the Constitutional Court'.

16 STC 42/2014, of 25 March.

17 Article 166 of the Spanish Constitution establishes that 'The right to propose a Constitutional amendment shall be exercised under the terms contained in clauses 1 and 2 of Article 87', in accordance to Article 87.2, 'The Assemblies of the Autonomous Communities may request the Government to pass a bill or refer a non-governmental bill to the Congressional Steering Committee and to delegate a maximum of three Assembly members to defend it'.

18 Cf. a very comprehensive reference to the rulings in Francisco Balaguer Callejón (Coord.), *Manual de Derecho Constitucional* (Tecnos 2020).

Constitutional Court marked a very relevant jurisprudential line[19] which partially upholds the claim lodged by the Government of Spain against a decision on the 'Declaration of Sovereignty and the Right to Decide of the People of Catalonia'[20]. The Constitutional Court established that the so-called first principle entitled 'Sovereignty' of the Declaration approved was 'unconstitutional and void'. At the same time, the Court affirmed that the references to 'the right to decide' of the citizens of Catalonia are not unconstitutional if it is interpreted in the sense set forth in legal foundations 3 and 4 of this ruling. Thus,

> The proposal of conceptions that seeks to modify the very foundation of the constitutional order is possible in our legal system, provided that it is not prepared or defended through an activity that violates democratic principles, fundamental rights or other constitutional mandates, and the attempt to achieve them effectively is carried out within the framework of the constitutional reform procedures, since respect for these procedures is always and in any case inexcusable.

In 2015 there were other pronouncements from the Constitutional Court, most notably the last one of that year, related to the result of the 'plebiscitary' elections to the Catalan Parliament called for 27 September of that year.[21] The secessionist sectors that had given these elections a plebiscitary nature clearly lost the 'plebiscite', as they failed to exceed 48% of the vote. However, they obtained the majority of seats in parliament and began a complicated drift towards sovereignty incompatible with minimum respect for democratic rules, since a minority cannot impose independence on the majority of society (independence being a matter that would in any case require a reinforced majority of no less than the two-thirds required to reform the Statute of Catalonia). Another decision of the Constitutional Court[22] states the unconstitutionality and nullity of Resolution 1/XI of the Catalan Parliament, adopted on 9 November 2015, 'on the start of the political process in Catalonia as a result of the electoral results of 27 September 2015'. The Court clearly indicates in FJ7 of that ruling that

19 STC 42/2014, of 25 March.

20 Resolution 5/X of the Parliament of Catalonia, approving the 'Declaration of Sovereignty and the Right to Decide of the People of Catalonia'. The first section of that Resolution states: 'The people of Catalonia have, for reasons of democratic legitimacy, the character of a sovereign political and legal subject'. On the basis of this self-attribution of sovereignty, the keys to exercising the right to decide are defined, indicating: 'the Parliament of Catalonia agrees to initiate the process to make effective the exercise of the right to decide so that the citizens of Catalonia can decide their collective political future'.

21 Paloma Biglino Campos, 'Cataluña, federalismo y pluralismo político' (2016) 37 Teoría y Realidad Constitucional 449–459.

22 STC 259/2015 of 2 December.

> [t]he autonomous chamber cannot establish itself as a source of legal and political legitimacy, to the extreme of claiming the power to violate the constitutional order that sustains its own authority.

The jurisprudential lines of the Constitutional Court were maintained in 2016 and 2017, with new pronouncements[23] that were to continue in 2018, 2019 and 2020.[24] Of particular relevance were the Constitutional Court's two rulings, both on 2 July 2019,[25] in relation to the application of Article 155 SC.[26] The application of Article 155 followed repeated disobedience by the Catalan secessionists as regards the resolutions of the Constitutional Court and as a consequence of Catalonia's declaration of independence which, although subsequently suspended by the President of the *Generalitat* himself several seconds after it was pronounced, generated great political tension that could only have been resolved without state intervention by calling elections to the Parliament of Catalonia, which the President of the *Generalitat* finally refused to do. The national government then decided to request authorisation from the Senate (upper house of the national parliament) on

23 The jurisprudential pronouncements of 2015 have to do with the consultation promoted by the Generalitat on 9 November 2014. They are the Constitutional Court's sentences 31/2015, of 25 February (in which some precepts of the Law of the Parliament of Catalonia 10/2014, of 26 September, of non-referendum popular consultations and other forms of citizen participation, are annulled), 32/2015 of 25 February (in which the Decree 129/2014 of 27 September on calling the non-referendum popular consultation on the political future of Catalonia is annulled) and the STC 138/2015 of 11 June (in which the actions of the *Generalitat* of Catalonia regarding the calling of the consultation are declared unconstitutional).

24 As regards 2018, the ATC 5/2018 of 27 January, the ATC 68/2018 of 20 June or the SSTC 10/2018 of 5 February; 46 and 47/2018 of 26 April and the STC 136/2018 of 13 December and others can be mentioned. In 2019, we must consider the STC 19/2019, of 12 February, which declares the provision for the investiture of a candidate for President of the *Generalitat* in his or her absence as unconstitutional. In the same sense, the STC 45/2019 of 27 March declares the unconstitutionality of several provisions of the Law of the Parliament of Catalonia 2/2018, of 8 May, annulling the legal precepts of the autonomous community that made it possible for a candidate to the presidency of the *Generalitat* of Catalonia to be invested without being present in person, as well as for remote meetings of the governing council to be held.

25 SSTC 89/2019 and 90/2019 of 2 July 2019.

26 Article 155 of the Spanish Constitution (inspired by Article 37 of the German *Grundgesetz*) was used to intervene the *Generalitat* of Catalonia and call for elections. Accordingly to this Article:

1. If an Autonomous Community does not fulfil the obligations imposed upon it by the Constitution or other laws, or acts in a way seriously prejudicing the general interests of Spain, the Government, after lodging a complaint with the President of the Autonomous Community and failing to receive satisfaction therefore, may, following approval granted by an absolute majority of the Senate, take measures necessary in order to compel the latter forcibly to meet said obligations, or in order to protect the above-mentioned general interests.
2. With a view to implementing the measures provided in the foregoing clause, the Government may issue instructions to all the authorities of the Autonomous Communities.

21 October 2017 to apply this constitutional precept after its request to the President of the Autonomous Community of Catalonia was not heeded. The Senate granted its approval, and the Government of the Nation dismissed the Government of the Autonomous Community of Catalonia and called for elections to form a new government in that Community. Two appeals of unconstitutionality were lodged against the Senate Agreement, one by members of Congress (lower house of the national parliament) of the parliamentary group Unidos-Podemos-En Comú Podem-En Marea,[27] and the other by the Parliament of Catalonia, which also challenged all the provisions issued in implementation or application of the measures authorized by the Agreement.[28] In both cases the Constitutional Court rejected the appeals except for one very specific aspect: the attribution of a lack of validity of rules or acts published without authorization because the Constitutional Court understood that they could affect legal certainty.[29] As regards the rest, the Court declared full compliance with the constitution in the implementation of Article 155 already carried out recalling, in the face of the appellants' allegations to the contrary, that the constitutional conditions required for their application were indeed met, taking into account the repeated failure of the Government and Parliament of the *Generalitat* to comply with the decisions of the Constitutional Court itself.[30] In any event, the Court also defined the general conditions to which it must be submitted, indicating that

> This norm allows the temporary alteration of the functioning of the autonomous institutional system, but in no way can it lead to the indefinite suspension of autonomy and, still less, to the institutional suppression of the autonomous community itself.

27 Resolved through STC 89/2019 of 2 July.

28 Resolved through STC 90/2019 of 2 July, which on the other hand dismisses the challenge to these provisions, thus limiting the scope of the recourse to the Senate Agreement by rejecting 'the alleged existence of an alleged "normative unit" in which what was agreed by the Senate and the provisions or acts adopted in its execution would seem to be included'.

29 For the Constitutional Court (STC 89/2019), it is legitimate for these acts to be subject to authorization while Article 155 is being applied so as to ensure that such application is effective and to establish prior controls to that effect in relation to what is officially published 'but in the event that such controls are circumvented or are ineffective, legal certainty (Article 9.3 EC) prevents the remedy from being that such publication is deemed to be unverified'.

30 STC 89/2019: 'To reach this conclusion, it is enough to recapitulate what this Court has declared in the pronouncements issued in relation to provisions and acts that form part of the so-called "constituent process aimed at the creation of an independent Catalan state in the form of a republic" (STC 90/2017, 5 July, FJ 3, among others). This process was launched by the resolution of the Parliament of Catalonia 1/XI, of 9 November 2015 "on the initiation of the political process in Catalonia as a consequence of the electoral results of 27 September 2015" (declared unconstitutional and null and void by STC 259/2015 of 2 December, which in turn was repeatedly violated by the *Generalitat*: AATC 141/2016, of 19 July; 170/2016 of 19 December; 24/2017 of 14 February and 123 and 124/2017 of 19 September)'.

The implementation of Article 155 SC cannot give rise, therefore, to a limitation of indefinite autonomy over time, but that it must have a determined or determinable time limit. For the Constitutional Court,

> Art. 155 CE is not an end in itself, but an instrument to guarantee the validity and effectiveness of the constitution in cases in which it is evident that only this way is it possible to restore the constitutional order.[31]

Among the latest pronouncements of the Constitutional Court in relation to this issue of separatist tensions in Catalonia, it is worth noting those related to monarchy.[32] In addition to these judgments, there are others that have to do with particular situations related to the judicial processes that have taken place in the criminal jurisdiction or with appeals for legal protection of rights motivated by actions of the Parliament of Catalonia.[33]

Especially noteworthy is the high number of applications for enforcement that the Constitutional Court has had to rule upon due to non-compliance with its rulings by the secessionist sectors.[34] Such contempt shown to the Constitutional Court contrasts with the attitude of the rest of the Catalan and national political actors who do respect its decisions. Although the secessionists have never obtained the majority of the votes in the elections to the Catalan Parliament (never exceeding 48% of the popular vote), they do have the parliamentary majority due to the disproportionality of the electoral system. This has allowed them to continue forming a government and passing parliamentary resolutions that challenge the Constitutional Court

31 In addition to these pronouncements by the Spanish Constitutional Court, there have been two others by the ECtHR and one by the ECJ. (In the ECtHR in the case of *Aumatell i Arnau v. Spain* of 4 October 2018 and in the case *Maria Carme Forcadell i Lluis and others v. Spain* of 28 May 2019.) The claim was declared inadmissible in both cases. In the ECJ, in its ruling of 19 December 2019 (Case c-502/19, Junqueras case) on a question referred for a preliminary ruling by the Spanish Supreme Court, it was decided in favour of recognizing the immunity of Oriol Junqueras from the moment that he was elected a Member of the European Parliament.

32 STC 98/2019 of 17 July, in which two paragraphs of Resolution 92/XII of 11 October, of the Parliament of Catalonia, related to the disapproval of the Head of State carried out by the autonomous Parliament and with the abolition of the Monarchy are declared void. Likewise STC 111/2019 of 2 October, which annulled Resolution 298/XII of 7 March of the Parliament of Catalonia creating a 'Commission of Inquiry into the Monarchy'.

33 To mention a few examples, the STC 75/2019 of 22 May, the STC 155/2019 of 28 November, in both cases with three dissenting opinions on the court's decision; the STC 115/2019 of 16 October, with one dissenting opinion; the SSTC 3 and 4/2020 of 15 January, with two dissenting opinions; SSTC 2 and 5/2019 of 15 January; STC 22/2020 of 13 February, with three dissenting opinions; STC 9/2020 of 28 January, with three dissenting opinions; SSTC 10 to 12/2020, all of 28 January; SSTC 36 and 37/2020 of 25 February, with three dissenting opinions and STC 38/2020, also of 25 February.

34 Along with those mentioned in previous notes, in the year 2019 alone, we can mention those ruled on by the Constitutional Court in AATC 180, 181, 182, 183 and 184, all of them from December 2019. In 2020, AATC 9 to 11/2020, the two of January 28 and AATC 16 and 18/2020, both from 11 February.

by ratifying agreements that have been declared null by the constitutional jurisdiction. Examples of this attitude are very numerous; it is enough to point out the Constitutional Court Orders issued in execution of previous sentences with which the *Generalitat* of Catalonia has clearly not complied and to which we have previously referred.[35] So the fundamentalist nature of populist attitudes, which obviate the conditions of the rule of law to emphasize the unlimited will of parliamentary majority (even if the latter does not represent the majority of the population as in the case of Catalonia) against the current constitutional framework, is evident here. For this reason, they repeatedly fail to comply with the rulings of the Constitutional Court, while the controversial reform of the Constitutional Court Organization Act of 2015 (LOTC), which gave the Constitutional Court itself additional powers to enforce its rulings, has not served to prevent such non-compliance.[36]

In the case of Catalonia, this intention by the secessionists to represent the people as a whole, thereby nullifying pluralist democracy, is constant. For example, when it is stated [37] that 'the will expressed on many occasions by Catalan society to maintain Catalonia as one people shall be guaranteed', it is obvious that more than half of Catalan society does not want independence, so that more than half of its members end up being expelled from this concept of 'one people'. The truth is, however, that the people of Catalonia express themselves through democratic institutions within a constitutional framework that must be observed, because the legitimacy of Catalonia's institutions derives from this framework.

However, the secessionists accept this constitutional framework as regards whatever interests them, while infringing upon whatever goes against their political projects because they appeal to a superior will, that of the 'people' whom they alone represent. But it is not the will of the real, plural people, i.e. the people that express themselves through democratic institutions under the rule of law; rather, it is they themselves constituted as a unique 'people', from which they exclude the majority of citizens because they do not coincide with their political positions. For this reason, they repeatedly fail to comply with the resolutions of the Constitutional Court, because they do not accept any legal limit to their will, which is defined as the authentic will of the Catalan people.

35 Vid *supra* the ATCs mentioned in notes 24, 30 and 34.

36 By means of Organic Law 15/2015 of 16 October on the reform of Organic Law 2/1979 of 3 October on the Constitutional Court, for the execution of the decisions of the Constitutional Court as a guarantee of the rule of law. This Law would be challenged before the Constitutional Court by the Government of the *Generalitat* of Catalonia and the Basque Government, appeals that were rejected by the Constitutional Court in the SSTC 185/2016 of 3 November (that of the Basque Government) and 2015/2016, of 15 December (that of the *Generalitat* of Catalonia) although the debate on the reform was also raised in the Court itself leading to the presentation of dissenting opinions by various judges.

37 Resolution of the Parliament of Catalonia 5/X, of 23 January 2013, approving the 'Declaration of Sovereignty and the Right to Decide of the People of Catalonia'.

These populist groups thus consider themselves as a part of the people when it suits their interests (when they stand for election, form a government, lodge appeals with the Constitutional Court) and as a whole when it is more useful for their projects (when they do not respect the rules that establish limits to the power of the majorities or the government, or when they do not accept the Constitutional Court's resolutions). They exercise the political power of the ruling majority within the constitutional framework when it interests them, yet they cross the border of that framework by exercising a constituent power when it seems convenient for their purposes. In doing so, they break not only the current Spanish Constitution but also any possible constitutional and democratic organization of coexistence. This is clearly evidenced in Law 19/2017 of 6 September on the self-determination referendum, declared unconstitutional by the Constitutional Court,[38] in which the parliamentary majority of Catalonia intends to exercise sovereign power, stating in its Article 3.1 that 'the Parliament of Catalonia acts as representative of the sovereignty of the people of Catalonia'. But neither the Parliament of Catalonia nor the State Parliament represents the sovereignty of the people; proof of this is that its laws can be prosecuted by the Constitutional Court and annulled for violating the Constitution.

This attitude can be seen even more clearly in article 3.2 of the same Law 19/2017 of the Parliament of Catalonia, which indicates that this law 'prevails hierarchically over all the rules that may conflict with it, while it regulates the exercise of a fundamental and inalienable right of the people of Catalonia'. In other words, a law that is approved within the framework of the Constitution and the Statute of Autonomy by a narrow parliamentary majority that does not represent even 48% of the voters is above the Statute of Autonomy and the Constitution itself. In short, the legal framework by which Parliament has a series of powers is accepted, but the limitation of those powers by the legal framework is not accepted. What benefits the interests of populists (the rules that define a parliamentary majority) is accepted, but it is not accepted what does not interest them (the rules that define the limits established by the rule of law for that parliamentary majority).

All of this must be qualified, however, with two observations. The first is that the populist drift of the Catalan secessionist sectors is atypical in the sense that they do not share the radical political programmes of other European populist sectors. But what they do share is fundamental in being able to be classified as populists: the claim to represent the people as a whole, the use of a concept of democracy that rejects pluralism and constitutional democracy and the contempt for constitutional jurisdiction, the resolutions of which they systematically disregard.

The second observation is that, in the populist evolution of the Catalan secessionist movement, there is (as in many other populisms) an ultimate reason that is only partially attributable to them: the blockade of politics, the

38 STC 114/2017 of 17 October.

inability of the rulers to manage problems through the Constitution and to give political solutions to those problems within the constitutional framework. The responsibility here clearly lies with the Popular Party government, which allowed the political problem to grow without applying the means to solve it before it finally led to a radical confrontation. The context of an economic crisis, for its part, also contributed to the development of increasingly intense political tension.

13.4 The health crisis and the constitutional interpretation

One last aspect to consider is related to the health crisis we are experiencing. The health crisis itself carries with it a specific constitutional interpretation that has to do with the exceptional situation that we are experiencing in which rights such as life, health and physical integrity must be preserved. Populists in governments or in the opposition tend to question measures of social distancing and to propose options more favourable to the maintenance of economic activity or the exercise of certain freedoms than to the preservation of people's lives and health. This is a question that deserves to be analysed because it shows the incompatibility of populism not only with procedures but also with constitutional principles and values.

Although not all populist movements have taken this position, a truly relevant part of them is following it even if this means, as known from specific epidemiological reports, causing an extraordinary increase in lethality that would bring the number of deaths to over a million in some countries.[39] Examples of this attitude in governments can be seen in the President of the United States, the President of Brazil and the opposition in AfD in Germany, for example, or in VOX in Spain. Their motives are varied and range from mere political opportunism to deeper reasons that have to do with the diverse nature and the social and political context in which these conservative populisms have developed in the 21st century compared to previous political movements such as fascisms.[40] In the case of Spain, the protest against social distancing measures has been led by VOX, which has called for demonstrations against the government.

On the question of the right to demonstrate in relation to social distancing measures, the Constitutional Court had the opportunity to rule,[41] and it did

39 This is the case of the Imperial College report, which indicates that the mitigation strategy could cause, in the best of hypotheses, some 250,000 deaths in the United Kingdom and between 1.1 and 1.2 million deaths in the USA. Cf. *Report 9: Impact of non-pharmaceutical interventions (NPIs) to reduce COVID-19 mortality and healthcare demand*.

40 Francisco Balaguer Callejón, 'Crisi sanitaria, globalizzazione e diritto costituzionale' (2019) 10 Atti della giornata di studi in onore di Paolo Ridola, Rivista italiana per le scienze giuridiche 795–812; see also 'A crise da democracia na época de Weimar e no século XXI' (Instituto Brasiliense De Direito Publico 2020) and 'Crisis sanitaria y derecho constitucional en el contexto global' (2020) 46 Teoría y Realidad Constitucional.

41 ATC 40/2020 of 30 April.

not accept, to process a petition for constitutional protection of rights filed by a trade union organization. The Constitutional Court directly assessed the basis upon which the prohibition had been established to determine whether it was proportionate and whether the limitation of the right corresponded to the constitutional requirements. That is, it was not because the declaration of the state of alarm was in itself an impediment to exercising the right, but because in the specific circumstances of the case, the demonstration could endanger the rights to health, physical integrity and life. The Court concludes that the measures proposed by the organizers did not allow avoiding this danger.

Other lower courts have accepted appeals contrary to the denial of authorization for demonstrations by the governmental authority. This does not necessarily contradict the doctrine of the Constitutional Court, since each specific case must be assessed in relation to the justification of the prohibition and also to the measures proposed by the organizers to prevent the spread of the virus. However, the truth is that in the demonstration by VOX in motorized vehicles in Madrid and in other cities, the passage of ambulances was blocked,[42] which was one of the aspects that the Constitutional Court had considered relevant in its decision, taking into account the current health situation, in order to refuse the appeal.

13.5 Conclusions

In many countries that follow the model of normative constitutions, as is the case of Spain, the articulation of the constitutional jurisdiction is very technical, which makes it relatively impervious to new forms of constitutional interpretation that may arise with the arrival of populist movements. However, in the opposite direction, it should be noted that these populist stances are taking up more and more space in public debate, so that there may be a growing 'diffuse' influence of populism in constitutional interpretation, which ultimately ends up affecting the constitutional jurisdiction in countries where this has not yet happened.

Populism breaks up the constitution's space and time coordinates. Unlike constitutional parties, populist movements want to be both part and whole, constitutive moment and subsequent constitutional periods, suppressing conceptual boundaries and depriving the constitution of its essence and its very meaning. By resorting to preconceptions that they place above the constitution, they distort the norms of the constitution and turn it into an inert object, to be manipulated according to their political interests. The interpretation that populist and national populist movements make of the concepts of people and nation disconnects them from their constitutional context by

42 See for instance, *Huffington Post* and *Diario de Cantabria*: https://www.huffingtonpost.es/entry/ambulancias-manifestacion-vox_es_5ec93d8dc5b62d9c3d2953c7?ncid=NEWSSTAND0006; https://www.eldiariocantabria.es/articulo/santander/protestas-motorizadas-vox-bloquean-paso-ambulancias-santander/20200523155726076557.html

considering them as preconceptions that existed before the constitution and that can be placed above it in the event that those movements consider that there is a conflict with the constitution.

In Spain there has been until now no influence of populist movements on the jurisprudence of the Constitutional Court. There has been, however, control by the Constitutional Court over some such movements of regional scope whose actions have tried to distort the logic of the constitution. These movements appeal to a concept of people they claim to represent in its entirety, excluding the majority of the population, which has a different political approach, and rejecting the constitutional procedures of the rule of law. In these movements, the intentional manipulation of concepts typical of populisms is clearly perceived in that they intend to mix and confuse the constitutive with the constitutional moment and the whole with the parts, breaking up the logic of the constitutional state.

On the other hand, the health crisis is also generating a conflict in the prevailing constitutional interpretation in favour of the rights to health or to life, which is being questioned by populist movements whether in governments or in the opposition (in Spain, the latter is the case) that encourage the continuity of economic activity or the exercise of certain freedoms as opposed to measures of social distancing. Some jurisprudential responses to this tension have already been given in Spain, with the Constitutional Court ruling in favour of the preservation of the rights to life and health.

14 Populism, UK sovereignty, the rule of law and Brexit

John McEldowney

14.1 Introduction

The question addressed in this chapter is whether the UK courts have developed new specific constitutional theories or doctrines in addressing the issues raised by Brexit. The chapter begins by considering the implications of the result of the referendum vote in 2016 in favour of Brexit, and the possible influence of populism. Next, Brexit's impact is evaluated in its effects on the relationship between Parliament and government, the working of constitutional conventions and parliamentary procedure during the passage of the European Union (Withdrawal) Act 2018,[1] which is the cornerstone of the post-Brexit era. There follows a discussion of the two most notable Supreme Court decisions on Brexit, *Miller 1*[2] in 2017 on the question of the use of the prerogative and the necessity of parliamentary approval, and *Miller 2*[3] in 2019 on the application by the government of the royal prerogative enabling the prorogation of Parliament. Going forward, the decisive December 2019 election victory of the Conservative Party with a large majority government and a populist leader as Prime Minister has enabled the government to proceed to exit the EU in January 2020 and enter the transition stage of leaving, pending final negotiations by the end of December 2020. The 2019 election victory was a triumph for Brexit supporters over those that supported remain. However, significant questions remain about the Brexit legacy, if any, on the courts, government and Parliament and the future of populism in UK politics.

1 See: Paul Craig, 'Constitutional Principle, the Rule of Law and Political Reality: The European Union (Withdrawal) Act 2018' (2019) 82 Modern Law Review 319–366.

2 *R (Miller) v Secretary of State for Exiting the European Union* [2016] EWHC 2768 (Admin) and [2017] UKSC 5.

3 *R (Miller) v The Prime Minister and others* [2019] UKSC 41.

14.2 The Brexit referendum and populist politics

Support for a referendum, to be included in the UK's unwritten constitutional arrangements, has a long history.[4] A. V. Dicey[5] was one of the first advocates, describing the referendum as a 'veto of the people'.[6] Dicey's motives for a referendum have been attributed to his opposition to 'party' government usurping Parliamentary power at a time when Irish Home Rule was in its ascendancy and this might result in the break-up of the Union[7]. Late nineteenth-century Britain was a period of considerable constitutional conflict, and Dicey feared the concession of Irish Home Rule would weaken the unity of parliamentary sovereignty through the break-up of the United Kingdom.[8] Dicey also recognised, but accepted with some alacrity, that parliamentary sovereignty, a fundamental pillar of the constitution, might be at variance to any popular referendum vote. He skilfully argued that political expediency of the times necessitated 'the will of the people' to prevail over elected MPs. A referendum offered through politics and polemics 'only a conservative check on legislation which is clearly in harmony with those democratic principles which in the modern world form the moral basis of government'.[9]

In contemporary times, various referendums have been held.[10] Political expediency underpins reasons for holding a referendum. While a referendum may allow a form of direct democracy, it is often in opposition to representative or parliamentary democracy. The reconciliation of different forms of choice – the party political and the popular have proved difficult. In the UK the referendum is normally non-binding,[11] authorised by an Act of Parlia-

4 P. Norton, 'Resisting the Inevitable? The Parliament Act 1911' (2012) 31 Parliamentary History 444–459.

5 A. V. Dicey (1835–1922) See: A. V. Dicey, *Law of the Constitution* (Macmillan 1885) and A. V Dicey, *Comparative Constitutionalism, vol 2* (Oxford 2013) 149.

6 A. V. Dicey, 'Ought the Referendum to Be Introduced into England?' (1890) 57 Contemporary Review 489; R. Weill, 'Dicey Was Not Diceyan' (2003) Cambridge Law Journal 474.

7 A. V. Dicey, *A Leap in the Dark* (2nd ed., London 1893); A. V Dicey and R. S. Rait, *Thoughts on the Union between England and Scotland* (Macmillan 1920). See: W. Molyneux, *The Case of Ireland Being Bound by Acts of Parliament in England* (Pamphlet 1688).

8 See: R. A. Cosgrove, *The Rule of Law: Albert Venn Dicey, Victorian Jurist* (Macmillan 1980) 35, 103–104, 235–236; A. V. Dicey, *Law of the Constitution* (Macmillan 1893) chapter 3. Also see: Dylan Lino, 'The Rule of Law and the Rule of Empire: A.V. Dicey in Imperial Context' (2018) 81 Michigan Law Review 739–764.

9 Dicey (n 8) 147.

10 In 2011, on the use of an alternative vote system to replace the first-past-the-post electoral system. Also in 2011, to give more powers to the Welsh Assembly. In 2014, a referendum to give more power to the Scottish government through an independent state was narrowly rejected.

11 An exception under the European Union Act 2011 for a binding referendum was never held. The Northern Ireland Act 1998 provides for a form of referendum that is imposed on ministers depending on the outcome.

ment, triggered by a dissatisfaction with the politics of political parties[12] or an inability of groups within political parties to agree. The EU referendum in 2016 came about because of long-standing deep divisions in the Conservative Party[13] over Europe, but also excited by a diaspora of dissatisfaction and underlying tensions within the United Kingdom. The UK had not triggered a referendum to join the European Community in 1972 but a confirmatory referendum on membership was held in 1975.[14] The 2016 referendum vote to leave the European Union was largely unexpected by the mainstream political parties, as it was a rejection of their advice to remain. Many explanations are offered for what happened in the Brexit vote. The general consensus is that the referendum was an expression of dissatisfaction amongst many voters of a failure of successive governments to address their needs. The term 'populism' is often used to mean an expression or response or corrective dissatisfaction about elites or vested interests and a desire to create political platforms that challenge existing orthodoxy. Notable characteristics that seem to fit the successful Brexit campaign include political activism working outside traditional party structures and organisations; a propensity to replace conventional constitutional structures by the use of popular meetings and skilled manipulation of social media in order to propagate simplified versions of facts and 'sound bites' effective against complex governmental systems; the exploitation and clever manipulation of legal regulations, including the rule of law, to avoid too much scrutiny and oversight; negotiating the electoral system through popular forums to garner support and exploit ideas that find common form in terms of nationalism and patriotism; the exploitation of public fears and suspicions, particular hostility to immigration; the use of ethnicity and race to promote common cause through accentuated differences of 'foreigners'.[15]

Responses to the 2016 referendum fit the model of typical responses to populism, namely a counter-reaction: a fear that the rise in populism will be an unstoppable influence on the political system that may enable 'far right' groups to flourish and gain political momentum and success. There is concern that its success will expose the fragility of democratic systems of government and may even question the vitality of the rule of law itself. In

12 See the evidence to the House of Lords Constitution Committee, *Referendums in the United Kingdom*, 12th Report, Session 2009–10, HL Paper 99, London: The Stationery Office.

13 Similar political splits came with the then Labour Government before the referendum in 1975 to modify terms of UK membership agreed earlier by the Conservative Government in 1972.

14 See: Bernard Donoughue, *Downing Street Diary* (Jonathan Cape 2005) 403. In the referendum, 17,378,581 (67.2%) voted yes and 8,470,073 (32.8%) voted no. The then Labour Prime Minister Harold Wilson remained euro-sceptic.

15 Jan-Werner Muller, 'The People Must Be Extracted from Within the People: Reflections on Populism' (2014) 4 Constellations; Ernesto Laclau, *On Populist Reason* (Verso 2005). Also see: Andrew Arato, 'Political Theory and Populism' (2013) 80 Social Research; Nicola Lacey, 'Populism and the Rule of Law' (2019) London School of Economics Working Paper 28; Katrina Forrester, *In the Shadow of Justice: Postwar Liberalism and the Remaking of Political Philosophy* (Princeton University Press 2019).

the Brexit context, the referendum is increasingly seen as a popular vote against the advice of the establishment. 'Taking back control' was doubly nuanced to mean leaving the EU as well as against the views of the majority of elected members of Parliament and their accompanying political parties, who favoured remain. Liberal democracy is accused of failing to represent a sufficiently wide spectrum of opinion and a reaction against an austerity programme of public cuts and a reduction in public services since the financial crisis of 2008.

The UK's decision to leave the EU claimed on the basis of the need to assert sovereignty and 'bring back control'[16] provided a simple slogan that became a compelling political message. The implications of the Brexit message are clear that EU membership had put at risk the UK as a nation state, undermined its sovereignty and impacted on the day-to-day life of many citizens, leaving them less free and able to make decisions on their own behalf. Underpinning many of the concerns about the EU is the question of immigration and its control. Paradoxically, the perception of 'hordes' of EU migrants is not supported by the actual figures, provided by the House of Commons Library. The origin of migrants coming into the UK in 2017 was 13% British nationals, 38% nationals of other EU countries and 50% nationals of non-EU countries. Significantly, it means that at least 50% of all migrants were subject to immigration controls.[17] Perceptions appear to matter more than reality, and in many crucial areas of the Brexit decision, communities believed that they were overcrowded by unwanted and uncontrollable EU citizens. One explanation comes from the 2008 financial crisis. Katrina Forrester offers the analysis[18] that as a consequence, the current political crisis is opportunistic and aimed at displacing liberalism and challenging exiting orthodoxy in our institution of government. Considering how Brexit has impacted on the UK's institutions, government, courts and Parliament provide an insight into how populism, or at least populist causes, may force a change in our perceptions about law and society.

14.3 Brexit: parliamentary procedure and constitutional conventions

Events after the 2016 referendum highlighted the political complexity of a parliamentary system when faced with a non-binding referendum result that most MPs did not want or expect. The government, under the Prime Minister, Mrs May, treated the 2016 referendum result as politically binding,

16 See: J. F. McEldowney, 'The Constitution and the Financial Crisis in the UK: Historical and Contemporary Lessons' in Xenophon Contiades, *Constitutions in the Global Financial Crisis* (Ashgate 2013) 167–194.

17 House of Commons Library Briefing Papers, *Migration Statistics* SN06077 (11 December 2018).

18 Katrina Forrester, *In the Shadow of Justice: Post-War Liberalism and the Remaking of Political Philosophy* (Princeton University Press 2019).

mainly because of a vociferous group of pro-Brexit supporters within the government and the Conservative Party. The majority of MPs in the House of Commons were supporters of remain, although both parties had agreed to give effect to the referendum result. The UK itself was spilt; the 2016 referendum was won by a narrow majority, 51.89% to 48.11%. Scotland and Northern Ireland voted to remain, as did London, while Wales and England voted to Brexit. Faced with likely opposition in the House of Lords, in 2017, the Prime Minister obtained the agreement of the House of Commons (required under the Fixed Term Parliament Act 2011) to call an early general election for 8 June 2017 with the expectation that having triggered Article 50 a few months earlier on 29 March, she might win a larger majority with which to govern. Instead, the government lost its overall majority and there was a hung Parliament. This had two important consequences, outlined below that have significance for the government. First, normally the government controls Parliament but the election result largely left Parliament in control with little room for the government to exercise its own authority. Second, the UK entered an unprecedented period where traditional constitutional conventions began to break down, not least because of the fetter on the government to decide when to call another election under the Fixed-Term Parliament Act 2011. As we shall see, the implications of a weakened government set the background for the issues raised by Brexit in the courts.

After the 2017 election the Conservative government, with only minority parliamentary support, reached an agreement with the Northern Ireland Democratic Unionist Party (DUP), resulting in an additional 10 members in support of the Conservative Party on key votes connected with financial supply. Even with the additional support of the DUP, it was not clear that the government would be guaranteed support for a specific agreement with the EU.[19]

The government's ambition to implement the referendum proved more complicated and politically difficult than at first appreciated, as it faced sustained opposition in Parliament, including from its own MPs. Brexit resulted in some novel constitutional challenges. The most serious was that the 2016 Referendum result was silent on the process and mechanics of reaching agreement with the EU as part of withdrawal under Article 50. Control of policy-making, traditionally vested in the government of the day, underwent unprecedented challenge as the government struggled to secure agreement within its own ranks as to the best policy to pursue in negotiations with the European Union. Negotiating with the European Union, a unique, complex and technically difficult process, was being determined by political struggles within the UK Parliament. The latter had far-reaching consequences for constitutional convention and the procedures of the House of Commons. The

19 P. Norton, *Governing Britain: Parliament, Ministers and Our Ambiguous Constitution* (Manchester University Press 2020) Chapters 4 and 5 (hereinafter Norton). I am grateful for the opportunity to read an advance copy of this excellent book.

migration of retained EU law into UK law proved a major challenge, as the debates on the European Union (Withdrawal) Bill 2018 revealed.

In January 2017 the government suffered opposition to its use of prerogative powers when the United Kingdom Supreme Court, in the *Miller 1* case, held that triggering Article 50 required an Act of Parliament. This was duly passed in six weeks.[20] The status of the Sewel Convention in relation to Brexit, also arose in the *Miller 1* decision (discussed in more detail later in this chapter). Scotland and Northern Ireland,[21] both devolved nations that voted to remain, raised the question before the UK Supreme Court of the Sewel Convention that provided that the UK Parliament would not normally legislate with regard to devolved matters except with the agreement of the devolved legislature. In the case of Scotland, section 2 of the Scotland Act 2016 recognised the existence of the Sewel Convention, and it was strongly argued that Scotland's case for the convention to be enforced by the courts came from the 2016 Act. The Supreme Court in *Miller 1* concluded that a 'convention was a convention and could not be enforced by the Courts',[22] thus depriving the legislature of Scotland and Northern Ireland with the need to give consent to Article 50 being triggered. In the particular case of the Scottish Parliament, the majority in *Miller 1* concluded that the UK Parliament has not sought 'to convert the Sewel Convention into a rule which can be interpreted, let alone enforced by the courts'. Interpreting the purpose and aims of the Scotland Act 2016 in this way avoided the Supreme Court having to engage with a 'political convention' which it would otherwise have had to deal with. The Supreme Court's interpretation raises some caution about attempting to place restraints on the powers of the Westminster Parliament through statute but at the same time acknowledges the necessity for the UK Parliament to enact fresh legislation required to trigger Article 50. The Supreme Court's narrow interpretation of the Sewel Convention marked its reluctance to decide whether or not a Brexit Bill needed any form of consent of the Scottish Parliament.[23]

Lord Norton, a leading political scientist and Conservative peer, estimates that largely as a result of Brexit, 38 ministers including 11 cabinet ministers resigned between April 2018 and the end of September 2019; the majority, 22, resigned over differences over Brexit policy. Most embarrassingly, the

20 The European Union (Notification of Withdrawal) Act 2017 see the *R (Miller) v Secretary of State for Exiting the European Union* [2016] EWHC 2768 (Admin) and [2017] UKSC 5.

21 Previously, a Northern Ireland case, in a judgment delivered by Mr Justice Maguire in *McCord's (Raymond) Application* [2016] NIQB 85, had rejected the attempt for judicial review of the UK Government decision to leave the EU and trigger Article 50 regarding the matter as non-justiciable.

22 This is of course consistent with Dicey's view that conventions were not legally enforceable but moral and political understandings. See: A. V. Dicey, *An Introduction to the Study of the Law of the Constitution* (10th ed. ECS Wade ed., Palgrave 1959) 39–40.

23 See the analysis offered by K. Ewing, 'Brexit and Parliamentary Sovereignty' (2017) 80 Modern Law Review 685–745. 711.

government was held to be in contempt of the House of Commons when it failed to publish legal advice on aspects of the Brexit arrangements that applied to Northern Ireland.

The full constitutional implications of Brexit on the Executive and Parliament have yet to be fully evaluated. It is clear that the referendum result created 'seismic tremors' within the Westminster system. Some considered it a crisis, while others pointed to the weakness of Parliament's constitutional arrangements, namely its outdated rules of procedures and highly discretionary decision-making, particularly in the discretion enjoyed by the Office of Speaker of the House. A noticeable omission was the use of modern electronic voting, leaving time-consuming votes on procedural motions and amendments to archaic procedures impeding the smooth functioning of decision-making.[24] Government ministers found a large portion of their time was spent not in governing, but hanging around the House of Commons chamber. Other shortcomings[25] related to Erskine May,[26] the long-established authoritative parliamentary book of past 'precedent', which lacked procedures (electronic voting for example) and suitable guidance for the needs of the twenty-first century.

14.4 Brexit and the Courts

Brexit, supported by a popular referendum vote, gave rise to legal controversy over the government's decision to use the ancient prerogative power to trigger Article 50, rather than face parliamentary scrutiny. The history of prerogative powers is distinguished by conflict often fully unresolved and resulting in a considerable lack of legal clarity. Blackstone's definition of the prerogative was couched in very general terms: 'a special pre-eminence, which the King hath over and above all other persons and out of the ordinary course of the common law, in right of his great dignity'. John Locke thought the prerogative 'was the power to act according to discretion of the public good'.[27] Such powers were treated by subsequent writers[28] as defined

24 One exception is the successful use of e-petitions, allowing the public to trigger a wider form of discussion in Westminster Hall and a wide preparation of material and discussion, including the House of Commons Library Briefing Papers and Information Packs.

25 Political and Constitutional Reform Committee, House of Commons (2010), *Fixed-Term Parliaments Bill*, Second Report, Session 2010-12, HC 436, London: The Stationery Office. Political and Constitutional Reform Committee House of Commons (2013), *The Role and Powers of the Prime Minister: The Impact of the Fixed-Term Parliaments Act 2011 on Government,* Fourth Report, Session 2013-14, HC 440, London: The Stationery Office. The House of Lords Constitution Committee 2010, *Fixed-Term Parliaments Bill*, 8th Report, Session 2010–2011, HL Paper 69 (The Stationery Office).

26 Erskine May, Parliamentary Procedure and Practice edition London. Also see J. Redlich, *The Procedure of the House of Commons: A Study of its History and Present Form, Vol. 1* (Archibald Constable 1908).

27 J. Locke, *The End of Civil Government,* chapter 14.

28 See: J. Chitty, *A Treatise on the law of the Prerogatives of the Crown,* 1820.

in the common law in terms of nature and extent.[29] Modern theory of the prerogative[30] is substantially a legacy from the seventeenth century and the constitutional struggles of the Stuart period of kingship.

Sir Edward Coke's (1552–1634) influence was perhaps the most decisive and set the trend away from the absolutist nature of royal power, to one of increasing judicial oversight. The judges in the *Case of Proclamations*[31] defined the King's powers as having no legislative authority without Parliament. This was followed by the *Case of Prohibitions del Roy*[32] that the king 'could not judge except through the intermediary of his judges'. While Coke's influence was considerable, it is clear that different judicial approaches also prevailed and accepted a greater latitude to the King.[33] Contemporary discussion of prerogative powers mirrors some of the earlier conflicts and uncertainties. De Smith noted how difficult it was to determine the question over the extent of the justiciability of the prerogative:

> There are simply categories of questions, some but not all having a strongly political flavour, which they have decided for historical or policy questions, to treat as non-justiciable.[34]

In contemporary times,[35] prerogative powers have largely given way to statutory powers.[36] The precise limits of judicial review very much depend on the 'justiciability' of the power being exercised.[37] Justiciability is a very vague concept, leaving much scope for judicial discretion. Any exercise of

29 *Council of Civil Service Unions v Minister for the Civil Service* [1984] UKHL 9.

30 See: *Bancoult (no 2)* [2008] UKHL 61 in which the Order in Council prohibiting native Chagos islanders to return to their home were considered by the House of Lords as falling within judicial review.

31 (1611) 12CO.REP.74.

32 (1607) 12 CO.REP.63.

33 For example in *R. v Hampden* (1637) 3 St.Tr.825 Croke. J in his dissent relied on the absolutist power of the Monarch. The theory of the prerogative was further discussed. *Bate's case* allowed the Monarch King the right to raise duties to regulate trade rather than raise revenue, and the courts could not look behind the King's statement of motive. *Darnel's case* (1627) 3 ST.Tr. 1 (known as the Five Knights Case), allowing the detention of prisoners to pay a debt for a loan required under the Privy Seal, broadly favoured the King, allowing the prisoners to be remanded. *Hampden's case* drew much greater clarity from the judges that if the King were allowed to levy taxation (ship-money) without Parliamentary consent, this would inevitably leave Parliament without authority.

34 De Smith, *Judicial Review of Administrative Action* (3rd ed. Stevens and Sons 1973) 255. Also see G. Sawer, 'Political Questions' (1963) 15 University of Toronto Law Journal 49.

35 See: House of Commons Library Briefing Paper, *The Royal Prerogative* Number 03861 (17 August 2017).

36 The Constitutional Reform and Governance Act 2010 codified the convention applied since 1924 on the ratification of treaties, giving the House of Commons a veto over treaties. The same Act made the appointment and regulation of the civil service to be on a statutory basis, replacing the prerogative powers of appointment.

37 See A. W. Bradley, K. D. Ewing, and C. J. S. Knight, *Constitutional and Administrative Law* (Longman 2015) 260–261.

prerogative powers by the government also falls within ministerial responsibility to Parliament.

14.5 The interpretation of prerogative powers: *Miller 1* – can the government trigger Article 50 by making use of prerogative powers?

Article 50 (TEU) provides that any Member State might leave the European Union 'according to its own constitutional arrangements'. The use of the prerogative to trigger Article 50 without prior parliamentary approval proved controversial. Gina Miller, a businesswoman and pro-remain supporter, argued that such use of prerogative powers could be triggered only after the UK Parliament had given its express approval. Miller made an application to the Divisional Court which unanimously upheld her argument that Parliament's authority was required to authorise the triggering of Article 50. The decision to appeal the Divisional Court was odd as it was well known, within government, that in advance of the Divisional Court's decision, the European Union (Notification of Withdrawal) Bill was in the process of being drafted. On appeal, the UK Supreme Court upheld the Divisional Court and held that the government could trigger Article 50 only after having express approval from Parliament.[38]

The question arises as to whether the Supreme Court in reaching this decision created new constitutional doctrines or approaches by placing constraints on the Executive's use of the prerogative. The majority in *Miller 1* reasoned that as with the *Case of Proclamations*,[39] the authority of Parliament is paramount and without its consent, the UK could not leave the EU. In reaching this decision, the majority were consistent with earlier case law that prohibited the prerogative from taking away statutory rights.[40] Article 50 had one significant aspect, namely that its effect was to dismantle an entire source and system of law in the United Kingdom that had become embedded in the legal system, with accompanying rights and obligations that changed the relationship between the individual and the state such as the *Working Time Directive*. The majority reasoned that such was the scale of change that only statute[41] could authorise a departure from the various rights and obligations the assumed into UK law. Parliament had not in the 1972 European Communities Act envisaged any significant changes in domestic

38 *R (Miller) v Secretary of State for Exiting the European Union* [2016] EWHC 2768 (Admin) and [2017] UKSC 5.

39 (1611) 12 Co. Rep 74.

40 Ibid.

41 It is useful to look at *R (Wheeler) v Office of the Prime Minister* [2008] EWHC 1409 (admin). Section 12 of the European Parliamentary Elections Act 2002 preventing any Treaty from increasing the powers of the EU Parliament without the approval by the UK Parliament. The Court rejected the argument that this required a referendum and this matter had already been covered under the European Union (Amendment) Act 2008.

law that would end the relationship with the EU. This could occur only by explicit legislation and not the prerogative.

Lord Reed dissented and argued that triggering Article 50 was part of a Treaty obligation and fell within a long-standing acceptance of the Executive's use of the prerogative to sign and agree international Treaties. The question of existing rights and obligations created since the UK joined the EU was covered by section 2(1) of the 1972 Act that broadly accepted that rights under the Act could be revoked or amended and given effect under the Act. International relations fell within the category of Executive discretion and the conduct of foreign relations' long-standing areas which valued 'unanimity, strength and dispatch' fell within prerogative powers. Underlying Lord Reed's analysis is the assumption that the EU is no different from any other treaty relationship, and that the Executive is best used to make such decisions about withdrawal from a Treaty.

The majority's approach followed the leading case of *Attorney General v De Keyser's Hotel*[42] in 1920, affirming that the prerogative is part of the common law, a residual power and not one that could endure for all time in its ancient form. The judges made a number of findings. Once executive power had been applied in an Act of Parliament, the Executive could no longer rely on the use of the prerogative. The judges' role in construing the use of legal powers required a careful exercise of judicial discretion in favour of the subject. The majority in Miller reasoned that the *De Keyser* principle indicated a predisposition to statutory over prerogative powers and that Parliament assumed that it would be consulted before any change would be made to the status quo of membership, given the major consequences this might have for the rights of the subject.

Lord Reed considered that the *De Keyser* principle did not apply in this case as Parliament had not yet, at any rate, regulated the withdrawal from the EU; it only recognised the existence of Article 50 TEU, not the means of withdrawal.

Popular reaction to both the Supreme Court and the Divisional Court included newspaper headlines claiming that the judges were 'enemies of the people' and arguing that the judges had usurped the popular mandate of the people found in the 2016 referendum in favour of leaving. Social media became an active source of 'hate mail' against MPs and remain supporters including Gina Miller. Political criticism of the judiciary reached unprecedented levels in opposition to the decision. The government's defeat in *Miller* resulted in the European Union (Notification of Withdrawal) Act 2017, passed within a few days of the Supreme Court decision.

The *Miller* decision attracted a wide range of academic opinions.[43] Some claimed that it broke new ground in the role of constitutional scrutiny by the

42 [1920] AC 508.

43 See the Special Edition to (2018) Public Law. Paul Craig, 'Miller, Structural Constitutional Review and the Limits of Prerogative Power' (2018) Public Law 48. Also see 'A Special Section on *R(Miller) v Secretary of State for Exiting the European Union*' (2017) Modern Law Review 685, 745.

Supreme Court, while others claimed the case was wrongly argued or poorly justified. Interpreting the correctness of otherwise of the majority's approach in *Miller* became tainted by the dispute between remain and Brexit. This overlooks the obvious and more mundane, that the *Miller* decision is largely in line with the orthodox Diceyan analysis of parliamentary sovereignty and the use of prerogative powers. The reasoning of the unanimous decision on the Sewel Convention also fits that analysis by refusing to construct section 28 of the Parliament Act 1998 as creating a status for the Convention, the Court followed a long-standing tradition of not giving legal effect to a constitutional convention.

There were some missed opportunities in the *Miller* case.[44] On the Sewel Convention, there was authority from the Canadian case law[45] that the Court could have explored the political significance of a Brexit withdrawal in the light of Scotland having voted to remain in terms of what kind or degree of consultation Scotland might have expected, even if that consultation fell short of requiring consent of the Scottish Parliament. On the need for parliamentary authority, there is the significance of the European Union (Amendment) Act 2008 incorporating Article 50 of the Treaty of European Union which had already provided Parliament with the authority to leave the EU. Taken together with the 2015 Referendum Act, was the 2008 Act not sufficient to give authority to leave the EU? This question was not addressed by the Supreme Court, but the Court might have considered the implications of such a question in their reasoning. Finally, the Supreme Court might have made clearer the consultative nature of a non-binding referendum, the role of populism and support for the democratic principles of parliamentary consultation underlining the constitutional role of ministerial responsibility to Parliament as a check on arbitrary power, including any use of the referendum. It is hard to take from *Miller* any guidance, if a government in the future might wish to withdraw from the European Convention of Human Rights.

14.6 Prerogative powers: *Miller 2* – can the courts review the exercise of the prerogative to prorogue Parliament?

The second *Miller* case also involved a legal challenge to the government's use of prerogative powers, this time, to prorogue Parliament. The Supreme Court unanimously held that the prorogation of Parliament for a period of five weeks was unlawful, void and of no legal effect. The first question is

44 Contrast the analytical style of the Supreme Court in *R(on the application of UNISON) v Lord Chancellor* [2017]UKSC 51 to *Miller*. The Unison decision was truly pathbreaking in the way public law issues were integrated through a horizontal effect into disputes between private parties. See Alan Bogg, 'The Common Law Constitution at Work *R(on the application of UNISON) v Lord Chancellor*' (2018) 81 Michigan Law Review 509–538.

45 See the Supreme Court of Canada: *Re Resolution to Amend the Constitution* [1981] 1 SCR 753.

whether or not the prorogation of Parliament is justiciable. The answer was unanimously agreed by all eleven justices, the one and only judgment delivered by Lady Hodge. Notably, Lord Reed, who dissented in the *Miller 1* case, agreed with the unanimous decision, that the government's decision to prorogue Parliament was null, void and of no legal effect. The Supreme Court overturned an earlier Divisional court decision but upheld the Scottish Court of Session's decision in *Cherry.* Unsurprisingly, academic reaction to the decision was spilt, with some in support[46] and adverse criticism by others,[47] including the claim that the decision was 'unconstitutional'.[48] The government was strongly critical of the Supreme Court's decision and accused the Supreme Court of making political rather than legal decisions, suggesting that in the future political decisions should be immune from judicial review and that the powers of the Supreme Court would come under review at some future date by the government.[49]

The justiciability of prorogation has divided opinion.[50] Contemporary case analysis in the 1985 decision in GCHQ[51] drew a distinction between judicial recognition of the *existence* of a prerogative power and the question of having to offer justification. Opinions divided on the latter being reviewable while the former was accepted as reviewable. Significantly, the majority, Lords Diplock, Scarman and Roskill, emphasised the need for evidence to justify claims made by the minister, but Lord Diplock had some reservations of the need to give reasons in the area of national security, leaving some doubts as to the level of judicial scrutiny available and leaving the possibility that certain matters were non-justiciable. In the GCHQ case, the court accepted the government's claim that 'national security' justified a ban on trade unions at GCHQ, the government's main intelligence centre. Such

46 Paul Craig, The Supreme Court, Prorogation and Constitutional Principle, https://ukconstitutionallaw.org/.

47 Stephen Laws, http://judicialpowerproject.org.uk/stephen-laws-the-supreme-courts-unjustifiedlawmaking/; John Larkin, 'The Supreme Court on Prorogation and Its Justiciability' http://judicialpowerproject.org.uk/john-larkin-the-supreme-court-on-prorogation-and-its-justiciability/; Prorogation3.pdf; Martin Loughlin, *The Case of Prorogation, The UK's Constitutional Council Ruling on Appeal from the Judgment of the Supreme Court* https://policyexchange.org.uk/wp-content/uploads/2019/10/The-Case-of-Prorogation.pdf.

48 John Finnis, 'The Unconstitutionality of the Supreme Court's Prorogation Judgment', Policy Exchange, https://policyexchange.org.uk/publication/the-unconstitutionality-of-the-supreme-courts-prorogation-judgment/

49 The 2019 Conservative Election Manifesto included. See: *The Guardian*, 22 February 2020.

50 Stephen Tierney, 'Turning Political Principles into Legal Rules: The Unconvincing Alchemy of the Miller/Cherry Decision', http://judicialpowerproject.org.uk/stephen-tierney-turning-political-principles-into-legal-rules-theunconvincing-alchemy-of-the-millercherry-decision/; Richard Ekins, 'Parliamentary Sovereignty and the Politics of Prorogation', Policy Exchange, https://policyexchange.org.uk/wp-content/uploads/2019/09/Parliamentary-Sovereignty-and-the-Politics-of

51 *Council of Civil Service Unions v Minister for the Civil Service* (the GCHQ case) [1984] UKHL 9

justification was accompanied by *ex gratia* compensation paid to workers for the abandonment of their trade union rights.

However, in the GCHQ case, Lord Roskill suggested that there were certain powers that were non-justiciable, including the dissolution of Parliament. Dissolution needs to be distinguished from prorogation. The former is where Parliament is brought to an end and a general election is called. However, the latter, prorogation, does not permit either House to be recalled. Prorogation also brings to an end the current parliamentary session with the loss of Bills, unless specifically carried over. Parliament's consideration of secondary legislation is suspended and select committees may not meet, though they can continue limited inquiries. However, the government can exercise its lawmaking powers to make regulations.[52] Undoubtedly, the period of prorogation reduces the influence of Parliament over the way its country is governed, This means that both Houses are unable to formally debate government policy and legislation, submit parliamentary questions for reply by government departments, or scrutinise government activity through parliamentary committees or introduce legislation. Normally prorogation is no more than a formality and without much political dissent, the implication is that Parliament gives it tacit consent.[53] Legally, Parliament is unable to prevent a prorogation, but it is possible for Parliament to replace the prerogative through legislation such as the Fixed-Term Parliaments Act 2011. Though there are financial consequences of prorogation, since a government might run out of supply as it would not be able to pass votes on account. This may limit the time for prorogation.

The question is whether the category of non-justiciability applied to prorogation in *Miller 2*. The Supreme Court considered what might be the limits of prerogative powers. The answer may be gleaned from the key historical developments of the prerogative.[54] In the past the prerogative was used to grant immunities to the Crown and potentially unfettered powers. Over the years, the courts considered Parliament's powers should not be threatened through the use of prerogative powers which, they held, could be limited by the common law and statute.[55] The result was that the courts recognised that Parliament had exclusive powers of taxation, and that the prerogative could not override statutory powers. It was also settled that there could be no new prerogatives, and the extent of existing prerogatives[56] could be settled by the courts.

52 That is under the negative resolution procedure.

53 There are examples in Australia and Canada where prorogation has to be made for explicit political reasons at federal and state levels.

54 See A. Twomey, 'Article 9 of the Bill of Rights 1688 and its Application to Prorogation' *UK Const. Blog* (4 October 2019).

55 O. Hood Phillips and Paul Jackson, *O. Hood Phillips' Constitutional and Administrative Law* (7th ed. Sweet and Maxwell 1987) 262–263, 266–267.

56 Ibid.

Limiting the use of prerogative powers in this way was a notable constitutional achievement that helped define parliamentary sovereignty[57] while also recognising the role of Parliament in holding government to account.[58] Both aspects, sovereignty and accountability, were adopted by the Supreme Court for their reasoning in *Miller 2*. The Supreme Court reasoned that the use of the prorogation power challenged both aspects of Parliament's roles. Sovereignty because Parliament was unable to meet and vote or pass legislation, and accountability, because Parliament was deprived of the opportunity to scrutinise the government over its policies. The two roles are inextricably linked.

Contemporary, judicial attitudes to the prerogative reflected the view that whenever any public powers are being exercised, statutory or prerogative, both should be subject to the same standard and intensity of review. In the *Miller 2* case, the Supreme Court set the limit upon the prerogative prorogue on the principle of legality, namely that it 'will be unlawful if the prorogation has the effect of frustrating, preventing, without reasonable justification, the ability of Parliament to carry out its constitutional functions as a legislature and as the body responsible for the supervision of the Executive. In such a situation the court will intervene if the effect is sufficiently serious to justify such an exceptional course'.[59] Placing the review of the prerogative on the same par as discretion exercised under a statute sets the terms of review as well as the rationale for the decision based on the primacy of the courts to determine the legality of matters raised in the courts. Two background considerations that set the context of the Supreme Court's decision are relevant. First, as amply demonstrated in the earlier discussion, a minority government had been defeated in successive attempts to gain parliamentary support which at that time was not forthcoming and that de facto the government of the day had lost the confidence of Parliament. Second, the government was unable to sign any affidavit certifying reasons for the exercise of the prorogation powers. The latter may have tipped the balance the other way – if a reasoned opinion justifying the government's position had been advanced. On the basis of *Wednesbury*[60] unreasonableness such reasons might have been accepted as a justification. Arguments that the Supreme Court was acting in an unconstitutional fashion have little historical support as courts have invariably strayed into constitutional conflicts and asked to determine the legality of actions by one side or another.[61]

57 House of Commons Library, Briefing Paper Number 03861 *The Royal Prerogative* (17 August 2017) 7–9. Also see, House of Commons Library, Briefing paper Number 8589 *Prorogation of Parliament* (11 June 2019).

58 Also see: *R. v Secretary of State for the Home department ex parte Fire Brigades Union* [1995] 2 AC 513.

59 *Miller 2*. UKSC 41 at [50].

60 *Associated Picture Houses v Wednesbury Corporation* [1948] 1KB 223.

61 M. Detmold, 'The Monarch in the Room', U.K. Const. L. Blog (2 October 2019) (available at https://ukconstitutionallaw.org/).

14.7 Has Brexit resulted in new constitutional theories or doctrines?

The question of how to assess whether the courts in the UK have developed new specific constitutional theories or doctrines in addressing the issues raised by Brexit falls to be answered. The answer may well disappoint those who seek a new and possibly far-reaching normative answer. The reality is much more mundane.[62] Viewed through the law of the prerogative, both *Miller 1* and *2* have been subject to close scrutiny and criticism. Both cases are consistent with a long-established constitutional and judicial pathway of reviewing prerogative powers on the same basis as statutory powers. In both cases Parliament was given sovereignty and legal priority, not the government of the day. The question raised by the devolved nations on the Sewel Convention under the Scotland Act 2016, *Miller 1* rejected any special status to be accorded to constitutional conventions, even when such a convention was recognised in a statute, fully in keeping with the orthodox Diceyan view that conventions should not be given any legal enforceability by the courts. The reasoning in *Miller 1* follows the reasoning in *HS2*,[63] namely, that a significant statute, the European Communities Act 1972 should not be devoid of effect by the use of the prerogative. Similarly, consistent with the principles of ministerial accountability, *Miller 1* prioritises Parliament in its EU scrutiny functions over the Executive. It is hard to distil new or novel underlying principles that distinguishes *Miller 1* from other decisions.[64]

Both *Miller 1* and *2* are unlikely to set new precedent on the use of prerogative powers as the particular issue of leaving the EU is not likely to recur again and it is highly unusual to withdraw from a Treaty of such magnitude and significance. Parliament is surely the most appropriate forum to resolve closely contested political choices that arise from EU membership, as will be the case when considering what will be retained on leaving the EU.

Miller 2 is in line with some contemporary cases, but without extending their analysis, or developing their line of reasoning. In 2002, in the *Thorburn v Sunderland City Council*, Lord Justice Laws acknowledged that parliamentary sovereignty was a principle of the common law, reviewable by the courts, within the category of constitutional importance that might include the European Communities Act 1972, the Human rights Act 1998 and the statutory framework for devolution. In the case of devolution, far from resisting this approach in the Scotland Act 1998 the Scottish Parliament was made permanent, further

62 R. Hazell 'Out of Court: Why Have the Courts Played No Role in Resolving Devolution Disputes in the United Kingdom' (2007) Journal of Federalism 589.

63 *R (on the application of HS2 Action Alliance Ltd., v Secretary of State for Transport* [2014] UKSC 3.

64 See the controversial decision in *R (Evans) v Attorney General* [2015] UKSC 21 and the discussion in M. Elliott, 'The Supreme Court's Judgment in Miller: In Search of Constitutional Principle' (April 2017) Paper 23/2017 University of Cambridge Legal Studies Research Paper Series.

signifying the special status given to Scotland. Since *Factortame 2*,[65] when EU enjoyed primacy over domestic law, this created a hierarchy of laws including the existence of what Laws refers to as 'constitutional statutes'. In 2005 in *Jackson*,[66] a case involving a challenge to the validity of the 2004 Hunting Act passed under the procedure set out under the Parliament Act 1949 further confirmed the existence of a hierarchy of Acts. Lord Steyn and Lord Hope both observed that parliamentary sovereignty was 'a construct of the common law', thereby transposing Dicey's doctrine of the sovereignty of Parliament into contemporary times. The 'absolute' nature of sovereignty is qualified in terms of any attempt to 'subvert' the rule of law. This line of reasoning has continued in the *Axa case*[67] in 2011, on the legality and incompatibility of acts of the Scottish Parliament. The Court held that the rule of law enforced by the courts was the 'ultimate controlling' factor on which the constitution is based.

In *HS2* the Supreme Court[68] recognised that various significant and fundamental constitutional statutes could not be impliedly repealed, and that a statute, the European Community Act 1972, should not be impugned to have no effect by the use of the prerogative.

It is wrong to assume that *Miller 1* and *2* have set in train an expansionist judicial bid for legal rules to overrule political choices. Instead, the evidence appears to suggest the contrary. There have been other Brexit legal challenges,[69] but most have been unsuccessful and also highly predictable in the classification of non-justiciable issues because of the underlying political issues raised by the challenges. For example, a judicial review challenge from a crowdfunding group campaigning to halt Brexit negotiations was rejected because it raised highly political issues that were not justiciable.[70] Similar reasons were advanced in refusing a challenge in April 2019 by the English Democrats claiming that Article 50 was illegal.[71] There were many more similar cases, but all failed to gain any success in the courts.

In terms of normative theory, Ewing neatly summarised the existence of a political constitution with a preference for governments to be held accountable in a political arena rather than through the legal process. There is an alternative approach resting on the existence of a legal constitution that advances accountability in the courts under legal restraint.[72]

65 [1991] 1 All ER 70, [1991] 1AC603.

66 [2006] 1AC 262.

67 *Axa General Insurance Ltd., and others v Lord Advocate* [2011] UKSC 46.

68 *R (on the application of HS2 Action Alliance Ltd., v Secretary of State for Transport* [2014] UKSC 307. Also see: *Thoburn v Sunderland City Council* [2003] QB 151.

69 House of Commons Library Briefing Paper Number 8415, *Brexit Questions in National and EU Courts* (1 November 2019).

70 *R (on the application of Webster) v Secretary of State for exiting the European union* (June 2018).

71 *The Queen on the application of the English democrats v Prime Minister and the Secretary of State for Exiting the European Union* Case no C)/1322/2019.

72 See Jonathan Sumption, *The Trials of the State: Law and the Decline of Politics Policy* (Profile Books 2019).

This may provide some promise to those who argue that *Miller 1* and *2* offer an expansionist view of the juridical and legal constitution triumphing over the political constitution.[73] Little guidance may be gleaned from both cases that in any clash between the Executive and the courts, the courts would fail to follow the Executive if needed and avert a constitutional crisis. More likely than not the courts will exercise self-restraint for Parliament's authority. Undoubtedly judicial oversight has undergone noticeable changes in the past twenty years, partly because of the growth of legislation particularly through the Human Rights Act 1998. A more active use of judicial review and a greater public awareness of the role of judges than in the past is more evident. Brexit has given greater visibility to such developments as well as a public perception that legal controls over the Executive have incrementally increased proportionate to greater legal and judicial controls.

14.8 Conclusions

The Covid-19 epidemic in 2020 has conspired to overtake Brexit in national significance, as the pandemic with a resultant health and economic crisis serves to re-calibrate what matters most and what will have enduring effect. In common with the history of medieval plagues, Covid-19 will undoubtedly adjust the status quo and realign law, the state and how people are governed. Covid-19 has restored technical expertise to its importance. Populist[74] ideology is likely to be reinvigorated as injustices become apparent by the revelation of deep-rooted startling inequality through the pending economic recession.

Brexit is not a single event but a continuous process. The UK exited the EU at the end of January 2020, and the transition stage is time-tabled to be completed by the end of December 2020, with considerable uncertainty as to the agreements that will be reached if any for the future relationship. De Smith writing in 1973 anticipated that the UK's accession to membership of the European Communities as 'entailing a major reappraisal of basis constitutional doctrines' including the question of obedience to the most recent Act of Parliament when a manifest inconsistency might arise. The *Factortame I*[75] case fulfilled this expectation. He also predicted the readiness of the courts to draw adverse interference from failure to give reasons for decisions.[76]

73 See: Loughlin (n 47).

74 *The Economist* 26 October 2019, p.79. Also see: Emmanuel Saez and Gabriel Zucman, *The Triumph of Injustice* (W. W. Norton and Company 2019); Heather Boushey, *Unbound* (Harvard University Press 2019); United Nations *Human Rights Council Visit to the United Kingdom of Great Britain and Northern Ireland: Report of the Special Rapporteur on Extreme Poverty and Human Rights* (22 May 2019) 1–4. House of Commons Briefing Paper, *Poverty in the UK: Statistics Number 7096* (5 September 2019); Joseph Stiglitz, *The Price of Inequality: How Today's Divided Society Endangers Our Future* (Pontifical Academy of Social Science Acta 19 Vatican City 2014); 'Paths from the Past: Historians Make Sense of Today's Political Turmoil' (*The Observer Review* 30 March–1 April 2019).

75 [1990] UKHL 7.

76 De Smith (n 34) 7–8.

Historians of the seventeenth century might find Brexit a modern example of the process of continuous adjustment of constitutional norms to accommodate new sources of power, politics and authority. In a minor way, that process has already begun in the UK because of Brexit. The referendum result has challenged the way elected MPs view their role and purpose.

Two aspects of Brexit's direct impact on the constitution are in the use of constitutional conventions and in the use of prerogative powers. Any attempt to codify each might only result in greater powers to the Executive, thereby replacing political controls with legal ones. This would be the default position of any government anxious to maintain its residual discretion. Paradoxically, this may create a greater expansion for the judicial role, something that might be resisted, at the expense of legislative checks and balances through parliamentary scrutiny. Another, perhaps, unintended consequence of Brexit is that executive controls through a plethora of Henry VIII clauses have given greater control to the Executive than before Brexit under the European Union (Withdrawal) Act 2018. How long lasting will all this be for the UK's constitution? Future historians are likely to relegate Brexit to the same category of constitutional development that historical study ascribes to the period of the Stuarts, noting its continuing constitutional influence and lasting significance in the power relationship between, then the King, Parliament and the courts. Contested accounts prevail as to who gained and lost and the legitimacy of the winner's victory.

The constitutional reform debate has also been re-ignited by Brexit. One possibility is to take the opportunity of dissatisfaction over Brexit to reform parliamentary procedures and/or to consider the merits of a written constitution. The latter is advanced as a means of clarifying the role and function of each element – the legislature, the executive and the judiciary.[77] The government has already signalled a review into the role of judicial review and the Supreme Court, that has yet to be established and its terms of reference announced.

77 Vernon Bogdanor, *Beyond Brexit: The British Constitution* (Hart 2019).

Part III

An outlook

15 Born populist

The Trump administration, the courts and the Constitution of the United States

Mark A. Graber

15.1 Introduction

Louis Hartz in *The Liberal Tradition in America* famously declared that American liberalism differed from European liberalism because the United States, as Tocqueville maintained, 'was born equal, instead of becoming so'.[1] European liberals in the seventeenth and eighteenth centuries had to fashion a liberal constitution and liberal institutions out of decidedly non-liberal materials. They sought a powerful state that would batter down the strong feudal institutions that had entrenched various status hierarchies. This experience left the liberal European bourgeois with a natural affinity for state authority as a major bulwark of bourgeois liberty and equality. American liberals in the eighteenth century had the happier experience of fashioning a liberal constitution and liberal institutions out of decidedly liberal materials. They did not require a powerful state to uproot entrenched status hierarchies in the absence of an established church and landed nobility. This experience left Jefferson, his political allies, and his political descendants with a natural antipathy to state authority which they were more inclined to view as the enemy of liberty and equality. Or so Hartz argued.[2]

This essay explores the possibility that right-wing populist constitutionalism in the United States differs from right-wing populist constitutionalism in Europe and South America because the United States was born populist. The literature on contemporary populism commonly links Donald Trump with such other right-wing populists as Viktor Orbán in Hungary, Nicolas Maduro in Venezuela, and the PiS party in Poland.[3] Right-wing populists in the United States and elsewhere scorn elites, insist on an ethnocentric understanding of the people, reject cosmopolitanism, and seek to centralize power

1 Louis Hartz, *The Liberal Tradition in America* (Harcourt Brace and Company 1955) x; Alexus de Tocqueville, *Democracy in America* (Vol. 2, ed. Philips Bradley, Vintage Books 1990) 191.

2 See Hartz (n 1) 35–66.

3 See, i.e., Tom Ginsburg and Aziz Z. Huq, *How to Save a Constitutional Democracy* (University of Chicago Press 2018); Steven Levitsky and Daniel Ziblatt, *How Democracies Die* (Crown 2018); Mark A. Graber, Sanford Levinson, and Mark Tushnet (eds.), *Constitutional Democracy in Crisis?* (Oxford University Press 2018).

in either the executive branch or, in the case of Poland, a political party.[4] If Trump, Orbán, Maduro, and other right-wing populists were writing a constitution from scratch, they might produce similar texts that include similar rules for staffing the national judiciary. How Trump and his political allies implement their right-wing populist constitutional vision differs from how right-wing populists in other regimes implement a similar right-wing populist constitutional vision because Trump faced different institutional challenges and had different constitutional options upon gaining power than his analogues in other regimes. Right-wing populists in such countries as Venezuela, Hungary, Poland, Turkey, and Israel when implementing their constitutional vision had to tear down a regime and various institutions with some degree of commitment to what I have called thickened progressive cosmopolitan constitutional democracy.[5] When reconfiguring the inherited political order, right-wing populists in power dramatically altered the national constitution, the dominant modes of interpreting or implementing the national constitution, and/or the people responsible for interpreting or implementing the national constitution. The Trump administration when taking office in 2017 did not confront a national constitution, interpretive practices, or a national judiciary with nearly the same degree of commitment to thickened progressive cosmopolitan constitutionalism. Trump found much to his liking in the inherited constitution, the dominant modes of interpreting or implementing the constitution, and the persons responsible for interpreting or implementing the constitution. He and other Republicans could build upon constitutional foundations established by mainstream conservative Republicans who had shared power in the United States for the previous fifty years. What other populists sought through radical transformation of the constitution, constitutional culture and constitutional judges, the experience in the United States suggests, a regime that is born populist may achieve by minor tweaks.

This essay examines the similarities and differences between constitutional manifestations of right-wing populism in the United States and elsewhere by examining the life, death, and jurisprudence of Supreme Court Justice Antonin Scalia. Scalia's opinions in *Morrison v. Olson*[6] and *Romer v. Evans*[7] hit many right-wing populist themes. Scalia in those opinions and elsewhere championed executive power, celebrated traditional morality, attacked elite cosmopolitans, and cast aspersions on using universal norms to interpret a domestic constitution. Unlike right-wing populists in other regimes, who

4 See Cas Muddle and Cristobal Rovira Kaltwasser, *Populism: A Very Short Introduction* (Oxford University Press 2017); Jan-Werner Muller, *What Is Populism?* (Penguin Books 2017).

5 Mark A. Graber, 'What's in Crisis: The Postwar Constitutional Paradigm, Transformative Constitutionalism, and the Fate of Constitutional Democracy' in Mark A. Graber, Sanford Levinson, and Mark Tushnet (eds.), *Constitutional Democracy in Crisis?* (Oxford University Press 2018) 686.

6 487 U.S. 654 (1988) (Scalia, J., dissenting).

7 512 U.S. 620 (1996) (Scalia, J., dissenting).

were uprooting constitutions committed to some version of thickened progressive cosmopolitan constitutional democracy, Scalia insisted, often dubiously, that his constitutional commitments were derived entirely from originalism, a method of constitutional interpretation that insists constitutional decision makers are bound by the meaning of constitutional provisions at the time they were ratified. In sharp contrast to right-wing populists in Europe and South America, who have had to resort to 'abusive' constitutional practices in order to fashion a supportive national judiciary, all Republicans have had to do in the past half decade to gain a strong judiciary majority on the Supreme Court is ensure one staunch conservative (Scalia) was replaced with another (Neil Gorsuch), replace a moderate conservative (Anthony Kennedy) with a more committed conservative (Brett Kavanaugh), and replace an elderly progressive who died (Ruth Bader Ginsburg) with another committed conservative (Amy Coney Barrett).

The following pages discuss only contemporary right-wing populism in the United States. Populism in the United States has a long history and is mostly though not exclusively associated with more left-wing movements.[8] While Scalia was on the bench, a populist constitutional movement developed among many law professors that was decidedly opposed to the conservative turn taken by the Supreme Court under Chief Justice William Rehnquist.[9] A fair case can be made that Senator Bernie Sanders of Vermont, the most prominent democratic socialist in the United States, is a far better representative of the American populist tradition than Donald Trump. Nevertheless, Trump is far better representative of the right-wing populist movement that is gaining power across the globe and is the subject of this volume. Whether a populist constitutional practice exists that is not simply a right-wing or left-wing populist practice is a topic for a different essay.

15.2 The populist jurisprudence of Antonin Scalia

Justice Antonin Scalia's influence on the course of American constitutional law helps explain why Donald Trump and Republicans in 2016 inherited constitutional doctrine and a judiciary that was largely born populist instead of becoming so. Scalia served as an associate justice on the Supreme Court of the United States from 1986 to 2016. During that time, he became a hero to a generation of right-wing lawyers by frequently articulating what in

8 See Michael Kazin, *The Populist Persuasion: An American History* (Basic Books 1995).

9 See, i.e., Mark Tushnet, *Taking the Constitution Away from the Courts* (Princeton University Press 1999); Richard Parker, *'Here, the People Rule': A Constitutional Populist Manifesto* (Harvard University Press 1988); J. M. Balkin, 'Populism and Progressivism as Constitutional Categories' (1995) 104 Yale Law Journal 1035. For a critique of this literature, see Mark A. Graber, 'The Law Professor as Populist' (2000) 34 University of Richmond Law Review 373.

other countries would be considered a right-wing populist jurisprudence.[10] Scalia in *Morrison v. Olson* championed a unitary executive capable of exercising the entire executive power. His dissent in *Romer v. Evans* insisted that the Constitution of the United States be interpreted consistently with what right-wing populists regard as traditional moral values. He scorned the use of international standards for interpreting domestic law. When Scalia died the year before Trump took the oath of executive office, his pro-executive, traditional values, anti-cosmopolitan jurisprudence enjoyed strong support on the Supreme Court and throughout the federal bench in the United States.

Scalia's dissent in *Morrison v. Olson* is his most influential opinion. The issue in that case was the constitutionality of the provision in the Ethics in Government Act that authorized the appointment of an independent counsel to investigate corruption in the executive branch of the government. The independent counsel was appointed by a judicial panel and could be removed from office by the Attorney General/President only for good cause. The judicial majority in *Morrison* had little difficulty sustaining this measure. Chief Justice Rehnquist's majority opinion ruled that the independent counsel was an 'inferior officer' whose appointment according to Article II, Section 2 Congress could vest in 'the Courts of Law'.[11] The 'good cause' requirement, Rehnquist asserted, left the executive with 'ample authority to assure that the counsel is competently performing his or her statutory responsibilities'.[12] Scalia, dissenting alone, rejected any diminution in executive authority, even one designed to ensure executive officials were obeying the law. His dissent insisted that executive power in the United States is absolute unless the text of the Constitution plainly specifies otherwise.

Scalia in *Morrison* championed a 'unitary executive'. The crucial premise of this understanding of the constitutional separation of powers is that the provision in Article II, Section I declaring 'The executive power shall be vested in a President of the United States' 'does not mean *some of* the executive power, but *all of* the executive power'.[13] Presidents may take any action free from interference from other governing institutions, whether those actions be firing government watchdogs or torturing suspected terrorists, as long as that action was traditionally considered executive in nature and the Constitution does not explicitly grant that executive power to the judiciary or legislature.[14] The Constitution, Scalia asserted, did not permit the Supreme Court to 'determine how much of the purely executive powers of

10 See Saikrishna Bangalore Prakash, 'A Fool for the Original Constitution' (2016) 130 Harvard Law Review Forum 24 ('Justice Antonin Scalia was one of my heroes'); Ted Cruz (@tedcruz), Twitter (February 13, 2016, 2:27 p.m.), https://twitter.com/tedcruz/status/698634625246195712?lang=en [https://perma.cc/PEM7-SEW3] ('Justice Scalia was an American hero').

11 See *Morrison*, at 671–673.

12 *Morrison*, at 692.

13 *Morrison*, at 705 (Scalia, J., dissenting).

14 See Steven G. Calabresi and Christory S. Yoo, *The Unitary Executive: Presidential Power from Washington to Bush* (Yale University Press 2008); John Too, *The Powers of War and Peace: The Constitution and Foreign Affairs After 9/11* (University of Chicago Press 2005).

government must be within the full control of the President'. 'The Constitution', he proclaimed, 'prescribes that they *all* are'.[15] In his mind, the constitutionality of the independent counsel statute raised only two questions. Was 'criminal prosecution ... the exercise of purely executive power' and had the president been deprived 'of exclusive control over the exercise of that power'.[16]

The independent counsel law, Scalia asserted, had two constitutional flaws. First, the independent counsel was appointed unconstitutionally. Article II, Section 2, declares the President 'shall have Power ... to ... appoint ... all other Officers of the United States ..., but the Congress may by Law vest the Appointment of such inferior Officers ... in the Courts of Law'. Scalia claimed that the independent counsel was a principal officer of the United States who had to be appointed by the president. 'Because appellant is not subordinate to another officer', he stated, 'she is not an "inferior" officer and her appointment other than by the President with the advice and consent of the Senate is unconstitutional'.[17] Worse, Scalia wrote, the statute ignored how 'Government investigation and prosecution of crimes is a quintessentially executive function'. Presidents had to have the absolute power to fire any federal prosecutor, even prosecutors commissioned to ferret out executive corruption. 'If the removal of a prosecutor, the virtual embodiment of the power to "take care that the laws be faithfully executed" can be restricted', he stated, 'what officer's removal cannot?'[18]

Scalia gave two responses to those who worried that executive corruption would thrive in the absence of independent authority to investigate the executive. First, the public would hold a president accountable for failing to prosecute corruption. '[W]hen crimes are not investigated and prosecuted fairly', Scalia declared, 'the President pays the cost in political damage to his administration'.[19] Second, absolute power was a fact of political life. Scalia's dissent concluded, 'A system of separate and coordinate powers necessarily involves an acceptance of exclusive power that can theoretically be abused'.[20] Viktor Orbán would have been pleased.

Romer v. Evans gave Scalia an opportunity to display his commitments to the cultural commitments of right-wing populism. The issue in that case was the constitutionality of an amendment to the Colorado constitution forbidding localities within the state and the state legislature from passing laws prohibiting discrimination on the basis of sexual orientation or otherwise providing legal protections to persons on the basis of sexual orientation. Veterans could secure an ordinance from a local town council, a county government, or the state legislature forbidding businesses from discriminating

15 *Morrison*, at 709 (Scalia, J., dissenting).
16 *Morrison*, at 705 (Scalia, J., dissenting).
17 *Morrison*, at 723 (Scalia, J., dissenting).
18 *Morrison*, at 726 (Scalia, J., dissenting).
19 *Morrison*, at 729 (Scalia, J., dissenting).
20 *Morrison*, at 710 (Scalia, J., dissenting).

against persons who served in the military. After the passage of Amendment 2, sexual minorities could gain such protection only by convincing their fellow citizens to ratify a state constitutional amendment. The judicial majority on the Supreme Court of the United States regarded a state constitutional ban on any state institution providing any protection to gays and lesbians with respect to any action or any right anywhere in the state as so overbroad as to compel the conclusion that the measure was based on unconstitutional animus towards sexual minorities.[21] Scalia, this time speaking for Justices Clarence Thomas and Chief Justice William Rehnquist, disagreed. He insisted state prohibitions against anti-discrimination laws was a constitutional expression of traditional sexual mores.

Scalia's dissent interpreted the comprehensive prohibition of anti-discrimination laws as 'a rather modest attempt by seemingly tolerant Coloradans to preserve sexual mores against the efforts of a politically powerful minority to revise those mores through the use of the laws'.[22] This effort to preserve long-standing traditions was justified on both substantive and procedural grounds. Scalia's constitution did not distinguish between sexual minorities and psychopaths. His *Romer* dissent stated, 'one could consider certain conduct reprehensible—murder, for example, or polygamy, or cruelty to animals—and could exhibit even "animus" toward such conduct'.[23] Amendment 2 prevented powerful elites from uprooting the traditional morality of the people. Sexual minorities in Colorado, Scalia insisted, 'possess political power much greater than their numbers, both locally and statewide'.[24] Putting state constitutional obstacles in the way of anti-discrimination laws was a vital means for average citizens to prevent this perceived powerful elite from running roughshod over Colorado politics by making such demands as having a right to employment when they had the skills necessary to perform the job in question.

The *Romer* dissent feeds into a common right-wing populist narrative that sees straight white male Protestants as the victims of laws than ban discrimination on the ground of sexual orientation, race, gender, and religion. Scalia insisted Colorado had prohibited only 'special protection for homosexuals', even though laws banning discrimination on the basis of sexual orientation routinely provide the same protections for heterosexuals as homosexuals. The underlying logic is that while the law typically permits a multitude of discriminations, such as discriminations on the basis of test scores or even hair color, legal rules typically carve out exceptions for such matters as race, gender, and religion. 'Ordinary' Americans, in this view, are disadvantaged by anti-discrimination laws that give persons of color, women, and sexual minorities the right to sue when they are denied admission to a university because of their race, gender, or sexual orientation, but do not permit straight

21 See *Romer*, at 632.
22 *Romer*, at 636 (Scalia, J., dissenting).
23 *Romer*, at 644 (Scalia, J., dissenting).
24 *Romer*, at 646 (Scalia, J., cdissenting).

white Protestant males to sue when they are denied admission because their parents did not attend that institution. Or so right-wing populists claim.

Scalia concluded his *Romer* dissent with some right-wing populist anti-elitism. He accused the Court of 'tak[ing] sides in the culture wars', by siding with 'the lawyer class from which the Court's members are drawn'.[25] This lawyer class furthered the marginalization of straight white Protestant males when exhibiting special solicitude for gays and lesbians. Scalia scornfully observed that law firms interviewing at law schools could discriminate on the basis of 'prep school', 'eat[ing] snails', and 'hat[ing] the Chicago Cubs', but not because the 'interviewer ... disapproves of the applicant's homosexuality'.[26] Fortunately, from his perspective, 'more plebian attitudes' still reigned in the national legislature which at that point had been 'unresponsive to extend to homosexuals the protection of federal civil rights laws ... and which took the pains to exclude them specifically from the Americans with Disabilities Act of 1990'.[27]

Seven years later, Scalia elaborated on these right-wing populist themes when dissenting from the judicial decision in *Lawrence v. Texas*[28] that forbade states from criminalizing homosexual sodomy. As in *Romer*, Scalia castigated elites while celebrating traditional morality. He described claims that constitutional privacy rights encompassed consensual behavior by adults as 'the product of a law-profession culture, that has largely signed on to the so-called homosexual agenda'.[29] Ordinary Americans knew better. Scalia expressed sympathy for the 'Many Americans [who] do not want persons who openly engage in homosexual conduct as partners in their business, as scoutmasters for their children, as teachers in their children's schools, or as boarders in their home' who could no longer throw same-sex couples in prison.[30] Scalia's *Lawrence* dissent combined anti-elitism with anti-cosmopolitanism. Justice Anthony Kennedy's majority opinion pointed to decisions protecting same-sex intimacy in other constitutional regimes as evidence that any moral consensus against homosexuality had long dissipated.[31] Scalia would not hear of such foreign influence on American constitutional law. 'The Court's discussion of these foreign views', he complained, was '[d]angerous dicta ... since this Court ... should not impose foreign moods, fads, or fashions on Americans'.[32]

Scalia's votes in other cases were consistent with right-wing populism, even as they sometimes demonstrated distinctive Republican Party and right-wing American populist twists. His religion jurisprudence was orthodox right-wing

25 *Romer*, at 652 (Scalia, J., dissenting).
26 *Romer*, at 652–653 (Scalia, J., dissenting)
27 *Romer*, at 653 (Scalia, J., dissenting).
28 539 U.S. 558 (2003).
29 *Lawrence*, at 602 (Scalia, J., dissenting).
30 *Lawrence*, at 602 (Scalia, J., dissenting).
31 *Lawrence*, at 576–577.
32 *Lawrence*, at 588 (Scalia, J., dissenting).

populism. Scalia claimed a constitutional commitment to monotheism[33] that justified state aid to religious organizations,[34] voluntary religious exercises in schools,[35] and the construction of religious monuments in public spaces.[36] His jurisprudence on democratic rights relentlessly served the interests of the Republican Party. Scalia insisted that million-dollar donations to political campaigns had the same constitutional status as reasoned discourse (even if the money was spent buying food for volunteers),[37] maintained that states had the right to require persons to have a state identification card in order to vote, even when no evidence indicated such measures were necessary to prevent fraud,[38] and asserted that federal courts had no business adjudicating egregious gerrymanders that enabled Republicans to control state legislatures while gaining substantially less than the majority of popular votes.[39] On other matters, most notably gun rights, Scalia advanced the distinctive world views of right-wing populism in the United States. Right-wing populists celebrated when Scalia in *District of Columbia v. Heller* issued a majority opinion holding that the Second Amendment of the Constitution protected an individual right to have a handgun for self-defense.[40]

Where Scalia was most distinctively American was in his justification of constitutional right-wing populism. Right-wing populists must often oppose tradition to constitutionalism. They commonly claim to speak in the name of a long-standing people, whose traditions have sometimes been suppressed by new progressive constitutions sponsored by cosmopolitan elites. Scalia united tradition and constitutionalism. He claimed to be speaking for the long-standing people who codified their traditions when framing and ratifying the ancient Constitution of the United States.

15.3 Originalism and American right-wing populism

Scalia claimed the United States was born right-wing populist and, barring constitutional amendment or replacement, had a legal obligation to remain right-wing populist. He insisted that his constitutional understanding of the separation of powers, federalism, fundamental rights, religion, guns, and freedom of speech were grounded in the original understanding of the Constitution of the United States. Government could provide certain forms of support for religion, he claimed, because '[t]hose who wrote the Constitution believed that morality was essential to the well-being of society and

33 *McCreary County, Kentucky v. American Civil Liberties Union of Kentucky*, 545 U.S. 844, 893–894 (2005) (Scalia, J., dissenting).
34 *Zelman v. Simmons-Harris*, 536 U.D. 639 (2002).
35 *Lee v. Weisman*, 505 U.S. 577 (1992) (Scalia, J., dissenting).
36 *Van Orden v. Perry*, 545 U.S. 677 (2005) (Scalia, J., concurring).
37 *Citizens United v. Federal Election Commission*, 558 U.S. 310 (2010) (Scalia, J., concurring).
38 *Crawford v. Marion County Election Board*, 553 U.S. 181 (2008) (Scalia, J., concurring).
39 *Vieth v. Jubelirer*, 541 U.S. 267 (2004).
40 554 U.S. 570 (2008)

that encouragement of religion was the best way to foster morality'.[41] Scalia insisted further that ascertaining the original meaning of the Constitution or original public meaning[42] was the only legitimate method of interpreting the Constitution of the United States. A 1989 lecture and essay declared,

> originalism seems to me more compatible with the nature and purpose of a Constitution in a democratic system. A democratic society does not, by and large, need constitutional guarantees to insure that its laws will reflect 'current values'. Elections take care of that quite well. The purpose of constitutional guarantees—and in particular those constitutional guarantees of individual rights that are at the center of this controversy—is precisely to prevent the law from reflecting certain changes in original values that the society adopting the Constitution thinks fundamentally undesirable. Or, more precisely, to require the society to devote to the subject the long and hard consideration required for a constitutional amendment before those particular values can be cast aside.[43]

Scalian originalism is the official method of constitutional interpretation of right-wing American constitutional populism. The *Guidelines on Constitutional Litigation* issued by the Department of Justice during the Reagan Administration declared, 'constitutional language should be construed as it was publicly understood at the time of its drafting and ratification'.[44] Scalia and his acolytes insist they are guided by the original meaning of the Constitution of 1789, even as several generations of scholars have demonstrated the incoherence of originalism as a means for interpreting an eighteenth century at the turn of the twenty-first century and that originalism does not explain the decisions Scalia and others actually make.[45] Such protestations of originalism are largely unique to right-wing American constitutional populists. Right-wing populists in other regimes are not interested in the original understanding of constitutions they correctly perceive were drafted by progressive cosmopolitans. The framers of the Constitution of the United States were also progressive cosmopolitans by the standards of their day. Nevertheless, because the Constitution of the United States is very old and knowledge of the framing is slight, distorted understandings of framing intention and language can often be wielded against contemporary progressive cosmopolitans.

Right-wing populists in the United States claim to be bound by the original meaning of constitutional provisions. Professor Adrian Vermeule observes,

41 McCreary County, at 887 (Scalia, J., dissenting).

42 See Lawrence B. Solum, 'Originalist Methodology' (2017) 84 University of Chicago Law Review 269.

43 Antonin Scalia, 'Originalism: The Lesser Evil' (1989) 57 University of Cincinnati Law Review 849, 862.

44 Office of Legal Policy, U.S. Department of Justice, *Guidelines for Constitutional Litigation* (Government Printing Office 1988) 3.

45 The most recent entry is Jonathan Gienapp, *The Second Creation: Fixing the American Constitution in the Founding Era* (Harvard University Press 2018).

> allegiance to the constitutional theory known as originalism has become all but mandatory for American legal conservatives. Every justice and almost every judge nominated by recent Republican administrations has pledged adherence to the faith. At the Federalist Society, the influential association of legal conservatives, speakers talk and think of little else.[46]

Even Trump purports to be an originalist. His Constitution Day message in 2017 'call[ed] on all citizens and all branches of government to reflect on the original meaning of our Constitution, and to recall the founding principles we too frequently forget'.[47]

This American emphasis on originalism is exceptional. Kim Lane Scheppele observes, '[i]nquiring this closely into a constitution's original meaning is done almost nowhere else in the world'.[48] Constitutional decision makers in other regimes rarely spout originalist justifications for their rulings. Right-wing populists are particularly disinclined to be originalists. The reason is obvious. As Zachary Elkins, Tom Ginsburg, and James Melton note, most constitutions last barely more than a generation, if that.[49] When populists come into power, they are likely to be confronted with a constitution written by more progressive cosmopolitans.[50] Their constitutional project is to subvert, revise, or replace that constitution, as was done in regimes such as Hungary, Poland, and Venezuela.[51] The last thing most right-wing populists want is to pledge allegiance to a constitution written by their mortal enemies. Right-wing populist constitutionalists in Israel, for example, are committed to undoing the constitutional revolution initiated by Aharon Barak and his cosmopolitan progressive allies.[52]

46 Adrian Vermeule, 'Beyond Originalism' *The Atlantic* (March 31, 2020) https://www.theatlantic.com/ideas/archive/2020/03/common-good-constitutionalism/609037/

47 Donald J. Trump, Proclamation 9639 – Constitution Day, Citizenship Day, and Constitution Week, 2017 Online by Gerhard Peters and John T. Woolley, The American Presidency Project https://www.presidency.ucsb.edu/node/331107.

48 Kim Lane Scheppele, 'Jack Balkin is an American' (2013) 25 Yale Journal of Law and the Humanities 23.

49 Zachary Elkins, Tom Ginsburg, and James Melton, *The Endurance of National Constitutions* (Cambridge University Press 2009).

50 For a claim that many recent constitutions and constitutional reforms sought to entrench a related neoliberal vision, see Ran Hirschl, *Towards Juristocracy: The Origins and Consequences of the New Constitutionalism* (Harvard University Press 2004).

51 See Wojciech Sadurski, *Poland's Constitutional Breakdown* (Oxford University Press 2019); David Landau and Rosalind Dixon, 'Abusive Judicial Review: Courts Against Democracy' (2020) 53 University of California, Davis Law Review 1313; David Landau, 'Abusive Constitutionalism' (2013) 47 University of California, Davis Law Review 189.

52 See 'Justice Minister to Radical Former Chief Justice: Your Path Leads to the Tyranny of the Minority' *The Jewish Press* (February 4, 2018) https://www.jewishpress.com/news/politics/justice-minister-to-radical-former-chief-justice-your-path-leads-to-the-tyranny-of-the-minority/2018/02/04/ ('Every day at the Justice Ministry I take another step in creating a democratic alternative to the constitutional revolution'). Yaniv Roznai, 'Israel: A Crisis of Liberal Democracy?' in Mark A. Graber, Sanford Levinson, and Mark Tushnet (eds.), *Constitutional Democracy in Crisis?* (Oxford University Press 2018) 363–367.

Right-wing populists in the United States seemingly face a similar difficulty. A long literature from Charles Beard to Gordon Wood to Michael Klarman depicts the constitutional revolution of 1787 as an elite struggle against the populist impulses unleashed by the American Revolution.[53] The details vary from scholar to scholar, but broad agreement exists that the Constitution of the United States was designed to privilege elite rule and elite political commitments. One of those elite commitments was international law. In sharp contrast to contemporary right-wing populists, who insist that no external standard limit their country's governance,[54] the American framers were fanatics on the subject of international law. Early Supreme Court justices routinely charged juries that they had the same obligation to maintain customary international law as they did to maintain domestic positive law.[55]

The primary populist solution to this problem is the selective use of history.[56] As a general rule, Scalia, Thomas, and other originalists cite history extensively when history provides strong support for right-wing populist positions. When contemporary historians dispute original understandings, right-wing populists in the United States cite only those historians who support right-wing populist positions, even when the weight of historical analysis cuts against right-wing populism. When the historical evidence is clearly against a right-wing populist position, right-wing populists ignore history. The end result is that the more right-wing populist justices on the Supreme Court in the United States who espouse originalism are as likely as the more progressive justices on that tribunal who claim to be guided by other principles of constitutional interpretation to make decisions based on contemporary constitutional visions and values.

Comparing how right-wing populists analyze the constitutional status of abortion and affirmative action illustrates this selective use of history. When Scalia and his judicial allies discuss abortion, practice when the relevant constitutional amendment, the Fourteenth, was ratified is decisive. States in 1868 routinely banned abortion, so none of the majestic generalities of the Fourteenth Amendment should be interpreted as protecting abortion

53 Charles A. Beard, *An Economic History of the Constitution of the United States* (The Free Press 1986); Gordon S. Wood, *The Creation of the American Republic 1776–1787* (University of North Carolina Press 1998); Michael J. Klarman, *The Framer's Coup: The Making of the United States Constitution* (Oxford University Press 2016).

54 See (n 7) and the relevant text.

55 See John Jay, 'John Jay's Charge to the Grand Jury of the Circuit Court for the District of New York, April 12, 1790' in *The Documentary History of the Supreme Court of the United States* (Vol. 2, Columbia University Press 1985–2007) 29; Martin S. Flaherty, *Restoring the Global Judiciary: Why the Supreme Court Should Rule in U.S. Foreign Affairs* (Princeton University Press 2019) 50–63; Jonathan Gienapp, 'Historicizing the Constitution: Originalism and the Original Constitution' 47–48 (unpublished manuscript on file with author).

56 This paragraph summarizes Mark A. Graber, 'Justice Thomas and the Perils of Amateur History' in Earl Maltz (ed.), *The Jurisprudence of the Rehnquist Court* (University of Kansas Press 2003).

rights.[57] This recourse to framing practice disappears when the more conservative justices on the Rehnquist and Roberts Court discuss affirmative action. The persons responsive for the Fourteenth Amendment frequently adopted race-conscious programs designed to help all person of color (and not merely former slaves).[58] Scalia and Thomas ignore this evidence. They rest their opposition to affirmative action on general principles of color-blindness that are nowhere to be found in the constitutional text or framing practice.[59]

Right-wing populists in the United States are nevertheless loath to admit the role values play in their constitutional analysis. A rare exception occurred in early 2020. Adrian Vermeule, a prominent Harvard Law professor, published an essay in a popular journal urging conservatives to abandon originalism for a jurisprudence rooted in Catholic integrationalism. Vermeule declared, 'such an approach—one might call it "common-good constitutionalism"—should be based on the principles that government helps direct persons, associations, and society generally toward the common good'.[60] 'Common-good constitutionalism' played core right-wing populist themes. Vermeule stated, 'the state will enjoy authority to curb the social and economic pretensions of the urban-gentry liberals who so often place their own satisfactions (financial and sexual) and the good of their class or social milieu above the common good'.[61] Again, Viktor Orbán would have approved, but not right-wing populists in the United States. The essay was dutifully condemned by conservatives across the conservative political spectrum, even as Vermeule's proposal probably better explained the path of right-wing populist constitutional decision-making than sincere efforts to determine the original public meaning of constitutional provisions.[62]

Populist embrace of originalism, if not particularly true to the framers either in result or in method,[63] is true to some important features of right-wing populism. Constitutional veneration is a form of authentic Americanism.

57 See *Planned Parenthood of Southeastern Pennsylvania v. Casey*, 505 U.S. 833, 952–953 (1992) (Rehnquist, CJ., concurring and dissenting); *Planned Parenthood*, at 980 (Scalia, J., concurring and dissenting)

58 See Eric Schnapper, 'Affirmative Action and the Legislative History of the Fourteenth Amendment' (1985) 71 Virginia Law Review 753, 755–758.

59 See, i.e., *Grutter v. Bollinger*, 539 U.S. 306, 349–350, 353–354 (Thomas, J., concurring and dissenting); *Grutter*, at 349 (Scalia, J., concurring and dissenting); *Adarand Constructors, Inc. v. Pena*, 515 U.S. 200, 239 (1995) (Scalia., J., concurring); *Adarand*, at 240–241 (Thomas., J. concurring).

60 Vermeule (n 46).

61 Ibid.

62 See Randy E. Barnett, 'Common-Good Constitutionalism Reveals the Dangers of Any Non-originalist Approach to the Constitution' *The Atlantic* (April 3, 2020), https://www.theatlantic.com/ideas/archive/2020/04/dangers-any-non-originalist-approach-constitution/609382/; Dan McLaughlin, '"Common-Good Constitutionalism" Is No Alternative to Originalism' *National Review* (April 2, 2020), https://www.nationalreview.com/2020/04/common-good-constitutionalism-is-no-alternative-to-originalism/.

63 See H. Jefferson Powell, 'The Original Understanding of Original Intent' (1985) 98 Harvard Law Review 885.

A political movement that sought to dispense with the Constitution or with the framers would be inconsistent with populist understandings of national identity in the United States. A constitution that is almost two hundred and fifty years old is more likely to provide support for more right-wing populist constitutional commitments than one that is twenty-five years old and ratified during the heyday of thickened progressive cosmopolitan constitutional democracy. Eighteenth-century texts do not embrace environmentalism, feminism, or the sexual revolution. The values underlying an ancient text can more easily be imagined or fabricated than those underlying texts framed and ratified within recent memory. Constitutional originalism benefits from the ease with which a history for right-wing populist claims that are not enshrined in the Constitution can easily be invented.

The Constitution of the United States is a symbol of authentic Americanism in a way almost no other national constitution can be an analogous national symbol. Most national constitutions are of recent vintage. In seeking their reinterpretation or destruction, right-wing populists argue that the recently adopted national constitution is not the true expression of the real people. Conservatives opposed to the constitutional revolution in Israel oppose the constitutional revolution initiated by a series of Basic Laws and judicial decisions interpreting those Basic Laws to the actual historic and present will of the true Israeli people.[64] The Constitution of the United States cannot be presented as an inauthentic representation of the historical will of the American people. For more than two centuries, Americans have for the most part revered the Constitution.[65] A right-wing populism that purports to represent authentic Americanism must claim to be true to the original spirit of the Constitution of the United States. Even some prominent left-wing populists are embracing a living originalism partly as a means of demonstrating their appropriate American bona fides.[66]

Most American populists, most of the time, on the left and the right, have had a romance with the Constitution of the United States. Gordon Wood documented a democratic revolution that took place in the United States, at least with respect to white males, during the first part of the nineteenth century.[67] This revolution was done in the name of the Constitution, even as the revolutionaries sought to overthrow the persons responsible for the Constitution. Martin Van Buren performed the remarkable task of detailing both how elites had seized control of the constitutional convention in 1787, but how a mass-based populist party was the best institutional means for preserving the Constitution those elites framed.[68] The Populist Platform of

64 See (n 52) and the relevant text.

65 See Michael Kammen, *A Machine That Would Go of Itself: The Constitution in American Culture* (Alfred A. Knopf 1986).

66 See Jack Balkin, *Living Originalism* (Harvard University Press 2011).

67 Gordon S. Wood, *The Radicalism of the American Revolution* (Alfred A. Knopf 1992).

68 Martin Van Buren, *Inquiry into the Origin and Course of Political Parties in the United States* (Augustus M. Kelley 1867/1967).

1892 similarly pledged allegiance to the Constitution of the United States as creatively interpreted by members of that agrarian movement. Party members sought 'to restore the government of the Republic to the hands of the plain people; with which class it originated' and declared their 'purposes to be identified with the purposes of the National Constitution'.[69] In wrapping themselves around the Constitution of the United States and insisting on a return to an imagined past, contemporary right-wing populists are exhibiting the same behaviors and employing the same justificatory logics as past generations of American populists (and the vast majority of popular movements in the United States).

Originalism is also useful for right-wing populists (and their conservative allies) in the United States because many items on the contemporary progressive (or left-wing populist) agenda could not be specifically imagined in the late eighteenth century. The culture wars of the eighteenth and nineteenth centuries were over prohibition rather than sexuality. Some version of Protestant Christianity was presumed to be the law of the land.[70] Sexual expression was heavily regulated. Affirmative action was unheard of and government had very little administrative capacity. For these reasons, claiming that the Constitution supports important parts of the contemporary conservative agenda is often effective rhetoric. The distance between the late eighteenth century and the early twenty-first century provides the historical fodder from common right-wing populist claims that the American framers did not risk their lives for [insert some progressive right or progressive government power]. The persons responsible for the Fourteenth Amendment did not self-consciously intend to protect abortion rights. The persons responsible for the commerce clause were not thinking of national health care. Progressives and left-wing populists have made originalist arguments for abortion rights and federal power to pass national health care laws,[71] but these assertions require more constitutional sophistication than the blunt decree that Abraham Lincoln was not at all concerned with reproductive choice or the Affordable Care Act of 2010.

In this respect, again, the Constitution of the United States is far more favorable to right-wing populism than other national constitutions. Newer constitutions typically make explicit mention of second- or third-generational constitutional concerns. They protect rights to gender equality. They announce rights to health care.[72] Vague clauses are naturally interpreted in light of practices of a few years ago, when those clauses were ratified.[73] What is explicit in new constitutions must be inferred when interpreting the

69 'Populist Party Platform' in Henry Steele Commager (ed.), *Documents of American History* (Vol. I, 7th ed., Appleton-Century-Crofts 1962) 594.

70 See *Holy Trinity Church v. United States*, 143 U.S. 457, 471 (1892) ('this is a Christian nation').

71 See Balkin (n 66) 174–177, 214–219.

72 See Peter E. Quint, 'What is a Twentieth-Century Constitution' (2007) 67 Maryland Law Review 238.

73 See Scheppele (n 48) 29–39.

Constitution of the United States. That constitution makes no mention of the equality rights of persons associated with the minority rights revolution. The text tends to focus on negative rights.[74] Originalists would have a vague clause interpreted in light of practices in 1787 or, perhaps, 1868, but certainly not practices after World War II when most foreign national constitutions were adopted.

Right-wing populists in the United States find originalism more attractive than right-wing populists in other regimes find originalism because the history underlying older constitutions can more easily be manipulated to support desired outcomes than the history underlying constitutions framed within recent memory. Claiming Lech Walesa was a right-wing populist is a challenging task when Walesa and many of his political supporters are still around to contest that designation. Neither George Washington nor Abraham Lincoln can magically appear to contest their appropriation for contemporary political projects. Walesa and other framers of post-Communist constitutions in Eastern Europe were clearly identified as progressive cosmopolitans. Neither the persons responsible for the Constitution of 1787 or the post-Civil War Amendments fit neatly into a 'progressive cosmopolitan' or 'right-wing populist' category. The American framers largely bequeathed their descendants quotations that, taken out of historical contexts, can be used by right-wing populists (or anyone else) for whatever political purposes they think best.[75] Consider framing attitudes towards social pluralism, a central concern of both right-wing populism and progressive cosmopolitanism. *Federalist* 10 seems progressive when claiming the Constitution of the United States will work because a large nation will enable a diverse people to share a common civil space.[76] *Federalist* 2 seems (right-wing) populist when insisting that the Constitution will work because Americans are 'one united people—a people descended from the same ancestors, speaking the same language, (and) professing the same religion'.[77] Pick your poison.

Historical distance influences strategies for interpretating constitutional provisions and past decisions. George Washington and Abraham Lincoln may be reimaged. Aharon Barak must be overcome. Jamal Greene suggests originalism is an easy sell for right-wing populists because originalism offers a vastly simplified account of American history that reverberates among Americans who distrust social pluralism.[78] Few Americans who do not study the Constitution for a living have any clue about what the framers thought about the status of international law. Hence, claims that Americans should not be enamored of foreign law may gain far more support among citizens suspicious

74 See *Jackson v. City of Joliet*, 715 F.2d 1200, 1203 (7th Cir. 1983).

75 See *Youngstown Sheet & Tube v. Sawyer*, 343 U.S. 579, 634–635 (1952).

76 Alexander Hamilton, James Madison, and John Jay, *The Federalist Papers* (Clinton Rossiter, ed.) (New American Library 1961) 77–84.

77 Ibid. 38.

78 Jamal Greene, 'Selling Originalism' (2009) 97 Georgetown Law Journal 657, 708–714.

of cosmopolitan elites than among constitutional historians.[79] Steven Griffin documents the contortions conservatives engage in when claiming that the constitutional framers in 1868 committed the United States to contemporary notions of racial and gender equality.[80] These legal gymnastics are possible because few Americans know or care about the history of the Reconstruction Amendments. Such appeals to oversimplified or mythological histories function better to subvert than reinterpret more recently adopted constitutions. Orbán and Fidesz preferred adopting a new constitution that reflected their conception of Hungarian nationalism rather than adopting the pretense that the post-Soviet Hungarian Constitution committed the Hungarian regime to some version of right-wing populism.[81]

15.4 Judicial populism before (and a bit after) the rise of right-wing populism

Scalia's influence on constitutional jurisprudence in the United States highlights the strength of right-wing populist jurisprudence in the United States before a self-conscious right-wing populist became chief executive. Trump upon taking office faced a far more sympathetic judiciary than did most other new populist leaders. A generation of Republican presidents and senators had staffed the courts with jurists sympathetic to a right-wing populist agenda, even though few labeled those justices or that agenda populist. These previous Republican efforts enabled Trump and his political allies to complete the task of consolidating a populist judiciary in the United States by relying on fairly normal processes of judicial replacement, which at most entailed what might be described as a more intense politics as usual. Republican efforts to secure a friendly judiciary often engaged in unprecedented actions that scholars described as 'constitutional hardball'.[82] Still, these actions were never inconsistent with plain constitutional text even as they uprooted long-standing constitutional conventions. The main challenge Republicans successfully overcame through unconventional legal behaviors was replacing one Supreme Court justice (Scalia) sympathetic to right-wing populist constitutionalism with another Supreme Court justice (Neil Gorsuch) sympathetic to right-wing populist constitutionalism.

Republicans became committed to remaking the Supreme Court when Richard Nixon became president in 1968 and more aggressively pursued that commitment after the election of Ronald Reagan in 1980. Nixon's court strategy was largely limited to finding justices who interpreted narrowly

79 Ibid. 713–714.

80 Stephen M. Griffin, 'Optimistic Originalism and the Reconstruction Amendments' (2020–2021) 95 Tulane Law Review.

81 See Muller (n 4) 64–66.

82 See Joseph Fishkin and David E. Pozen, 'Asymmetric Constitutional Hardball' (2018) 118 Columbia Law Review 915. See generally, Mark Tushnet, 'Constitutional Hardball' (2004) 37 John Marshall Law Review 523.

constitutional protections for persons accused of criminal activity.[83] Reagan's strategy was more comprehensive. The Reagan Justice Department called for justices committed to the original understanding of constitutional provisions, and sought to wield originalism in favor of what conservatives claimed were traditional moral values and executive power.[84]

What in 2020 looks like a right-wing populist agenda had a more complicated pedigree from the vantage point of 1980.[85] The Republican Party at that time was becoming a coalition of evangelicals, white ethnics opposed to further integration, foreign policy hawks, and new entrepreneurs opposed to federal regulations. The first two might be considered right-wing populist. The latter two were not. Republicans in the late twentieth century were more often thought to represent American elites than the lower middle classes that form the backbone of populist movements.

Republican cultural commitments in the late twentieth century reflected the increasing strength of the more right-wing populist wing of the party.[86] Republican party platforms supported bans on abortion, 'voluntary' prayer in public schools and providing public funding for parochial schools. When gay and lesbian rights became more prominent, Republicans called for continued bans on same-sex relationships and same-sex marriage. Republican party platforms initially called for judicial restraint, but over time, several activist programs were added. Republicans aggressively favored judicial decisions declaring unconstitutional affirmative action programs, gun control measures, and laws that restrict the participation of religious groups in public programs.

Republican commitments to executive power in the late twentieth century better reflected the more elite wing of the party. Most commentators in the late twentieth century thought the structure of American constitutional politics privileged Republicans running for president and Democrats running for Congress. Hence, as a matter of partisan advantage, Republicans had an interest in promoting presidential power, less because of a commitment to anti-pluralism than because presidential power was thought likely to be Republican power. Republican commitments to executive power had two other non-populist foundations. First, the Republican Party in the late twentieth century was committed to a far more muscular foreign policy than the Democrats. Americans had 'lost' Vietnam, prominent conservatives maintained, because Congress had interfered far too much in presidential policymaking. The separation of powers needed to be interpreted to give the president unilateral power to wage the Cold War as the president saw fit. Second, Republicans were concerned with what they perceived as out-of-control bureaucracies that

83 See Kevin J. McMahon, *Nixon's Court: His Challenge to Judicial Liberalism and Its Political Consequences* (University of Chicago Press 2011).

84 See David Alistar Yalof, *Pursuit of Justices: Presidential Politics and the Selection of Supreme Court Nominees* (University of Chicago Press 1999) 133–167.

85 For the changes in Republican commitments and coalition, see John Gerring, *Party Ideologies in America 1828–1996* (Cambridge University Press 1998).

86 All Republican Party Platforms can be found on the website of the American Presidency Project, https://www.presidency.ucsb.edu/.

they believed were dedicated to more liberal, Democratic principles. Again, increases in presidential power to control the bureaucracy were seen as measures likely to advance Republican policy commitments, populist or otherwise.

Republicans were quite successful at gaining at least partial control over the federal bench in the years before Donald Trump became president. From 1969 to 2016, Republicans appointed eleven Supreme Court justices, while Democrats appointed only four. The last three Chief Justices of the United States, Warren Burger, William Rehnquist, and John Roberts, have been Republican appointees. This disparity was partly a consequence of disproportionate Republican control of the presidency. From 1968 until 1992, Republicans controlled the presidency for all but four years. Some of this disparity was luck. Chief Justice William Rehnquist happened to die while President George H. W. Bush was in office. No justice left the bench during the Carter administration. Ruth Bader Ginsburg ignored President Obama's hints that she should retire at a time when she could be replaced by a liberal justice.[87]

Republicans also had a greater impact than Democrats on the direction of judicial decision making because Republican strategies for staffing the courts differed from those of Democrats.[88] Democrats tended to focus on diversity. Presidents James Carter, Bill Clinton, and Barack Obama sought to increase the percentage of women and persons of color on the federal bench. None would appoint a black women conservative to achieve that end, but none was interested in appointing a movement progressive with a distinctive leftish agenda. Ruth Bader Ginsburg, who had led the fight for gender equality in the 1970s, was the closest to a movement liberal on the Supreme Court. Her cause had gone mainstream long before Ginsburg joined the federal bench. Republicans were far more concerned with ideology when making judicial appointments. Presidents Ronald Reagan, George H. W. Bush, and George W. Bush, or their justice departments, intensively screened possible judicial nominees to ensure their commitments to the Republican constitutional vision. The result was a conservative bloc that regularly sought to pass the court in more right-wing populist directions on matters such as federalism, religion, and gun rights, and a more progressive bloc that on matters other than same-sex intimacy tended to engage in what Mark Tushnet described as 'defensive-crouch liberalism'.[89]

Republican efforts to control the federal bench before 2016 placed Trump and his political allies in a much better position than most right-wing populists upon assuming political office. Trump did not need to conduct a purge

87 See Susan Dominus and Charlie Savage, 'The Quiet 2013 Lunch That Could Have Altered Supreme Court History' *The New York Times* (September 25, 2020), https://www.nytimes.com/2020/09/25/us/politics/rbg-retirement-obama.html.

88 For comparisons between Republican and Democratic strategies for judicial appointments, see Henry J. Abraham, *Justices, Presidents, and Senators: A History of the U.S. Supreme Court Appointments from Washington to Bush II* (5th ed. Rowman & Littlefield Publishers 2007); Yalof (n 84).

89 Mark Tushnet, 'Abandoning Defensive Crouch Liberal Constitutionalism' *Balkinization* (May 6, 2016), https://balkin.blogspot.com/2016/05/abandoning-defensive-crouch-liberal.html.

of hostile justices or fundamentally restructure the federal judiciary. Rather, he and his supporters could fashion a more supportive right-wing populist judiciary largely by practicing what might be considered a more intense politics as usual. This more intense form of politics as usual was on full display during the struggle to fill Justice Scalia's seat, the confirmation battle over Brett Kavanaugh, and the staffing of the lower federal courts. Republicans repeatedly took actions that were unprecedented, but none in any sense violated the letter of the constitutional text.

Partisan warfare broke out when Scalia suddenly died on February 13, 2016, nine months before the next presidential election. Senate Majority Leader Mitch McConnell promptly announced the Republican-controlled Senate would not even consider confirming another Supreme Court nomination until after the identity of the next president was known. Republicans successful carried out this threat. The Senate refused to consider whether President Obama's nominee, Merrick Garland, a judicial moderate, should join the high court. McConnell's refusal to hold hearings was unprecedented. As Democrats repeatedly pointed out, the Senate had never refused to consider a presidential nomination to the Supreme Court. Still, while McConnell's ploy might have provided political cover for Republicans who did not want to vote against a Supreme Court nominee, his behavior was not a clear constitutional violation. The Constitution of the United States might be interpreted as requiring the Senate vote on a judicial nomination, but text hardly compels such a reading. Garland's eventual nomination was hardly a sure thing. Republicans might have followed a previous script and filibustered the nomination to death. All Republicans might have voted against the Garland nomination.

Trump in office and his political supporters played variations on this more intense politics as usual when fashioning a more right-wing populist federal bench. Trump and Senate Republicans moved more quickly than any previous regime to fill all federal judicial vacancies but did not attempt to create new judicial offices. Republicans urged senior conservative justices to resign so that they could be replaced with younger conservative justices, but made no effort to remove more senior liberal justices from the federal bench. In a less polarized environment, Republicans might have regarded the charges of sexual assault against Brent Kavanaugh as disqualifying, particularly when Kavanaugh appeared to commit perjury repeatedly at the Senate hearing to determine whether he was qualified to sit on the highest court in the land. With one exception, however, Republican senators decided to support the Kavanaugh nomination rather than require President Trump to nominate another justice who might be a less reliable judicial conservative.

This more intense politics as usual was on full display when Justice Ruth Bader Ginsburg died on September 18, 2020, less than seven weeks before the next national election. President Trump immediately announced that he would nominate a justice to fill that seat within a week and did so eight days later. McConnell immediately announced the Senate would hold hearings on that nomination. These announcements were consistent with the constitutional text, which says nothing about how quickly a justice may be nominated and confirmed. No past precedent existed, given that no justice had ever died less than two months before a national election during a time of substantial political polarization. The most that could be said was that Republican efforts to increase the influence of right-wing populism on the Supreme Court were hypocritical, given Republican claims in 2016 that no replacement should be made for a Justice who died nine months before a national election by the incumbent, and unseemly, given their declarations were made even before funeral services for Ginsburg had taken place.[90]

15.5 Populist pasts and presents

The past structures the present. Regimes that have similar aspirations and constitutional visions implement those aspirations and constitutional visions in different ways in light of different constitutional and regime inheritances. Stephen Skowronek observes that all new regimes are fashioned by the political conditions and institutional structures of the old regime.[91] Political leaders that appear similar may also differ in the justificatory logics available to them. Quentin Skinner notes how all revolutionaries must 'march backwards into battle'.[92] The differences between Trump and other right-wing populists capture the different ways right-wing populists implement constitutional visions in regimes that are born and not born populist.

Regimes that are born populist have an easier time implementing a constitutional vision than regimes that not so 'advantaged'. Populists in regimes not born populist must often engage in a complete restructuring of the national judiciary, which typically includes wholesale replacement of hostile judges. Trump merely tweets when he dislikes a judicial ruling and, with his allies in the Senate, fills up immediately all judicial vacancies that occur in the normal course of events. Populists in regimes not born populist must often engage in whole replacement of judges in order to challenge the long-standing use of comparative and international law as legitimate sources for interpreting the national constitution. The Supreme Court of the United States rarely used such materials before Trump took office. One judicial appointment was sufficient to guarantee that such materials will play no role in Supreme Court majority opinions for the foreseeable future. Where populists in other regimes must reverse entrenched practices, Trump at most must tweak (and tweet).

Trump also inherited a far more populist constitution than did right-wing populists in Europe, the Middle East and South Asia. The Constitution of the United States was framed, ratified, and significantly amended long before anyone had ever heard of the constellation of ideas that comprise thickened progressive cosmopolitan constitutional democracy. Twentieth-century progressives in the United States had developed modes of constitutional

90 See Dana Milbank, 'They Couldn't Even Wait until Ruth Bader Ginsburg Was in Her Grave' *The Washington Post* (September 20, 2020) (https://www.washingtonpost.com/opinions/2020/09/20/they-couldnt-even-wait-until-ruth-bader-ginsburg-was-her-grave/).

91 Stephen Skowronek, *Building a New American State* (Cambridge University Press 1982) 285.

92 Quentin Skinner, *Visions of Politics* (Vol. I: Regarding Method, Cambridge University Press 2002) 150.

interpretation that justified transforming the United States into a thickened progressive cosmopolitan constitutional democracy. Still, as vibrant interpretive traditions and practices provided Trump and his allies with the constitutional materials necessary for claiming that the existing constitution, without any changes, was committed to their distinctive populist vision and not the progressive vision of their political rivals. Right-wing populists in the United States could claim to be originalists, however bad their history. Other right-wing populists faced a far more daunting constitutional landscape when first taking office. Fidesz in Hungary and PiS in Poland confronted constitutions drafted within recent memory known to be committed to some version of thickened progressive cosmopolitan constitutional democracy. They could not be originalists because not even a bad constitutional history was available to justify their constitutional agenda. This inherited constitutional landscape explains America, and only American right-wing populists could adopt constitutional originalism as a governing philosophy without having to alter the constitution and constitutional politics significantly to maintain power and make their constitutional vision the official law of the land.

The extent to which the United States was born right-wing populist challenges those who would prefer a more progressive or left-wing populist regime. One challenge is gaining control over the federal judiciary. A coalition of progressive cosmopolitans and left-wing populists may have to emulate in part right-wing populists abroad if they wish to prevent a right-wing populist federal judiciary from playing havoc with their legislative agenda. President Biden will inherit a federal judiciary far more hostile to liberal constitutionalism than President Trump inherited a judiciary hostile to right-wing populist constitutionalism. Reconfiguring that judiciary may require tactics more similar to those that right-wing populists recently employed in Poland than those right-wing populists recently employed in the United States. The other challenge is providing a justificatory logic for that new regime in a nation that was arguably born populist. One path is that of being born again. American progressives and left-wing populists might imitate foreign progressives and populists by writing a new constitution that better expresses left-wing constitutional commitments and constructs the democratic institutions most likely to achieve that constitutional vision.[93] The more likely path is the distinctly American route of renaming the baby. Just as the person once known as Jonathan can be called John or even Jane, so with some tweaking in the particular persons and texts, the same ancient framers who right-wing populists ritually invoke when supporting presidential power and regulations on sexuality can be invoked by constitutional movements favoring legislation and sexual freedom.[94] The choice between these strategies is nevertheless contingent on progressives and left-wing populists gaining the power necessary to make their constitutional vision the law of the land. As the old saw goes, the first step in the recipe for rabbit stew is to find a rabbit.

93 See Sanford Levinson, *Our Undemocratic Constitution: Where the Constitution Goes Wrong (And How We the People Can Correct It)* (Oxford University Press 2006).

94 See Balkin (n 66).

16 Constitutional interpretation

What can Europeans learn from US debates?

Martin Loughlin

16.1 Introduction

We live in a constitutional age, an age in which the role of the Constitution in regulating the political life of the nation-state has never been greater. The growing influence of the Constitution is attributable to many factors but, whatever the causes, the effect has been to expand remarkably the power of constitutional courts. Across the world, constitutional courts are today determining disputes on highly charged political questions that a generation or two ago would have been regarded as beyond the court's jurisdiction. One consequence of this extension of judicial power is that many of the basic concepts of constitutional review, including doctrines of justiciability, standing and remedial powers, have had to be revised.

Of these various revisions, none is of greater significance than the change that has taken place in methods of interpretation. I will examine this issue of constitutional interpretation by addressing a series of questions, the most basic of which is: according to what methods are constitutions to be interpreted? But that question cannot adequately be answered without also addressing some of the underlying questions. How is the authority of the constitution established and maintained? Are there limits to constitutional interpretability? And, crucially, what is meant by a constitution?

Such questions are of universal significance, but I will address them more narrowly by considering how the American experience can help throw into relief some of the issues that European constitutional courts, especially those established post-1989, presently face. The reasons for considering the American example are not difficult to identify. The US Federal Constitution, drafted in 1787 and coming into force in 1789, is the world's first modern written constitution. Having been amended only seventeen times (if one excludes the Bill of Rights, the ten amendments adopted in 1791), it is also the world's longest surviving constitution and is now commonly regarded as being fixed and permanent. These features of the US Constitution, of course, might suggest that the American experience is thoroughly exceptional, not least in the way that their Constitution has acquired a status as one of the main symbols of national political identity. But it is precisely because of the status acquired by the Constitution that there exists such an unrivalled depth of intellectual energy and scholarly literature devoted to the issue of constitutional interpretation on which to draw.

16.2 What is a constitution?

All states are constituted, but not all have a Constitution. The distinction is significant. Dieter Grimm explains it by stating that constitution in the former sense 'refers to the nature of a country with reference to its political conditions', whereas in the latter it is 'a law that concerns itself with the establishment and exercise of political rule'. And he suggests that whereas the former meaning offers a descriptive account of the conditions of ruling authority, the latter connotes a normative concept.[1] Grimm is right to highlight the significance of these differences in meaning but is on less sound footing when suggesting that it rests on a descriptive-normative distinction. It is surely more accurate to say that although there are evident differences between the constitution of a regime and the regime's adopted Constitution, both are normative phenomena. The critical point is that these two conceptions of constitution derive their normative power from different sources.

A regime, it has been suggested, 'is the order, the form, which gives society its character'. It connotes simultaneously 'the form of life of a society, its style of life, its moral taste, form of society, form of state, form of government, spirit of laws'.[2] Regimes take a variety of forms and rest their authority on such sources as the customs, practices and historic experiences that go to make up a sense of collective identity of a people. From this perspective, the regime's normative authority, its sense of rightness, is a product of the degree to which the will of the ruling power is accepted by its subjects. Normative authority is therefore generated by the political and cultural practices of the regime, the relationship that evolves between the government and its subjects, and the degree to which a sense of political unity of a people is derived. These factors go towards establishing a sense of the constitution of the regime or, we might say, the constitution of 'the state'.[3]

The Constitution, by contrast, is a text that is drafted and adopted within the state at a particular moment in its development. This Constitution generally establishes the institutions of government, regulates their relations, and regulates relations between those institutions and the citizens of that state. The Constitution acquires its normative authority in part through the coherence of the governmental scheme it establishes and in part by virtue of the process by which, through an exercise of the people's constituent power, the Constitution is drafted and ratified.

What we refer to as the state's Constitution, then, is not to be equated to the constitution of the state. The distinction has a particular importance

1 Dieter Grimm, *Constitutionalism: Past, Present, and Future* (Oxford University Press 2016), 3.

2 Leo Strauss, 'What Is Political Philosophy?' in his, *What Is Political Philosophy? and Other Studies* (Free Press 1959), 9–55 at 34.

3 See Martin Loughlin, *Foundations of Public Law* (Oxford University Press 2010), ch. 8.

for my task because the difference between these two conceptions of constitution reveals why constitutional interpretation remains such a contested activity. The point may be highlighted by consideration of the political theory of constitutionalism. Constitutionalism, it might be said, aims to realise a state of affairs in which the written Constitution becomes consonant with the constitution of the state. This is a highly ambitious objective which, if it ever were to be realised, depends on time, experience, political action and the generation of a constitutional narrative that runs through that text and eventually is able to shape the political reality of the state. And only once realised could it be said that the Constitution has made 'a people'.

This relational claim is particularly important in helping us appreciate the significance of the American experience. Americans, it would appear, have come closest to realising the idea that the Constitution is constitutive of the political character of a people.

The ambition of the exercise on which they were embarked was signalled by Marshall CJ in the early phase of American state-building. In the landmark case of *Marbury v Madison*, Marshall stated that 'the whole American fabric' has been erected on the idea that 'the people have an original right to establish for their future government such principles as, in their opinion, shall most conduce to their own happiness'. This original right, he elaborated, requires 'a very great exertion' which cannot be 'frequently repeated', and it is for this reason that the basic principles it expresses are 'deemed fundamental' and 'are designed to be permanent'.[4]

When Marshall wrote, it was not self-evident that the Constitution had incorporated that ambition, let alone could achieve that status.[5] But a century later, another great American jurist felt able to claim that that ambition had since been realised. 'When we are dealing with words that also are a constituent act, like the Constitution of the United States', Holmes J stated, 'we must realize that they have called into life a being the development of which could not have been foreseen completely by the most gifted of its begetters'. He continued: 'It was enough for them to realize or to hope that they had created an organism; it has taken a century and has cost their successors much sweat and blood to prove that they created a nation'.[6] The US Constitution, Holmes was suggesting, had become an expression of the constitution of the American state.

This type of claim lends a heightened significance to the issue of interpretation within American constitutional practice. It explains in particular why

4 *Marbury v Madison* 5 US 137 (1803), at 176.

5 Consider, e.g., the 9th Amendment: 'The enumeration in the Constitution, of certain rights, shall not be construed to deny or disparage others retained by the people'. This would appear to indicate that there are certain rights vested in the people (i.e. that form part of the constitution of the state) that are prior (in time, if not in authority) to the rights prescribed in the Constitution. Recent American constitutional scholarship now contests that claim: see, e.g., John Hart Ely, *Democracy and Distrust: A Theory of Judicial Review* (Harvard University Press 1980), 34–41.

6 *Missouri v Holland* 252 U.S. 416 (1920), 433.

the constant refrain in contemporary American constitutional scholarship is that faith in 'the constitutional project' must be maintained. That project might have been initiated by the enactment of a Constitution, but it can be advanced only by subsequent political action. However liberal, democratic and rights-protecting the scheme laid down in the Constitution might be, that text is drawn into alignment with the constitution of the state only through nurture and the investment of a considerable amount of political capital.

Consider, by way of contrast, the Constitution of the Weimar Republic. Adopted in 1919, it established a model social democratic constitution for the German people, but in the thirteen or so years of its life it remained 'an idea seeking to become reality'.[7] The German people may have given themselves a Constitution, but it remained a Constitution without constitutionalists, a republic without republicans, and a democracy without democrats – at least in sufficient numbers to be able to establish the regime's authority as a constitutional and democratic republic. And it was brought to an end by the establishment, through constitutional means, of an evil dictatorship.

The amount of political investment required to establish the Constitution's authority is invariably huge. In the case of the United States, for example, the cost included the bloodiest civil war in modern history. But what is of significance for my task is that the gains made by that political investment must be consolidated through the means of constitutional (re)interpretation. Bruce Ackerman is therefore right to maintain that 'it is not the case that every important constitutional question ends up in the courts for full-dress resolution' because often the courts simply acknowledge the constitutional conclusions reached by others after long and bitter years of argument'.[8] The political work must first be carried out through more explicitly political processes that bring about changes in the constitution of the state which are subsequently recorded by the judiciary. But to achieve that consolidation, those changes generally need to be authorised through a judicial exercise in constitutional interpretation.

The challenges faced by this interpretative venture are indicated by the circumstances that invariably surround the enactment of a Constitution. Constitutions are most commonly drafted in the immediate aftermath of turmoil occasioned by such events as the collapse of the old order following defeat in war, the disintegration of empires, or revolutionary overthrow. Constitutional renewal without these fundamental breaks are exceptional, even though their incidence may be increasing.[9] But whatever the precise political circumstances, the constitution-making moment signals a break with the old order. If the aim is, through interpretation, to bring the Constitution into alignment with the constitution of the state, then the enormity of the challenge should not be underestimated. The Constitution is invariably drafted

7 Peter Gay, *Weimar Culture: The Outsider and Insider* (Norton 1968), 1.

8 See Bruce Ackerman, *We the People, vol.2: Transformations* (Belknap Press 1998), 252.

9 See, e.g., the modernising revisions of the constitutions of Finland (1999), Switzerland (1999) and Hungary (2011).

in the name of 'we, the people' but the political reality is that what some (the majority) experience as liberation in the adoption of the new Constitution, others (the minority/the old order) experience as defeat.

If the constitutive moment has strong emancipatory dimensions, as for example, in post-Apartheid South Africa, the circumstances leading to the enactment of the Constitution might yield a positive narrative on which to try to rebuild the constitution of the regime. But in other cases, as in the German Revolution of 1918–1919, it may be born of disillusionment. As Walter Rathenau wrote in 1919:

> It was not that a chain was smashed by the swelling of a spirit and a will, but that a lock rusted through. The chain fell off and the freed men stood dazed, helpless, disconcerted, and had to take action against their will.[10]

In these less elevating circumstances, building the Constitution's authority may be an insurmountable task.

The US is often regarded as a singular case, but the American experience of the founding and its aftermath might not actually deviate much from the general pattern of modern constitutional development. That this is not obvious today is attributable mainly to the work of the Constitution's great ideologues – the constitutional lawyers. American constitutional lawyers commonly treat the Constitution as a sacred text whose authority is not to be questioned, even in the course of investing it with new meaning through novel interpretation. Even sophisticated analysts, such as Jack Balkin, who accept that constitutions are 'flawed, imperfect compromises with the political constellation of the moment' and who recognise that the struggle is to improve the Constitution over time, still conceive the interpretative task as one of 'redemption'.[11] Redemption, it should be stressed, does not entail reform so much as realising past promises. Redemption, argues Balkin,

> does not mean discarding the existing Constitution and substituting a different one, but returning the Constitution we have to its correct path, pushing it closer to what we take to be its true nature, and discarding the dross of past moral compromise.[12]

Balkin here conveys two powerful messages. The first is the need to put political resources into bolstering the theory of constitutionalism and to work to try to ensure that the Constitution can be equated to the constitution of the state. The Constitution, Balkin writes, 'is not merely a document; it is also part of – and embedded in – a set of institutions and a cultural and political

10 Walter Rathenau, *Kritik der dreifachen Revolution* (Fischer 1919), 9–10; cited in Rupert Emerson, *State and Sovereignty in Modern Germany* (Yale University Press 1928), 211.

11 Jack M. Balkin, *Constitutional Redemption: Political Faith in an Unjust World* (Harvard University Press 2011), 5.

12 Ibid. 5–6.

tradition'.[13] The second is that once the Constitution is accepted as framing the entire regime, future political action might no longer be seen to be directed primarily towards achieving reforms through legislative initiatives; they might more appropriately come to focus on constitutional litigation designed to institute the 'correct' theory of constitutional interpretation, one that reinforces the Constitution's ambition.

These types of arguments flow from the exercise of investing the founding with sacred significance. They are expressions of what might be called 'aspirational constitutionalism'. Consequently, it is not surprising to find Balkin arguing: (i) that the Declaration of Independence is 'the constitution that our Constitution exists to serve'; (ii) that the 'Constitution creates a structure of government; but the Declaration tells us why governments are instituted'; and (iii) that the Revolution 'was not merely a political revolution' but also 'a social revolution' because, in addition to overthrowing imperial government, it 'threw off a form of society as well'.[14]

These claims highlight the tendency of constitutional lawyers to provide ideologically infused interpretations of political events. This type of claim about American history, for example, takes no account of incompatibilities in regionally differentiated conceptions of liberty espoused in revolutionary discourses,[15] or of the analysis of historians who maintain that 'the Constitution was intrinsically an aristocratic document designed to check the democratic tendencies of the period'.[16] Historians might now have jettisoned the idea of political history as a great and singular narrative (what in Britain is called 'the Whig interpretation of history'), but it most surely lives on in the works of constitutional lawyers.

16.3 The limits of interpretability

Once the distinction between the Constitution and the constitution of the state is highlighted, we are able to see more clearly what is at stake in competing theories of interpretation. Many jurists assume that the purpose of interpretation is to bring the relationship between these two conceptions into a closer alignment. But it should not be assumed without question that the Constitution actually has the capacity not just to establish a basic framework of government but also to give expression to the basic values on which the constitution of the state is founded. 'The legitimacy of our Constitution', notes Balkin, 'depends ... on our faith in the constitutional project and its future trajectory'.[17] Or, as he put it earlier, the aim must be to discard 'the dross of past moral compromise'. But what if the Constitution is, of its nature, a document of compromise? Compromise, the obverse of aspiration,

13 Ibid. 114.
14 Ibid. 19, 20, 21.
15 See David Hackett Fischer, *Albion's Seed: Four British Folkways in America* (Oxford University Press 1989).
16 Gordon S. Wood, *The Creation of the American Republic, 1776–1787* (University of North Carolina Press, rev edn 1998), 513.
17 Balkin (n 11) 2.

is far removed from redemption. Conceived as a document of compromise, there may be distinct limits to the Constitution's interpretability.

The idea that the Constitution should be treated as the outcome of a set of political compromises – that is, that it enables a people to live together despite basic disagreements about the collective good – tends nowadays to be suppressed within American constitutional scholarship. Once the Constitution is treated as a sacred text, the idea that it is a document born of compromise is supplanted by faith in the wisdom and virtue of its framers. And following on from this, we get Balkin's faith in a moral project. After *Marbury v Madison*, this type of approach leads us to conceive the court as the institution 'charged with the evolution and application of society's fundamental principles',[18] and to treat it as the institution 'that calls some issues from the battleground of power politics to the forum of principle'.[19] But does this provide a faithful depiction of the foundation on which the American republic was established? 'Just what our forefathers did envision or would have envisioned had they foreseen modern conditions', Justice Jackson remarked in *Youngstown Sheet*, 'must be divined from materials almost as enigmatic as the dreams Joseph was called upon to interpret for Pharaoh'.[20] The fact of the matter is that, in order to form 'a more perfect union', Americans had to engage in compromise on basic principles. That is, they were obliged to obscure the nature of the regime that they were establishing.

The American Constitution was, in actuality, a document made through compromise. Specifically, it was drafted to achieve a compromise over slavery, and it was able to maintain its authority only to the extent that that compromise, institutionalised through its articles, could be preserved. The silences and ambiguities of the text were deliberate aspects of its design. It may not have established constitutional protection for slavery explicitly, but it ensured that the governing authorities would not be able to regulate or abolish slavery without the consent of slave-owning states. Provisions such as the fugitive slave clause (Art. IV, s. 2, cl. 3), the moratorium on federal legislation banning the international slave trade until 1808 (Art. I, s. 9), and the provision counting every slave as three-fifths of a person for the purpose of legislative representation (Art. I, s. 2, cl. 3) were all designed to achieve this purpose. And as Daniel J noted in the *Dred Scott* case, slavery 'is the only private property which the Constitution has *specifically recognized*, and has imposed it as a direct obligation both on the States and the Federal Government to protect and *enforce*'.[21]

This overriding purpose of holding a compromise over slavery was maintained during the early decades of the republic. It was held in place mainly because of the political dominance of southern states, with slave-owning Virginians controlling the presidency for all but four of the first 36 years and every presidential election bar four between 1788 and 1848 putting

18 Alexander Bickel, *The Least Dangerous Branch: The Supreme Court at the Bar of Politics* (Yale University Press [1962] 2nd edn 1986), 109.

19 Ronald Dworkin, *A Matter of Principle* (Harvard University Press 1985), 71.

20 *Youngstown Sheet & Tube Co v Sawyer* 343 US 579 (1952), 592.

21 *Dred Scott v Sandford* 60 US 393 (1857), 490.

a southern slaveholder into the White House.[22] The compromise lasted until the mid-nineteenth century. It then became strained largely because of changing demographic patterns that resulted in the northern states gaining greater political power. And it is at this point that the question of whether the original constitutional compromise could be maintained came to the fore.

In the analysis of today's constitutional lawyers, there is an overwhelming consensus that the court's decision in *Dred Scott* flowed from the application of an incorrect theory of constitutional interpretation and stands as the single worst decision in Supreme Court history.[23] Yet what the Court decided in that case in fact maintained fidelity to the Constitution's original settlement. *Dred Scott* has acquired such notoriety because, having now apparently become constitutive of the political character of the people, the Constitution must today be (re)interpreted both as the expression of founding wisdom and the embodiment of the nation's fundamental values. It would be truer to say that in the mid-nineteenth century, because of social, economic, political, demographic and technological change, the nation was faced with an emerging conflict between constitutional obligation and the requirements of social justice. President Lincoln chose justice over constitutional obligation and, in order to vindicate that choice, chose war over peace. Whatever the rights and wrongs of that choice – and it was a choice that led to the death or injury of millions in the ensuing civil war – to say that this turned on a matter of constitutional interpretation is to adopt winner's history and, with it, the ideology of aspirational constitutionalism.

In a compelling account, Mark Graber argues that 'Lincoln failed the Constitution by forgetting that his obligation to adopt a plausible interpretation of the Constitution that preserved the social peace was constitutionally higher than his obligation to adopt an interpretation of the constitution the best promoted justice'.[24] Graber also draws certain conclusions from his study that touch on more general questions of constitutional interpretation. The first is that theories of constitutional interpretation are not adequate to address issues of what he calls 'constitutional evil'. Such evils can be adequately addressed only by a 'constitutional politics that persuades or by a nonconstitutional politics that compels crucial political actors to abandon an evil practice'.[25] Legal theories, in short, provide no substitute for practical politics. Secondly, that, like all Constitutions, the American Constitution was drafted at a particular moment in time, in the face of certain pressing conditions,[26] and inevitably was the product of compromise. And with so many different interests to be accommodated, there are distinct limits to the ability to construct a comprehensive theory of the values and principles on which

22 Domenico Losurdo, *Liberalism: A Counter-History* (Verso 2011), 12.

23 *Dred Scott v Sandford* 60 US 693 (1857); see Mark A. Graber, *Dred Scott and the Problem of Constitutional Evil* (Cambridge University Press 2006), 15–17.

24 Graber (n 23) 251.

25 Ibid. 18.

26 Note, e.g., Graber (n 23) 9: 'The various compromises reached in 1787 enabled Americans with diverse beliefs to form a state strong enough to forestall foreign invasion'.

that regime can be assumed to rest.[27] Thirdly, contrary to the orientation of aspirational constitutionalists who discover values in abstract expressions of principles, many constitutions achieve their purposes through more prosaic mechanisms of an institutional design that provide checks and balances. Fourthly, with respect to the American case, 'the Constitution caused the Civil War by failing to establish institutions that would facilitate the constitutional politics necessary for the national government to make policies acceptable to crucial elites in both sections of the country'.[28] Finally, that 'those responsible for creating and maintaining new constitutions in heterogeneous societies cannot be Lincolnians'.[29]

The logic of this argument is that we should not assume that the main purpose of the Constitution is to institute and promote a particular conception of social justice. The main purpose of the Constitution is surely to establish the authority of the state's system of government and that might dictate as its main function the necessity of maintaining social peace among a people who hold different visions of the good society. In a world in which Constitutions are commonly conceived as 'aspirational constitutions', this aspect of their role is in danger of being overlooked.

16.4 Methods of interpretation

The considerations that Graber identifies which are illustrative of the treatment of the American Constitution as an instrument of compromise impose significant limitations on the pursuit of interpretative fidelity. Yet they have not prevented the evolution of a huge industry involved in the business of constitutional interpretation. The US Constitution, at fewer than 8,000 words, is a relatively short text, but over the years Supreme Court justices 'have written tens of thousands of pages ... explicating those words' and the Court has created 'a vast amount of meaning that is not contained in the text of the document or its original understanding'.[30] To which one might add that the Supreme Court's tens of thousands of pages have been glossed in commentaries by American constitutional law professors that cover hundreds of thousands of pages. From the outside, this seems to verge on

27 See, e.g., Madison's contortions in trying to explain the principle underpinning the provision that assesses slaves as three-fifths for the purpose of allocating legislative representation: James Madison, Alexander Hamilton, & John Jay, *The Federalist Papers* (Penguin, 1987), No 54: 'Let the compromising expedient of the Constitution be mutually adopted which regards them [slaves] as inhabitants, but as debased by servitude below the level of free inhabitants; which regards the *slave* as divested of two fifths of the *man*. ... Such is the reasoning which an advocate for the Southern interests might employ on this subject; and although it may appear to be a little strained in some points, yet on the whole, I must confess that it fully reconciles me to the scale of representation which the convention have established' 333–335).

28 Graber (n 23) 167.

29 Ibid. 251.

30 Jeffrey M. Shaman, *Constitutional Interpretation: Illusion and Reality* (Greenwood Press 2001), 4.

madness, especially once we note Judge Posner's observation that, since most Supreme Court decisions 'are written by law clerks a year or two away from graduation', American constitutional law professors are spending their considerable intellectual energies in writing critiques of the work of their recent students.[31] The question is: what is at stake?

The first point to note is that the US Constitution may be the product of political deliberation and compromise, but once it had been adopted, it was quickly conceived to be 'fundamental law'. Its meaning, it was soon established, must be determined as a matter of legal interpretation. In the *Federalist Papers*, Alexander Hamilton noted that 'there can be few men in the society who will have sufficient skill in the laws' to qualify for the judicial role and fewer still 'who unite the requisite integrity with the requisite knowledge'.[32] Since the Constitution can establish its authority only when it is accepted as transcending partisan politics and setting out the basic rules of political engagement, Hamilton was alert to the danger that those impressed with these special interpretative responsibilities might be tempted to shape the text according to their own political views. Emphasising that they must never be disposed 'to exercise will instead of judgment',[33] he maintained that this danger is averted by professional discipline. A consistent body of constitutional knowledge must be built up, so that when engaging in interpretation, judges 'should be bound down by strict rules and precedents'.[34]

The problem here is that this attempt to fix one type of threat to the establishment of its authority (that those entrusted with interpretative responsibilities will impose their own political beliefs) exposes another: that the Constitution will be unable to establish its authority unless it is somehow perceived as expressing the basic principles, values and aspirations of the regime. Its instrumental function, that of providing a clear, consistent and objective structure of rules regulating the exercise of political power, sits in tension with its symbolic function, that of presenting certain general, abstract and ambiguous principles around which the regime's identity can be negotiated. This dilemma was clearly expressed by Dieter Grimm who noted that 'a constitution's symbolic power increases with its interpretative ambiguity, although its legally determinative power decreases to the same degree'.[35]

These tensions pervade the task of constitutional interpretation. The Constitution must seek symbolically to express the basic values of the regime but, as a device of political compromise, these values of necessity must remain at the level of abstraction and ambiguity.[36] At the same time, the fact that the

31 Richard A. Posner, 'Democracy and Distrust Revisited' (1991) 77 Virginia Law Review 651.

32 *The Federalist Papers*, No 78 (Hamilton) (n 25) 442.

33 Ibid. 440.

34 Ibid. 442.

35 Dieter Grimm, 'Integration by Constitution' (2005) 3 International Journal of Constitutional Law 200.

36 See Sanford Levinson, *Constitutional Faith* (Princeton University Press 1988), arguing that no institution has a monopoly of authoritative meaning of the Constitution and that its legitimacy rests on this continuous openness to contestation by citizens.

Constitution is expected also to establish a relatively clear and impartial set of rules of political engagement makes the enterprise of realising these symbolic aspirations doubly challenging. In *McCulloch*, Marshall CJ propounded that: 'We must never forget that it is a constitution we are expounding'.[37] The ambiguities of the document, Marshall was suggesting, mean that generally it cannot be the subject of strict construction. But he otherwise offers few clues as to appropriate interpretative method.

These tensions highlight the extent of the gulf between the two main schools of constitutional interpretation: those of the strict constructivists and the aspirationalists. The former exist under a variety of designations, including textualists, originalists and doctrinalists, but the common core of their method is that the Constitution, as a type of law, must be interpreted in accordance with the canons that are applied to all legal texts. They therefore maintain that the text should be accorded its plain meaning, that special attention should be given to the original meaning intended by its drafters, and that adhering to judicial precedents is essential to the task of ensuring consistency and stability of constitutional meaning.

Whereas the strict constructivists accentuate the value of *stability* – the fixity of the Constitution through time[38] – the aspirationalists emphasise *change*. Aspirationalists, sometimes called 'living constitutionalists', argue that the meaning of the text changes in accordance with changing social and political conditions of the time. They argue that the Constitution must be the subject of re-interpretation in accordance with the prevailing conceptions of social justice of the day.

A good illustration of this interpretative method is provided by Kennedy J's opinion for the Court in *Lawrence v Texas* 539 US 558 (2003), a case holding that a Texas statute that made it a crime for two persons of the same sex to engage in intimate sexual conduct was unconstitutional. In reaching its determination, the Court overruled its previous ruling in *Bowers v Hardwick* 478 US 186 (1986). With respect to this aspect of the case, Kennedy J noted that while the 'doctrine of *stare decisis* is essential to the respect accorded to the judgments of the Court and to the stability of the law', it is not 'an inexorable command'.[39] He also referred specifically to the work of the framers, those who drafted and adopted the 5th and 14th Amendments, stating that: 'They knew times can blind us to certain truths and later generations can see that laws once thought necessary and proper in fact serve only to oppress'. Consequently, he elaborated: 'As the Constitution endures, persons in every generation can invoke its principles in their own search for greater freedom'.[40] Having disposed on the issues of precedent and original meaning of the framers, Kennedy then explained that 'our laws and traditions in the past half century are of most relevance here' and these 'show an

37 *McCulloch v Maryland* 17 US 316 (1819) at 407.

38 Antonin Scalia, *A Matter of Interpretation: Federal Courts and the Law* (Princeton University Press 1997), argues that the main purpose of the Constitution is to prevent change.

39 539 US 558 (2003) 577.

40 539 US 558 (2003) 579.

emerging awareness that liberty gives substantial protection to adult persons in deciding how to conduct their private lives in matters pertaining to sex'.[41]

This distinction between the two schools of strict constructivism and aspirationalism is – confusingly – sometimes referred to as one between 'interpretivism and noninterpretivism'.[42] This makes sense only to the extent that interpretivism is equated to textual exegesis. Consequently, interpretivists argue that, far from engaging in interpretation, 'non-interpretivists' confer new meaning on the text. We might note that its main proponent, who was not an 'interpretivist', seems now to have abandoned the distinction.[43]

Seeking to transcend the basic differences between constructionists and aspirationalists, Balkin has argued for what he calls 'living originalism'.[44] He claims that 'originalism' and 'living constitutionalism' are complementary rather than antagonistic concepts. Originalism expresses the point that the semantic meaning of the words in the constitutional text remains fixed, resulting in some rules (such as the requirement that the President must be 35 years old) having a fixed and determinate meaning. But others, the abstract principles such as the requirement that no person shall be denied 'the equal protection of the laws', may be interpreted differently in different times. Since almost no one doubts the existence of certain specific rules (such as Presidential age limits, or the provision providing for each state to elect two senators), he argues that even living constitutionalists accept originalism with respect to basic rules and that originalists recognise that the meaning of some of the more abstract general principles does evolve through interpretation.

Balkin's attempt to reconcile these two different methods of interpretation is inventive, but it underplays the extent to which these different methods are expressions of two fundamentally antagonistic theories of law. Constructionism and its varieties express a legal positivist jurisprudence that conceives rules as the basic conceptual building blocks of law, whereas aspirationalism expresses a rights-conception that argues that principles (which acquire weight through their moral authority) are higher-order items that shape the meaning even of basic rules. This jurisprudential dimension opens up a set of more complex distinctions that are not so easily susceptible of reconciliation.

This jurisprudential aspect provides one clue to the proliferation of theories of constitutional interpretation. These various theories range beyond those of these two basic schools. They include process theories as is illustrated in John Ely's influential work which, concerned that aspirational theories are open to the broadest forms of interest balancing, aims to replace them with an intent-based analysis that focuses on constitutionally forbidden

41 539 US 558 (2003) 571–572. Cf Scalia's dissent: 'It is clear from this that the Court has taken sides in the culture war, departing from its role of assuring, as neutral observer, that the democratic rules of engagement are observed'. 602.

42 Thomas Grey, 'Do We Have an Unwritten Constitution?' (1975) 27 Stanford Law Review 703. This nomenclature was taken up by Ely (n 5); see chapter 1: The Allure of Interpretivism.

43 Thomas Grey, 'The Constitution as Scripture' (1984) 37 Stanford Law Review 1.

44 Jack M. Balkin, *Living Originalism* (Belknap Press 2011).

legislative intentions and claims that legislation should be struck down only when it is necessary to ensure equal access to the political process.[45] They also comprise more pragmatic approaches such as Cass Sunstein's methods of overlapping consensus and judicial minimalism,[46] and Richard Posner's claim that, since no theory of constitutional interpretation has the power 'to command agreement from people not already predisposed to accept the theorist's policy prescriptions', judges should be much more attentive to the social implications of the decisions they make.[47] We conclude, then, with a proliferation of methods, none of which come close to commanding authority within the field.

16.5 Imitative constitutionalism

The final issue I want to address is: what lessons might we draw from this account of the American experience to assist Europeans in thinking about appropriate methods of constitutional interpretation? Specifically, what insight does the American experience offer those regimes of central and eastern Europe which since 1989 have established a Constitution on the liberal democratic model?

I began by suggesting that we are living in a constitutional age. It might now be added that this is also an age in which many judges and scholars now seek to interpret contemporary Constitutions according to the canons of aspirational constitutionalism. In conceiving the Constitution as a vehicle for expressing the rights of citizens and the duties of government, jurisprudential theories derived from the American literature have been influential. But the point of my argument is to emphasise that American constitutionalism is a unique achievement which has been the product of a singular historical experience. Americans began their collective journey with a Constitution crafted as a device of political compromise. Later, in the post-civil war period of reconstruction, the Constitution took the form of negative constitutionalism, that is, one that was directed towards the constitutional protection of individual autonomy *from* the government. And only since the mid-twentieth century has it become a battleground of aspirational, or positive, constitutionalism, that is, of a theory that asserts that the Constitution should be interpreted as imposing duties *on* government through the advancement of constitutional claims to autonomy.

Whatever the merits or otherwise of this development, the general point is that American constitutionalism can properly be understood only when situated in the context of a history of struggle. And for this reason, its contemporary

45 Ely (n 5).

46 Cass R. Sunstein, *The Partial Constitution* (Harvard University Press 1993); 'Incompletely Theorised Agreements'.

47 Richard A. Posner, 'Against Constitutional Theory' (1998) 73 New York University Law Review 3; Richard A. Posner, *The Problematics of Moral and Political Theory* (Harvard University Press 2002).

practices cannot easily be imitated. If that claim is correct, then the attempts by those who seek to use recently enacted Constitutions to promote aspirational constitutionalism by imitation are likely to face an uphill struggle.

This point has a particular relevance with respect to the post-1989 European revolutions. Jürgen Habermas has maintained that the these were 'rectifying revolutions', in that the purpose of these was to bring eastern Europe into alignment with the models of liberal democracy that had already been established in the west.[48] But 'rectification' remains a hugely ambitious undertaking. It required these newly independent nation-states without having much prior historical experience on which to draw, simultaneously to establish functionally effective market systems, vibrant civil society networks, and democratic governmental arrangements. When the Federal Republic of West Germany had been constituted after the Second World War, a huge amount of energy (and US capital) was invested in strengthening the political stability of the regime, and this included the need to maintain a degree of continuity (of practice and personnel) with the discredited Nazi regime. The post-1989 responses have generally been different; following the end of the Cold War, in many regimes former communists were excluded from governing positions and, in accordance with the dominant economic philosophy of the time, industries were rapidly privatised and market mechanisms instituted. In some cases, these practices seemed closer to Naomi Klein's 'shock doctrine' than an incremental transition to a new type of constitutional order.[49]

These new liberal democratic Constitutions were enacted alongside these radical social and economic changes. Hungary's experience is exemplary. As Gábor Halmai explains, 'Hungary was one of the first and most thorough political transitions after 1989' and it 'provided all the institutional elements of constitutionalism'.[50] A powerful Constitutional Court was established which, under the influence of its first President, László Sólyom, promoted the philosophy of aspirational constitutionalism. Sólyom and many academics, Halmai notes, 'argued that the text of the 1989 constitution and the jurisprudence of the Constitutional Court made a new constitution unnecessary'.[51] In a case in 1990 concerning the death penalty, Sólyom made explicit the basis of his constitutional jurisprudence. The Constitutional Court, he declared,

> must continue its efforts to explain the theoretical basis of the Constitution and of the rights included in it and to form a coherent system with its decisions, which as an 'invisible Constitution' provides for a reliable standard of constitutionality beyond the Constitution.[52]

48 Jürgen Habermas, 'What Does Socialism Mean Today? The Rectifying Revolution and the Need for New Thinking on the Left' (1990) 183 New Left Review 5.

49 Naomi Klein, *The Shock Doctrine: The Rise of Disaster Capitalism* (Henry Holt 2008).

50 Gábor Halmai, 'A Coup against Constitutional Democracy: The Case of Hungary' in Mark A. Graber, Sanford Levinson, & Mark Tushnet (eds), *Constitutional Democracy in Crisis?* (Oxford University Press 2018) 243.

51 Ibid. 245.

52 Decision 23/1990; cited by Halmai (n 50) 245.

Aspirational constitutionalism, according to which the Court was motivated by the Constitution's 'spirit' or underpinning moral principles rather than by closely adhering to the text, was promoted. That these liberal aspirations did not fully take root is indicated by the election in 2010 of a Fidesz government on the back of growing dissatisfaction by ordinary citizens with the effects of the post-1989 transition. Since then, not only have the jurisprudential advances made by the Court been put into reverse; Fidesz has also moved directly to undermine the Court's independence, has effectively nullified many of its rulings and has taken action to institute a self-styled regime of 'illiberal democracy'.[53] The Hungarian government's policies are now threatening to extend into a pan-European crisis of constitutional democracy.[54]

Hungary is not a unique case, as other essays in this volume demonstrate. My point is that, as the American study indicates, the task of establishing constitutional government requires much more than adopting a liberal Constitution and establishing a Constitutional Court as its guardian. As Hamilton explained in *Federalist* No 78, lacking the power of the purse and the sword, the judiciary relies on neither force nor will but only on its judgment. And if that exercise of judgment is not in accordance with the popular sentiment and with those holding governmental power, it is unlikely to carry authority.

The post-1989 revolutions are in certain respects different from all other modern revolutionary movements. And it is not just, as Habermas suggested, that these are rectifying revolutions. Whereas the losers – American empire loyalists, French aristocrats or White Russians – were the ones required to leave the country in the aftermath of the American, French and Bolshevik Revolutions, those who left the country after the post-1989 velvet revolutions were the winners. Finding that 'changing countries is easier than changing one's country', Ivan Krastev and Stephen Holmes have argued that, after 1989, it was the young educated intellectuals who left to study, work and live in the west.[55] Between 1989 and 2017 Latvia lost 27% of its population, Lithuania 22.5%, Bulgaria 21% and 14% of GDR residents moved to West Germany. Since Romania joined the EU in 2007, 3.4 million of its citizens, the great majority of them under 40, have left the country. This exodus has had 'profound economic, political and psychological consequences', and it has left eastern Europe 'home to the fastest shrinking populations in the world'.[56] The question is: what might be the constitutional implications?

53 See Fareed Zakaria, 'The Rise of Illiberal Democracy' (1997) 76 Foreign Affairs 22–43; Marc F. Plattner, 'Illiberal Democracy and the Struggle on the Right' (2019) 30 Journal of Democracy 5–19.

54 Most recently, following the Covid-19 crisis, on 30 March 2020, the Hungarian Parliament passed an emergency law granting the Government broad-ranging powers of indefinite duration to rule by decree. This led to the European Commission, without mentioning Hungary, immediately issuing a statement reminding Member States that the European Union is founded on 'the values of freedom, democracy, the rule of law and respect for human rights' which must be upheld and defended 'even in these challenging times': Statement by President von der Leyen on Emergency Measures in Member States, European Commission Statement 20/567 (31 March 2020).

55 Ivan Krastev and Stephen Holmes, *The Light that Failed: A Reckoning* (Allen Lane 2019), 32.

56 Ibid. 33–38.

Presently, one can only speculate, though it does not seem controversial to suggest that, under such conditions, any attempt to build constitutional authority on the foundation of an emancipatory narrative will be very challenging. It is symptomatic of that failure that regimes have retreated from universalist aspirations and sought to bolster their authority by falling back on some ethnically based sense of national identity. Once this type of narrative is promoted, fear of mass immigration into the country by foreigners is touted as posing a threat to identity. Given the low levels of immigration into eastern European countries, this might seem ill-founded, but it can serve a purpose. 'Hysteria about non-existent immigrants about to overrun the country', Krastev and Holmes argue, 'represents the substitution of an illusory danger (immigration) for the real danger (depopulation and demographic collapse) which cannot speak its name'.[57] Populist expressions of national identity become the basis of constitutional identity in place of a cosmopolitanism that has taken the form of a constitutional patriotism, as is expressed today (by liberals) in western regimes like Germany's.[58] But many who condemn this emerging populism fail to appreciate that establishing a bounded political community is a precondition of democracy and securing the loyalty of ordinary citizens is a precondition of establishing a stable constitutional democracy.

16.6 Conclusion

The general argument I have been advancing draws on a distinction between the constitution of the regime and the regime's Constitution. It therefore draws on the differing requirements of constitutional government and those of constitutionalism.

Constitutional government is a historical achievement; it is a practice that evolves through a historic struggle of imposing institutional checks and limits on the powers of public authorities so as to ensure that public power is exercised with due regard to the liberties of the people. Since the practices of constitutional government vary from regime to regime, it is unlikely that we can appreciate the achievement without having regard to the underlying social, political and economic conditions of their success.

Constitutionalism, by contrast, is a political ideology. It is a rationalist project which aims to establish the Constitution as the medium through the authority of governing institutions is determined, citizens are able to speak authoritatively about their public values, and collective political identity understood. Constitutionalism is an ideological project which aspires to make the values and principles laid down in the enacted Constitution constitutive of the political character of a people. And when, as is generally the case, the Constitution is assumed to be 'fundamental law' and constitutional

57 Ibid. 38.

58 See, e.g., Jürgen Habermas's argument that the only patriotism that can be coherently embraced today is what he calls 'constitutional patriotism' (*Verfassungspatriotismus*), an allegiance to the principles inscribed in the constitution: Jürgen Habermas, *Between Fact and Norms* (Polity Press 1996).

lawyers present themselves as possessors of special knowledge of the Constitution's true meaning, it is also a decidedly elitist project.

This paper is directed towards the attempt to establish constitutionalism as a governing ideology in those regimes of central and eastern Europe that experienced 'rectifying revolutions'. I have, however, focused in this chapter on American debates on the status and meaning of the Constitution. I have done so because within constitutional studies, Americans are the original people of the book, by which I mean that they have travelled much further than any other regime in absorbing the ideology of constitutionalism. American constitutional lawyers readily accept that the Constitution founded their state, that their civil war was a war over constitutional interpretation and that justice is to be achieved not primarily through political action leading to legislative enactment, but through the peddling of an interpretative technique that is able to convince a majority of the Justices of the Supreme Court that they have discovered the ideals implied by the text (section II). But I have also sought to show the limits of interpretability, of how in reality the US Constitution, like all Constitutions, are documents born of compromise. This is not to undervalue the significance of Constitutions, but rather to emphasise that their real value may lie not in establishing substantive values but in establishing a framework through which political differences can be negotiated (section III). Nevertheless, I have also argued that the ideology of constitutionalism is so powerful in the US that it has now itself become highly politicised: that is, it has given rise to intense disputes about constitutional interpretation that are no longer able to mask the fact that they are expressions of major differences in political beliefs (section IV).

Finally: what might Europeans learn from the American experience? One message is that, given the contemporary power and influence of American-style constitutionalism, there is a real danger in adopting constitutionalism as a technology of governing rather than being attentive to the conditions that are needed to advance the task of establishing practices of constitutional government. This is the danger alluded to in the section on 'imitative constitutionalism' (section V). The reasons for the rise of populism are undoubtedly complex. But, as Krastev and Holmes argue, 'they lie partly in the humiliations associated with the uphill struggle to become, at best, an inferior copy of a superior model', especially one promoted by consultants 'with an anaemic grasp of local realities'.[59] Alternatively, as Michael Ignatieff has expressed it, one of the reasons might be that there has an over-reliance on universalist values in preference to 'the ordinary virtues'.[60] That some regimes which have gone through a rapid and radical process of constitutional renewal are now experiencing a populist backlash may therefore be because they have seriously underestimated the challenges entailed in establishing and maintaining the practices of constitutional government.

59 Krastev and Holmes (n 55) 22.

60 Michael Ignatieff, *The Ordinary Virtues: Moral Order in a Divided World* (Harvard University Press 2017).

17 Populist and non-democratic reading of the Constitution

Sad lessons from Latin America

Pablo Riberi

17.1 Foreword

The Argentine Supreme Court along with several high tribunals and Constitutional Courts in the region offer multiple examples of biased non-democratic case law interpretation, a phenomenon which, unfortunately, is nowadays on the rise. Civilian and military dictatorships and a myriad of populist experiences throughout Latin American history have undoubtedly been supported by whimsical anti-normative readings of the Constitution.

In line with mainstream legal scholarship associated with what we currently call neo-constitutionalism, many of the highest tribunals, as well as the Inter-American Court of Human Rights, have together consolidated a pundit understanding of rights; a view that has also randomly been opposed to democratic values.

From a deep global south perspective, through a theoretical and comparative analysis, this chapter aims to develop a critical argument against two ways of acknowledging the fabric of constitutional law. I am referring to two interpretative stances that have been sliding towards undemocratic and anti-republican discursive practices. These are, on the one hand, non-democratic legalist perspectives, and on the other, populist approaches. These trends feel at odds with the political and ideological setting that took shape during the constitutionalization process in countries like Argentina. In analytical terms, therefore, I will explore general principles – and some concrete judicial doctrine – that have brought about an inconsistent record of interpretative solutions in constitutional law. This situation has gradually triggered tensions between case law developments and people's civic-democratic aspirations.

17.2 Thesis and main inferences

My concern is to unravel a principal argument and to cope with another ancillary one which stems from it. The core idea is to better understand and assess the specific factors that have gradually lessened our constitutional culture in general, as well as thwarted some thriving interpretative trends of constitutional rights in particular. I will dwell on some key elements, both epistemic and doctrinal, which help us understand how courts and individuals have perceived constitutional interpretation as a task that goes beyond the content of the Constitution. From there, and by reviewing some interpretative trends, my concern is to shed light on the main challenges preventing cogent democratic and republican interpretation as regards constitutional rights. What this chapter attempts to highlight is a clear watershed dividing well-established constitutional polities with unstable ones. My view is that in Latin America in general and in Argentina in particular, failures, mistakes, and all sorts of intellectual straying when it comes to the defense of constitutional rights have been unfortunate outcomes resulting from a prior misconception. This basic shortcoming has impaired constitutional stability and its legitimacy much more than any other moral incapacity and/or any wrongful interpretative technique.

My thesis, thus, is that in most countries in the region, the main problem is that both power-holders and power-recipients *have failed to understand or to make a difference between the practical meaning of constitutional politics and ordinary politics*. This blunder has had, and still has, an obvious negative impact on constitutional interpretation.

Concerning this situation, the first corollary provides that both 'populist' responses and other moderate views, either 'conservative' or 'liberal', reflect 'agonal' claims based upon self-interested short-term agendas, which, voluntarily or involuntarily, have all ended up neglecting or manipulating the constitution, or imposing a biased reading of it.

Among other things, having acknowledged the thesis and the first corollary, it is plain to see that civic trust appears to be in constant jeopardy.[1] A second corollary arises when the aforementioned statements are taken into account. When 'ordinary politics' and 'Constitutional Politics' are mixed up, as a consequence of the degrading of the latter, the so-called 'Linz's nightmare' is likely to come true. What does this mean? It means that Linz's fear of hyper-presidentialism is very telling of Latin America's constitutional decay.

In Bruce Ackerman's words, the nightmare refers to a recurrent traumatic phenomenon that depicts constitutional design failures in the region.[2] Incidentally, the copying of the USA separation of powers model has driven many Latin American democracies to throw themselves on the horns of a wicked dilemma. Experiencing weakness in checks and balances

1 In any community, it is important to generate public trust. Trust in the Constitution is an essential asset. We must consider that political institutions' public and private contracts and every institutionalized agreement do nothing else but technically consolidate the necessary collective trust in our future behavior. Mainly, it eases social cooperation by allowing us to be part of our fellow citizens' expectations. See Pablo Riberi, 'Disenso, Pesimismo y Desconfianza dentro de los Límites de las Reglas Constitucionales' in C. Rosenkrantz & M. Bergman (eds.), *Confianza y Derecho en América Latina* (Fondo de Cultura Económica 2009) 195–214. See also Russell Hardin, *Trust & Trustworthiness* (Russell Sage Foundation 2002) 10–52.

2 Bruce Ackerman, 'The New Separation of Powers' (2000) 113 Harvard Law Review 633–725.

or succumbing to an authoritarian momentum seem to be the unavoidable options during random cycles of constitutional frustration.

Whatever the reasons, the lack of any difference between constitutional and ordinary politics is the source of this demise. In short, in several Latin American countries, especially in Argentina, this trend has gradually undermined institutions that could boost trustworthiness and loyalty to the Constitution.

17.3 Analysis

Claiming that everyone is free to have their own interpretative theory of the Constitution is not only a reductionist view. In my opinion, it is a blatantly wrong one. This is because an underlying and necessary interpretative practice regarding the Constitution must always be postulated in its normative dimension. This must be so because the interpreter must assume that its fulfillment will convey a positive or a better effect on the referred constitutional order. Moreover, any attentive observer can acknowledge the close connection between institutional ways of reading and enforcing the Constitution and the underlying political/legal foundation in place.[3]

Hence, regardless of the interpreter's intelligence or willingness, a far-fetched theory of constitutional interpretation will inevitably impair the likelihood of justice, liberty, and equality in the community involved. If this is so, it is crystal clear why constitutional interpretation does not depend on the method but works in the opposite way: the method depends on constitutional interpretation.[4] Furthermore, constitutional interpretation is far from being a sub-species of the whole range of legal interpretations. In fact, it does not correspond to any mechanical task of subsumption, unraveling, or content-meaning revelation.

What is plain is that, as interpretation is constitutional, it must engage with the Constitution in one way or another. Then, if 'observation is loaded with theory', in Hanson's words, it is also plausible that the forging of constitutional culture in Latin America has been a servant of two masters.[5] An observation of both political and constitutional facts proves this. As a matter of fact, on the one hand, the historical process of independence and decolonization has developed peculiar riddles in economic, social, and religious terms. Moreover, such puzzles have turned out to be key elements of the demystification of the constitutional phenomenon. On the other hand, it is also evident that the constitutional phenomenon has always been tainted

3 For example, concerning the so-called 'rule of recognition', see Herbert L. A. Hart, *El Concepto de Derecho*, (Abeledo Perrot 1992) 117–125.

4 David Davidson (quoted by Marmor) underlines the idea that every understanding of the other's discourse involves a radical interpretation. See Andrei Marmor, *Interpretation and Legal Theory* (Clarendon Press 1992) 37.

5 See M. Lund & N. R. Hanson, *Observation, Discovery and Scientific Change* (Humanity Books 2010).

by the ideological hue provided by political forces representing hegemonic beliefs and interests.

Be that as it may, from the early 19th century, it is true that in several areas of Central and South America, constitutional narratives provided prestige to a political discourse that promised the benefits of liberty, equality, and justice. Along the same lines, the reading of authors committed to the 'Enlightenment', the quest for republican ideas, the call for popular sovereignty on the basis of consent and/or the struggle for popular participation as free and equal subjects, all – in different combinations – ended up bequeathing a bold constitutional mindset in the region.

What was the great challenge? The most fundamental goal was to guarantee the stability of all-new State formations. All things considered, however, concerning every single constitutional experience, a clear divide separates principles and values enshrined within the formal constitution vis-à-vis actual constitutional practices.

17.3.1 Brief methodological remarks

When it comes to comparative constitutional law, it is important to agree on two key issues. Firstly, we need to know 'what' we are comparing and 'how' we are observing the subject we analyze. This needs complete accuracy. In the present hypothesis, it is important to know what we mean when we talk about 'constitutional interpretation' and what it looks like in countries like Argentina.[6]

Following the path of the aforementioned thesis and its corollaries, another remark seems plausible. It is of utmost importance to examine the organic part of the Constitution. In other words, the gears and levers that hasten the functioning of the main branches of government have a far-reaching impact on rights enjoyment.[7] In other words, even though in terms of individual liberty the soundness of constitutional interpretation might be construed from the dogmatic part of the Constitution, a pure case law reading of those provisions says very little about actual rights enforcement. My view is that far more important than case law sophistication are those institutions of power that effectively secure rights protections.

17.3.2 Starting points

Bearing the thesis and corollaries in mind, and acknowledging the methodological remarks mentioned previously, there are three other principles, or axioms, that shape this chapter's argument. Although there could be room for other subtleties, the chosen principles are very telling of the interpretative constitutional practices in the region.

6 See Mark Tushnet, *Comparative Constitutional Law* (Edward Elgar 2014) 94.

7 See Roberto Gargarella, 'Latin American Constitutionalism and the Engine Room of the Constitution' in Pablo Riberi & Konrad Lachmayer (eds.), *Philosophical or Political Foundation of Constitutional Law? Perspectives in Conflict* (Nomos 2014) 97–115.

As far as this chapter is concerned, however, a constitutional study of consequences drawn from populism's interpretative abuses as well as any review dealing with the consequences of the recurrent weakness of institutional checks and balances will certainly need to rely on basic methodological caveats. Let me stress three of them:

1. No descriptive statement must lose sight of the diversity of social, economic, and cultural experiences that have taken place in different historical and political processes in context.
2. Although the US Constitution has had an overriding influence on the region, it is sensible to pay attention to other constitutional models as well as to other eclectic and original local influences. For example, there is the *amparo* which was first introduced in Latin.[8]
3. Finally, underlying political ideologies have brought about the thriving appreciation and/or justification of the constitutional interpretative task carried out by Courts and other State bodies.

Following these three basic statements, let me highlight their main meanings. In the first place, we need to understand how different experiences concerning social, economic, and cultural diversity have muddled through different political processes of constitutionalization in Latin America. From Central America to the South, for instance, we cannot overlook the Mexican Revolution (1910–1917) as a meaningful political stepping-stone in the quest for civic equality through the enshrinement of social and economic rights. These changes naturally account for an atavistic story of ongoing political conflicts. Social constitutionalism, introduced early in the Querétaro Constitution of 1917, reflects, without a shadow of a doubt, a true token of transformative vanguardism.[9] Another element that may claim our attention is Brazil's political path toward constitutionalization. Before being a republic, the country had experienced imperial rule until the end of the 19th century.[10]

In the second place, it is worth noticing how deeply influential the US Constitution was in the region. However, in terms of the institutional design of the Judiciary, and specifically concerning the strengthening of the Court's independence, as well as judges' authority and accountability, there are many windows and reference factors that must be analytically studied.

In the third place, it is interesting to explore how the ideological backdrop, often reflected by parallel legal developments, has opened the gates to a comprehensive normative assessment through incidental interpretative activity. The mimetic link consolidating mirrored relations between dominating political beliefs and constitutional programs has been very evident in several

8 See Roberto Gargarella, *Latin American Constitutionalism 1810–2010* (Oxford University Press 2013) 81.
9 See Gargarella (n 8) 41–43.
10 Ibid. 36–38.

countries of the region. In that context, the willingness to compromise has undoubtedly been widespread during the process of constitutional drafting.

For example, a political phenomenon that took place in several Central and South American countries during the 19th century is rightly labeled 'fusion-constitutionalism'.[11] Due to the compromise of diverse political stances, as a collective opus, constitutional drafting or reforms have repeatedly been spawned during successful political negotiations.

17.3.3 What kind of foundations?

Before going into the dilemma between the philosophical and the political grounds for constitutional law, a good strategy would be to focus our attention on a basic question, namely: are there different genealogies of claims and/or practical foundations to justify the Constitution? This is where an unavoidable division of possibilities arises. If the only way to uphold the normative value of a Constitution were to rely on a theory of justice and/or the postulation of a certain set of well-protected individual rights, it would seem that only the right philosophical speculation can lead us to that objective.[12]

If, however, the primary goal were to arrive at a civilized justification of constitutional norms to ensure higher levels of responsibility and social cooperation, then the realm of politics looks more suitable. If this were correct, purely collective processes of negotiation and compromise would provide imperfect though more stable foundations to the Constitution. My guess is that constitutional legitimacy has stronger foundations when these are rooted in the realm of politics. Hence, in the end, it seems to be a democratic public will, rather than an enlightened content-based checklist of principles, which provides a foundation for the duty of political obedience to the Constitution.

We should not disregard the fact that institutionalized deliberative practices within the State aim principally at clarifying legal and political decisions. Naturally, any acceptance and consolidation of constitutional values, principles and rules unavoidably need to undergo high levels of popular consensus.

The tension between political vis-à-vis legal constitutionalism is inevitable. Accordingly, insofar as political-deliberative byproducts could be subjected to epistemic conditions of validity, my feeling is that philosophical reason or legal conformity inevitably becomes an attempt to restrain and/or displace political-democratic aspirations.[13] Even when dogmatic belief in unblemished constitutional values, principles, and rules could have been fiercely

11 As regards Latin American constitutional history, it is worth mentioning, for instance, Roberto Gargarella's interesting description of the political alliances held by seemingly irreconcilable elites. See Gargarella (n 8) 27–34.

12 Pablo Riberi, 'An Uncertain Dilemma: Philosophical or Political Foundations for the Constitution' in Pablo Riberi & Konrad Lachmayer (eds.), *Philosophical or Political Foundation of Constitutional Law? Perspectives in Conflict* (Nomos 2014) 61.

13 For democratic and republican thinking, the political boundlessly stands above any kind of constraint. See Hannah Arendt, 'Culture and Politics' in Hannah Arendt, *Thinking Without a Banister* (Schocken Books 2018) 167.

supported by majorities, the truth is that from the very moment in which free and equal citizens willingly submit their own constitutional preferences to transcendental normative principles, the political meaning of popular sovereignty turns into an opaque abstraction.[14]

17.3.4 Which rights are meant to be constitutional rights?

I believe that in terms of constitutional interpretation, the legal view, together with the so-called neoconstitutionalism in its all variations, brings some undesired side effects.[15] Guastini, for example, has summarized the basic characteristics which, in his opinion, must be acknowledged by everyone who stands for a normative threshold in the field of constitutional interpretation.

Hence, as such, the Constitution should always fit into an objective normative template. According to the Italian author, in this version of constitutionalism every constitution must have the following characteristics: (1) it must be written; (2) there must be a jurisdictional guarantee; (3) the binding force of the Constitution itself must be assumed; (4) as to its content, beyond the formal text, overinterpretation of the Constitution must be admitted in order to draw principles from rules; (5) the likelihood of the direct application of constitutional principles is also unquestionable; (6) every law must conform to the Constitution.[16]

Against this view, my claim is that in Latin America, excessive scholarly zeal to develop stringent normative patterns has developed into a harmful constitutional culture. My claim, in this regard, is that some legal or jus-philosophic insights have proved to be insensitive to democratic-republican complaints. Neo-(*crypto*)constitutionalism, however, has been and still is acknowledged as a hegemonic trend among legal operators and most legal scholars.

In sum, it is not an exaggeration to state that the lack of faithfulness to the constitution, together with the low level of political, governmental, and bureaucratic exemplary behavior is somehow draining into a detrimental dilemma. I am referring to the swaying game that is restricting constitutional

14 As regards this idea, Waldron has an insightful reference to Aristotle's 'doctrine of the wisdom of the multitude'. He notes that 'the connection between DWM and a constitutional order respectful of the rule of law is not merely contingent'. See Jeremy Waldron, *The Dignity of Legislation* (Cambridge University Press 1999) 99.

15 I call 'crypto-constitutionalism' the scholarly epistemic stream that sees constitutional interpretation as a technical undertaking whose appropriateness or accuracy depends on the agent's skill or ability to dive into a kind of hermeneutical whirl. For further clarification concerning this concept, see Pablo Riberi, 'Límites sobre el Poder Constituyente – Agonìas y subjetividades del Criproconstitucionalismo' in I. Nuñez Leiva (ed.), *Nuevas Perspectivas en Derecho Público* (Librotécnia 2011) 94.

16 See Paolo Comanducci's reference to the Guastini template. Paolo Comanducci, 'Formas de (Neo)constitucionalismo: Un análisis meta-teórico' in Miguel Carbonell (ed.), *Neoconstitucionalismo(s)* (Editorial Trotta 2005) 81.

debate to the waste products left by populism – among other authoritarian forms – and its counterpart, a kind of aristocratic legal criticism.[17]

The key idea in this legalist and/or philosophical scholarly approach is that when they are rationally and properly understood, rights operate as a shield of immunity in favor of the will and interests of the person whose absolute individuality is being taken seriously. According to this view, rights must always stand in harmony, particularly when the right interpretation provides fair constitutional solutions. In a conflict of law, a proper legal interpretation must, therefore, find one and only one answer: the right one.

To my knowledge, this is awkward. And it is so because it is wrong to consider the sum of all civil relations subordinated to constitutional law to be a fair and harmonic pattern where insular points of contact are perfectly entwined. Besides, concerning constitutional conflicts, it does not seem reasonable to rely on hegemonic uses of trained scholarly reason as the exclusive and/or dominant source of the adjudication of rights.

Opposing this portrayal, I would choose an alternative approach. My insight is that constitutional rights in motion are likely to be better represented as dynamic defensive strongholds. If these are usually meant to operate as deterrents which prevent unacceptable personal sacrifices, perhaps it would be more reasonable to think of them otherwise. If constitutional rights were deemed to be the epitome of collective interests encapsulated in positive legal formulas, then, more humbly, constitutional interpretation could reflect a more basic practical goal. The chief concern of constitutional interpretation would be to provide narrowly tailored normative solutions preventing hegemonic uses of the statement 'I have this subjective-right'.[18]

Behind the constitutional discourse on rights, therefore, there must always be some basic collective interest that has deserved a kind of immunity. Legal provisions encapsulate those collective interests as rights.[19] Faced with foreseeable conflicts, political legislative debate first, and the interpretation of Courts later, must encourage the development of a body of coherent decisions, all of which must enable the foreshadowing of the fairest possible solutions at hand.

17 Very dauntingly, several countries of Latin America are witnessing a variety of political stances saddled with constitutional ravings of different shades which are usually labeled 'populist'. These utterances are used to reject some liberal principles; to blame the ideas and goals of 18th- and 19th-century constitutionalism; to denounce European ethnocentrism and to confront colonialism, not to mention all sorts of legal imperialism as well. Liberal constitutionalism – they complain– implies the protection of the established social and economic order. See Pablo Riberi, 'Non-Democratic Constitutionalism and the Uneasiness of the Crowds' (2020) Ossimori Costituzionali – Constitutional Oxymorons, Percorsi Costituzionali 299.

18 Jeremy Waldron, *Political Political Theory* (Harvard University Press 2016) 210–245.

19 On major and subtle differences in Jeremy Waldron, *Theories of Rights* (Oxford University Press 1984).

In short, the conflict of rights seems to weave a series of partial legal responses within a tapestry of broader institutional solutions.[20] When the dispute involves constitutional or fundamental rights claims, the interpretation must always be oriented toward prudent legal solutions.[21] From time to time, therefore, the interpretative warp can end up yielding disruptive outcomes. Concerning the importance of case law precedents, new interpretative doctrines may randomly disavow other previous normative engagements.

17.4 Constitutional interpretation and legal conflict

In this context, it is appropriate to single out which conflicts deserve to have constitutional relevance. Basically, they might fall into three main groupings:

1. 'Ad-Intra', within the same category of rights conflicts. These take place when, in a legal dispute over the same good or object or a subset thereof, or when in a controversy among those who claim equality in the distribution of a good/goods or services, courts and legal operators engage themselves to find out who must be excluded or who must have priority in the use of the very same right. An example of this could be the following: when there is a shortage of public resources and through a writ of protection, like the *amparo*, a Court renders a decision fulfilling certain demands of services associated with the right to health.[22] In Latin America, the potential success resulting from such a legal process will inevitably bring about a later shortage of resources. And naturally, together with that looms a lack of funding or coverage for other subjects whose requests for assistance are doomed to be ignored.
2. 'Inter-right conflicts'. In litigation over an allegedly thwarted constitutional right, in acknowledging that right, this happens when the triumphant claim causes the unavoidable sacrifice of another right entrenched within the constitution. For instance: when P's right to freedom of speech outweighs Q's right to have his image unaffected.
3. Finally, 'conflict between rights and collective interests'. This alternative takes place when abiding by the required condition of legality and reasonableness; by using its lawmaking powers, the Parliament, as well as other political authorities, encroach, restrict, or erode the individual

20 See Pablo Riberi, 'Qué (no) son los derechos constitucionales' in Rivera, Grosman, Elías, & Legarra (eds.), *Tratado de los Derechos Constitucionales, Tomo I* (Abeledo Perrot 2014) 5–52.

21 Cass Sunstein, *Radicals in Robes* (Basic Books 2005) 27–31.

22 *Amparo* is a writ that stands for the protection of constitutional rights violations. When a constitutional right is thwarted or in actual jeopardy and no other suitable remedy is available, *amparo* turns to be an exceptional constitutional action that allows a right-holder to seek the Courts' protection though a swift legal proceeding.

The Argentine Supreme Court acknowledged it firstly in two cases *Siri s/recurso de habeas corpus*, Fallos 239: 459 (1957), and *Kot Samuel SRL s/recurso de habeas corpus*, Fallos 241: 291 (1958), it was later entrenched within Art. 43 of the Constitution.

rights at stake. For example, this may happen when – on the basis of an extraordinary situation – a legally declared emergency impairs the enjoyment of some basic rights.

17.4.1 Constitutional interpretation, the method, and its ideological backdrop

As stated, before rushing into determining which method of interpretation is more suitable for full enforcement of constitutional rights, we should resort to a previous theoretical and practical set of options. In other words, although it may sound illogical, the enjoyment of constitutional rights depends on an integrated set of elusive underlying insights.

Depending on the idea of the constitution, instilled by the political or theoretical conceptions nurturing different streams of constitutionalism, the interpretative task, certainly, will foster different civic expectations. Depending on the goals of the constitutional design (e.g. concerning a polity's aims: how legitimate or independent or technically sophisticated Courts' byproducts should appear), then judicial review and/or rights-adjudication are likely to develop. Likewise, depending on which pragmatic horizon is hovering in the background of the practice of constitutional interpretation – nuanced by political or philosophical approaches – the very nature of constitutional rights is likely to be based upon different sorts of normative discourses. In sum, the random combination of all of these elements is very telling of how interpretation will enhance or prevent a democratic reading of the Constitution.[23]

If there is a platonic ideal of the Constitution and/or if any engaged legal operator subscribes to legal or philosophical constitutionalism, a solipsistic reading of the text is very likely to occur. Naturally, alongside this, it is more likely for such a dominant hypothesis to provide one and only one true or right answer; one and only one accurate or fair interpretation of the case.

A fair grasp of constitutional interpretation needs to take notice of some of the underlying concepts at stake. It also needs to spell out a set of complementary practices and aims. My impression is that the correct understanding of all these elements is elusive. Were this true, my view is that both 'interpretativism' and 'non-interpretativism' do not provide a comprehensive approach to all would-be reasonable readings a Constitution may have. My attempt involves paying more attention to subtle details. Beyond methodology, interpreting the Constitution requires the awareness of a coherent concert of other concealed factors. Which ones?

23 As regards possibilities of interpretation, it is wise and useful to pay attention to the following classification which follows Cass Sunstein's ideas on the matter. The author points out there are at least four alternatives, namely: (1) 'Perfectionism'; (2) 'Majoritarianism'; (3) 'Fundamentalism'; and (4) 'Minimalism'. Sunstein (n 21) 23; Cass R. Sunstein, *One Case at a Time* (Harvard University Press 1999); Cass R. Sunstein, *Legal Reasoning and Political Conflict* (Oxford University Press 1996).

As stated, the latitude and value of constitutional interpretation depend on the prior meaning the interpreter attaches to the term 'Constitution'. Naturally, this is so without leaving aside the fact that interpretative toils will logically differ depending on how constitutional rights are *a priori* conceived; not to mention, as well, that either epistemic or more political assumptions would provide them with different shades of meaning.

Besides, there are some questions that both constitutional theory and comparative constitutional law should never forego. I would like to mention at least three of them. (1) Is it possible to reach something like truth and/or justice by means of comprehensive interpretative techniques? (2) Do judges deserve, or do they have enough legitimacy, to be the final interpreters of the Constitution? (3) And, as some supporters of the economic analysis of law might claim, is this even desirable?

The Romans used to say: '*in claris non fit interpretatio*'. This is because, naturally, as H.L.A. Hart has pointed out, the first virtue of law is 'clarity'. However, no matter how accurate a legislator's legal writing may be, or how plausible case law outcomes appear to be, language traps and deceptions of the senses are unavoidable in the world of human beings.

As previously stated, the method depends on interpretation and not the other way around. Hence, constitutional interpretation brings to the surface a clear dividing line in the biases usually conveyed by any interpretative activity. This watershed drives towards an objectively oriented perspective vis-à-vis a subjectively oriented one. As a matter of fact, semantic theories – in their various forms – usually have interpretative goals that are opposed to these types of hermeneutic alternatives.[24] As accurately as possible, broadly speaking, the former attempts to understand the plain linguistic meaning of the text under the interpreter's scrutiny. Incidentally, it requires information on the legislator's intent.

From another point of view, supporters of hermeneutic constitutional readings, clearly closer to judicial activism, would rather overvalue the context of the enforcement of the norm under study. In this trend, they see the right-adjudication processes within a 'chain' and/or within a spiral of interconnected meanings. It would seem that full integration of each case law interpretative outcome must rely on an entwined, expansive, and never-ending process of construction.

It is a well-known fact that most Latin American highest courts have not only developed a Kelsenian controlling role as a negative legislator. They have engaged themselves in the process of the adjudication of rights as well. And it is not my wish to pry into the promises and weaknesses of the so-called activism, although it is clear that in any constitutional order where

24 As regards this concept within the law, Gadamer underscored that 'In this manner, the hermeneutic problem is naturalized in every legal science'. See H. G. Gadamer, *Verdad y Método, Volumen II* (Editorial Sígueme 2004) 109.

adjudication of rights is granted by judges, the normative consequences of this trend have a sound political impact on the balance of powers.[25]

Following Marshall's seminal *dictum* granting the judicial review of legislation, every normative assessment concerning constitutional supremacy over other branches' decisions has driven supreme courts and constitutional tribunals to undergo some legal hazards. For example, as regards the writ of habeas corpus, in 1887, in (Eduardo) Sojo's case, a landmark in Argentine constitutional history, similar to *Marbury*, apart from being the first time in which the Argentine Highest Court struck down a law passed by Congress as unconstitutional, the ruling's 'holding' also provides that constitutional interpretation should fit the rule of liberty.[26] In this ruling, the Supreme Court established a normative standard whose key formulation can appear as follows: 'if there was any doubt in the interpretation of the constitution, it had to be solved in favor of Liberty ... concerning the person and property'. From this case onwards, the Argentine Supreme Court claimed for itself a so-called 'diffuse control of constitutionality'.

In short, whoever adopts or puts forward a particular interpretative theory understands that as from its application, the constitutional order will convey a greater load of justice. All things considered, we must remember what Schauer has rightly pointed out: 'the existence of an interpreter with restricted powers is imposed by the very idea of the rule or by the idea of a system of rules'.[27]

17.4.2 Textualism, constructivism, hermeneutics revisited

The Argentine Supreme Court has had prominent justices and has bequeathed some excellent rulings to the country. Based on this fact, nevertheless, it is also plain that for many reasons, Argentina's highest court has managed to be neither sufficiently coherent nor institutionally independent throughout its history. A series of unfavorable circumstances have damaged its reputation and authority. The following are at least three of those significant circumstances.

Firstly, from 1930 to 1983, the Supreme Court – and the Judiciary in general – experienced the daunting effects of the impact of coups d'état. Secondly, the ongoing and distressing cycles of political, economic, and social instability were the leeway by which constant 'emergency responses' ended up weakening republican controls. Finally, the lingering effect of

25 Vicki C. Jackson & Jamal Greene, 'Constitutional Interpretation in Comparative Perspective: Comparing Judges or Courts?' in Tom Ginsburg & Rosalind Dixon (eds.), *Comparative Constitutional Law* (Edward Elgar 2011).

26 See the *Sojo* case, Fallos 32:120 (1887).

27 Frederick Schauer, *Las Reglas en Juego* (Marcial Pons 2004) 293.

hyper-presidentialism, due to design errors and/or a legacy of authoritarian practices, ended up impairing the Judiciary's independence as well.[28]

On the other hand, whether as a consequence of these factors or not, the lack of reliability and the excessive malleability of case law precedents also seems a plausible cause of its damaged authority.[29] For instance, the account of a lengthy dispute between jus-naturalists and jus-positivists has gained more complexity as more nuanced stances are perceived in an ever-changing set of legal disputes. Naturally, new differences driven by 'interpretativism' and 'non-interpretativism', or between those claiming a greater 'formalism' and those whose views are align with 'content-based substantivism'; or between those who support courts' 'self-restraint' and those who favor judicial 'activism', in the end, and taken together, have randomly brought about a non-independent Judiciary usually ready to endorse the overwhelming power of the Executive.[30] Truth be told, the records of Argentina's Supreme Court – with democratic periods included – do not yield a coherent and predictable constitutional narrative to enhance civic expectations of fairness and responsiveness.[31]

All things considered, ever since the last quarter of the past century, hermeneutics and judicial interpretativism have come to be very influential in the country. Besides, even though analytical philosophy and semantic theories of the law were deeply rooted in Argentina's legal scholarship, the Supreme Court's case law doctrine has been deviating towards neo-constitutionalist stances.[32] As this chapter explains, this perspective is currently shaping not only the way the interpretative task is being performed but also the whole understanding of what the Constitution and human rights should look like.

28 For further insights on the detrimental influence of the USA's constitutional model in Latin America, see Cindy Skach and Alfred Stepan, 'Presidencialismo y Parlamentarismo; Perspectiva comparada' in Juan Linz and Arturo Valenzuela (eds.), *La Crisis del Presidencialismo: Perspectivas Comparadas* (Alianza Universidad 1997) 189.

29 In *Ramón Jasso y. José Fragueiro s/amparo*, Fallos 310 (1987), the Supreme Court said that 'interpretation must be practiced in the light of the general context and the normative ends' and the 'Peralta's holding' it said that 'the value of the Constitution is not entrenched within the written texts; ... it has to be drawn from the realistic practice that enables the harmonizing of different interests, passions ... and so on'. See *Peralta, Luis A y otro s/amparo*, Fallos 313:1513 (1990)

30 For instance, in *Benes Monica v Bernasconi Coop. Ltd.* (1985), the Supreme Court favored a strict juridical formalism to work out the case. In this precedent, it states that *the first source of interpretation of the law is its wording.*

31 In this regard, Justice Carlos Rosenkrantz, current President of the Argentine Supreme Court, has an interesting point of view regarding the negative effects brought about by the excessive use of foreign precedents and legal transplants. See Carlos Rosenkrantz, 'Against Borrowing and Other Non-Authoritative Uses of Foreign Law' (2003) 1 International Journal of Constitutional Law. See also Pablo Riberi, 'A Constitutional Caveat: How Much Legitimate Meaning Comes When Implementing Legal Transplants?' (2003) Diritto Publico Comparato Europeo.

32 The Hart/Dworkin dispute has also been replicated in Argentine scholars' debates. Dworkin's influence has been thriving with neo-constitutionalist support. See Ronald Dworkin, *Taking Rights Seriously* (Harvard University Press 1978) 17. Hart's famous 'Postcritum' elapsed this dispute. See Hart (n 3) 242–243.

According to this outlook, it is evident that for many judges and legal operators, the reconstruction of legal meaning has become far more important than the legal text itself.[33] Thus, many courts' rulings seem to give in to the transformative power of hermeneutics in an entwined process of the adjudication of rights.[34] The 'interpretative turn' actually dwells where theory and practice meet. And there is little respect for democratic concerns. This happens even when it comes to some 'moderate interpretativism' *à la* Dworkin, for example. For every appropriate 'theory of interpretation', therefore, the meaning seems more important than the text.

Attractive as the statement may be, my concern is that, at least in Argentina and other countries of the region, activism, hermeneutics, and 'interpretativism' have delivered serious inconsistencies and have left a trail of unfair spoils. A wholesale assessment reveals that these trends fall short of what is desired. As a final remark, then, let me single out two major weaknesses. Firstly, these stringent legal views have usually overestimated judges' ability to deliver impartial decisions. In several countries in the region, it is striking to learn how the adjudication of rights is straightforwardly biased by the judge's moral, cultural, economic, and/or social prejudice. Secondly, as is shown by the repeated winding path of many high courts' case law in the region, it is also crystal clear that another overestimated assumption is the likelihood of an objective normative theory of constitutional rights.

17.5 Inspecting the engine room

In Latin America, in general, and particularly in Argentina, we have witnessed a relentless phenomenon of constitutional mutation. I would like to highlight that most of the Latin American countries have struggled to replicate the clear 'separation of powers' model inspired by the USA's Constitution of 1787. The greatest difference concerning the original template lies in the Executive's plethoric development and the subsequent breakdown of the actual institutional game of checks and balances.

In this setting, balanced expectations as regards the interplay of the different branches have been overwhelmed by the Executive's leadership. As a matter of fact, the Executive is usually called upon to carry out its governmental promises, and to do so, it tends to elude both legislative and Courts' constraints. Besides, the President must exercise leadership over the bureaucracy and must propose a budget and be responsible for most of the expenditure. And finally, for different reasons, other controlling institutions and/or agencies are also likely to fit and/or decline their vigilance or benchmarking commitments upon the Executive.

33 As Ricoeur once claimed, the 'writer is (only) the first reader'. Paul Ricoeur, *Hermeneutics and the Human Sciences: Essays on Language, Action and Interpretation* (Cambridge University Press 1981).

34 In this regard, Carlos Nino provides some inspiring insights for moral constructivism and the Law. Carlos Nino, *Etica y Derechos Humanos* (Editorial Astrea 1989) 92–129.

In line with this chapter's concerns, it is important to learn how the imbalance of the political branches is an outcome derived from a flawed constitutional design which, among other detrimental secondary effects, has brought about a wide range of constitutional blunders that, in the long run, have ended up undermining constitutional allegiance among ordinary individuals.

In this context, it is worth noting that whimsical adaptations have had a negative impact on political and constitutional practices. And so from a comparative constitutional law perspective, it is important to recall some methodological caveats which have already been highlighted. Despite levels of language randomly involved in descriptive, normative, and/or in political-philosophical spheres, the fair understanding of what the 'rule of law', 'constitutional order', and 'constitutional rights' are relies heavily on the actual functioning of the branches of government.[35]

From the observer's perspective, it is no less important to delve into further traits that might help us examine the constitutional *ethos* of a given polity. My concern, however, is to explore how institutionalized deliberation operates; how legislative decisions are implemented and how, in particular, the Judiciary renders its legal decisions in a troubled setting. In terms of comparative case law, there can be no reliable accounts unless the observer can grapple with the connection between deficits in the enjoyment of rights and the influence of a hyper-presidential distorted model in such an outcome.

17.5.1 Constitutional weakness by institutional design

To set standards of 'democratic accountability', it is therefore necessary to have a realistic awareness of the civic expectations at stake. In the case of a breach, the Judiciary, naturally, is less likely to be blamed. Broadly speaking, in Argentina, however, arbitrariness and low prestige encompass all branches of government to an equal degree. The State at large appears disoriented in its bureaucratic mazes. It appears to be overwhelmed by high levels of corruption and impunity, while the Judiciary lacks transparency. It is commonplace, then, that private interests and soft powers usually curb, undermine, and/or outweigh the intentions of brave judges. It is also plausible that the summation of the cyclical failures of the branches of the State paints a very somber picture, which depicts the failure of the whole constitutional setting.[36]

As regards the Judiciary, in addition to internal uneasiness related to shortcomings in human resource areas and weaknesses of character among

35 Gargarella (n 8) 172.

36 As regards the Judiciary, concerning institutional goals, it is sensible to compare the performance in different constitutional settings. Alec Stone Sweet, 'Constitutional Courts' in Michael Rosenfeld & András Sajó (eds.), *The Oxford Handbook of Comparative Constitutional Law* (Oxford University Press 2013).

many magistrates, the truth is that the court's performance resembles a piece of peripheral machinery consolidating the impunity of hegemonic political actors as well as of egotistic private interests. In this context, two basic elements may well summarize the current degradation associated with the Judiciary's loss of public esteem.

In the first place, the Judiciary's indifference toward republican values is a direct path to impunity and a lack of legal accountability. In this regard, it is often remarkable to see how a significant number of judges have recklessly displayed a 'partisan' approach while providing legal shelter to those who become their cronies. In many countries in the region, we have witnessed how puppet-magistrates hasten the dissolution of liberal and republican values by wiping out the very principles that had once given birth to a sound constitutional tradition. For instance, such servile support has played a major role in 'Chavism's' strategy of taking overall power in Venezuela.

Secondly, there is another negative element that calls for attention. An imbalanced system, saddled with weak democratic mechanisms of accountability, provides a blurred domain for civic altruism and legal trustworthiness. In some countries like Argentina, it is certainly usual to find a significant number of judges who are willing to turn their courts into a strategic field so that those pushing for or resisting political encroachment or the seizure of private interests may find a friendly environment to master the untamed dynamics of political conflict.

17.5.2 Case law, examples

In Latin America, the development of political constitutional history has been played out against a backdrop of constant states of emergency, exceptions, revolutions, military coups, and so forth. Basically, political and institutional responses grappling with various populist and anti-democratic assaults might be better understood if we also portray people's fears and expectations.

As previously stated, Bruce Ackerman developed a sound criticism of the Latin American model of the separation of powers. In the text mentioned earlier, he stressed that faltering democratic mechanisms provide the so-called 'Linzian nightmare', which has been utterly detrimental to Latin American constitutional culture. According to Ackerman, the 'separationist response' is a doctrine of political legitimacy which relies on a single key normative proposition. The core idea is that a single electoral victory is sufficient to vest plenary lawmaking authority in the victorious political movement. He underscored that

> this proposition yields one of the most distinctive features of the separation of powers: the fact that the different lawmaking powers often operate on a staggered electoral schedule.[37]

37 Ackerman (n 2).

Even if party A wins big at time one (T1), it may have to win 'n' times more before it can gain plenary lawmaking authority. A fortiori, following Ackerman's assessment, Juan Linz has adequately proved that the 'separation of powers' was one of the USA's most dangerous exports to Latin America. This is why he complains that:

> generations of Latin liberals have taken Montesquieu's dicta, together with America's example, as an inspiration to create constitutional governments that divide lawmaking power between elected presidents and elected congresses - only to see their constitutions exploded by frustrated presidents as they disband intransigent congresses and install themselves as caudillos with the aid of the military and/or extra-constitutional plebiscites.[38]

Therefore, such an attitude has brought about several manipulations of and breakdowns in constitutional rule. Such a trend has eventually ended up impinging upon fallacious interpretations of the political foundations of the constitution. This record of failures has turned constitutional practices into a calamity.[39] Thus, in agonistic terms, non-democratic or even populist-like solutions have confronted the Judiciary with a sort of Manichean logic. On the one hand, one horn of such a dilemma shows how some judges are carelessly hastening hyper-presidentialism. Even worse, the second path shows how some other judges are actively engaged in dismantling atavistic republican practices. To put it simply, copycatting the USA's original constitutional model of separation of powers has brought about unforeseen behaviors in the region, which can be described as follows:

1. Firstly, *judges with no ties, whatsoever*. These are not Herculean judges who, far from following the hero's mythical epics – and Dworkin's vagaries – unscrupulously behave like Procrustes.[40]
2. Secondly, *out-of-control executives*. These are Presidents who boldly break the circle of limits and controls legally entrenched in the Constitution. In line with what has already been emphasized, in some cases they came to

38 Ibid.

39 Unlike extraordinary forces of nature, which may harm human groups (cataclysms, earthquakes, droughts, fires, floods), calamities are catastrophic events, though caused by human agency. Ernesto Garzón Valdés, *Calamidades* (Editorial Gedisa 2004).

40 According to Greek mythology, Procrustes had an adjustable iron bed and he invited tired 'guests' to lie down. Passersby usually suffered from his terrible whims. Pablo Riberi, 'La Constitución democrática-republicana: dos imágenes un mismo espejo. En torno a la Política y el Poder Constituyente' (2016) LIV El Derecho – revista de doctrina y jurisprudencia 916.

transform the political structure into a device for an endless 'state of emergencies'. Closer to the demands of messianic populisms, some leaders even dare to reinvent the Constitution so as to keep hold of power at any cost.

3. Finally, ***indolent representatives***. These are bureaucratic, submissive legislators who are neither engaged with people's well-being nor have developed deliberative skills. They include Representatives and Senators whose future and political career depend on their ability to obtain favors from the President.

Along this line of thought, both populist readings and those expressing non-democratic commitments have been similarly responsible for undermining citizens' loyalty to the Constitution. Mistrust towards political participation as well as a reluctance to engage in political debate is usually justified under the cloak of greater concerns, such as the quest for abstract conditions of social justice. Hyper-presidentialism, in this context, opens the gates to an authoritarian platform by which aggressive and hegemonic readings of the Constitution allow arbitrary shares of injustice for everyone.[41]

In brief, besides democratic institutions' low performance and beyond the hideous legacy of some authoritarian regimes, judges' and some other legal operators' lack of republican commitment has become a key factor in the process of constitutional backsliding. Concerning this assessment, let me consider three different cases that can illustrate the (negative) influence of courts in the aforementioned process of political and democratic decay. In a certain way, these decisions unveil how judges' constructions often manipulate or stand carelessly aside from the democratic affiliation of the Constitution they are called on to interpret.

Firstly, in *Fayt* the Argentine Supreme Court rendered a decision by which a reformed section of the Constitution was strikingly deemed unconstitutional.[42] After the 1994 reform, the Argentine Constitution required new Senate consent for federal judges who were willing to continue in their positions after 75 years. Bear in mind that following the US constitution, the Argentine historical text also provided that once appointed by the Executive and confirmed by the Senate, judges were granted a life tenure in their offices. Addressing his own case, Fayt, a Supreme Court justice, challenged the constitutional section which had unanimously been approved during the constitutional convention. In an

41 Gargarella (n 8) 27–34.

42 *Fayt, Carlos c/ Estado Nacional*, Fallos 322 II: 1616 (1999). See also See Antonio M. Hernandez, *El caso Fayt y sus implicancias constitucionales* (Edición de la Academia Nacional de Derecho de Córdoba 2001).

unprecedented ruling, the Supreme Court – led by justice Fayt – said the section did not apply to those who were already in office. Fortunately, a new leading case – the *Schiffrin* case – prevented this doctrine from affecting other judges who had been appointed after the 1994 constitutional reform.[43]

Secondly, the *Gelman* case introduced an Inter American Court of Justice's controversial legal doctrine.[44] This Supranational Court, exercising 'conventionality control', issued a very daring sentence against Uruguay. This case refers to 'transitional justice' in the democratization period that took place in the region at the end of the 20th century. In order to hold back the unrest among the Armed Forces, the Uruguayan Congress wanted to strengthen a peace process in the country. They did so first by an amnesty law, which was later ratified by a popular referendum.[45] However, following the San José de Costa Rica Human Rights covenant, the Inter American Court ruled on the 'unconventionality' of said amnesty. This decision has become yet another milestone in its consolidated jurisprudence on the matter.[46]

The third case involves the Bolivarian Supreme Court of Venezuela. This event is unprecedented in the annals of comparative constitutional law. After the legislative elections in 2015, when the opposition obtained a majority in Congress, institutional conflict broke out between the latter and the government.[47] In a puzzling ruling, the Venezuelan Supreme Court was not only receptive to the government's complaints concerning the election results, but it went further by upholding a shocking decision. What came to be a bold and unfathomable decision was that through a senseless construction,

43 *Schiffrin Leopoldo H. c/ Poder Ejecutivo Nacional s/ acción meramente declarativa*, Fallos 340:257 (2017).

44 Uruguay is part of the Inter-American System of Human Rights protection. Unlike Europe where there is a tridimensional system, most of the countries in the Americas have engaged themselves in a bidimensional system of protections.

45 *Gelman v. Uruguay, Merits and Reparations*, Judgment, Inter-Am. Ct. H.R. (ser. C) No. 221, 45 (Feb. 24, 2011). Corte IDH. Serie C No. 221.

46 It is worth noting that the Inter American Court of Justice has developed a cogent legal doctrine against self-amnesties passed by waning dictatorships and also against amnesty laws which would have had a lingering effect through all democratic transitions. For further insights, see the following cases: *Barrios Altos vs Perú* (sentencia del 14 de mayo de 2001); *Almonacid Arellano y Otros vs Chile* (sentencia del 26 de septiembre de 2006), *Gomes Lund y Otros – Guerrilha do Araguaia – vs Brasil* (sentencia del 24 de noviembre de 2010).

47 The sentence 155/217 was delivered on 29 March 2017 by the Venezuelan Supreme Court, which outrageously decided to take away from the Legislative some powers that were entrenched within the Legislative Power. Later, the Court reversed its own decision.

the Venezuelan Supreme Court decided to temporarily take on the legislative powers of Congress.[48]

17.6 Epilogue

Ordinary politics and an incorrect balance of powers have downgraded the constitutional *ethos* in several polities in the region. Thus, citizens and law operators are reluctantly prone to sharing collective strategies in defense of the Constitution. They are seldom willing to make civic virtues thrive in public service. Given these circumstances, and abusing their *counter-majoritarian* biases, some engaged supporters of the rule of law have nonetheless recklessly despised the nuts and bolts of democratic constitutionalism.

Moreover, various versions of populism – in different disguises – are randomly reappearing in the Latin American political setting. In general, this ideological slant shares a common behavioral pattern with the leader's reveries. Those holding office, representatives, and judges are willfully or unintentionally emptying the Constitution of its normative meaning.[49] And this is what I want to stress from a deep global south perspective.

What is, then, the important cause which is at once so harmful and yet we have lost sight of? We are failing to realize something very basic. Something obvious in countries where respect for human rights is deeply entrenched within the constitutional mindset. In those countries where there is full compliance with and respect for the rule of law, one may also notice that sound political-democratic conditions for civic deliberation and participation are drawn from an upper level of collective decision-making. Here is where constitutional politics dwells. And clearly, the radical difference between 'constitutional politics' and 'ordinary politics' has been, and is still, the key for law-abiding people to respect and cherish the Constitution they have all accomplished together.

48 On 5 June 2020, the Bolivarian Supreme Court of Venezuela produced another preposterous decision. It held that the Venezuelan Congress – controlled by the opposition majority – had incurred a kind of 'constitutional omission' by failing to duly appoint the new directors of the CNE (National Electoral Committee). This meant that, as required by the Constitution, the members of the CNE were not timely appointed by the Legislative Power. Therefore, replacing the Legislative branch, the Justices of the court had decided to take over those powers of appointment. It is worth mentioning that due to political disarray coupled with Covid-19 restrictions, it was almost impossible for congressmen to rally together.

49 Bobbio has sharply highlighted the existence of informal powers or 'hidden powers', which have been acknowledged from ancient times to the present day. Norberto Bobbio, *Teoría General de la Política* (Editorial Trotta 2013) 431.

Part IV

Summary

18 Populist challenges to constitutional interpretation

An assessment

Fruzsina Gárdos-Orosz and Zoltán Szente

18.1 Introduction

The problem-setting of our book was based on the recognition that one of the most characteristic political tendencies in contemporary Europe is modern populism, which seeks to realize its power ambitions as well as its values and aspirations through constitutional changes. Consequently, according to all indications, the populist agenda influences constitutional development not only when populists are in government, but also when they are in opposition and when the government, often under pressure from public opinion, takes on and pursues similar policy objectives.

Nevertheless, real constitutional moments occur only rarely, and formal constitutional changes often lack the appropriate majority support. In such circumstances, the importance of the use of informal tools and procedures to change the constitutional design increases. Among them, constitutional interpretation can have a crucial role, because if new methods are used to reveal the meaning of the constitutional text, or certain substantive constitutional concepts are reinterpreted, significant reforms can be performed even without amending the constitution. In addition, as Fruzsina Gárdos-Orosz's study reports, even when specific political expectations are reflected in a constitutional amendment, they do not necessarily prevail in reality. In sum, our presumption was that if populist constitutionalism is a real phenomenon with certain common features, it will certainly have an effect on previous, well-developed ways of constitutional interpretation.

Although our research focused on the interpretive practice of constitutional and other high courts, it should not be forgotten that constitutional interpretation is not the exclusive domain of these courts, as other public bodies also carry out such activities and often seek to influence the constitutional jurisprudence accordingly. As Wojciech Brzozowski points out in relation to Poland, for example, 'the populist revolution relied greatly on constitutional arguments and interpretations put forward by the political branches of government and by their committed supporters'.

Moreover, we must distinguish between political demands, proposals, and judicial practice, because our study focuses not on political rhetoric but on the actual effects of populism on constitutional interpretation. In other words, populism as a political movement, style or rhetoric cannot be identified with populist constitutionalism, as the latter covers only the constitutional dimensions of populist political aspirations.

Below, when analysing the chapters of this volume, we first discuss the various forms of populism in the countries examined, before exploring how courts performing constitutional review have responded to the populist challenge by constitutional interpretation. Next, we attempt to give explanations for why certain courts have changed their interpretive practice, while others have not, and in this way, whether they support or resist populist aspirations. In the last section, we briefly summarize our most important findings and conclusions.

18.2 National varieties of populism

Populism is present in different forms in different political systems. Among the countries where populism has emerged as an organized political movement, populists have gained a constitution-making majority only in Hungary, while in some other countries they have a parliamentary majority and a dominant position in government but they alone cannot achieve formal constitutional changes. In other states, although populists have joined the governing coalition, they do not have a parliamentary majority, while in most countries they are in opposition. But even in the last group of countries, there recently have been constitutional or legislative changes, or simply attempts at reform, that have followed or realized typically populist purposes. Another similarity is that in spite of the different national contexts and the varying policy objectives and goals, these changes have often been inspired by wide-ranging dissatisfaction with the political establishment and their vested interests; such anxiety has been expressed in Britain by the Brexit campaign and referendum, while in Spain the Catalan secession movement has indicated the emergence of a revolt against the existing political order in Catalonia. Whatever has caused social discontent, populism has offered new and distinctive political platforms challenging the pre-existing frameworks of political decision-making.

Nevertheless, self-evidently, the stronger the populists' position in government, and the greater their political support, the greater their chances of accomplishing the populist agenda through constitutional changes.

18.2.1 Populists in government

In this respect, Hungary is in a special situation, because it is the only state among the countries examined in this book where the populist government has had a constitution-making majority in parliament for a long time. Thus, for our subject, the impacts made by populist constitutional policy on the methods of constitutional interpretation can be best examined by analysing the recent constitutional developments in Hungary. There is a broad consensus that the major governing party, Fidesz, and its charismatic leader, Viktor Orbán, embody the archetypes of populism and populist politics. The consecutive Orbán governments, with the exception of the period between

2015 and 2018, have had a qualified majority in the legislature since 2010, so they have had a continuous opportunity to pursue their constitutional ambitions almost without any limitation. The government coalition has made wide use of this situation: the government majority, despite the protests and boycott of the opposition parties, adopted a new constitution (Fundamental Law) in 2011, which has been amended no less than nine times since then, and in parallel, by extensive legislation, they have reshaped the entire legal system. In addition, since the regulation of many elements of the public law system can be adopted only by a two-thirds majority, the government has probably managed to cement for a long time to come a constitutional system that is mostly characterized in the literature as right-wing nationalist populism. Indeed, the government pursues a confrontational domestic policy, it is EU-sceptical emphasizing national sovereignty, it sharply opposes immigration and it centralizes public power. The almost continuous constitution-making activities and the considerable transformation of the legal system has provided ample opportunity for the Constitutional Court to respond to all these changes through its interpretive practice.

Many claim that Poland has been following the path trodden by Hungary in many respects since the right-wing nationalist Law and Justice Party (PiS) came to power in 2015. Since then the PiS has been the major party of the government coalition, but the government has never had a large enough majority to modify the Polish Constitution. Even so, the development that Brzozowski calls 'statutory anti-constitutionalism' has brought about important constitutional changes, from packing the Constitutional Tribunal to judicial reforms that undermine judicial independence. As extensive and significant reforms have taken place without any formal change to the Constitution, constitutional interpretation has played an important role in this process.

Modern Italian populism emerged as a result of the decline of the traditional party system in the mid-1990s, when the coalition of *Forza Italia*, formed by Silvio Berlusconi, the Northern League (*Lega Nord*), and the National Front came to power in 1994. Although these parties have not disappeared, contemporary Italian populism has a new leading party, the Five Star Movement (*Movimento5Stelle*), which formed a government coalition with the so-called Centre-Right Coalition (including the right-wing populist *Lega Nord*) after the 2018 general elections, and although this government was toppled in August 2019, populism is still very strong (the analysis in our volume refers to the period of this populist government). This is proved by the constitutional reforms initiated in recent years, which were, as Demuro and Montaldo argue, populist in nature, given that the first, the initiative to reduce the number of members of the two chambers of parliament, as well as to expand direct participation in legislation, would have weakened the representative nature of the political system, while the other proposal would have linked immigration to internal security, which is a hallmark of contemporary populism. Both cases had constitutional implications and reached the courts.

In the Czech Republic, the presidency of Václav Klaus is usually associated with a shift in the Czech political system towards populism, while its latest wave is linked to the government led by Andrej Babiš, which shares the Hungarian and Polish governments' scepticism towards the EU's immigration policy. It is important, however, that the populist stance of the government has not led to serious attacks on the system of the rule of law in this country.

Populism is not a new phenomenon in Austria either, where Jörg Haider's far-right populist party, the Austrian Freedom Party, which became more and more popular in the 1990s, formed a coalition government with the Conservative People's Party in 2000 at the federal level, an alliance which lasted until 2006. Between 2017 and 2019, these two parties governed together again. However, as Konrad Lachmayer claims, the presence of populism in Austria does not end with the Freedom Party's involvement in the federal government, as is proved by certain policy elements of the Sebastian Kurz-led government, such as the restriction of NGOs, the strong, determined leader, and most importantly, the anti-immigration policy.

18.2.2 Populist aspirations under non-populist governments

Experience shows that demands, decisions or policies of a populist nature can be born and become the subject of constitutional controversies not only through the policies of a populist government, but also by other channels, for example, under external political influence or the pressure of public opinion. This is particularly likely if the constitutional framework provides favourable circumstances for anti-elitist or anti-institutional initiatives. As Djordje Gardasevic points out, in Croatia, for example, the constitution offers several opportunities for direct popular participation. One of them is a constitutional amendment by constitutional referendum, a process which has been initiated several times in recent years. Some of these were particularly populist in nature, such as those that had an anti-elitist purpose or wanted to influence identity politics. Interestingly, whereas populist pretensions can find the appropriate tools, political circumstances have had adverse effects on these claims in recent times, as, on the one hand, in the fragmented party structure, populists have not been able to gain a majority capable of achieving constitutional changes, and, on the other hand, the EU accession process has not favoured populist policies.

As Alexandra Mercescu explains, it is arguable whether the ethno-nationalist features of the Romanian political system can be considered populist, but, as she adds, at least a 'mild' form of populism is a recurring feature of Romanian politics, and certain populist-like legislation may challenge the normal method of constitutional interpretation.

In Spain, in recent years, there have been significant changes in the political system at both national and regional levels. In national politics, bipartisanship, i.e. the dominant position of traditional parties, seems to have finally disappeared, and the party system has become significantly fragmented. In addition, Catalan separatism has become stronger, which is important for our subject because it has led to a constitutional crisis and posed serious challenges to constitutional interpretation. Francisco Balaguer Callejón discovers populist traits in both trends. At the national level, he argues, the latest wave of populism is linked to the Covid-19 pandemic as the protest against social distancing measures has been led by VOX, a populist party, organizing demonstrations against the government's measures to handle the health crisis. He claims that populism permeates Catalan secessionism even more, because the pro-independence Catalan parties 'appeal to a superior will, that of the "people" whom they alone represent', but in fact, this is only an imagined popular will, rather than one that the people would have expressed in an institutional way. Probably this view will be disputed by many, but it is worth noting that Balaguer Callejón's argumentation continues, stating that the adherents of separatism fail to comply with the relevant rulings of the Constitutional Court, 'because they do not accept any legal limit to their will, which is defined as the authentic will of the Catalan people' expressed by a regional referendum and the parliamentary majority in the Catalan legislature. His final assessment is that these political forces adhere to legal norms only as long as they coincide with their own interests.

John McEldowney's study sees populist trends in the national debate on an extremely divisive political issue, Brexit. In Britain, as he points out, the typical signs of populism were combined in the Brexit campaign from buzzwords such as 'taking back control' to anti-immigrant feelings. The British example is particularly interesting because populism, mostly represented by the UK Independence Party, is not present in the UK Parliament, so it is only a marginal force in this country, but at the same time its main political objective, exit from the EU, has dominated British domestic politics for years.

Apostolos Vlachogiannis's chapter shows that the Greek situation is also very special, as the Greek Council of State, which has the exclusive competence to judge the constitutionality of legal rules, flirts with populism and communitarian constitutional ideals and values. As he explains, during the years of economic crisis (between 2010 and 2018), strong populist tendencies prevailed in this country, but the role of the Council of State was even more significant in this respect, as the practice of this court in the past few years has been permeated by populist ideas. After the turbulent years of tackling the negative effects of the crisis, the Court changed its attitude and tried to stand up for the people's interests against international actors, such as the EU institutions or foreigners in general.

The perspectives of the chapters by Pablo Riberi and Mark A. Graber well illustrate that populism has different effects on constitutionalism in Latin America and the United States than it does in Europe. In many Latin American countries adopting patterns of American constitutionalism, strong populism significantly distorts the original principles and practices of these borrowed constitutional principles and institutions, the main reason for which is the shortcomings of the constitutional culture. Regarding the present-day right-wing populism in the United States, Mark A. Graber draws attention to the fact that, due to the basically different institutional settings, the constitutional vision of President Donald Trump and his allies differs significantly from that of their European and Latin American counterparts. While the European nationalist, right-wing populists have had to restructure the national constitutions in order to consolidate and expand their power, the Trump administration has not had to abuse the constitutional frameworks or to refashion the dominant mode of constitutional interpretation, because both the inherited constitution, as well as originalism, favour the traditional values preferred by populists. Briefly, to borrow Graber's expression, the U.S. constitutional polity and the judiciary is largely 'born populist instead of becoming so'.

In summary, we can state that in those countries which are discussed in our book, right-wing, authoritarian populism has raised issues that have affected the well-accepted way of constitutional interpretation, and in one way or another, the courts adjudicating constitutional cases have directly encountered populist aspirations everywhere.

18.3 New interpretive doctrines or methods?

18.3.1 How to assess interpretive responses to populist-inspired constitutional issues?

The country studies in this volume show that no matter how populism is present in a national political system, populist-inspired changes have reached constitutional review to varying degrees, so the previously elaborated methods of constitutional interpretation might have been affected in one way or another by populist reforms.

Exploring how the constitutional and the equivalent courts have responded to these challenges, and whether they have developed and applied new interpretive methods or judicial constructions, we primarily examined, as a first step, whether the practice of constitutional interpretation has changed in the cases that our authors consider to be part of the populist agenda in their country, that is, in the cases involving constitutional reviews of legislation inspired by populism.

We assumed that one theoretical possibility was that the interpretive practice of the courts has remained unchanged, that is, they have used the same principles and methods of interpretation in these cases as in others. Therefore, as a first step we examined whether there has been any change in the methods of interpretation.

Then, in the second phase of our analysis, assuming that interpretive practice has changed, we examined what kind of change(s) have taken place, and

- whether new 'technical' interpretive modes have come to the fore, or the emphasis has been placed on methods already used by the courts, or
- whether certain substantive constitutional concepts have been reinterpreted or new substantive categories have been used (possibly created or borrowed) by the courts.

Certainly, the courts may reply to the populist challenges by combining these mechanisms, using, for instance, a mixture of interpretive methods as well as evoking dormant constitutional provisions or inventing new substantive concepts. The attitudes towards activism and deference represent another dimension of possible judicial strategies, as the same methods can be applied extensively, or moderately.

Finally, as the third step, we summarized the authors' assessments on how the continuity or the changes in constitutional interpretation have had repercussions on populist claims; that is, whether the courts, by way of constitutional interpretation, have resisted or supported populist aspirations, or, possibly, had a neutral effect on them.

18.3.2 No interpretive changes: the business-as-usual model

Analysing the national case studies in this volume, it can be stated that the interpretive practice of some constitutional courts or other equivalent supreme courts has not changed even when they have encountered populist-inspired cases. Paradoxically, this does not represent an unchanged judicial strategy, but only the continuity of the techniques or substance of constitutional interpretation. However, behind the application of the same interpretive tools may lie different judicial strategies or behaviours.

As Konrad Lachmayer reports, for example, even though there are no perceptible changes in the interpretive methods used by the Austrian Constitutional Court, the Court has become more self-restrained in the past decade than it was before, in particular in the protection of fundamental rights. Prior to 2008, the Court pursued an activist stance for promoting basic rights, boldly using teleological reasoning and interpreting substantive concepts such as equality. As a result of this kind of judicial activism, the body was able to be an effective barrier to the first wave of populism in Austria. Now, however, due to the more deferential approach of the Court, it has lost its earlier role in this respect. This illustrates that even when there is no change in the interpretive methods applied, there can be different outcomes depending on whether the courts pursue an activist or self-restraining practice.

Gianmario Demuro and Riccardo Montaldo evaluate the Italian Constitutional Court's responses to populist initiatives in a similar way, claiming that the Court has not taken the opportunity to curb populist aspirations – although in some cases this would have been possible – but has evaded responsibility for the decision on procedural bases. Interestingly, however, some ordinary courts have acted against populist attempts and annulled individual decisions using a constitutionally conforming interpretation that used to be applied otherwise by the Constitutional Court.

Alexandra Mercescu draws a similar conclusion, saying that the interpretive practice of the Romanian Constitutional Court has remained unchanged in cases that can be considered populist 'mostly because of their outcome'. However, this jurisprudential continuity, as she argues, means the perpetuation of weaknesses in standard reasoning such as the argumentative fallacies of '*non sequiturs*, tautologies, contradictions and selective treatment of case law'. The results of the low-level judicial reasoning ultimately weaken constitutional guarantees and control mechanisms, even if the Court's rulings do not comply with the objectives of the populist political agenda.

In the Czech Republic, as Zdeněk Kühn supposes, although the populist trends have had little effect on the jurisprudence of the Constitutional Court, the body observed the coming new wave of populism and embarked on a more moderate practice, at least in the sense that it ceased to extend its powers, and some of its decisions have not been 'in line with the earlier case law'. The self-restraining practice culminated in refusing the justiciability of the declaration of the state of emergency in 2020, but the interpretive toolkit and the self-understanding of the Court have remained unchanged.

As opposed to the cases discussed so far, the continuity of constitutional jurisprudence has obstructed populist ambitions in Spain. In this country, as Balaguer Callejón states, neither Catalan separatism, nor the national populist parties have 'managed to generate a jurisprudential line of interpretation of the constitution that can be defined as populist', because the Spanish Constitutional Court has resolutely resisted such aspirations. This means that the existing interpretive practice has provided appropriate tools for the Court to combat populist constitutionalism. Essentially, the Court has taken the position that unilateral legislative actions that do not respect the constitutional framework, even on the basis of the popular will, are unconstitutional.

In Britain, according to McEldowney's analysis, during the protracted Brexit controversies, the Supreme Court's decisions were consistent with the well-established judicial practice reviewing the prerogative powers of the Executive, giving priority to the principle of parliamentary sovereignty, and rejecting the special legal status and judicial enforceability of constitutional conventions.

18.3.3 Changing interpretive practice to promote populist aspirations

In those cases in which populist issues have triggered changes in interpretive practice, these effects have taken a variety of forms. The outcomes of our research show that most often some substantive concepts have come into the mainstream of constitutional interpretation, in some cases bringing real innovations into jurisprudence. In Greece, for example, when the Council of State (endowed with the power of constitutional review of laws) sought to act as the protector of the people's interests, it fulfilled this mission primarily through the interpretation of the concept of constitutional identity. According to Vlachogiannis, the development of this substantive concept needed a holistic approach, but only after the turn in its practice. Previously, when dealing with the debt crisis, the Court had raised sovereignty issues rather than the concept of constitutional identity. In 2018, however, the Court reactivated the 'prevailing religion' clause of the Constitution, yielding normative power to this provision that had previously been considered a purely declarative clause, claiming that the Greek Orthodox religion is a centrepiece of Greek constitutional identity. It is also worth noting that, in contrast to the jurisprudence of the German Federal Constitutional Court, the Council of State did not invoke the eternity clause of the Constitution when it evolved the new concept of constitutional identity. This new approach postulates national selfhood as a pre-constitutional phenomenon which can be contrasted with external threats to the nation's existence. In addition, the Court, similar to its Hungarian counterpart, considers the Preamble of the Constitution to be an aid to interpretation. It is worth noting that the Court, in the relevant part of its jurisprudence, preferred the contextual interpretation of the constitutional text. However, neither constitutional identity as a newly discovered substantive concept nor the contextual method have become general or pervasive modes of constitutional interpretation. Yet these interpretive tools are now available and can be revived at any time in the future, not just in cases in which they have been used so far (i.e. judgments on nationality, Sunday laws and religious education).

The Greek Council of State is not the only court examined in this volume that has used some new interpretive tools to pursue a populist stance. The invention of new substantive concepts and the reinterpretation of older ones have been characteristic of the jurisprudence of the Hungarian Constitutional Court in recent years as well. As Fruzsina Gárdos-Orosz explains, here, the 'historical constitution' (in effect the one existing before the end of World War II) and 'constitutional identity' are the most preferred new magic words, while the concept of 'human dignity' has been significantly reinterpreted. In this country, the Constitutional Court, fully packed by the government parties, has assiduously favoured the legislative policy of the government, which is widely believed to be the archetype of populist rule. Notably, in this country, the right-wing populist government has always exploited its constitution-making majority unscrupulously whenever it has needed to, so even an independent Constitutional Court would have lacked the weapons to deal with the government-dominated legislature. In addition, Hungary is the only country where the constituent power also sought to influence constitutional interpretation by including the preferred interpretive methods in the constitutional text. In such circumstances, it might be surprising that these modes do not play a prominent role in the recent jurisprudence of the Court. The current judicial deference uses a mixture of interpretive modalities in the same way as it did in its activist era in the past, but this time to support the governmental power rather than to counterbalance it. Overall, the overwhelmingly populist political course, which has overcome all institutional barriers and resistance, has ultimately led to significant changes in the content of the constitutional interpretation without radically reshaping its methods.

Populism has also had a very significant effect on constitutional interpretation in Poland because, as Wojciech Brzozowski puts it, 'the populist revolution relied greatly on constitutional arguments and interpretations put forward by the political branches of government … interpretations which were proposed and enforced precisely against the judges and the courts'. In this country, the Constitutional Tribunal was quickly packed by the populist government, and it has used old techniques for new purposes. Thus, the Court has not abandoned the practice of giving guidelines to courts on the proper interpretation of constitutional provisions. However, the Constitutional Tribunal has used this tool only in a narrowly tailored way, namely to defend the controversial measures of the populist majority. While the interpretive techniques applied have not changed, if the previous practice obstructs the governmental will, it is rapidly changed by the Court. Brzozowski argues that there is no consistency in the interpretive practice, which he characterizes as a 'cherry-picking model'.

18.3.4 Changing interpretive practice to counteract populist initiatives

While constitutional interpretation using new substantive terms has not been used by constitutional courts in Greece and Hungary to prevent or counteract populist aspirations, the Croatian Constitutional Court has sought to resist some populist initiatives by applying similar interpretive tools. For this country, Gardasevic examined the methods and changes in constitutional interpretation in connection with the constitutional review of popular constitutional initiatives, based on the assumption that some of them pursued populist goals such as anti-elitism, the restriction of minority rights and backing of identity politics. According to his analysis, the Croatian Constitutional Court has also used contextual interpretation to develop certain substantive concepts, bestowing upon them high constitutional values, such as constitutional identity or unconstitutional constitutional amendments. Likewise, it has reserved some unenumerated powers for itself, such as the constitutional review of popular constitutional initiatives, although this can be seen as a manifestation of the constituent power (since successful referendums result in an immediate amendment of the constitutional text). It is noteworthy that these substantive categories are not included in the text of the constitution, so in this case the populist challenge has provided an opportunity for the Constitutional Court to strengthen its position and, in many cases, to break with its previous practice, to establish a kind of hierarchy among constitutional values. As to the modalities of constitutional interpretation, the Constitutional Court has used several different methods inconsistently; the interpretive tools applied have 'varied significantly from case to case' in relevant review procedures, but as Gardasevic argues, the Court has used the various methods always against populist demands; it rejected the popular constitutional initiatives aimed at restricting minority rights by the proportionality test, refused the initiative to change the electoral system on the basis of a grammatical interpretation, and then, referring to the systematic interpretation, also declared the referendum to prevent the outsourcing of certain public services unconstitutional.

18.4 Explaining different judicial strategies

As we have seen, constitutional courts and other high courts exercising constitutional review have reacted to populist legal aspirations in different ways. The diverse judicial strategies may be manifested not only in the outcome of the constitutional interpretation but also in its method. If we accept that the aims and means of populist constitutionalism challenge the constitutional system of liberal democracies, undermine the functioning of traditional institutions and seek to establish an alternative constitutional design, it is reasonable to assume that they also affect the well-accepted forms and methods of constitutional interpretation. Presumably, the power of interpretation is therefore greatly appreciated in the eyes of populists. And if this is the case, it is plausible to presume that they seek to develop a specific interpretive method that will most effectively help them to achieve their goals.

However, Anna Gamper, based on a wide-ranging comparative analysis, has found no evidence that populists would favour any particular method of constitutional interpretation. As she demonstrates, although the new constitutions prescribe mandatory interpretive methods more often than the old ones, wherever this occurs, populism is not the main explanatory variable. Presumably, their approach is a target-oriented one, that is, it does not matter how the desired result is achieved. Interestingly, she has concluded that when constitutions contain binding guidelines for interpretation, they are mostly intended to establish and promote liberal democracy (at least on paper). What can make a difference is that 'established liberal democracies rarely entrench such rules in their constitutions, because they rather consider constitutional interpretation to be the domain of independent courts', while populist or illiberal constitutionalism calls into question whether the courts should really be the ultimate interpreters of the constitution. Among the countries examined in this book, only in Hungary have the populists become so strong that they were able to adopt their own constitution, which included preferred methods of constitutional interpretation. However, this has not had a decisive effect, even in this country.

Beyond the fact that comparative analysis has not proved that different political systems would have their own specific rules of constitutional interpretation, Mark Tushnet is sceptical about whether the nations of the world would have autochthonous interpretive methods. All the signs show that national constitutional and supreme courts use the same modalities. Nevertheless, there may be some room for national peculiarities in that the same interpretive methods are used in different combinations in various countries, establishing a specific hierarchy between them. In this sense, different meanings can be attributed to the same substantive concepts depending on the national legal culture in which they operate.

Martin Loughlin's study, exploring the American debates on constitutional interpretation, highlights the difference between the 'strict constructivist' and the 'aspirational' interpretations, resting on diverse approaches to the constitution. This kind of conceptualization can be an appropriate way of characterizing populist constitutionalism, supposing that the prevailing authoritarian populism, with its eagerness for power and zeal for comprehensive political and social reforms, prefers to take the aspirational approach to constitutionalism and constitutional interpretation.

Analysing the country studies in this book, the most plausible explanatory variable of judicial behaviour is the political context that surrounds the courts. Where populists have been strong enough to pack the constitutional courts, such as in Hungary and Poland, they have taken this opportunity to replace judges with their own nominees. However, the new judges have not developed new interpretive methods to legitimize the majority will; at most, they have placed some new legal concepts or constitutional provisions at the centre of their jurisprudence, or creatively resorted to the methods available, choosing the one best suited to justify the preferred decision. It is also interesting that the political subordination of a constitutional court does not necessary involve judicial deference, but also depends on the given political circumstances. In Hungary, where the government majority may write anything in the constitution that they want, the Constitutional Court has pursued a self-restraining stance in recent years, while in Poland, where the governing parties do not have a sufficient majority to amend the constitution, populists have urged judicial 'passivism' only in opposition, but in government, they have needed a fairly activist Constitutional Tribunal to reinterpret the unchanged constitution.

In a number of countries, the mainstream parties have succeeded in preserving the support of their voters, or the fragmentation of the party structure has prevented populist movements from coming to power or reaching a position in which they could influence the composition of the high courts. Yet, as the Austrian, Czech and Italian examples illustrate, some constitutional courts have started a more self-restraining practice, showing deference to the decisions of political branches, even if they have otherwise remained intact. We assume that if such a court relinquishes its earlier activism in the hard cases generated by a populist agenda, this can be better explained by its own institutional interest or the pressure of public opinion, rather than by the national legal culture. Nevertheless, constitutional traditions can play a decisive role, as can be seen in the United States, where the ancient constitution and the well-accepted methods of constitutional interpretation favour populist aspirations.

Furthermore, some authors in this book have argued that although the existing interpretive toolbox has provided appropriate instruments for the courts to resist populist aspirations which seek to reshape the constitutional framework, only some high courts have used these instruments for this purpose. As a matter of fact, only a few of the constitutional and supreme courts we have examined have undertaken decisive action against populist initiatives, even if the latter have challenged the traditional constitutional framework; perhaps the high stakes involved (such as the unity of the state against Catalan separatism in Spain, or EU membership in Croatia) have encouraged these courts to do so.

Overall, where populists are in opposition, and where the constitutional or supreme court is in a strong position, the business-as-usual model is most likely; and vice versa, where populists rule and have been able to change the competence or composition of the court(s) reviewing the constitutionality of legislation, there has been a change in constitutional jurisprudence in favour of populist objectives.

18.5 Our major findings and conclusions

All country studies show that where populism has influenced the interpretive practice of the courts, no new theory of interpretation has evolved, and no close connection can be established between populist constitutionalism and any specific method of constitutional interpretation. In short, populists do not have any favourite interpretive method or theory. Even the rubber-stamp courts do not need to use specific interpretive methods or judicial philosophy; this does not mean, however, that such courts would be reluctant to find the most appropriate ways to be deferential to the political will of the government. However, in these cases, the choice of the modalities of interpretation applied is made on a pragmatic basis, from case to case, depending on the desired end result, and there is no consistent interpretive theory or practice behind it. In other words, even if populists are able to achieve informal constitutional changes by influencing the high courts' jurisprudence, the methods of constitutional interpretation play a merely instrumental role. In these countries, even the most sophisticated and elaborate interpretive theories and methods can be used to justify blatantly unconstitutional laws and initiatives.

Putting our research results in a broader context, we can also draw an important conclusion. As has been said earlier in this chapter, our presumption was that if populists are not strong enough to achieve formal constitutional changes, they are likely to want to influence the way the constitution is interpreted in order to reach their goals. We also assumed that if 'populist constitutionalism' is an analytically useful tool, the methods of constitutional interpretation must be its crucial domain. However, we have not been able to confirm this presumption; we have concluded that no substantive theory or specific mode of constitutional interpretation can be ascribed to populist aspirations, and populist constitutionalism does not, in effect, have a special constitutional toolbox. In other words, populism, as a political phenomenon, although it can achieve real constitutional changes, does not achieve them in any particular way, by elaborating a new constitutional theory.

The growing literature on populist constitutionalism is based on the assumption that, firstly, populism is a worldwide trend, and that secondly, it has made significant constitutional changes whenever populists have been able to. The term 'populist constitutionalism' may at most refer to this relationship, but we have not found any evidence that these achievements have elaborated any specific constitutional ideas or methods which would be characteristic only of populism. All indications are that populism considers constitutional interpretation only in a purely instrumental way, handling every legal concept and procedure, including constitutional adjudication and – as an element of this – constitutional interpretation, as a tool to achieve political objectives and goals.

Index

Page number followed by “n” refers notes numbers.